RECRAFTING A LIFE

RECRAFTING A LIFE

Solutions for Chronic Pain and Illness

Charlie Johnson
Denise Webster

Brunner-Routledge
New York & London

Published in 2002 by
Brunner-Routledge
29 West 35th Street
New York, NY 10001

Published in Great Britain by
Brunner-Routledge
11 New Fetter Lane
London EC4P 4EE

Brunner-Routledge is an imprint of the Taylor & Francis Group.
Copyright © 2002 by Brunner-Routledge

Printed in the United States of America on acid-free paper.

10 9 8 7 6 5 4 3 2 1

Library of Congress Cataloging-in-Publication Data
Johnson, Charlie.
    Recrafting a life : solutions for chronic pain and illness / Charlie Johnson and
Denise Webster.
        p. ; cm.
    Includes bibliographical references and index.
    ISBN 1-58391-356-4
    1. Pain—Treatment. 2. Brief psychotherapy. 3. Chronic diseases—Psychological
aspects. I. Webster, Denise. II. Title.
    [DNLM: 1. Pain—psychology. 2. Psychotherapy, Brief—methods. 3. Chronic
Disease—psychology. WM 420.5.P6 J66r 2002]
    RC480.55 .J635 2002
    616'.0472—dc21
                                                              2001052499

To my father George E. Q. Johnson Jr., a "chronic" optimist, whose unconditional support has made all the difference.

—Charlie Johnson

To all my Friends and family.

—Denny Webster

CONTENTS

FOREWORD

So. Whenever I can stand back and am able to be (somewhat) of an observer, I am amazed at how Solution-Focused Brief Therapy (SFBT) has evolved and/or developed in the past 20 or so years. This form of Brief Therapy was originally developed by therapists/researchers observing what seemed to work with our clients. Once we had identified what worked, we would deliberately do more of it. This led us to develop, with our clients, a practice that was both effective and efficient within our specific context (a private, not-for-profit, research-oriented, teaching and training focused general practice). We could, of course, never be sure that our way of doing SFBT could be transferred to other contexts.

Over the years we saw anybody and everybody that came (or was forced to come) to see us. Thus we saw the wide range of clients that would be seen by any out-patient mental health clinic. It did not take us too long to find out that the most important thing for effective and efficient therapy was helping the client figure out what exactly it was that they wanted from therapy. "To stop drinking," "to stop fighting," "to stop the voices in my head" seem to express what they want but these kinds of statements are actually complaints. All they tell us is that the client has failed to stop something. And, as we all know from personal experience, stopping something is the most difficult way to change. Goals, as we came to see them, involve the *consequences* of this kind of change: What, exactly, will the client be *doing instead* of drinking, fighting, hearing voices, and so forth.

Johnson and Webster have figured out and tell us clearly how to do this in some special kinds of situations by asking "who," "what," "when," and "where" questions that will help the client describe the consequences of goal achievement in some detail. In general, therapists fear the clients in these kinds of situations will respond to the Miracle Question with impossibilities: the lupus patient will say (they fear) that the lupus will be gone! Of course, this would seem to be a reasonable thing for the patient to say and in that sort of situation, I would be surprised if he/she did not say that. I am reminded of a client I saw many years ago, just at the time we were starting to develop the Miracle Question. We were not yet sure about its scope and whether or not there were times when we should not use it. The client had lost his left arm in an industrial accident. I was afraid to ask the Miracle Question because I was sure he would want his arm back. If I were in his shoes, that's what I would do. But, nonetheless, I asked it, and when he responded that he would have his left arm back, I did not know what to do and so I just sat there, waiting for him to continue. After a brief pause he did: "Ah, but you mean something that can happen," and talked about his wife smiling more so that he could smile more in response.

Webster and Johnson have figured out how to use the Miracle Question with patients with chronic illnesses and pain, and their case examples are wonderful. In each case it is clear that what the patient wants involves something of his/her choice; something they can control. I think this will be of great interest and use to young therapists trying to figure out how to be useful with clients in these situations. I was particularly struck with how Johnson and Webster use the EARS acronym as a way to structure and organize second and later sessions. This helps to keep the therapist's focus where it belongs; on change, difference, and getting better. Working with clients in a situation involving chronic pain and illness, focusing on what's better and how it got that way seems central and very, very difficult. When you perceive yourself to be in pain for 24 hours a day, 7 days a week, week after week, month after month, it is quite difficult to pay any attention whatsoever to minor variations and fluctuations. It's easy and reasonable to start to believe that "it is forever." The Eliciting of a description of differences that happen between sessions and then Amplifying the descriptions of anything better, and then Rewarding these in some way seem crucial to clients in these kinds of situations. (Of course, it is useful to Start the process over again with description of another difference.) Knowing the difficulties involved with helping clients in these kinds of situation notice differences, Webster and Johnson developed *The Solution Identification Scale for Health*, which can be given to clients at the end of the first session. This can add to the therapist's toolbox some topics worth talking about in subsequent sessions since the 34 items seem to cover the areas most clients talk about when they are talking about things getting better in their life.

I have watched SFBT spread into domains that I never could have expected. For instance, there are some schools and residential treatment centers (for adolescents) in Switzerland and Sweden who have used SFBT as a starting point for designing their entire programs. Goals and choices are central to their approach both in the classroom and in day-to-day living. More reasonably, from my point of view, is its spread into programs focused on drug and alcohol abuse. Again, goals and choices are the primary focus. And both effectiveness and efficiency is increased by focusing on what it is that clients want.

I think this is an important and interesting book that is bound to be useful to therapists and their clients/patients when the situation involves chronic illness and pain. Certainly these clients need therapy that is both effective and efficient.

Steve de Shazer
August 2001
BFTC
Milwaukee, Wisconsin

ACKNOWLEDGMENTS

This book is the reflection of many years of collaboration, teaching, and most importantly learning in the field of health-related psychotherapy. First, and foremost, we would like to thank our clients for sharing their humanity, knowledge, and inspirational courage over the years. We are also indebted to our colleagues that have faithfully participated in what we affectionately refer to as "Friday afternoon team." This solution-focused, one-way-mirror therapy team has served as a catalyst for many of the clinical interventions presented in this volume. During its 18-year history this team has been creatively inspired by Jeff Goldman, Marty Waters, Teri Pichot, Yvonne Dolan, Evelyn Braithewaite, and Edie Israel, along with such innovative visitors as Steve de Shazer, Insoo Berg, Steve Gilligan, Lynn Johnson, and Michael Hoyt.

We are also grateful for the major contributions of research participants from across the United States. Their willingness to share their solutions to the challenges of chronic pain and illness has immeasurably advanced our understanding of the many options available in recrafting a life. We are equally appreciative of all the graduate students and the participants in our professional workshops and supervision groups over the years. Knowledge gained from our teaching (and more importantly learning) experiences with these groups is integrated throughout this book.

Finally, we would like to thank Judy Roybal for her patient and invaluable technical assistance in helping us complete this manuscript.

Charlie Johnson and Denise Webster

Introduction and Overview of the Book

Chronic illness and chronic pain conditions are among the major health problems seen in the current health care system. They also are among the least responsive to conventional medical therapies. Almost by definition, conditions that are not eradicated by antibiotics or surgery are seen as elusive, mysterious, and/or something other than the usual human condition. Paradoxically, these conditions and the suffering they bring can be seen as the essence of the human condition. Hoffman, Rice, and Sung (1996) reported that between 80 and 90 million U.S. citizens have at least one chronic illness. Although many with these conditions included children with asthma and other chronic illnesses, the majority of those with ongoing health problems are adults. Eighty-six percent of those over age 65 have at least one chronic illness. Among the most prevalent conditions are arthritis, diabetes, respiratory diseases, hypertension, and mental illness. The leading causes of death in adults—heart disease, cancer, and stroke—are also among the leading causes of disability among those who survive. Other estimates suggest 39 million live with more than one chronic illness; 50% of men and 70% of women over 80 are reported to have two or more chronic conditions. The estimated direct and indirect cost of these chronic conditions during 1990 was more than $650 billion dollars.

At the same time that the public health document *Healthy People 2000* was setting goals for reducing the prevalence of these diseases, concerns were mounting about the rising costs of providing health care (U.S. Department of Health and Human Services, 1990). The Clinton Plan for providing health care for all was seen as too radical by many legislators and their constituents—an intrusion on the freedom of patients* and health care providers. Nevertheless, the growing influence of managed care has made its mark on the delivery of care for a majority of the population. The message of managed care is clear to provider and consumer alike: Keep costs down (Fishman, VonKorff, Lozano, & Hecht, 1997). In the area of mental health care, the result has been a new respect for a range of effective brief and/or intermittent approaches to treatment that have largely replaced therapies that were open ended or directed toward goals beyond resolution of the immediate complaint. For those with physical illnesses that do not respond to medical interventions, a mixed array of options exists, depending on the particular health care plan and/or the resources of the consumer. Among the options are packaged "programs," using a variety of medical and cognitive–behavioral protocols offered by "pain clinics" and a wide range of self-help groups dedicated to providing information and support for those with ongoing health problems.

☐ The Purpose of the Book

This book is intended to offer immediate guidance to "fill the gap" for those mental health professionals who are seeing people with long-term physical concerns and for health care providers who are perplexed about how to deal with the multiple challenges that accompany the experiences of long-term illness and/or pain and their sequelae. It is not yet clear what effect the parity law requiring equivalent health insurance coverage of mental and physical illnesses will have on the delivery of care and reimbursement for services. Given the tendency for medicine to separate body and mind, classifying problems as either physical or mental, the bill will probably do little to diminish the stigma associated with seeking care for psychological and emotional pain, whatever the source. However, there is a growing recognition that attention to mind–body phenomena is essential to providing quality care that is effective, efficient, and respectful of individual needs and resources. Both improved health outcomes and reduced costs have been found following implementation of a variety of psychosocial interventions. There is also evidence that "alternative" health treatments are increasingly acceptable to the public, particularly for managing chronic health problems. Among the approaches considered "nonconventional" in a 1993 study were many commonly used approaches to "self-care," including diet, exercise, vitamins, folk rem-

---

*Given ongoing debate about terminology, we use the terms "patient" and "client" interchangeably in this text.

edies, and prayer. Other approaches, such as chiropractic, massage, acupuncture, spiritual, and energy healing, were dependent on ongoing contact with a provider (Eisenberg et al., 1993). Follow-up studies find increasing numbers using what we now call "complementary" therapies (Eisenberg et al., 1998; Sobel, 1995). Some of these approaches have only recently begun to be evaluated using methods generally accepted by the scientific community. However, a consensus conference, sponsored by the National Institutes of Health, provided strong support for some of the interventions included in this book for managing chronic pain: relaxation approaches, cognitive reframing, imagery, meditation, and hypnosis. The panel identified one of the barriers to use of these methods was the relative lack of information most health professionals have about their use and effectiveness. Another identified barrier was the inability to introduce psychosocial interventions in ways that are sensitive to individual beliefs and differences in response (Chilton, 1996).

The authors, a social worker and a nurse, are therapists who have worked for many years with people having a variety of conditions that have forced them to live with pain and/or disabilities. Our personal experiences have been greatly enriched by the stories we have heard from patients, our students, and our colleagues. In our practices, workshops, and research, we have learned much from them about the courage of the human spirit and the limitations of the human body. Over many years we have developed approaches to helping patients that validate the individuality of clients, empower them with personally meaningful tools and skills, and honor the ebb and flow of available energy for managing on a day-to-day basis. Many of these approaches are an outgrowth of practicing solution-focused therapy as well as other approaches that emphasize the importance of individualizing care, accessing conscious and unconscious resources for healing, and the centrality of caring relationships.

☐ The Search for the Story

There are many articulate and poignant stories by and about those who have suffered from poorly understood and difficult-to-manage conditions. But few provide the dramatic effect necessary to stimulate compassion in others. Many of these stories stress the process of becoming ill and the stages related to grieving loss of roles, autonomy, or any future at all. Sometimes telling one's "story" and feeling heard can be healing in and of itself. But for many, simply telling the story (or hearing another's story) again and again can become a mantra keeping them focused only on the presence of all that is absent in their lives.

In an attempt to introduce the topic to health professionals, the authors did an extensive search of popular media (videos, movies, and books). We wanted to find presentations that sensitively represented the experiences of chronic pain and chronic illness. We found, perhaps not surprisingly, that the most sympathetic images were of young athletes who had lost mobility following a tragic accident, or young parents or children who were dying of a fatal illness. Those with ongoing, lingering complaints were more often portrayed as burdens to others or as seeking "secondary gain," a position unfortunately supported by many health care professionals. Often the role was played by a background figure providing comic relief, à la the hypochondriacal characters in Woody Allen movies (e.g., *Hannah and Her Sisters)* or the bizarre grandparents in *Willy Wonka and the Chocolate Factory*. Apparently the continued presence of characters who suffer, but neither recover nor die, detracts from a foreground plot, pace, mystery, or adventure.

People with chronic or debilitating illness live with their hopes and fears on a daily basis. In the best of worlds they have others who can and do support them in their efforts to maintain the best quality of life possible. Sometimes there are few supports. Often those in support roles need reinforcements along the way. Even with the support of others, the experience of "living apart" can be one of the most devastating aspects of being ill. The analogy we use for both the person with chronic pain/illness and the therapist/helper comes from the archetypal story of Robinson Crusoe. This classic novel presents a powerful image of a man who finds himself suddenly alone on a distant island—to remain for nearly 27 years. There are several aspects of this nearly 300-year-old story that are inconsistent with contemporary values about class, race, religion, and gender. Despite these inconsistencies, we believe the archetype provides a moving example of how one learns to survive in unexpected, often dangerous circumstances, and what role a therapist might have in providing needed assistance and companionship as the adventure unfolds (Defoe, 1719/1994).

☐ The Journey

While in practice we stress the individual's unique experiences and needs, we have found some themes in the stories we hear from clients when they first come to us. These themes include an initial sense of disorientation, a search for safety and rescue, seeking to understand, and eventually, a distressing descent into despair. Following brief descriptions of these themes is a synopsis of the story of Robinson Crusoe illustrating parallels to the journey into chronic illness/pain and, additionally, providing invaluable directions for how to live adventurously in an unknown land.

Disorientation: What's Happening to Me? Where Am I?   For the person who has a serious accident or gets a devastating medical diagnosis, the circumstances can be disturbingly similar to being catapulted into unknown territory. Even concerted attempts to provide patients with information, support, and resources may not diminish the existential isolation of being in a body that may suddenly seem foreign. The feeling of being cast adrift without a compass may be accentuated by the related experience of being thrust into a health care system that tends to focus on the illness rather than on the person who is experiencing it.

Trying to make initial sense of the situation comes late for some people and is an almost immediate response for others. When we become ill or have a serious injury, we usually have a number of previous experiences by which to measure the current one. We come to know that a cold lasts 7 to 10 days—that if we rest and do exercises and lift carefully, our sore backs will hurt less, and that the flu may make us feel that we will perish but we know we will be good as new in a matter of days or weeks at the most. But chronic pain and chronic illness are different. We can't even be sure we have a chronic illness until things don't improve within the normal time frame. When a chronic condition develops insidiously the experiences seem—at first—quite similar to those we've had in the past, only they don't respond as they did in the past. Sometimes symptoms or other markers seem totally unfamiliar; and we have to search our memories to try to "place" this new experience and to feel some sense of understanding regarding what this experience has to do with us—at least as we have known ourselves up to this point.

This need to orient oneself can be one of the most pressing tasks of managing the illness. The person diagnosed with cancer who was asymptomatic may find it difficult to know what *not* having any symptoms means. She didn't have symptoms before and that didn't mean she was healthy. The person with chronic pain may have considerable difficulty knowing if increased pain signals structural damage that needs attention, or meaninglessness pain that cannot be connected with physical signs or diminished by usual methods. It becomes difficult to know the "meaning" of the signs we use to orient ourselves—does pain mean we should seek help, worry about a worsening condition, or ignore it and try to get from where we are to a place we hope will be better (Costa & VandenBos, 1990; Crigger, 1996)?

Another source of disorientation is a shift in the perception of time. Without markers to define the passing of time, the days take on a different quality—merging into one another and seeming interminable. We all know that physical pain, nausea, fear, and other aspects of the illness experience can make time take on very different meanings. While we may still be counting the hours and days until we can get back to our "real lives," the experience of time can be greatly distorted. Some medications and treatments cloud consciousness or contribute to a changed sense of time. Moments without pain, or without the centrality of the illness experience, seem to pass fleetingly, while the objective time spent in pain or waiting for test results seems to bear no relationship to the subjective experience of time (Charmaz, 1991).

Many people with chronic illnesses also have impressive histories of previous illness, stressors, and losses. Researchers in the field of psychoneuroimmunology are finding important links between stress and illness, while social scientists are sometimes able to link issues of violence and abuse to subsequent illness. For some, then, the new life chapter on chronic illness will be part of an ongoing series of problems. For others, this is entirely new territory and they look desperately for a map to tell them where they are and how they might get back to where they came from (Kiecolt-Glaser & Glaser, 1995; Koss, 1993).

☐   Seeking Safety and the Search to Be Rescued

How best to find "safe haven" in chronic illness is not always apparent. Even if one has health care options, they may be limited in access, coverage, or ability to adequately diagnose or treat the newly defined "patient's" condition. When it is unknown whether a condition is potentially life threatening, attempts to control one's life in every way possible reflect a primal need. Some stay close to home, with only trusted family and friends. Others may keep things to themselves, preferring to control their environment by not talking about their fears. Physical "guarding" against pain is a nearly universal response that can ultimately become part of the problem. How does one learn to "relax" in the presence of signals that are intended to alert us to danger?

When faced with crisis and ongoing stresses, we all tend to use the tools that we know best. In some cases these can be highly valuable, providing us with tried and true ways to manage many of the challenges brought about by chronic pain and chronic illness, that is, the need to reduce anxiety, promote relaxation, determine priorities, and make decisions. We will use whatever has protected us in the past and try to keep on hand what we think may be helpful in this new situation. Few, however, will have well-developed ways to manage ongoing stressors or pain that doesn't respond to minor pain relievers and a good night's sleep. Friends and family try to help. We may be given any number of suggestions that others have found helpful. In some cases these suggestions provide valuable information and hopefulness. In other cases, however, they are like the clothes that fit someone else pretty well, but look and feel ridiculous on another person.

Most of all, we hope to be rescued. It is this hopefulness that often sends patients into desperate "doctor shopping." This phenomenon is often viewed with displeasure by health professionals, who see it as evidence of a lack of confidence in the health care provider and a source of frustration for the patient. In fact, it is confidence in the health profession that often keeps patients in an endless cycle of looking for a medical miracle and rescue by a savior who will be able to provide the prayed-for miracle. The search also may lead to a growing sense of despair and confusion, if treatments that are held out as "sure cures" fall short of the claims. Over time, patients may become disillusioned at the limitations of medicine for "curing" many chronic illness and most chronic pain (Lubkin, 1999).

☐ Seeking to Understand

When a condition resists cure, other questions come to the fore. Why me? The question is one that is central to the human experience, as evidenced by the titles of many contemporary self-help books, such as *When Bad Things Happen to Good People* (Kushner, 1981) and hundreds of books all purporting to answer the question "Why me?" Many religions, cultures, and families have belief systems that support serious consideration of offenses one might have committed—purposely or otherwise—against parents, ancestors, behavioral codes, taboos, and so on. Beliefs in predestination, karma, and "I told you so's" often merge into a sense that one must be guilty of something—even if it's not clear what the transgression might have been. For some this belief may provide a sense of predictability and continuity in life, as well as possible directions to take toward appeasement or restitution. For others, the question can become an added source of torture—pitting one against any and all who would impose their belief systems on an already suffering self (Spector, 1996).

More mundane attempts to understand involve trying to identify patterns by tracking symptoms and keeping lists of what tends to "trigger" flares or reduce pain. Many cognitive–behavioral programs build on this innate tendency of some to document and measure their experiences. We may be encouraged to list what makes the symptoms worse and to note how treatments are (or aren't) working. Some find these lists comforting—a way of trying to control experiences that seem unpredictable or immutable. Others may find that focusing on the problem and reporting fears makes the symptoms more prominent. Often it is difficult, in the short run, to know if treatments/interventions are having any effect (Mishel & Braden, 1988; Webster & Brennan, 1995).

Part of trying to understand involves wondering how to think and feel about the situation and fluctuations in the experience. The "good news/ bad news" phenomenon is all too familiar to many patients. It's good news that it hasn't gotten worse or spread, and it's bad news that it may not be responding to treatment as hoped. We want instant relief, and as time drags on, it may become more difficult to add "good" things to our lists. Gratitude is not the overriding or immediate response of many who are diagnosed with a chronic disease or wake to find themselves in a hospital following a serious injury. But for many, the realization that things could have been worse leads them to feel both gratitude and a range of other feelings: fear, anger, hopelessness, isolation. And thus begins a dialectic between the thankfulness and sense of outrage (Barasch, 1993).

☐ Despair

Despair, in all of its forms, is what usually brings people to therapy. Most people experiencing chronic illness or chronic pain are not objectively alone in the world. Nevertheless, the inherent subjectivity of pain and suffering seems to bring about a sense of being separate from others that is difficult to bridge. The tendency to physically isolate, noted in much of the pain literature, seldom addresses the existential dimension of feeling unable to escape from a "state" of time and place known only by pain, despair, depression, anxiety, and outright panic (Morris, 1994).

The Adventures of Robinson Crusoe: Saved or Cursed?

> September 30, 1659. I, poor miserable Robinson Crusoe, being shipwrecked, during a dreadful storm . . . came on shore on this dismal unfortunate island, which I called the Island of Despair, all the rest of the ship's company being drowned, and myself almost dead.

Thus begins the story that has been told and retold throughout the centuries in adventure novels, as well as historical and science fiction literature. Some of the stories, such as *Swiss Family Robinson* (Wyss, 1977), the 1965 to 1968 television series *Lost in Space* (Allen), and the movie *Castaway* (issued in 2000), are obvious derivations. Others, such as *Into the Forest* (Hegland, 1998), reflect contemporary concerns about how we would survive without the modern resources on which we have come to rely. The following brief overview of the story parallels the stages already described and introduces many of the concepts associated with "recrafting" a life.

Robin's Dilemma: Castaway and Lost.   Robin began trying to orient himself in his first hours on the island. With no one else to consult, he tried to fit this experience into similar ones he'd had in the past. He had been on several voyages and had earlier adventures—some of which had seemed to be as desperate as his current state. But in each case he had been befriended or escaped, and he had always had the outcome of returning to life as he had previously known it. Once enough time had elapsed, each event faded into dim memory, with no lasting effect on his expectations for himself or his life.

Robin also tried to locate himself in space and time. He desperately wanted what he did not have: a detailed map that would lay out the risks of taking one direction over another. Fierce tides, steep cliffs, hostile inhabitants, and innumerable unnamed dangers were very real possibilities. As a sailor, however, he was able to use the sun and stars to determine his approximate longitude and latitude. Based on this knowledge, he was aware that passing ships would be few and far between.

Once partially oriented in space, Robin realized it would still be a problem to orient himself in time. When he began to keep a journal, he recorded his strategy for keeping track of the days. He gathered large pieces of wood and carved on one: "Came on shore here on the 30th of September, 1659." He formed the wood into a great cross near the place where he had landed and each day cut a notch on the side of the post. Every seventh day he cut a longer notch, and marked the first day of each month with another longer notch, allowing him to track the passage of time that would become weeks, months, and years.

Robin Seeks Safety and Searches for Rescuers.   After his initial attempts at orientation, Robin began to plan how best to survive what he hoped would be a brief ordeal. His overwhelming need was to seek safety from known, imagined, and unknown threats. If he did not provide for these, he correctly assumed that he would soon meet a fate similar to his shipmates—death at the hands of the elements and Fate. Thus, finding shelter and identifying possible threats to safety became paramount concerns.

After searching for a safe place to stay, Robin found a nearby cave that would protect him from the elements and where he could hide if he needed to. Then Robin began to gather what could be salvaged from the ship, before it sank. During several trips to the doomed craft, he salvaged everything he hoped had any remote possibility of improving his chances of survival—from weapons and food to sails and anchor lines that could be modified for other uses. He even retrieved clothing that didn't fit him (but might be altered) and money, for which he knew he now had no use.

Not surprisingly, Robin was reluctant to go far from shore once he had found a safe cave in which to live and store his goods. He worried that other areas of the island might bring more dangers and—more importantly—if he were not on shore and scanning the horizon, he might miss his one opportunity to signal a ship and be rescued.

Those who are only superficially aware of the story of Robinson Crusoe assume the footprint Robin found on the shore was that of his longed-for companion, Friday, and that it somehow heralded the end to his awful island ordeal. A more careful reading reveals that the footprint was the source of terror for Robin, who had thought himself alone on the island, and now feared that the presence of other humans was not necessarily a sign of his rescue and salvation. On the contrary, he was so frightened by the footprint that he retreated to his cave for another few years. When he finally ventured out it was with great care as he eventually discovered a pile of human bones. The finding supported his worst fears: Any humans on the island were more likely to eat him than to send him back to England.

Robin Tries to Understand.   Why me? Robin revisited this question uncounted times during the 27 years he lived on the island. The question seemed always to lurk in the background, demanding continual reappraisal. Why had he been shipwrecked and why had he been spared? Early in his search for meaning, Robin recalled, with sadness and regret, that his father had warned him against the path he was taking in life. His discontent with the "middle way" of life had led him to seek adventure far from his home. His father predicted that God would not bless him if he took this course. His ruminations seemed at first to support his belief that his father's warning was also a curse—one that had doomed him to his now miserable existence. Yet he alone had been spared from death. For what purpose had his life been saved?

Even while feeling devastated by his new circumstances, Robin was acutely aware that he might well have suffered a worse fate. In the midst of his fear he also was grateful for the opportunity to survive and, perhaps, to change his ways. Impressively early in his ordeal, Robin began to keep a ledger that helped him maintain perspective. He noted not only his fears and losses (under "evil") but also how things could be much worse (under "good"). Emotional shifts between gratitude and despair became part of the challenge and stress of his new life.

Robin's Despair.   Much of Robin's despair during his time on the island was a result of his sense of total isolation from the outside world and other human beings. Although he had many pets on the island, he felt most keenly the loss of conversation, of being able to share ideas and feelings with another human being. Until he found Friday, isolation was the most consistent source of his distress. He wrote in his journal, "And now I began to enter into a melancholy silent life, such perhaps as was never heard of in the world before."

Turning Points.   Despite having been lost at sea, abandoned and alone on an island, without companionship and with fears for his safety and ultimate rescue, the point at which Robin reached bottom was when he fell ill. Not knowing what was wrong or what he could do for himself, his own resources seemed woefully inadequate to meet the new challenge of bodily breakdown. In this state of ultimate vulnerability he was presented with gifts from the Unconscious—fevered dreams that initially terrified him and ultimately gave him hope and direction. The dream figure who sought to kill him succeeded in killing his single-minded desire to return to his old life and left him with a growing trust in Fate, as well as his own skills and intuition. He began to consider the possibility that he might create a satisfactory life on the island.

After the turning point, Robin became more aware of the small blessings around him. He was astounded to see that, indeed, Nature was providing for him, in the shape of new growth from old seeds. Some grain had seeded itself from the stores he brought from the ship. He began to appreciate the wonder of life that could emerge from what had seemed barren and formidable.

Recrafting a Life

Robin had to be willing to leave his perpetual vigil at the shore's edge before he was open to exploring what the rest of the island might hold for him. Only after he had diminished his reliance on hope of rescue was he freed to find the beauty and abundance that he would never have imagined possible from his post near his small cave. Robin developed his powers of observation and carefully planned how he might discern and create some sense of predictability in his new circumstances. He ascertained the best ways to work with the growing cycles for his crops. He honored his need to seek shelter during the rainy seasons to protect his health. He began to raise goats, rather than hunt and kill them, thereby developing another replenishable source of energy. He took care to conserve and store the resources he had. He anticipated the possibility of a poor growing season and kept in his stores always more than he expected he would need. As he developed these skills, he became even more appreciative of the small blessings he had.

Over time, Robin engaged in a series of experiments intended to improve his options and quality of life. His first experiments were attempts to create the resources he needed and didn't have. He experimented in making pots for carrying water and storing what he grew. Many of his experiments failed repeatedly as he refined his skills. His first boat, carved out of a whole tree, was too heavy to drag to water. A second attempt floated but was difficult to steer. He engaged in the time-honored process of trial and error, learning from each mistake and noting his progress so that he might improve his methods over time. He took considerable pride in his accomplishments, while maintaining a good sense of humor about the inevitable failed experiments. Once Friday became part of the story, his skills were also incorporated in the experiments, building on what Robin had already learned.

Further Adventures

Robin's adventures as a castaway formed the major focus of Defoe's novel *Robinson Crusoe*. But there was a sequel, *The Further Adventures of Robinson Crusoe* (Defoe, 1719), as there are sequels to all of our adventures. Many of these sequels will tell of lives lived quite differently, and of adventures never before imagined. For some, as a consequence of the experience of chronic illness or chronic pain, questions about the possibilities of life in the hereafter may become more prominent—and signal the beginning of a new or newly energized spiritual quest. Clarifying priorities is nearly universal. For all of us, the quality of life we are able to lead in the present moment greatly depends on the skills and efforts we can muster to recraft our lives in the face of changing circumstances. As one client described her turning point: "One day I noticed that I was still alive. So I decided that I'd better get on with my life."

Recrafting a life is ultimately an individual endeavor, but not one that must be undertaken without companionship. It is to that adventure and the role of the worthy companion that the remainder of this book is dedicated.

☐ How to Use This Book

While this book is not intended to substitute for appropriate medical care, we know that our quality of life is closely related to an ability to care and be cared for by ourselves and others. Toward that end, part I provides a broad overview of some of the underlying issues and principles to consider when working with people having chronic illness or chronic pain. The therapist's philosophy of care and beliefs about health and healing may or may not be consistent with clients' cultural, religious, or idiosyncratic beliefs about why they become ill and what is likely to foster relief, if not a cure. These perspectives define the context of therapy and invariably influence outcomes of care as well as what happens in therapy sessions.

Part II provides more detailed explanations of our therapeutic approaches for working with clients in therapy sessions. In addition to providing examples of the first meeting and the use of a range of in-session approaches, including ways to utilize hypnosis and other states of consciousness, we have also provided several tools that clients have found are helpful in identifying their goals, resources, and progress. It is possible to use these tools without integrating their use into a unified approach to working with clients. However, their best use will be in combination with ongoing, intermittent contacts to track progress, reinforce strengths, and learn new skills. In our experience, people come into therapy for many reasons and describe having fluctuating energy to invest in therapy or self-care. We recognize that "readiness" is neither consistent nor invariably unidirectional, particularly for those with chronic conditions. We have nevertheless been impressed that some people are able to move from being simply curious about what they might do to improve their quality of life to becoming active explorers—always seeking new tools and skills that might someday come in handy. Selected experiments are described and illustrated in the context of therapy sessions in part II. Part II ends with attention to the need for therapists to also practice self-care.

Chapter 11 lists resources for clients and therapists for use either in sessions or between sessions. Included are a number of "experiments" in self-care that others have found helpful in managing symptoms, clarifying priorities, or fostering personal growth. Some combination of intermittent meetings and the use of "experiments" between these meetings meets the requirements of reducing costs and sensitivity to the unpredictability of living with chronic illness. In addition, we provide a listing of selected resources, such as books, websites, and organizations dedicated to providing information and/or services for those with chronic health problems. We hope you will find that each of the sections provides information and perspectives to enrich your clinical work and diminish the sense of helplessness that patients and therapists often experience in the face of human suffering.

Here is a brief overview of the remaining chapters:

Part I

Chapter 2. Becoming a Worthy Companion: Clarifying and Refining a Philosophy of Care

"Friday" provides the model for becoming a worthy companion and the centrality of the healing relationship. Characteristics of healing relationships are presented in the context of personal, cultural, and philosophical perspectives on health and healing.

Chapter 3. Caring and Self-Care

Several models of self-care and care of the self are linked with cultural belief systems and different definitions of relevant "outcomes" of care in chronic illness.

Chapter 4. Creating a Meaningful Life

This chapter explores different perspectives on meaning in illness and paths for creating a meaningful life. Several models are presented for helping clients shift, focus, order and/or expand consciousness. Attention to ultradian rhythms and states of flow are emphasized.

Part II

Chapter 5. Stages of Recrafting a Life

Clients suffering from chronic pain and illness come to therapists at many different levels of readiness for change. This chapter outlines the five stages that reflect the available energy, hopefulness, curiosity, and willingness to risk that are necessary for recrafting a life. This stage-of-change framework is utilized to inform therapists of types of interventions and therapeutic relationships that will be most helpful in relation to the client's current view of the world, level of energy, and access to available resources.

Chapter 6. The First Meeting: Exploring the Landscape: The Solution-Focused Approach

This chapter introduces the solution-focused framework as the principal mechanism in conducting the initial interview with clients suffering from chronic pain and illness. The reader is introduced to the core components of this approach along with their application to shift the client's focus away from an ineffectual entrenched view of the problematic past toward a proactive and hopeful outlook in regard to solutions in the present and future.

Chapter 7. Solution Building

This chapter outlines solution-focused interventions in the second and subsequent clinical sessions through "framing in" the foundation constructed by the therapist and client in the first session. This is accomplished by three (interrelated) clinical interventions. The first utilizes a structured, solution-focused interview to elicit, amplify, and reinforce the resources the client is already employing to improve his or her condition. The second draws upon instruments to evoke present and future possibilities that the client might employ to improve her condition. Finally we offer a number of "experimental" tasks that can significantly enhance the solution-finding process from the beginning stages experienced by sufferer/victims through to the maintenance process employed during the recrafter stage.

Chapter 8. Recrafting Consciousness: Clinical Hypnosis for Pain and Chronic Illness

This chapter reviews the history of hypnosis in the treatment of pain and chronic illness, its phenomena, and applications for chronic pain and illness. Expanding on the clinical applications of hypnotic and nonhypnotic altered states of consciousness, we present a three stage-clinical model integrating the work of Milton Erickson and solution-focused therapy. Finally, specific self-hypnosis applications are provided to relieve clients suffering from pain and chronic illness.

Chapter 9. Suggestive Therapeutics: Hypnotic and Posthypnotic Suggestion to Treat Chronic Pain and Illness

This chapter presents principles, components, and techniques of hypnotic suggestion along with ways to integrate them into the self-hypnosis protocols. Specifically, a clinical intervention framework for hypnotic and posthypnotic suggestions is presented as a continuum of suggestion strategies ranging from Erickson's microdynamics of pacing to direct behavioral injunctions that provide relief to clients suffering from chronic pain and illness. Additionally, strategies for posthypnotic suggestion are presented with specific applications that address time-, symptom-, and event-related contingencies that are common to this clinical population. These principles and techniques are illustrated by lengthy case examples.

Chapter 10. Caring for the Caregiver

A brief overview of caregiver stress and burnout. Risk factors and mediators of burnout are described, as well as examples of self-care for caregivers.

Chapter 11. Experiments

A range of self-care "experiments" is suggested for therapist to use in session or for client homework. Tools are suggested for identifying general approaches to self-care use and effectiveness and for evaluating experiments. A cross-reference table guides readers to chapters in which experiments are referenced and/or illustrated with clinical examples. Selected resources for caregivers and clients are also provided.

☐ References

Allen, I. (1965). *Lost in space*. CBS television series.

Barasch, M. (1993). *The healing path*. Los Angeles: Jeremy Tarcher.

Charmaz, K. (1991). *Good days, bad days: The self in chronic illness and time*. New Brunswick, NJ: Rutgers University Press.

Chilton, M. (1996). OAM report: Panel recommends integrating behavioral and relaxation approaches into medical treatment of chronic pain, insomnia. *Alternative Therapies, 2*(1), 18–26.

Costa, P., & VandenBos, G. (Eds.). (1990). *Psychological aspects of serious illness: Chronic conditions, fatal diseases, and clinical care*. Washington, DC: American Psychological Association.

Crigger, N. (1996). Testing an uncertainty model for women with multiple sclerosis. *Advances in Nursing Science, 18*(3), 37–47.

Defoe, D. (1994) *Robinson Crusoe*. London: Everyman. (Original work published 1719.)

Defoe, D. (1999). *Further adventures of Robinson Crusoe (great stories)*. Carol Stream, IL: Tyndale House.

Eisenberg, D., Davis, R., Ethan, S., Appel, S., Wilkey, S., Van Rompay, M., & Kessler, R. (1998). Trends in alternative medicine use in the United States, 1990–1997: Results of a follow-up national study. *Journal of the American Medical Association, 280*(18), 1569–1575.

Eisenberg, D. M., Kessler, R. C., Foster, C., Norlock, F., Calkins, D., & Delbanco, T. L. (1993). Unconventional medicine in the United States. *New England Journal of Medicine, 328*(4), 246–252.

Fishman, P., VonKorff, M., Lozano, P. S., & Hecht, J. (1997). Chronic care costs in managed care. *Health Affairs, 16*(3), 239–247.

Hegland, J. (1998). *Into the forest*. New York: Bantam.

Hoffman, C., Rice, D., & Sung, H. (1996). Persons with chronic conditions: Their prevalence and costs. *Journal of American Medical Association, 276*(18), 1473–1479.

Kiecolt-Glaser, J., & Glaser, R. (1995). Psychoneuroimmunology and health consequences: Data and shared mechanisms. *Psychosomatic Medicine, 57,* 269–274.

Koss, M. (1993). The negative impact of crime victimization on women's health and medical use. *Journal of Women's Health, 2*(1), 67–72.

Kushner, H. (1981). *When bad things happen to good people*. New York: Schocken.

Lubkin, I. (Ed.). (1999). *Chronic illness: Impact and interventions* (4th ed.). Boston: Jones & Bartlett.

Mishel, M., & Braden, C. (1988). Finding meaning: Antecedents of uncertainty in illness. *Nursing Research, 37,* 98–103, 127.

Morris, D. (1994). Pain's domain: What we make of pain. *Wilson Quarterly*, 8–26.

Sobel, D. (1995). Rethinking medicine: Improving health outcomes with cost-effective psychosocial interventions. *Psychosomatic Medicine, 57,* 234–244.

Spector, R. (1996). *Cultural diversity in health and illness* (4th ed.). Norwalk, CT: Appleton & Lange.

U.S. Department of Health and Human Services, Public Health Service. (1990). Healthy people 2000. Diabetes and chronic disabling conditions. In *Healthy people 2000: National health promotion and disease prevention objectives* (pp. 441–478). Washington, DC: U.S. Government Printing Office, DHS Publication No. (PHS) 91-50212.

Webster, D., & Brennan, T. (1995). Use and effectiveness of women's psychologic self-care strategies for IC. *Health for Women International, 16*(5), 463–475.

Wyss, J. D. (1977). *The Swiss family Robinson.* New York: Bantam.

I

THEORY

Becoming a Worthy Companion: Clarifying and Refining a Philosophy of Care

What is a worthy companion? In this chapter we discuss the centrality of the healing relationship and characteristics of healing relationships. An overview of some of the personal, cultural, and philosophical factors that shape therapists, clients, and the therapeutic process are described, as well as contrasting models of helping and coping.

☐ Friday's Conversion

Friday was not the story's hero nor even a particularly central character. Contrary to some modern interpretations of *Robinson Crusoe*, Friday played a very small role, only entering the story after Robin had already learned most of the skills he needed to survive on the island. To be sure, Friday had specialized information about island living from having spent many years surviving and prospering in similar conditions, but this was of less importance to Robin than might be expected. Robin wished, above all, to have someone who would take the time to learn his language and hear his thoughts. Friday was most useful to Robin once he had learned how Robin had survived and how he had organized his life on the island. Friday first needed to learn how Robin had developed the resources and skills to manage his life on a day-to-day basis.

21

There is much at which to take offense in the story of Robin's relationship to his trusted "man 'Friday.'" By today's standards, the image of the great white male "saving" the indigenous "savage" provides an astonishing singular example of racism, sexism, classism, and oppressive fundamentalism. If it is possible, however, to look beyond the 17th-century historically bound assumptions of Defoe, there are important lessons to be learned from the "instruction" of Friday on how to be a worthy companion.

An important aspect of the story was Friday's own personal transformation as he turned away from what was presented as his native culture's acceptance of cannibalism. Whatever the historical accuracy of the claim related to Friday's culture, it might be asked if a form of cannibalism continues today in the psychotherapy community. Several critics have noted that one aspect of longer term therapies is the propensity for encouraging, with varying degrees of subtlety and intent, a dependence on the therapist. When patients are desperate and vulnerable the therapist has considerable potential power to take over a client's life. "Taking over" can include an unconscious expectation that the client will accept the therapist's values or be successfully indoctrinated into the dominant culture. Other examples of "taking over" include having clients memorize lists of what someone else considers "irrational beliefs" or someone else's list of desirable beliefs (often in the form of predetermined "affirmations"). Although either of the latter examples can be immensely helpful to an individual client, to the degree that they discourage or drown out the client's own voice they are more likely to diminish, rather than enhance, the client's sense of self-confidence.

☐ Fear and Trust

All clients bring to the therapy relationship their expectations and unique beliefs about health and illness. Too often, they also bring with them the scars of failed therapeutic relationships in which they may have felt unheard and disrespected. It is important to note that Robin, at first, very much distrusted Friday. Others had come to the island with their own agendas, and were found to be untrustworthy. Despite hopes of aid and support, Robin learned to watch carefully for signs that Friday might prove more intent on meeting his own needs than on helping Robin. So it is with many who come to therapists seeking some comfort and assistance and fearing that they will lose more than they may gain in the transactions. Many have had a series of disappointing or even degrading experiences in their previous contacts with the health care system. Patients who continue to complain of distress, despite the best efforts of health care providers, often leave everyone involved feeling helpless and hopeless. In too many cases this frustration is turned on the client, who is told "there is nothing more we can do for you. You will just have to learn to live with it." This view may be reinforced by family, friends, or coworkers who urge clients to "snap out of it" or to "stop feeling sorry" for themselves.

Furthermore, learning how to "live with it" often seems impossible or overwhelming. Clients, who have often been led to believe that each new treatment or treatment provider will be able to successfully rescue them, bring with them the scars of having been more than once "seduced and abandoned." It is not unusual for clients to commence telling their story with the dissociated sense of reading a script that has ceased to have any personal meaning. At the other extreme are clients whose distress is palpable and who seem desperate to convince the listener of the depth of their despair. Either extreme may be interpreted by the weary and time-pressed provider as evidence of hysteria or "la belle indifference"—leading to diagnoses of an underlying personality disorder, "somatization," or "conversion" disorder.

Depression and anxiety generally are seen as understandable consequences of serious illness, associated with relative helplessness, loss of function or role, worry about the future, and so on. Sometimes symptoms are dismissed as being "natural" when one has had a serious or lingering health problem. But in many cases, clients tell their story in a dissociated manner that may be less "la belle indifference" than a recognizable response to inescapable stressors. If we think of the metaphor of having been thrust onto an unknown shore and having difficulty telling friend from foe, it seems quite likely that some clients also may be suffering from a form of posttraumatic stress disorder (PTSD). The possibility seems particularly plausible if their illness or pain seems to "come out of nowhere" or to "sneak up" on them, or if it is experienced as a senseless form of torture for reasons beyond knowing. Sometimes it's related to memories of painful or debilitating treatments. Part of reducing clients' distrust is learning how they see their situation and what they expect, hope for, or may fear.

☐ Ideas about Health and Illness

Philosophies about life, death, purpose, meaning, suffering, health, and healing are intricately woven into the fabric of consciousness. To some degree the trust a client has in any health care provider may be dependent on having shared definitions of health and illness, and beliefs about how an ill person should be treated. Only recently have health care professionals become more familiar with alternative models of health and healing. Exposure to other belief systems has become a matter of greater importance since a widely cited article by Harvard physicians reported that more than $13 billion was being spent annually, out of pocket, in the United States for what they labeled "unconventional medicine" and what others might call "alternative" or "complementary therapies" (Eisenberg et al., 1993).

The dominant Western views about health and illness, called allopathic medicine, are based on the biomedical model of disease. The "Decade of the Brain" has begun to reduce Descartes's split between body and mind to a problem of insufficient information. This perspective holds, for many, the promise that eventually consciousness itself and all behavior will be explained anatomically and physiologically. For example, depression, in the biomedical model, is explained by relative deficiencies in the neurotransmitters norepinephrine and serotonin, and is treated by providing exogenous medications that affect the manufacture, processing, or utilization of these chemicals. The biomedical model relies on the scientific method and epidemiologic data to track down the sources of problems and find biologically based solutions. Acceptable evidence of problems, in this model, appear in the form of observable deviations from norms. These norms are assumed to be shared by most, if not all, humans. In contrast, psychodynamic models would suggest the importance of attending to the emotions related to losses, particularly those occurring in the formative years that might be reactivated in the present. In cognitive–behavioral models, one is encouraged to change one's thoughts or behaviors to increase facilitative thoughts and diminish distressing ones and/or to improve function by practicing certain behaviors, irrespective of the related thoughts or emotions involved (Roth & Fonagy, 1996). Stress-response theories, gate-control theories, and psychoneuroimmunology theories all attempt to bridge the either–or thinking of the body–mind split, emphasizing different aspects of known relationships among thoughts, feelings, behavior, and their physiologic correlates (Lovallo, 1997).

The simplified models just described represent only a few of the approaches to understanding health and illness that are recognized by therapists. In turn, therapists work with clients who have their own beliefs about illness, and these beliefs may bear little resemblance to any of these models. Clients may embrace energy-based theories of health and illness or feel attracted to homeopathic, chiropractic, transpersonal, and other nonallopathic ideas about health and illness (Dossey, Keegan, & Guzzetta, 2000; Weil, 1995). Each of these models has different explanations for the experience of illness and incorporates different views of the roles and responsibilities of clients and therapists, as well as of families and other health care providers.

The relationships between illness and disease are also complex. *Disease* is the problem from the practitioner's perspective. In the narrow biological terms of the biomedical model, this means that disease is recognized only as an alteration in biological functioning or structure. In contrast, *illness* is the subjective experience of symptoms and suffering. As a broader concept, illness carries with it a society's views of how a sick person, family members, and social network should perceive and manage various symptoms and disabilities. Illness perceptions include how one determines if specific symptoms, such as a runny nose, pain, or fatigue, should be seen as an expected part of life or signals to seek treatment.

The ways we understand and treat illness are based on local cultural orientations, usually described as "common sense." When complaints of subjective illness are brought to health professionals, they are usually recast into biomedical models of disease, which seek explanations based on objective abnormalities of biologic structure and function. These abnormalities are presumed to cause the symptoms and complaints that brought the patient (Kleinman, 1998, pp. 5–6).

In Western society, the "sick role" must be conferred by an expert in the health care profession. Only after this occurs may a sick person be exempt from performing expected social obligations, including caring for oneself while ill. Accepting help from others is expected as part of the sick role. Legitimization of the sick role is often temporary, however, as being sick is seen as undesirable and one is expected to recover as rapidly as possible and to return to one's duties (Parsons, 1972).

Each of us carries around multiple and often conflicting theories related to health and illness. For example, as either helper or recipient of help, we usually have beliefs about who or what is responsible for a particular illness and about who is responsible for doing something about it. These often unexamined models also incorporate ideas about what people need and about what will happen if help is not forthcoming. By developing a 2 × 2 grid of responsibility for cause and responsibility for solution as in table 2.1, four models are derived.

In the *medical* model, patients are not held responsible for either the

TABLE 2.1. Model of Helping and Coping

Problems	Solutions	
	Client	**Other**
Client	Moral model	Enlightenment model
Other	Compensatory model	Medical model

Note. From Brickman et al. (1982), p. 370.

cause or the solution, and the expected response of others is to provide treatment. In the *compensatory* model, clients are not seen as responsible for the cause but are responsible for the solution, associated with the belief that having more power will make it possible. In the *enlightenment* model, clients are held responsible for the cause but are viewed as unwilling or unable to provide a solution to the problem unless they develop more discipline. The *moral* model holds that clients are responsible for the cause and solution to the problem and only need to be more motivated (Brickman et al., 1982). Many sophisticated models have been described to help therapists match their beliefs and attitudes about patients and problems with the theories they use in practice. When these attribution models conflict with clients' belief systems about when improved coping is needed, rather than help, the results can be frustrating to both parties and potentially lethal. When combined with differing beliefs about the relationships between body, mind, and spirit, the probability of miscommunication increases exponentially. Much of the professional name-calling of patients (e.g., "crocks," "frequent fliers") derives from these types of mismatched expectations. When people reject professional advice or don't respond to treatment as expected, there can be a tendency all too often to "blame the victim" for unexplained symptoms or treatment nonresponse.

Miscommunications have become of greater concern as we move toward a global society in which the cultural and religious beliefs of different groups (both patients and providers) may be totally incongruent. The terms *culturally sensitive, culturally congruent,* and *culturally safe* are used by those who are concerned about improving communication and quality of life. The term *politically correct* is more often used by those who are either frustrated with the enormity of the demand to honor all differences or who believe differences should be of secondary concern when scientific evidence exists. Sometimes we are alerted to possible differences in beliefs when there are obvious ethnic or racial differences between patient and provider. Other differences are more subtle and may be based on gender, age, personality, life experience, and so on. Even within the same family, one often sees competing explanations vying for acceptance. A person who becomes ill frequently or doesn't recover as expected may be seen as overtired, fragile, lazy, bad, spoiled, needy, deluded, misdiagnosed, or possessed by malevolent spirits at different times and/or by different people.

The model we describe is intended to work with the differences people bring to the therapy situation, without overclassifying them based on any particular characteristics. Many examples of how to put this principle into practice are described in part II of this book. At the same time, we would encourage providers to become knowledgeable about possible differences in health beliefs and clients' preferences for understanding and treating health problems. Even the most well-intentioned questions may be seen as insulting if, for example, they are asked automatically of the family member with the best ability to communicate. If that person is considered by the family to be too young or the wrong gender, or is asked very personal questions about an elder, the family may feel disrespected before the intake has even begun.

☐ Health and Healing

When you ask people what being "healthy" means, most will describe an absence of illness or symptoms, having the ability to carry out desired roles and functions, or having the capacity to adapt to stressors based on effective coping. Westernized people will less often describe health as a harmony of body–mind–spirit, sometimes called a *eudaemonistic* (quality of life) model of health, which emphasizes a subjective sense of well-being, harmony, or fitness (Watson, 1988; Woods, 1989). Many indigenous groups have maintained this sense that health is more than the absence of disease; rather, it is seen as a reflection of being in "right relationship" with oneself, one's community, and one's sense of the transcendent.

A German ethnologist noted:

> There are three things our [Western] culture has forgotten: basic health, healing, and holiness. All three words have the same linguistic root, and the concepts have same goal: sanity, integrity, completeness, salvation, happiness, liberation, magic. . . . Basic health and well-being means the panoramic perception of all levels of being. Healing means healing culture first, then people, and finally sickness. Holiness means feeling many—all—spheres of existence within oneself. We have lost this triad with its qualities of wisdom, happiness, and magic. (Kalweit, 1992, p. 1)

The word *health* comes from *Haelen*, meaning "whole," or "holy." Anthropologist Jean Achterberg's study of healing found several common threads that seemed to unite women healers across cultures and across time. They tended to "see body, mind, and spirit as the inseparable nature of humankind" and their work as aspiring to "wholeness or harmony within the self, the family, and the global community." Rather than an experience to simply be halted, "They regard sickness as a potential catalyst for both emotional and spiritual growth, among other things." They "support the virtues of nature as healing resources, and the curative aspects of caring." And "They view healing not as something one does to another, but as a process that takes place through the healer/healee relationship" which must be made of trust, love and hope" (Achterberg, 1990, pp. 3–4).

This view is remarkably similar to that held by Florence Nightingale, who wrote nearly 150 years ago that "all disease, at some period or other of its course, is more or less a reparative process" (Nightingale, 1860/1969, pp. 8–9). Through careful observation of what helps and what hinders the reparative process, she counseled nurses to pay particular attention to the effects of noise, lack of variety, choice of food, exposure to sunlight and clean air, and visitors filled with "chattering hopes and advice." Further, she concluded, knowledge of

> pathology teaches the harm that disease has done . . . [and] nothing more. We know nothing of the principle of health . . . except from observation and experience. And nothing but observation and experience will teach us the ways to maintain or to bring back the state of health. It is often thought that medicine is the curative process. It is no such thing . . . [medicine and surgery] can do [nothing] but remove obstructions; neither can cure; nature alone cures. . . . And what nursing has to do . . . is to put the patient in the best condition for nature to act upon him. (p. 133)

Nightingale's description of "curing" is synonymous with what others define as healing. For example, Whitmont wrote: "Seen from a wider perspective, the diseased subject and the invading process are like protagonist and antagonist in the staged performance of the life drama of evolution that is meant to usher in new realities." He noted that, although disturbing or painful, improved immune responses may be the result of an acute illness and depression or severe illness often fosters a new outlook on life (Whitmont, 1993, pp. 125–126). Models that view healing as having the potential for change and growth are sometimes referred to as transformative or transcendent models of health and healing (Miller & C'deBaca, 1994). The goal of Western medicine and of most patients who seek help from health professionals is generally far less ambitious. Most patients want relief from their symptoms and elimination of the underlying disease. They want to be cured, once and for all, and to feel well again. The vast majority of patients come to us with this single desire. And yet, once the hope for cure is relinquished, the call to healing/wholeness can be a profound experience: As one client said: "I would never have asked to have this illness. But neither would I want to go back to being in my old life—I have learned too much and become aware of dimensions of life that I might otherwise have known nothing about."

☐ Healers and Healing Relationships: Characteristics of Healers

The metaphors of Robinson Crusoe and of Friday are intended to elicit compassion for both characters—for our clients and for ourselves. In some ways we are stranded together and our fates are, however temporarily, inextricably linked. We can become worthy companions, in part, by developing a caring philosophy, by listening, and by doing what clients define as helpful. In part II, the emphasis is on what we can do to help clients directly and to help them help themselves.

At least as important as our "doing," however, is our way of being when we are with them and in our daily lives. For example, when asked the qualities of a good nurse, some Sioux indicated that having a "clean heart" was essential (Selzler, 1996). Having a clean heart is important to health and involves being respectful to yourself and others, knowing how to behave, respect for environment and other people, generosity to others, seeing each individual as unique, and knowing each possesses a special purpose in the universe. A clean heart means "living at the right moment," that is, thinking ahead about what your actions will do. Having a clean heart also means having the ability to communicate positive healthy feelings to the one who is sick, and being free of negative thoughts or intentions when attending to the sick person in order to bring intentional thought to the healing process. To be able to do so requires, preferably, attending to one's own personal problems and issues prior to coming to work or, minimally, clearing one's mind in order to focus positively on the patient.

There is a growing desire among health care professionals to reassume their identity as healers. To many the notion of "healing" is either synonymous with "curing" or decidedly too New Age to be appealing. Worse, many take on the mantle of "healer" as a form of grandiosity implying that the power to heal lies with the health care "provider," rather than in the client or "nature." With some trepidation, then, a selected review of the characteristics of healers and the healing relationship follows.

The concept of intention and the importance of the healer's consciousness are seen as important in most healing models. Although some believe that the healer must bring a peaceful centeredness to the relationship, others believe that conscious control of thoughts and feelings is necessary. Envisioning clients as whole and having positive intentions for them would be an example of the latter. LeShan claimed that many of the antecedents of today's therapies are derived from spiritual values and related models of healing—for example, Rogers's client-centered therapy is related to Taoist concepts, while the ability to change consciousness is valued in psychoanalytic therapy, hypnosis, biofeedback, and many forms of relaxation (LeShan, 1966). Clearly, some models focus on the consciousness of the healer, and others emphasize the consciousness of both healer and client.

The importance of intention and consciousness is underscored by the voluminous literature on patients' expectations for healing. The role of expectations in healing is often described in terms of the *placebo effect*. Controversies abound concerning the role of the placebo effect in response to treatments (Brody, 2000; Harrington, 1997). The dominant biomedical view of the powerful therapeutic effects associated with positive expectations is that they are nuisance factors to be controlled for in clinical research, in order to determine whether interventions are actually effective. For others, who would agree with Nightingale, this inherent capacity for self-healing is the essence of healing. Also called the *Haelen effect* (Quinn, 1989), or *remembered wellness* (Benson, 1996), *placebo* means "I will please" and builds on the positive expectations of the patient which usually reflect the expectations of the provider. Benson cautioned, however, that negative expectations are equally powerful, and the *nocebo* effect can be quite deleterious to the patient's condition.

The placebo effect, which is credited with between 30 and 60% of all treatment responses (Brody, 2000) can be mobilized by trust in the provider (sometimes this means oneself) and a belief in the treatment. Although in most cases this means a treatment has to "make sense" within a client's beliefs about health and healing, in some cases, it is precisely that which is foreign, exotic, or mysterious that carries with it a powerful ability to mobilize the healing response (Harrington, 1997). In most cases, the latter model is based on faith in the mysterious abilities of an external healer, or shamanic figure (i.e., an outside "expert"), who has access to information that is not generally known to others. Sometimes healing involves the healer's ability to heal by altering the client's and/or the healer's consciousness.

☐ Healers and Healing Relationships: Healing Roles

Multiple roles may be taken by caregivers at various points in time and in response to fluctuating client needs. The role of the healer as expert may be an important one in some cultures and for some clients. In our model, the role of healer is probably more consistent with the concept of being an educator in the fullest sense, that is, through educing—drawing out something hidden, reserved, or latent (Palmer, 1993).

The stages of "recrafting," described in chapter 5, address the shifts we see in clients. Therapists also experience these shifts. Roles are partly a function of time, in the sense they parallel the development of any relationship. We start out as strangers with the goal of coming to know one another. Sometimes we function as a resource person, making referrals, suggesting contacts or references. At other times we may serve as a surrogate for parents or friends who may be no longer present or for those who, though present, sometimes cannot bear to hear their loved one's greatest hopes and deepest fears. We may be seen as a support person when needs are minimal. At other points we may have to make the necessary connections for more complete care in the case of increasing disability or hospice care for those nearing the end of life.

Flexibility in shifting roles is essential to being a responsive practitioner. During a single contact we may find ourselves taking, by turns, the roles of advocate, validator, advice giver, counselor/consoler, and journey guide. More often than not, we play the role of a cheerleader, fanning the dying embers of passion for life. When we try to learn what clients are motivated to do, we feel like detectives, sifting through clues to find the single piece of information (a phrase, a subtle change in affect, a gesture) that could bring energy to the process or hold the promise of growth. One of our most important roles is being a second set of eyes and ears attuned to seeing and hearing strength in apparent weakness and hope in the midst of despair. And we must combine the ability to be flexible "shape shifters" with being authentic—only one of the paradoxes inherent in a healing relationship.

☐ Healers and Healing Relationships: Characteristics of Healing Relationships

A healing relationship is one characterized by a desire to be of service. The overall question underlying a healing relationship is "How can I help?" (Dass & Gorman, 1991). For the current illness care system to become a true health care system, there must be a move toward more "relationship-centered care" (Pew-Fetzer Task Force, 1994). Providing the possibility for a healing relationship requires an exquisite balance between extremes and a high tolerance for ambiguity and paradox. We must be dependable without fostering dependence. We stand up for our clients by assuring them they are complete and "enough" even as we encourage them to become more and to risk growing and changing. We take seriously the pain and suffering of our clients without succumbing to their own despair. We may personally maintain holistic views of health and still be able to suspend these to work within the client's perspective. We help clients expand limited definitions without diminishing the centrality and dignity of their own perspectives. Although addressing the dimension of psychological, rather than somatic, illness and pain, Linehan (1993) spoke eloquently to the dialectic tension and potential paradoxes inherent in having simultaneously held beliefs. The message given to clients is, in essence: "You are fine just the way you are" (i.e., you know what you need) *and* "you must change" (you need to expand your repertoire of ways of being, knowing, and doing).

Perhaps the most important paradox in our model is the requirement that we demonstrate our expertise by acknowledging that we are not experts. Humility is not a quality that is often encouraged in graduate school or in contemporary life. Humility is what working with people who live in pain and debilitating or life-threatening illnesses will teach us, if we are willing to learn. It starts with remembering who lives with the problem every day and acknowledging the client's expertise as central.

The openness necessary to learn from clients is the opposite of the "mindlessness" that occurs when we rush to classify a person, diagnose a problem, and prescribe a treatment without being truly present in the relationship (Langer, 1989). The pressures to do more with less and to quickly "diagnose" and "prescribe" are omnipresent in most health care settings. Similarly, the focus on population-based care and encouragement to develop cost-effective "programs," designed to treat the mythical average patient with "x" problem, carry with them the risk of fostering mindless relationships and mindless results. Having preconceived ideas about clients and their problems predisposes us to spend whatever limited time we have either assuming others accept our reality or trying to convince them of our position—that is, our view of what's really wrong. When we rush to judgment, however well intended, there is a closing of options and a tendency to "half-listen" as we worry about the next client and the ticking of the clock.

True presence is only partially a function of available time. Maintaining a sense of "mindfulness" involves having what Buddhists call "beginner's mind"—a way of being in the world as if everything were being seen for the first time, without the automatic labeling or non-seeing of the familiar. Change is constant. Having and maintaining a genuine curiosity about a client's experience is the first step. Being willing to be surprised by the expected and open to the unexpected brings energy to a relationship that a limited concern with treatment compliance can destroy.

When clients no longer need us to be of service (and along the way) we often ask them what has been helpful. What we hear has less to do with our techniques than with our acceptance, respect, and caring. We are more likely to hear, "You were always telling me that I was okay, that the ways I feel are normal. After a while I began to believe it myself." Or, "You were able to see more than my problems and you helped me see that some of what I thought were weaknesses were actually strengths." We believe the most powerful "interventions" are those that clients provide themselves—often when they reframe their experiences in ways that challenge us to change and grow. A woman with chronic pain from a work-related injury concluded: "If I can't fight it, perhaps I can learn to somehow enjoy it—as strange as that may sound."

☐ Personal Philosophies and Frameworks of Care

Much of the foregoing and what follows reflects the philosophies the authors have developed over many years about what makes one a good therapist and a worthy companion. Certainly there are many characteristics, roles, and ways of helping we did not identify that are equally important and may be more consistent with the reader's own philosophies and practices. Working with clients who are ill, in pain, and/or are dying is invariably challenging. To do so, we believe it is important to have a well-developed philosophy regarding health and healing without imposing that belief on clients. We seek to remain open to modifying our own views and curious about others, without reducing that philosophy to an ill-conceived "technique-of-the-month" approach. We try to listen without judging. We take seriously the need to practice responsible discernment, knowing when to seek supervision, suggest referrals, or recognize serious risks.

We believe that the "best practice" can take many forms, as long as it is reflective practice—that is, as long as the practitioner is able to remain conscious about the process used and reflect on the effects of that process on clients and ourselves. If we successfully avoid commitment to any particular position, it becomes impossible to bring authenticity to the healing relationship. Consciously identifying our own belief systems provides some protection against the unconscious imposition of beliefs on clients and makes it possible to answer with honesty if clients ask our positions (which is likely). For example, we may be asked where we stand in the "battle against death." Do we see death as the enemy? As a culture committed to perpetual youth, physical fitness, "quality time," and "better living through chemistry," many of us no longer know how to face the finiteness of life or how to comfort those who have lost loved ones or are dying. We treat death as an aberration, rather than as a certainty in life. Often, we must help clients hope for the best and prepare for the worst. Which is which? To be a worthy companion we must know the answer for ourselves and cherish our ignorance about how others might answer.

☐ References

Achterberg, J. (1990). *Woman as healer*. Boston: Shambhala.

Benson, H. (1996). *Timeless healing*. New York: Scribner.

Brickman, P., Rabinowitz, V., Karuza, J., Coates, D., Cohn, E., & Kidder, L. (1982). Models of helping and coping. *American Psychologist, 37*(4), 368–384.

Brody, H. (2000). *The placebo response*. New York: HarperCollins.

Dass, R., & Gorman, P. (1991). *How can I help?* New York: Alfred A. Knopf.

Dossey, B., Keegan, L., & Guzzetta, C. (2000). *Holistic nursing: A handbook for practice* (3rd ed.). Rockville, MD: Aspen.

Eisenberg, D. M., Kessler, R. C., Foster, C., Norlock, F., Calkins, D., & Delbanco, T. L. (1993). Unconventional medicine in the US. *New England Journal of Medicine, 328*(4), 246–252.

Harrington, A. (Ed.). (1997). *The placebo effect: An interdisciplinary exploration*. Cambridge, MA: Harvard University Press.

Kalweit, H. (1992). *Shamans, healers and medicine men*. Boston: Shambhala.

Kleinman, A. (1988). *The illness narratives: Suffering, healing and the human condition*. New York: Basic Books.

Langer, E. (1989). *Mindfulness*. Reading, MA: Addison-Wesley.

LeShan, L. (1966). *The medium, the mystic and the physicist: Toward a general theory of the paranormal*. New York: Viking Press.

Linehan, M. (1993). *Cognitive–behavioral treatment of borderline personality disorder*. New York: Guilford Press.

Lovallo, W. (1997). *Stress and health: Biological and psychological interactions*. Thousand Oaks, CA: Sage.

Miller, W., & C'deBaca, J. (1994). Quantum change: Toward a psychology of transformation. In T. Heatherton & J. Weinberger (Eds.), *Can personality change?* (pp. 253–280). Washington, DC: American Psychological Association.

Nightingale, F. (1969). *Notes on nursing: What it is and what it is not*. Toronto, Ontario: Dover. (Original work published 1860.)

Palmer, P. J. (1993). *To know as we are known: Education as a spiritual journey*. San Francisco, CA: HarperSanFrancisco.

Parsons, T. (1972). Definitions of health and illness in the light of American values and social structure. In E. Jaco (Ed.), *Patients, physicians, and illness: A sourcebook in behavioral science and health* (2nd ed., pp. 97–117). New York: Free Press.

Quinn, J. (1989). On healing, wholeness, and the Haelan effect. *Nursing & Health Care, 10*(10), 552–556.

Roth, A., & Fonagy, P. (1996). *What works for whom?* New York: Guilford Press.

Selzler, B. (1996). *The health experiences of Dakota Sioux and their perceptions of culturally congruent nursing care*. Unpublished doctoral dissertation, University of Colorado Health Sciences Center, School of Nursing, Denver.

Tresolini, C. P., & Pew-Fetzer Task Force. (1994). *Health professionals education and relationship-centered care*. San Francisco, CA: Pew-Fetzer Health Professions Commission.

Watson, J. (1988). *Nursing: Human science and human care: A theory of nursing*. New York: National League for Nursing.

Weil, A. (1995). *Health and healing*. Boston: Houghton Mifflin.

Whitmont, E. D. (1993). *The alchemy of healing: Psyche and soma*. Berkeley, CA: North Atlantic Books.

Woods, N. (1989). Conceptualizations of self-care: Toward health-oriented models. *Advances in Nursing Science, 12*(1), 1–13.

Caring and Self-Care

In chapter 2 we described the characteristics of healing and the healing relationship. In this chapter we focus on ways to think about self-care and how to help facilitate clients' self-care. Exploring different models of self-care, we differentiate between self-care and care of the Self. Our model of care is grounded in the delicate and ever-changing balance between caring and self-care, between what can best be developed in relationship and the strategies clients often develop in highly personal and unique ways. Our model focuses on self-care for two reasons. First, the approach is highly consistent with the philosophy of solution-focused therapy; second, managing any chronic condition requires awareness about the ways we take care of ourselves and an expansion of our self-care skills, precisely at a time when the energy required may seem inaccessible. In many ways, our role is that of becoming a compassionate "self-care coach."

☐ Chronic Illness and Self-Care

All humans and animals have practiced self-care. We carry out certain activities to maintain life and protect ourselves from obvious dangers. We also carry out certain practices when we are ill or injured. We often take for granted these activities and our ability to engage in them. It is only when food, clothing, and shelter are not available that it becomes all too clear how essential these "essentials" are to life. When daily existence is in question, as a consequence of war, violence, or life-threatening illness, our bodies mobilize to deal with the threat. When illness in some form becomes part of our experience we first must notice that something is wrong. This usually is followed by trying to figure out what is happening and what we can do about it. Only after exhausting these resources are we likely to turn to others—most often family and friends. Consulting a health professional, during most historic periods and across cultures, has been a distant second or third choice. Because most health problems are self-limiting, occasional fluctuations in energy, comfort, and ability to function are usually temporary, and resolve with or without outside assistance. There are no national statistics on self-care; however, a study of young adult women found they managed (minor acute) illness with "over-the-counter" medication, alteration of activity, use of prescription medication, and home remedies. Only 3% of activities involved consulting a health professional, and only 1% involved actually visiting a health professional (Woods, 1995).

When health problems persist despite professional attention, people may be at a loss to know what else to do. Although modern medicine has been quite successful in treating many of the acute infectious and traumatic health problems that once led to untimely death, the largest category of problems now includes those considered chronic health problems. Much of the research on self-care addresses acute conditions or the latter stages of caring for a chronic illness. Less is known about self-care in the earlier phases of chronic illness. One challenge in studying and providing care for chronic illness is that there is no precise or agreed-on definition of chronic illness (Curtin & Lubkin, 1998). The boundary between acute and chronic illness is seldom clear. Not all chronic illnesses are progressive or fatal, although most are seen as irreversible. Chronic care is differentiated from acute care in many ways. The goal of chronic care is not to "cure" or "fix," but to facilitate social and personal adjustment, minimize potential physical and mental deterioration, and maintain independent living, to the degree possible. Although acute care is associated with specific health care agencies, chronic care often involves many different sources of support, including families and community agencies. Specific outcomes of care have been defined for most hospital-based acute conditions, whereas there are fewer measures for evaluating the quality of care provided for chronic conditions (Institute of Health and Aging, 1996).

In some traditional cultures, the persistence of the condition might signal that the problem derives from the spiritual realm and requires spiritual interventions. Most modern cultures have no consensual ways to understand how chronic illness should be managed—other than being endured and trying to handle each symptom as it presents. Some authors describe specific learning needs and tasks for managing any chronic illness. Those considered "necessary tasks" are organized around adjustment to lifestyle changes, the illness and treatment for it, and maintaining an identity apart from the condition (and any stigma attached to it). Family relationships and social support must be addressed, along with ways to deal with illness-related discomfort. Learning needs are very specifically identified by authors who emphasize cognitive approaches, that is, organizing time for treatments, developing strategies for controlling symptoms, and learning about the anatomy, physiology, and pathophysiology of the body systems affected by the condition (Pollin & Kanaan, 1995).

The fear of developing health problems and the necessity of learning how to live with existing health problems have spawned a growing market providing consumers with health-oriented self-help information and resources. These books are a small but growing portion of the burgeoning self-help/do-it-yourself industry. Self-help books can provide important information and validation for someone who is struggling with the "tasks" thrust on one by having a chronic illness. At the same time, the highly individual act of seeking self-help information in books is seen by some as socializing people to see their problems as individual problems, requiring individual actions, thereby reducing demands for social responsibility and accountability (Simonds, 1992). Access to computerized health care information and "self-administered interventions" have the same potential for isolation; whereas, paradoxically, computer-based support groups can reduce isolation for home-bound persons with chronic health problems.

☐ Politics of Self-Care and Danger of Abandonment

In the United States, the growth of the self-help movement has been attributed by some to a diminished trust in the health care system, and/or the loss of personal connection with a particular provider. Societies have become more mobile and there are fewer extended and multigenerational families. These shifts often mean that the experience and advice that might have been offered by older family members are not readily available. Many parents in recent generations have learned more about child-rearing from Dr. Spock and other gurus of parenting than from their parents, grandparents, and older relatives. Understandably, then, we often feel adrift when someone in the family becomes ill. Global migration has meant that traditional ways of staying healthy and treating illness may be disrupted, devalued, or misunderstood in a new culture. And in the United States, the rising cost of health care has resulted in several different trends. One trend has been greater attention to health promotion activities, including public education about risk reduction (e.g., related to smoking, obesity, seat belts, alcohol and substance abuse, violence). The other trend has been for the millions of uninsured and underinsured in the population to postpone seeking care from health professionals until there is no choice, and many acute conditions have become chronic. Limited access to formal health care makes self-care a nonchoice.

The model of helping and coping described in chapter 2 is useful in identifying some of the opposing interpretations of contemporary health care trends (Brickman et al., 1982; Dean, 1998). For example, conservatives tend to support concepts of self-determinism and self-responsibility. Liberals have tended to identify the sources of problems as lying more in the environment than in individuals and to see the appropriate interventions as being the responsibility of institutions as well as individuals. From either of these positions, individuals may or may not be responsible for the problem, but they have some responsibility for the solution. The moral model would exhort people to be strong, and the compensatory model would encourage people to reach out to one another to change the situation (e.g., in self-help groups and disease-specific lobbying groups). Most approaches to self-help for chronic illness reflect these models. However, for many with chronic illnesses and chronic pain, the additional expectation that they should be politically active in changing the environment, policies, or laws is unrealistic. The idea of self-help support groups appeals to some, whereas to others the thought is repugnant or irrelevant. To some, the emphasis on self-care is seen as legitimizing the abandonment of those who are most vulnerable (Northrup, 1993). Furthermore, Ruzek warned, "as self-help, self-care, and social support are increasingly recognized as valuable to the maintenance of health, [some] are concerned that these aspects of the traditional female role will be expected of [women] either without compensation in the home or in the form of low-paid paraprofessional work in the formal health care system" (Ruzek, 1986, p. 190).

For those who believe that there must be cures for their health care problems and that they have not yet found a competent person to treat the problem, the concept of self-help and self-care can be experienced as demeaning, insulting, and/or abandoning. The burden of having to do self-care may be seen as overwhelming by those who are exhausted by their illness and worried about its consequences. Chu raised the important question of whether people who have experienced abuse or neglect have any concept of self-care—either a sense of a self worthy of being cared for, or any experience with the kinds of self-nurturing behaviors that constitute the essence of self-care (Chu, 1998). For these clients the idea of self-care must be approached carefully and with clear assurance that the therapist is not abandoning them to fend for themselves.

☐ Definitions of Self-Care and Examples

To some degree the mixed feelings about what self-help and self-care should or should not involve can be traced to the many different overlapping concepts and terms related to self-care. The World Health Organization defines self-care as referring to the "activities individuals, families and communities undertake with the intention of enhancing health, preventing disease, limiting illness, and restoring health. These activities are derived from knowledge and skills from the pool of both professional and lay experience. They are undertaken by lay people on their own behalf, either separately or in participative collaboration with professionals" (Konrad, 1998, p. 9).

Levin and others (Ehrenreich & English, 1973; Levin, Katz, & Holst, 1977, p. 24) saw self-care part of the larger self-help social movement that was revived in the 1970s and resembled in many ways the "social hygiene movement" of the mid and late 1800s. "Social hygiene" emphasized the use of spas, health education, public sanitation, and personal hygiene. Both eras were associated with major social change movements intended to shift the balance of power between the haves and have-nots in society. For example, within the larger resurgence of women's movement beginning in the 1960s, the women's health movement was fueled by the call for women to have the right to control their bodies. The underground pamphlet *Our Bodies, Ourselves*, now in at least its 6th edition (Boston Women's Health Book Collective, 1998) and a worldwide bestseller, was intended to provide women with the information they needed to provide self-care in several ways, such as by being knowledgeable about their bodies, sharing information about how to take care of themselves (through nutrition, and exercise), and providing information and options related to reproductive health, treatment of breast cancer, childbearing and child rearing, healthy relationships, self-defense, and when and how to seek professional help. Readers were given examples of ways to empower themselves and others by becoming politically active to change the external conditions of women's lives. The motto "knowledge is power" was central to this work and foreshadowed major changes in the patient–provider relationship by creating alternative clinics, providing "patients" heretofore relatively privileged information, and emphasizing the rights of "consumers."

Several definitions of self-care are incorporated in the preceding example. *Medical self-care* is directed at making patients responsible for certain types of self-assessment, monitoring, treatment, and compliance, with the intent of improving communication with physicians when consultation is appropriate. Goals of medical self-care include decreasing inappropriate use of resources and increasing active participation. Physicians are still seen as the experts, who must utilize patients' reports to make diagnoses and decide on treatments. Both monitoring activities and patient education tend to be organized around symptoms and problems, such as glucose monitoring for diabetics, teaching about lowering cholesterol levels, and performing proper breast self-examinations. Health promotion activities in this model tend to be directed at risk reduction by modifying personal habits related to diet, exercise, smoking, alcohol and substance use, and so on (Gantz, 1990).

Overlapping with this model are behavioral medicine and health psychology models of self-care that use the language of self-efficacy, self-management, and self-regulation. Increasing a personal sense of control is the goal of self-efficacy programs. Perceived self-efficacy refers to a person's belief that that he or she has the necessary capability to manage situations in the future. Such positive expectations and hope for success affect the actions people choose, the effort they expend, and their perseverance and resiliency in the face of adversity, as well as their thought patterns, emotional responses associated with their situation, and accomplishment of health behaviors (Bandura, 1997). Development of this experience of self-mastery is often linked to participation in self-management programs that introduce patients to skills and processes for dealing with the demands of chronic illness (Philips & Rachman, 1998). Self-management "refers to those processes, internal or transactional, that enable individuals to guide goal-directed activities over time and across settings. Self-management entails modulations of thought, affect, behavior or attention through use of specific mechanisms and skills" (Creer & Holroyd, 1997, p. 225). These processes include goal selection (with clearly defined behavior change goals the client is working toward), information collection (including self-monitoring), information processing and evaluation, decision making (the steps to be taken to work toward the goals), action (sometimes involving rehearsal and feedback prior to application in the real world), and self-reaction (evaluation of one's performance). The success of self-management programs is often measured in relation to compliance with the program as well as progress toward specified goals (Tunks & Bellissimo, 1991, p. 25).

Among the skills/actions often taught as part of self-management are a collection of what are called "self-regulation" activities. Based on the concept of homeostasis, Cannon described how humans maintain their health by making constant biologic adjustments in response to changes in stimuli. These internal or external stimuli are now called *stressors* (Cannon, 1932). The "fight or flight" reactions of the sympathetic nervous system associated with the stress response were recognized as essential for managing acute threats to an organism's integrity. It also became clear to researchers (as it long had been to shamans and grannies) that maintaining a high level of stress over a long period of time is ultimately detrimental to health. Selye later described the "general adaptation syndrome," based on these physiologic responses to stress, that could lead to an organism's breakdown and eventual death (Kaplan & Sadock, 1997).

In 1969, Green first proposed self-regulation theory based on the effects on human behavior of cognitive processing of information (Green Walters, Green & Murphy, 1969). The theory proposed that perception (or imagery) is intricately related to biochemical changes in the limbic, hypothalamic, and pituitary areas in the brain, which are involved in modulating emotional responses. These, in turn, bring about physiologic changes that are subsequently perceived and responded to, that is, forming a cybernetic feedback loop. Self-regulation approaches are directed at the mental images or schema (involving the focus of attention, thoughts, memories) that can be accessed, reinforced, or reframed to bring about positive changes in physiologic response—reducing sympathetic response and/or increasing parasympathetic (relaxation) responses. Self-regulation practices include various exercises associated with autonomic relaxation, such as certain breathing practices, progressive muscle relaxation, biofeedback, and autogenic training (invoking a sense of warmth and/or heaviness in extremities) (Smith & Nicassio, 1995).

Self-management programs also utilize cognitive–behavioral approaches for determining whether a client's beliefs, attitudes, and expectations are likely to facilitate or interfere with healing (i.e., whether they enhance or diminish the placebo effect). For example, thoughts related to pain may be labeled "cognitive errors" if they represent "catastrophizing" (jumping to negative conclusions), "overgeneralization" (extending implications beyond the evidence), "personalization" (seeing a neutral event as personal), or " selective abstraction" (seeing only failure as relevant). Programs based on self-management, self-regulation, and self-efficacy are sometimes marketed as "stress-reduction" programs with the intent of changing cognitive, behavioral, and/or situational sources of stress. Often the relevant "psychiatric" diagnosis for these universally observed mind–body phenomena is "psychological factors affecting a medical condition." The *DSM–IV* criteria for this diagnosis require an Axis III diagnosis (general medical condition) and evidence that psychological factors affect the course or treatment of the illness and that stress-related physiological responses are associated with onset or exacerbations of the condition (DeGood & Shutty, 1992).

Although these self-management approaches might broadly be called "coping" practices, not all coping or self-care actions are directed at achievement of mastery or self-efficacy, nor are these always relevant goals for those with extreme debilitation or terminal conditions. Given a terminal diagnosis, there are many ways to cope that do not fit neatly into the preceding models. Some will manage by active suppression or total denial, while others may search far and wide for any "proven" or "unproven" strategy that holds out any hope for survival. Some will channel efforts toward preparing for death in whatever manner is consistent with their personal, cultural, and/or spiritual belief systems. Some will vacillate among all three approaches, depending on the day and the progression of the condition (Tunks & Bellissimo, 1991, p. 13).

For example, when Ellen was told her latest recurrence of ovarian cancer was not responding to treatment, she continued her practice of drinking large quantities of purified water, eating a macrobiotic diet, and practicing healing imagery. She vehemently discouraged any conversation that might invite "negative thoughts." When Dan was given a similarly dismal cancer prognosis, he chose to channel his waning energy toward attending every hike, dance, and concert he could, while continuing to explore what other treatments might be considered. Much of his time was spent trying to study the various medications and treatments being given to him so that he could interpret his symptoms and determine which might be attributed to the treatments themselves. Only when he could not attribute his growing weakness to chemotherapy or overexertion from his activities would he fleetingly wonder if it might be due to the metastatic process.

☐ Other Self-Care Models

Nursing has used the language of self-care more than other health-related professions and has several models of self-care. One of the earliest and most widely used is Orem's self-care deficit theory, which describes when and how nurses provide care to those who can no longer provide it for themselves (Orem, 1991). According to this model, self-care is an essential human function for the purpose of establishing and maintaining conditions that support life processes, development, and integrated functioning. Self-care needs are seen as universal (those supporting life), developmental (to meet special needs at points of transition), or health-deviation self-care needs (those required when one has different or special needs as a consequence of illness). Most applications and research using this model have tended to focus on the capacity to carry out activities of daily living (ADLs), particularly in the presence of an illness (Orem, 1991).

Our model of self-care builds most closely on the self-care theories of Erickson, Tomlin, and Swain (1983). In the theory of "modeling and role modeling" (concepts similar to Ericksonian "pacing and leading" discussed in chap. 9), self-care is defined as the process of "managing responses to stressors through self-care actions directed toward health, growth, development, and/or adaptation." Starting from the position that clients are the most relevant experts on their own lives, "modeling" is defined as gaining a holistic understanding of the client's world from the client's perspective, whereas "role modeling" is the process of planning interventions/designing strategies to meet client-defined needs, based on the client's self-care knowledge and resources. *Self-care knowledge* is conscious or unconscious knowledge *from the client's perspective* that explains why the client became ill and what the client thinks will contribute to his or her healing or growth. For example, in Denny's pilot study of women with interstitial cystitis (IC), a chronic pain condition involving the bladder, all of the women interviewed spontaneously described stressful events that they believed contributed to their becoming ill/developing IC (Webster, 1997a). *Self-care resources* are either internal or external. These may include internal resources, such as specific skills, abilities, or past experiences that can be built on, as well as external resources such as social support, concrete forms of assistance, and material resources. In a healing relationship, then, the role of the health care provider is to facilitate clients' self-care. Helping clients recognize their unique resources and knowledge is more important, from this perspective, than "patient education" approaches that presume what clients need to know. Many of the experiments in chapter 11 are ways to facilitate self-care actions. Our model utilizes several strategies for facilitating self-care, including solution-focused interviewing, using self-care checklists, keeping self-care diaries or journals, or engaging in self-care "experiments" to expand one's repertoire of self-care strategies. Specific examples of using these strategies in therapy sessions and as homework appear in chapters 6, 7, and 11.

An individual's knowledge and resources for self-care include shared knowledge and resources (such as cultural, family, or religious beliefs and accessible information sources), as well as highly unique resources (reflecting personality, life experience, and idiosyncratic health practices) (see table 3.1). Cultural definitions of health are highly related to what is considered culturally "appropriate" self-care, and effectiveness of self-care is determined within the definition. Providing "culturally congruent" self-care is usually seen as dependent on understanding cultural beliefs about health and illness—an ambitious goal, given the rapidly changing world demographics (Young & Zane, 1995).

Holistic concepts of health often form the basis for what are labeled *alternative* or *complementary* healing modalities. These approaches to healing and self-care attend to more than the physical deviations from the norms that are the focus of Western allopathic/conventional approaches. "Traditional" healing approaches are often deeply embedded in beliefs about the purpose of life, the obligations of individuals, and the behaviors that support life. For example, in a study of health beliefs and practices of elderly Hispanics in southern Colorado, Martinez identified the belief that "health is creating balance in life by living your beliefs and that health is faith that one will be cared for by God, family and community." The concept of "self-care" in this culture was not confined to what one did to maintain individual health, but incorporated the perspective that "one fulfills obligations to self through fulfilling obligations to others" (Martinez, 1995, p. 184).

Southern Appalachian widows echoed similar beliefs that their health was influenced by staying busy/physically active, staying connected with other people, and being able to "keep one's mind" (enjoying life, not worrying). "Keeping one's mind" meant retaining the ability to make good decisions and was maintained by such activities as playing bridge, reading, doing puzzles, and playing word games. Staying healthy was directed at maintaining independence as long as possible, while also staying closely connected with one's family and friends. Remaining active in the community and having a moral sense of concern for others were seen as essential to a healthy life. Having a strong commitment to God was important to fostering health and essential as one prepared for impending death (Hardin, 1990).

Among the Northern Dakota Sioux, a healthy lifestyle was evidenced by the activities one engaged in (i.e., the self-care activities themselves were indicators of health). These included being active, eating natural foods, being related to family and tribe, being relaxed, showing respect, and valuing spirituality. These and many other studies of health beliefs provide definitions of health and self-care that challenge the idea that health can be restored by simply finding the right medication, eating a low-fat diet, or participating in regular aerobic exercise (Selzler, 1996).

Spector (1996, pp. 10–12) reviewed the health beliefs from many cultures and identified nine interrelated facets, representing traditional methods of maintaining, protecting, and restoring health. In these models, the individual is seen as multifaceted and integrated into larger contexts of health. Sometimes these models are described in terms of systems theories. In culturally based systems models, health is defined as being in a state of balance within (i.e., the body, mind, and spirit) and in context, that is, in relation to one's family, culture, work, community, history, and environment, including the natural world. Tables 3.1 and 3.2 show the range of approaches found in many cultures to maintain health/balance.

☐ Self-Care Knowledge and Resources

Based on these differing models of health and beliefs about self-care, clients will describe their self-care activities in innumerable ways. In a series of studies on self-care, we found different answers to two apparently similar questions. When we ask people what they do to keep healthy or

TABLE 3.1. Personal Methods to Maintain, Protect, and Restore Health

	Physical	Mental	Spiritual
Maintain health	Proper clothing Proper diet Exercise/rest	Concentration Social and family support systems Hobbies	Religious worship Prayer Meditation

Protect health	Special foods and
	   food combination
	Symbolic clothing
		Avoid certain
		   people who can
		   cause illness
		Family activities
			Religious customs
			Superstitions
			Wearing amulets and
			   other symbolic
			   objects to prevent
			   the "Evil Eye" or
			   defray other
			   sources of harm

Restore health	Homeopathic
	   remedies,
	   liniments
	Herbal teas
	Special foods
	Massage
	Acupuncture/
	   moxibustion
		Relaxation
		Exorcism
		Curanderos and
		   other traditional
		   healers
		Nerve teas
			Religious rituals—
			   special prayers
			Meditations
			Traditional healings
			Exorcism

From Spector (1997, p. 11), with permission.

to take care of their health, we often hear relatively narrow definitions of health and health practices. If we ask, "What do you do to take care of yourself?" the range of responses becomes unlimited. The latter list usually includes using internal and external resources and knowledge. By definition, what is readily described is information primarily available at a conscious level. Accessing unconscious knowledge and resources involves practices that may be unfamiliar from the perspective of conventional self-care approaches, but may be highly consistent with models of self-care from holistic and some cultural perspectives (e.g., self-hypnosis, attending to dreams). Other types of resources that may be relatively unconscious are the kinds of information and observations that family and friends may provide based on long-term relationships and caring concern. We often encourage patients to bring supportive others to therapy sessions to provide their unique insights and to positively reinforce strategies to improve the situation.

In a study of self-care for interstitial cystitis, we found patients made conscious decisions about self-care in nearly every aspect of their lives. These strategies included special diet, exercise, stress reduction, helping-seeking, and various body comfort strategies. We learned that they often did different things to manage different aspects of their conditions. For

TABLE 3.2. Nine Interrelated Facets of Health (Physical, Mental, and Spiritual) and Communal Methods to Maintain, Protect, and Restore Health

	Physical	Mental	Spiritual
Maintain health	Availability of proper shelter, clothing, and food Safe air, water, soil	Availability of traditional sources of entertainment, concentration, and "rules" of the culture	Availability and promulgation of rules of ritual and religious worship Meditation
Protect health	Provision of the knowledge of necessary special foods and food combinations, the wearing of symbolic clothing and avoidance of excessive heat or cold	Provision of the knowledge of what people and situations to avoid Family activities	The teaching of : Religious customs Superstitions Wearing amulets and other symbolic objects to prevent the "Evil Eye" or how to defray other sources of harm
Restore health	Resources that provide homeo-pathic remedies, liniments, herbal teas, special foods, massage, and other ways to restore the body's balance of hot and cold	Traditional healers with the knowledge to use such modalities as : relaxation, exorcism, storytelling, and/or nerve teas	The availability of healers who use magical and supernatural ways to restore health, including religious rituals, special prayers, meditation, traditional healings, and/or exorcism

From Spector (1997), with permission.

example, they might do some things to prevent symptoms, others to manage symptoms on a daily basis, and still other things to handle acute flares of the condition. Because we asked not only if they used these self-care approaches, but also how often and how they would rate the effectiveness of each of these activities (Webster & Brennan, 1998), the simple act of completing this questionnaire often provided a new awareness. Clients may note that they use certain strategies repeatedly, but actually find them relatively ineffective. It's also common for clients to "remember" that a practice they tend to use infrequently is highly effective when it is used.* A shorter version of this instrument, intended for clinical use, is shown in part II.

---

*Studies supporting the findings here were funded by the University of Colorado Health Sciences Center, School of Nursing, intramural and BRSG studies (SO7 RR05809-03-06).

☐ Definitions of Health and Self-Care Outcomes

What difference does self-care make? What difference does any type of care make? These questions have become increasing important as decisions are made by third-party reimbursement and public funding agencies regarding what care should and shouldn't be provided. One distinction that complicates outcome research in chronic illness is that conditions often wax and wane in presentation, making it difficult to attribute improvement or deterioration to specific treatments (Charmaz, 1991). Typically, self-care "outcomes" include measurement of symptoms (such as pain or shortness of breath), ability to carry out daily functions, degree of adaptation to living with the condition, or general quality of life or life satisfaction. Given the unlikelihood of imminent cure for many long-term conditions, some believe that satisfaction with care or a reduction in uncertainty should be relevant as a health outcome to consider when evaluating any health-related intervention.

Equally challenging is the need to recognize that some highly valued self-care activities, undertaken to meet specific goals and unique definitions of health, may have a negative impact on other dimensions of life and health. For example, those with chronic illness are often accused of "isolating" themselves and efforts may be made to get them to increase their social activities. At least at some points in the illness trajectory, this strategy of reducing stimuli may be seen as essential to managing the day-to-day demands of an illness. It is often this type of "solitude" (from the standpoint of the patients) that is seen as invaluable in helping them come to terms with their situation and bring about the evolution from who they have been to who they can become. If, on the other hand, conserving energy is seen as important by others (family or health care providers) and living life to its fullest is important to the client, there may be constant disagreements about the kinds of self-care choices clients make. Avoiding certain situations that trigger pain (e.g., avoiding temperature extremes and taking special precautions to avoid painful intercourse) was correlated in our study of self-care for interstitial cystitis with reduced uncertainty, but also was correlated with reduced recent life satisfaction. The vigilance required to continually scan the environment for possible triggers seems, understandably, likely to diminish the ability to appreciate life fully in the moment (Webster & Brennan, 1998).

Outcome studies focusing on symptoms, adaptation, function, and quality of life in chronic conditions seldom address definitions of health based on the person in context, that is, the balance of body, mind, and spirit, and of the person within his or her family, community, and environment. Nor do they address concepts of healing as movement toward wholeness. If it is possible that, for some people in some situations, illness is a call to attend to one's "wholeness," how might that be explored with respect to health outcomes? In our study of chronic pain, most respondents believed they had "changed" as a result of having pain. The vast majority (72%) indicated that the changes they had undergone were negative—that they had become impatient, irritable, hopeless, and unforgiving. These are the kinds of changes that have come to be expected in chronic illness and chronic pain. These are seldom considered signs of "transformation," and yet, they are experiences that undeniably are experienced as transformations from the person they used to be to someone they scarcely recognize or would want to know. To imply to someone in pain and despair that their illness is a wonderful opportunity for growth is likely to be taken as minimally unsympathetic and, quite possibly, as sadistic. Another 12% in our study described their experience as "mixed," either because they went through cycles of depression and hopelessness, followed by a cycle of strength, or because they could discriminate that some days were better than others and they appreciated the better days. An amazing 16% characterized their experience of having a pain condition as "positive"—which meant they had developed much more compassion for others, and learned to live in the moment. They saw themselves as having come to appreciate each day, seeing life as "fragile and precious." This last group was more likely than others to find certain self-care activities especially effective. Among these were prayer, having trust, and accepting the illness, as well as managing acute flares with several hypnotic strategies. These findings would imply that patients who have a basic sense of trust, are active in their self-care, are able to stop "fighting" the diagnosis and the disease, and are open to trying self-care strategies associated with changing one's state of consciousness are more likely to find some positive aspects to their illness (Webster & Brennan, 1998).

☐ Self-Care and Care of the Self

Chronic illness, chronic pain, and/or a life-threatening illness bring with them not only the discomfort and distress of the condition itself, but the associated experiences of stress, trauma, and suffering. Each of these dimensions of the experience may be more prominent at some times than others. The same experience that feels like a crisis on Monday may feel like a burden on Tuesday and an opportunity on Wednesday. The shifting meanings and energy needed to deal with them can feel crazy-making at first. Later these shifts may be recognized as part of the rhythm of life, with its characteristic ebb and flow. A growing number of stress-management, pain-management, and similar programs are incorporating holistic concepts into their programs and honoring the diverse ways that people "manage" unexpected life changes, both in the moment and over time (Benson & Stuart, 1992; Kabat-Zinn, 1990). Many of the "experiments" described in chapter 11 are based on the wide range of self-care approaches described by our clients, students, and others who study and work with people having chronic pain and chronic illness. Taken as a whole, we find it is helpful to conceptualize self-care, broadly, into two interdependent categories: self-care and care of the Self.

The concept of care of the Self is grounded in several different literatures, traditions, and practices. One approach to conceptualizing self-care as developmental is based on Maslow's hierarchy of needs. From this perspective, self-care would be first concerned with meeting basic physiologic needs (air, food, water), safety and security, and later love and belonging, self-esteem, and ultimately self-actualization. This type of prioritization seems to parallel the concerns of many with chronic health problems and to reflect the Western focus on the self from an individualistic perspective.

In contrast, when visiting New Zealand (Aotearoa), Denny was told that, from the traditional Maori perspective, decisions about appropriate treatments for medical/psychiatric/spiritual conditions would not necessarily consider the individual patient's perspective as central. Rather, these decisions would be made by the collective, giving greater weight to the opinions of family and respected community members. "We know you would have some difficulty with this in your culture," she was told. This practice is consistent with a belief that health is always seen in context, and staying healthy involves, among other activities, one's ability to recite one's whakapapa (the genealogy linking the individual to the collective by tracing one's descent from immediate to distant ancestors). Similarly, in many indigenous and immigrant cultures, knowing the culture's creation stories and mythologies is a valued way to honor the "old ways" and diminish the unhealthy possibility of seeing oneself as disconnected from one's people, culture, and history—or abandoned on an island.

Jung's theory of personality and development is one of the few Western psychological theories that has a definition of Self that incorporates concepts transcending the individual and providing a model of human development that assumes the potential for growth. For Jung, the potential for growth involves awareness and integration of the human unconscious and the experience of the collective unconscious (with its mythologically based archetypes of human experience). Although thoroughly grounded in the centrality of the *personal* self, the larger concept of Self is a major departure from most Western psychologies. The Self is seen as the center of the psyche (the whole of one's personality comprising the various contents and relationships that exist between conscious and unconscious life). The Self as an archetypal concept has been seen to represent "unifying images that convey the awe and wonder of the 'wholly other,'" or in more obvious language, "the God within" (Spoto, 1995, p. 194), or "the inborn personality that it takes a lifetime to grow into . . . a [flexible] template for the person we are intended to become" (Robertson, 1992, p. 109). Combining this perspective of the Self with theories about healing/ wholeness suggests that illness (as well as other life transitions) sometimes can be seen as a call to wholeness, that is, a situation that frequently forces one to reprioritize what is important in one's life and to confront some of the larger questions about the purpose and meaning of life (Kreinheder, 1991).

The model of consciousness described by Jung and developed in the Myers–Briggs Type Indicator (MBTI) by Isabel Myers and described by others (Myers, McCaulley, Quenk, & Hammer, 1998) may be an important tool for understanding "ways of knowing" and the range of self-care activities that people spontaneously choose when faced with an illness. Further, the concept of type development may be helpful in understanding both the reticence to try unfamiliar things and the powerful responses that may accompany the discovery of an aspect of oneself and one's previously untapped abilities. Jung's theory of personality is actually a model of consciousness, partially described in terms of "psychological type." Based on his clinical observations, Jung noted that people tend to focus most of their psychic energy either inward (introversion) or toward external objects (extraversion). He further noted that people usually displayed marked tendencies to perceive either through their physical senses (*sensation*) or through a more abstract process of knowing that he called *intuition*. The data perceived then are most often processed using a preferred type of decision making. Those preferring "thinking" are more likely to use objective facts and theories to organize and problem solve, whereas those preferring the "feeling" function are more inclined to make decisions based on personal values, including the effects of decisions on others. To Jung's model, Isabel Myers added her observation that some people prefer to seek closure, and are more comfortable with predictability, discipline, and organization, while others prefer to keep their options open and value spontaneity over structure.

Jung's theory of psychological type can help identify possible preferences for the use of self-care strategies based on individual perceptual and decision-making preferences (Webster, 1997b, 1999). Psychological type also can provide a framework for linking self-care actions to the potential for growth. Jung described growth as involving first differentiation, which is using your more preferred (dominant) ways of knowing. Often at midlife, or sometimes in response to illness, there is greater development of one's less preferred (inferior) ways of knowing and being. This incorporation of the less preferred (and often unconscious) ways of knowing comprises the process Jung called *individuation*. Some preliminary studies indicate that people are more likely to use self-care strategies that "make sense" to them, that is, are consistent with their preferred ways of knowing. However, there is also some evidence that the perceived effectiveness of self-care strategies may reflect either these preferences or self-care actions that draw on inferior/unconscious resources. In other words, developing new and different patterns of self-care (i.e., expanding one's ways of knowing) may be more effective for some individuals.

Putting It Together: Solution-Focused and Growth-Oriented Self-Care

There are no clear boundaries between self-care and care of the Self. Both the concepts and the practices are highly interrelated. Consequently, there are no clear boundaries between the following descriptions of solution-focused self-care and growth-oriented self-care. They are best conceived of by a Venn diagram or perhaps the symbol of the Tao (fig. 3.1), emphasizing the mutual dependence of each dimension on the other. Examples abound of people who change their priorities in order to manage their symptoms and find that in the process they have changed themselves in a fundamental way. As in all paradoxes, it may be that the Western pursuit of "self-esteem" is doomed as long as the focus remains on the needs of the personal self. It may also be true that in attending to others' needs, the definition of the self/Self changes. At some point the withdrawal from others as a form of self-care contributes to the growth of the Self, while at other times, if experienced as disconnection, it may diminish the self/Self.

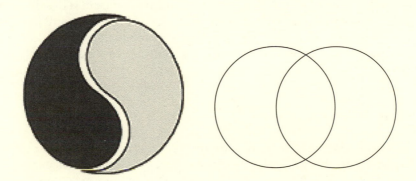

FIGURE 3.1. Mutual dependence of concepts.

☐ Solution-Focused Self-Care

Solution-focused therapy (SFT), discussed more fully in part II, is a form of therapy that shares many values with the modeling and role-modeling theory of self-care. Both provide clear and systematic approaches to helping clients identify what they are already doing right, how they might increase those activities, and what difference it makes to them and their relationships when they engage in these self-defined behaviors. Solution-focused self-care incorporates information known by clients at a conscious level about their preferred outcomes and utilizes clients' own observations to identify what they are already doing that "works" (i.e., what supports movement toward their preferred outcomes). Usually these are related to symptom management, prevention of symptoms, or a specific functional goal. Clients may become aware of their self-care knowledge and resources at a conscious level as a result of solution-focused interviewing, described in part II. When this self-generated information is insufficient, the therapist may provide information about what has helped others or explore with the client the possibility of trying self-care "experiments" to expand the client's repertoire of self-care activities without prescribing behaviors that may result in demoralizing "failures" or problems of "noncompliance."

There are many ways to facilitate self-care. Use of the Self-Care Responses (SCR) instrument (modified from A. Dan, B. McElmurry, & D. Webster, funded by Nursing Research Emphasis Grant, Doctoral Programs in Nursing, NU 0 1049-03, 1984-7) is one way to help clients identify what they are already doing or what they might explore to help them manage symptoms or move toward functional goals. Clinical examples in chapters 5–7 illustrate the close relationship between solution-focused therapy and concepts of self-care. The Solution Identification Scale for Health (SISH) bridges the concepts of solution-focused self-care and growth-oriented self-care. It can be helpful in tracking movement in relation to preferred "outcomes" of self-care. Instructions for using these in session appear in chapter 7, on solution building, and as "experiments" in chapter 11.

Clinical/Research

For several years, we have used solution-focused interviews to study how to facilitate effective self-care for chronic illness and pain. For example, Judy participated in the self-care study described in the next chapter. She has fibromyalgia (FMS), chronic fatigue syndrome (CFS), and grand mal seizures. One of the biggest challenges she faces each day is remembering what she needs to do. She has the cognitive difficulties many with FMS and CFS experience. Particularly when she gets overtired, she has problems concentrating and articulating her needs. The following communication is excerpted from an unsolicited e-mail she sent six months after she completed the process, documenting the observations she was making from her ongoing "solution-focused self-care experiments."

Date: Sat, 23 Jan 1999 09:45:11 -0800

From: Judy

To: Denny Webster <Denny.Webster@UCHSC.edu>

Subject: strategies

Denny —

I just figured out one of the problems I have been having with my self-care and, once I recognized the problem, a possible solution . . .

Background. There are a number of things that I can do each day or periodically that help me. . . . Some of these I can control—my scheduling and habits. I can decide to do my stretching tape when I first get up and before I have changed out of my night clothes. That means that will probably happen—unless there is some time-based schedule that is important and interferes with it. Others are things that should happen once during the day but it doesn't matter when—and it doesn't matter if I miss a day or two. These seem to be managed by a checklist (spreadsheet) tallied at the end of the day—when I am being diligent. The very act of not checking the box reminds me that I need to do this . . .

Problem. The category (newly recognized) that I really have trouble with is the things that I ingest. Remembering to eat three meals per day doesn't seem as hard as the things that I am just supposed to drink or eat throughout the day until I have had a certain amount. These turn out to be things that help me the most and yet they are the things I have the most trouble getting done.

- I want to drink ¾ gallon of water per day.
- Part of that I want to put cranberry concentrate in.
- Part of that I want to squeeze lemon in.
- I want to eat "a handful" (I need to look up how much it really is) of nuts per day.
- I want to eat a certain amount of different raw vegetables each day.

There will be some other things I want to ingest when I explore naturopathic ways to reduce my neurological issues (I started having trouble with my new drug and so had to reduce how much I was taking until it may start impairing my ability to drive).

I've tried keeping notes on how much I ingest, both in a static site (where I often am not) and in a little notebook I carried around (which I often forgot). I've tried keeping prepared raw vegetables close to hand—but again couldn't keep track because I couldn't really remember if it was yesterday or today that I had had that carrot stick. I have good water close to hand—but have had no successful way of tracking how much I had drank.

Solution Model. I run into the same problem with my pills and so have a pill container with four compartments of stuff to take four times per day. I can remember whether I have taken them by keeping this in a very visible spot—somewhere I have to look at it when I am getting ready to eat. If it has pills in it, I haven't taken them yet.

It occurred to me that I could do the same thing with these other things.

Solution? I could establish a shelf, or portion of the counter, or other obvious place, plus the most accessible shelf in the refrigerator. Each day I will set up pitchers, bowls, whatever, of the amount of each of these things I'm supposed to have—these will be only for me. During the day I will eat from these until they are gone. I may compel myself to eat/drink what is left at the end of the day.

I may still prepare several stalks of celery or several carrots at a time and have those elsewhere in the refrigerator—but I'll just set out the portion of those that I am eating the same day in my "special place."

I will schedule the "filling" of my stuff so that it happens. Doing so around dinnertime would be a good time, for example, because I can predict my condition then more than I can in the late evening or early morning.

Expected Outcome. I think this continual visual of what I still have to drink/eat that particular day will encourage me to ingest it. It's not that I don't want to drink/eat it—I just lose track and when I am nutritionally stressed I forget my priorities. Also, the availability of my "correct" foods will encourage me to choose that instead of what I formerly saw as handy.

This may be an obvious solution to you, but it suddenly seemed like a system that might work for me. What pitfalls do you see?

Date: Mon, 25 Jan 1999 22:45:50 -0800

From: Judy

To: Denny Webster <Denny.Webster@UCHSC.edu>

CC: Judy

Subject: Re: strategies

Denny Webster wrote:

Dear Judy-

I think your plan is ingenious! You've really alerted me to the dimension of cognitive problems with fibromyalgia and how difficult they make it to carry out any kind of program. Since you find this kind of organization makes your life better I'm sure it will be a useful experiment. I have found that many experiments that work can then become habits, which seems like another part of what you are saying. I appreciated your note saying that the process had been helpful. Do you mind if I share your ideas with others?

Denny

Response:

You can share anything I tell you unless I say otherwise. . . . The nice thing about using e-mail is I can send a copy of this to myself to remind me of what I said I'd do. Pretty cool, huh! Judy.

Judy's report illustrates nicely the results of helping clients notice possible solutions and find ways to do experiments in their daily lives. Even though Judy was already an active "recrafter" (described in chapter 5), she continues to refine her observations and approaches to self-care as a regular practice. Although cognitive challenges are not a prominent aspect of most chronic conditions, fatigue and pain may contribute to difficulty in "remembering" what works. For this reason, as we show in part II, there are distinct advantages to combining self-care practices with the process of solution-focused questioning to highlight and reinforce what helps.

Not surprisingly, approaches to accessing unconscious resources often "unearth" self-care strategies that have been "forgotten" or fallen into disuse. Specific approaches to remembering forgotten resources are covered in chapters 8 and 9.

☐ Growth-Oriented Self-Care

The concept of *growth-oriented self-care* acknowledges that many activities undertaken to care for the self also care for the Self, the inherent potential for growth toward wholeness and transformation described by many who are faced with chronic or terminal health problems. Often the activities that clients describe as most important to them are those that allow them to redefine and reprioritize their lives. In other words, they may have learned to do some things differently and to be unattached to a particular outcome for either the activity or their previous definitions of what constituted "good health." These activities often are dependent on accessing information that was previously unconscious. Accessing unconscious knowledge and resources contributes to growth at the individual level. Growth may also be horizontal, that is, in the development of relationships with others—family, friends, and community, others in similar circumstances—and may take many forms. It may be the development of greater compassion for others, as described earlier. It might involve a connection or reconnection with a supportive group, a cultural heritage, or an effort to change social conditions. Particularly when energy for reaching out is limited, these growth-oriented connections may involve allowing others to help you.

Finally, growth-oriented self-care may involve activities and ways of being that extend the boundaries of the personal self to allow the experience of the transcendent—whether that is a sense of connection with nature, a religious or spiritual connection, or a sense of place in time. These experiences are often associated with an expanded or altered sense of time and self. Many of the strategies described in chapters 8 and 9 involve ways to access unconsciousness resources through a variety of forms of "natural trance" and self-hypnosis. These hypnotic approaches and clinical examples also richly illustrate the ongoing struggles of patients with chronic conditions to integrate who they have been and what they do with what they value in their lives. The next chapter honors this struggle to move beyond being a victim or even a survivor to creating a meaningful life.

☐ References

Bandura, A. (1997). Self-efficacy and health behavior. In A. Baum, S. Newman, J. Weinman, R. West, & C. McManus (Eds.), *Cambridge handbook of psychology, health and medicine* (pp. 160–162). Cambridge, UK: Cambridge University Press.

Benson, H., & Stuart, E. (1992). *The wellness book: The comprehensive guide to maintaining health and treating stress-related illness.* New York: Simon & Schuster.

Boston Women's Health Book Collective. (1998). *Our bodies, ourselves, for the new century.* New York: Simon & Schuster.

Brickman, P., Rabinowitz, V., Karuza, J., Coates, D., Cohn, E., & Kidder, L. (1982). Models of helping and coping. *American Psychologist, 37*(4), 368–384.

Cannon, W. (1932). *The wisdom of the body* (2nd ed.). New York: Norton.

Charmaz, K. (1991). *Good days, bad days: The self in chronic illness and time.* New Brunswick, NJ: Rutgers University Press.

Chu, J. (1998). *Rebuilding shattered lives: The responsible treatment of complex post-traumatic and dissociative disorders.* New York: John Wiley & Sons.

Creer, T., & Holroyd, K. (1997). Self-management. In A. Baum, S. Newman, J. Weinman, R. West, & C. McManus (Eds.), *Cambridge handbook of psychology, health and medicine* (pp. 255–258). Cambridge, UK: Cambridge University Press.

Curtin, M., & Lubkin, I. (1998). What is chronicity? In I. Lubkin (Ed.), *Chronic illness: Impact and interventions* (pp. 3-25). Boston: Jones & Bartlett.

Dean, K. (1998). International perspectives on self-care research. In M. Ory & G. DeFriese (Eds.), *Self-care in later life: Research, program, and policy issues* (pp. 180–192). New York: Springer.

DeGood, D., & Shutty, M. (1992). Assessment of pain beliefs, coping, and self-efficacy. In D. Turk & R. Melzack (Eds.), *Handbook of pain assessment* (pp. 214–234). New York: Guilford Press.

Ehrenreich, B., & English, D. (1973). *Complaints and disorders: The sexual politics of sickness.* Old Westbury, NY: Feminist Press.

Erickson, H., Tomlin, E., & Swain, M. (1983). *Modeling and role-modeling: A theory and paradigm for nursing.* Englewood Cliffs, NJ: Prentice Hall. (Can be ordered from Lexington, SC: Pine Press)

Gantz, S. (1990). Self-care: Perspectives from six disciplines. *Holistic Nursing Practice, 4*(2), 1–12.

Green, E. E., Walters, E. D., Green, A. M., & Murphy G. (1969). Feedback technique for deep relaxation. *Psychophysiology, 6*(3), 371–377.

Hardin, S. (1990). *Let the circle be unbroken: Health of elderly southern Appalachian widows.* Unpublished dissertation, University of Colorado Health Sciences Center, School of Nursing, Denver.

Institute for Health and Aging, University of California, San Francisco, for the Robert Wood Johnson Foundation (1996). *Chronic care in America: A 21st century challenge.* Princeton, NJ: Robert Wood Johnson Foundation.

Kabat-Zinn, J. (1990). *Full catastrophe living: Using the wisdom of your body and mind to face stress, pain, and illness.* New York: Delta.

Kaplan, H., & Sadock, B. (1997). *Synopsis of psychiatry: Behavioral sciences/clinical psychiatry* (8th ed., pp. 797–818). Baltimore, MD: Williams & Wilkins.

Konrad, T. (1998). The patterns of self-care among older adults in Western industrialized societies. In M. Ory & G. DeFriese (Eds.), *Self-care in later life: Research, program, and policy issues* (p. 8). New York: Springer.

Kreinheder, A. (1991). *Body and soul: The other side of illness.* Toronto: Inner City Books.

Levin, L., Katz, A., & Holst, E. (1977). *Self-care: Lay initiatives in health.* New York: Prodist.

Martinez, R. (1995). *Close friends of God: An ethnography of health of older Hispanic people.* Unpublished dissertation, University of Colorado Health Sciences Center, School of Nursing, Denver.

Myers, I., McCaulley, M., Quenk, N., & Hammer, A. (1998). *MBTI Manual: A guide to the development and use of the Myers-Briggs Type Indicator* (3rd ed.). Palo Alto, CA: Consulting Psychologists Press.

Northrup, D. (1993). Self-care myth reconsidered. *Advances in Nursing Science, 15*(3), 59–66.

Orem, D. (1991). *Nursing: Concepts of practice* (4th ed.). St. Louis, MO: Mosby Year Book.

Philips, H., & Rachman, S. (1998). *The psychological management of chronic pain: A treatment manual* (2nd ed.). New York: Springer.

Pollin, E., & Kanaan, S. (1995). *Medical crisis counseling: Short-term therapy for long-term illness.* New York: W. W. Norton

Robertson, R. (1992). *A beginner's guide to Jungian psychology.* York Beach, ME: Nicholas-Hays.

Ruzek, S. (1986). Feminist visions of health: An international perspective. In J. Mitchell & A. Oakley (Eds.), *What is feminism: A reexamination* (p. 190). New York: Pantheon.

Selzler, B. (1996). *The health experiences of Dakota Sioux and their perceptions of culturally congruent nursing care.* Unpublished dissertation, University of Colorado Health Sciences Center, School of Nursing, Denver.

Simonds, W. (1992). *Women and the self-help culture: Reading between the lines.* New Brunswick, NJ: Rutgers University Press.

Smith, T., & Nicassio, P. (1995). Psychological practice: Clinical application of the biopsychosocial model. In P. Nicassio & T. Smith (Eds.), *Managing chronic illness: A biopsychosocial perspective* (pp. 1–31). Washington, DC: American Psychological Association.

Spector, R. (1996). *Cultural diversity in health and illness* (4th ed.). Stamford, CT: Appleton & Lange.

Spoto, A. (1995). *Jung's typology in perspective* (rev. ed.). Wilmette, IL: Chiron.

Tunks, E., & Bellissimo, A. (1991). *Behavioral medicine: Concepts and procedures.* New York: Pergamon Press.

Webster, D. (1997a). Recontextualizing sexuality in chronic illness: Women and interstitial cystitis. *Health Care for Women International, 18,* 575–589.

Webster, D. (1997b). Psychological type and self-care. In *Proceedings of the First Annual Clinical Conference* (pp. 73–88). Atlanta, GA: Center for Application of Psychological Type.

Webster, D. (1999). Psychological type and self-care in chronic illness: Experience sampling for activity and rest. In *Mind, body, and personality: The role of type in mental and physical health* (pp. 101–111). Proceedings of the Second Biannual Conference. Gainesville, FL: Center for Application of Psychological Type.

Webster, D., & Brennan, T. (1998). Self-care effectiveness and health outcomes in women with interstitial cystitis. *Issues in Mental Health Nursing, 19*(5), 495–519.

Woods, N. (1995). Women and their health. In C. Fogel & N. Woods (Eds.), *Women's health care* (pp. 1-22). Thousand Oaks, CA: Sage.

Young, K., & Zane, N. (1995). Ethnocultural influences in evaluation and management. In P. Nicassio & T. Smith (Eds.), *Managing chronic illness: A biopsychosocial perspective* (pp. 163–206). Washington, DC: American Psychological Association.

CHAPTER 4

Creating a Meaningful Life

Much has been written about meaning *in* illness and even more about the meaning *of* illness. Theories abound to explain the shared phenomena of illness, and a wide range of stories documenting personal journeys testify to the unique. Earlier chapters described the importance of clients defining what they think the illness represents and what should be done about it. The role of culture and belief systems in shaping what clients think should be done and by whom has also been addressed. In this chapter we look at the larger meanings that define and are defined by illness—the canvas on which the meaning of illness is drawn—and the different paths people take in finding, reshaping, remembering, and/or actively creating a meaningful life. The abilities to focus attention and shift contexts for understanding can be powerful strategies for shaping human experience. Because our model involves facilitating a patient's ability to naturalistically shift, focus, order, and expand consciousness, a number of naturalistic ways to modify consciousness are described in detail, along with case examples. Original adaptations of the work of Ernest Rossi on ultradian rhythms and of Mihalyi Csikszentmihalyi on flow are described to link naturalistic phenomena to the more formal experience of hypnosis.

The Many Meanings of Meaning

Although some would emphasize the challenge of creating a meaningful life *despite* illness and pain, others observe that life, itself, is about illness and pain—that suffering is part of being mortals who are destined to live imperfect and finite lives (Kabat-Zinn, 1990). Still others would say that the meaning of life—or of their lives—only became clear to them when they were faced with their own mortality, the fragility of human existence, or the enormity of suffering that can be endured. Probably most are like Robin, finding that meanings change over time. What first seemed to him to be a punishment was later seen as evidence of Providence's blessings. He wrote: "I began to see the merciful dispositions of heaven, . . . How wonderfully we are delivered when we know nothing of it."

The meaning of illness is inextricably embedded in meanings of life and death. A meaningful life does not commit the major sin of *Nimis simplicando*—making molehills out of mountains: the act of reducing tragedy to triviality, suffering to simpering, courageous acts into instances of stimulus and response, and passions into "the satisfaction of basic needs" or tension release (May, 1967, p. 180). But sometimes, as therapists, we do diminish others' meanings in our hurry to "fix" one problem and get onto the next one, forgetting that clients do not have the same option of easily moving on. When solutions to problems are forthcoming, there is little need to make mountains out of molehills. But in our haste, we may forget to ask one of the most important questions in any chronic condition: Is it the pain/illness that makes your life intolerable, or is it your life that makes the pain/illness intolerable (Bresler, 1979)?

People who are trying to figure out how to get through each day generally have little time or energy to contemplate the meaning of life. At least during an acute pain or illness or in the early phases of living with what eventually becomes a chronic health condition, the only "meaning" that seems important is the meaning of the symptoms: What do they indicate? What is wrong? If a diagnosis (by self or others) is accurate and treatments are successful, the incident is often forgotten in the bustle of returning to normal life. Only when symptoms persist does a more ominous sense of meaning insinuate itself.

☐ Why Do I Have This Condition?

We live in cultures that tell us that, on the one hand, illness has no meaning. The idea that some diseases carry a moral indictment is seen by some as superstitious and cruel, in a scientific age that can explain conditions at the cellular or even genetic level. Others see this type of analysis as cold and dehumanizing, condemning the hapless patient to meaninglessness at a time when it is meanings that are most desperately sought/needed (University of California, 1994). At the other extreme, Ken Wilber, in *Grace and Grit* (1991, pp. 46–49), described the litany of meanings to which he and his wife, Treya, were condemned when she was diagnosed with breast cancer, "all the various meanings and judgments that our different cultures and subcultures attached to this illness . . . that cloud of voices, images, ideas, fears, stories, photographs, advertisements, articles, movies, television shows, . . . vague, shapeless but dense, ominous, full of fear and pain and helplessness." The overlapping categories of meanings/judgments he identified included that illness is: (a) punishment for sin, (b) a spiritual lesson, (c) a purely biophysical disorder, (d) the purifying result of karmic past misdeeds, (e) the result of repressed emotions, (f) an illusory dream since Spirit is the only reality, (g) without meaning, (h) retribution for bad thoughts about another, (i) an inescapable aspect of the manifest world—to be transcended, (j) the product of intricately interrelated physical, emotional, mental, and spiritual factors, (k) traceable to a specific cause, or (l) entirely random. Treya's own list of possible "causes" of her cancer were equally contradictory, including many of these, as well as the possible consequence of having been depressed in the past, eating too much animal fat and caffeine, being too self-critical, worrying too much about finding her calling in life, a childhood sense of loneliness, needing to be in control and independent, and failing to consistently practice a spiritual discipline.

One can even "look up" the presumed underlying meanings for certain symptoms or illnesses, much as some people look to predefined dictionaries of symbols for interpreting their dreams. For example, one book lists "back symptoms" as related to problems with uprightness, the bladder with release of pressure, the throat with anxiety, and so on (Dethlefsen & Dahlke, 1993). "Unhappy" sexual organs are listed in another book as reflecting unhappy sexual relationships, and emphysema is a consequence of smoking, which reveals someone who "wanted to be filled up with love and mother's milk" (Rush, 1994).

Untangling the many "meanings of 'meaning'" can become a tautologic nightmare—both linguistically and for those engaged in the personal struggle to make sense of what is happening. The preceding lists incorporate many of the meanings of meaning: purpose/intention, significance/value, and sense/coherence. Yalom (1980) spoke of meaning of life issues as either cosmic or terrestrial. The cosmic view involves a design existing beyond the individual, a magical or spiritual ordering of the universe. Terrestrial meanings are not necessarily based on cosmic meaning systems and apply to an individual's perspective (i.e., the meaning of *my* life) and its organization around a sense of purpose, a function to be fulfilled, and/or an overriding goal or goals. Obviously the partial or complete acceptance of competing meaning systems can maintain a disturbing level of conflict and anxious quests for the "real" or the "right" meaning.

☐ **What Can Be Done about It?**

Learning about and responding to terrestrial and cosmic meanings may seem a bit far afield when someone has come to us seeking relief from their pain or ways to manage living with their illness. Certainly these are not realms that are of immediate concern to most patients. When we asked women with breast cancer what would have made their situation better, most answered, "not to have breast cancer" (Webster, Dan, & McElmurry, 1984–1987). Once the option of rewriting history is not available, we begin the process of figuring out what we can and can't do about the situation. Often we need support for making treatment decisions, weighing the costs and benefits of whatever options we can identify. Although these kinds of decisions are greatly dependent on the information available and the existence of real alternatives, the final decisions are often based on considering the "bigger picture," based on the meanings of life as well as the meanings of illness.

Problem solving and decision making are among the ongoing stresses of living with chronic pain and illness. There's a new treatment out there—should I try it? My insurance will no longer cover my provider—what do I want do to? What can I afford do to? What risks are there to whatever progress I've made so far in living with this? What are the risks to relationships? How will it affect my quality of life? The answers to these questions are always contingent on current perspectives and circumstances. New cycles of problem solving and decision making are required as there are changes in the trajectory of an illness over time and changes in treatment options become available. The decisions made at one point may be quite different from those made at another.

Seligman, best known for theories of learned helplessness and learned optimism, constructed a list of psychological and psychiatric conditions and evaluated the data related to the bases of the problems and the likelihood that behavioral and/or pharmacologic interventions will be effective ("curable" in his language). He explored many "myths" about conditions and provides a countering list of facts. Problems of greater "depth" are those less amenable to change. Deep problems include those with three factors: biological bases (often hereditary), a strong belief system easily confirmed or difficult to challenge, and the presence of explanatory theories having great power (i.e., theories that make great sense and explain much about the world, not just the problem). He takes the position that problems of the surface can be easily changed by psychotherapy and/or drugs, while problems of the soul cannot. Among the "problems" described as deep and unchangeable are sexual identity, sexual orientation, and being overweight. Posttraumatic stress disorder is listed as a "disorder of the soul" based on the understandable adoption of pervasive belief systems about the dangerousness of the world. In contrast, panic disorders and phobia are seen as surface problems (highly changeable), whereas anxiety and depression, with mixed biological and belief bases, are seen as only moderately modifiable (Seligman, 1994).

☐ Who Gets to Decide What to Call It?

Where does this leave the client with chronic illness or pain and the therapist who wishes to be helpful? Given very mixed evidence that personality and deeply held belief systems are disposed to change over the life span (Heatherton & Weinberger, 1994), we are disinclined to engage in efforts directed toward personality change. Clearly, there are also limits to what can be done to reverse or modify many of the physical factors/ conditions that manifest themselves as chronic illness and chronic pain. But working within clients' values and belief systems, it is still possible to help them to expand their range of possible interpretations and to reframe for themselves either the meanings of problems and/or the range of strategies and resources to deal with them.

From the perspective of social constructivists, meaning is created (or more accurately cocreated) between people (McNamee & Gergen, 1992). The continual process of refining and expanding, clarifying, and specifying meanings is the essence of therapeutic communication. Many would go so far as to say that therapy is inevitably about "meaning making" (Carlsen, 1988). Because the meaning-making process is inherent in all relationships, the meanings of the illness and of the relationships are continually being revised—an observation that makes it impossible *not* to modify meanings, to some degree, over time.

Language skills and benevolent intent can contribute to the directions these meaning shifts may take. Many of our clients have had the distressing experience of having the meanings of their experiences redefined by others in the process of reporting their symptoms and concerns. The language used in much of the chronic pain literature shapes the ways in which we may come to conceptualize our clients and their problems. Terms like *denial, catastrophizing, somaticizing,* and *resistant* are mixed liberally with classifications of *pain-amplifiers, ineffective/poor copers,* and *symptom-over-interpreters.* Such labels and classifications are predicated on the belief that there is a normative way to experience physical and emotional phenomena, and that some ways of dealing with problems are invariably superior to other ways.

Getting beyond pathologizing language is a goal of therapeutic approaches incorporating narrative and/or solution-focused questioning. Strong (1999) described a one-day workshop for caregivers and patients, based on the belief that "the way we converse with others and ourselves about problems is a key factor in shaping how we experience those problems." First, ground rules for sharing experiences and assumptions are made explicit. Among the assumptions are that "the language we use to describe experience organizes thoughts and behaviors in ways that become part of coping and can be oriented to resourcefulness or suffering," and "people are not their pain or illness. They have relationships with the sensations and impactful meanings they associate with pain and illness." Then a series of questions is raised, intended to foster conversations that may allow stories to be told, heard, and sometimes revised. Examples of these questions include: "What secondary effects has pain or illness had on your mood or outlook, and how has this interfered with the life you would prefer to have? Has this outlook made responding to pain or illness more difficult? If so, how?" From such stories and conversations, underlying meanings can be identified and explored.

In several articles and books, Griffith and Griffith (1994) described their approach to developing therapeutic dialogues for mind–body problems. They reviewed theory and evidence from cognitive science and philosophy about the relationship between language and the body, noting that this evolving view of language illuminates relationships between language, mental ideas, and physical bodies in the context of living within social organizations. They listed a number of ways that life stories can become "binding," because they are forbidden—politically, socially, culturally, religiously—or based on family myths. Other sources of binding may be fears about the possible disastrous consequences of telling one's stories. The goal of family therapy becomes assisting patients to "reauthor old self-narratives into a form that does not bind the body."

In our experience, it may be helpful to reframe negative labels (imposed by others) to meanings that are more respectful of the uniqueness of individual experience. People who have acute sensitivities to physical phenomena (which they may experience as symptoms) can be acknowledged for these abilities—and they are abilities—and queried about how this type of sensitivity/skill has been helpful to them and how it might be utilized in their healing. For example, perhaps they are able to notice small positive changes that others might not perceive. Often the client already has an identity of being particularly sensitive, physically and emotionally. Based on this self-awareness, clients may consciously choose the people, places, and situations that they are able to manage at different times. Several clinical examples of using these sensitivities are described in chapters 6 and 7.

Sometimes clients have been chastised for "giving in" to pain or for "enjoying their suffering." What do such interpretations mean? While the traditional Western view is one of action, antagonism, and fighting in the presence of an "enemy," there are other perspectives that see suffering as part of life—to be met with no more and no less acceptance than moments of joy (Allport, 1959). In this perspective, ways of being may be more important than "doing." While to some "surrender" means passivity and giving up on life, to others it means embracing a process that they acknowledge they cannot control and finding peace in that surrender.

This process of surrender was clearly described by Frank, who died while this book was being written after living with AIDS for 14 years. During the last year of his life he said:

> I didn't want to keep fighting with this illness—it is not the enemy. It is part of me now and I want to learn how to live with it. Often I even have an image of dancing with the pain—even though it sometimes seemed more like "slam-dancing" than the slow waltz that *I* had envisioned. I know death is not the enemy. More and more I find myself knowing that I am ready to go Home.

☐ Beginnings and Endings, Meaninglessness and Hope

Janet spoke of appreciating how a mutual friend, Dan, had spent his final months, after being diagnosed with cancer. He hiked and danced and went to concerts and had lunch with friends and met with a small prayer group on the rare occasions when he thought more about the future than living fully in the present. She said, "When faced with death he knew what was important. He shared his journey of the diagnosis and the process. . . . There was no scrambling at the end of life—no regrets or recriminations, so it was easy to be with him and a privilege to share his dying. It was a gift to all of us."

To be at peace at the end of life is a gift beyond measure, and one that seems increasingly elusive in contemporary society. Nor do we always know how to live with the illness and pain that can eclipse all other aspects of life. To those for whom life holds no meaning (value, significance, or purpose), there is no meaning in suffering, no comfort in the memories of the past or the hopes for the future—no appreciation for the small moments in which life is ultimately lived. But what makes a life meaningful?

Most of us inherit belief systems, based on family, religious, and/or cultural norms, that tell us what is important and how to live. However, some clients have long since rejected traditional viewpoints (if they were ever exposed to them) in favor of more existential perspectives on meaning. Many believe there is no inherent meaning in life and that we each have the responsibility to choose our values rather then inherit them

(Frankl, 1959). Many have not taken the time, nor do they have the inclination, to explore these questions until they become ill or find their belief systems cannot adapt to the challenges of living with a chronic illness/pain.

In addition to accepting or choosing values/meanings, there are those, like Jung, who embrace teleologic views—the doctrine that final causes exist, and that "purpose and design are a part of or are apparent in nature . . . [moving] us toward certain goals of self-realization" (Random House, 1967). From this perspective, meaning/significance is to be discovered/uncovered. Jung saw these meanings in mythical terms. In his memoir (1961), he wrote:

> The need for mythic statements is satisfied when we frame a view of the world which adequately explains the meaning of human existence in the cosmos, a view which springs from our psychic wholeness, from the cooperation between conscious and unconscious. . . . Meaninglessness inhibits fullness of life and is therefore equivalent to illness. Meaning makes a great many things endurable—perhaps everything. (p. 340)

Discovering meaning does not have to take on the enormity of being framed in mythic proportions. Whatever we feel passion for and have a commitment to has already assumed a position of significance and, not infrequently, has provided a sense of life purpose. Many parents will say that they "kept going" against great odds for the sake of their children. People engaged in social change efforts are often willing to make great sacrifices for a cause they believe in strongly.

Accepting, choosing, and discovering meaning are approaches to meaning making that are neither mutually exclusive nor exhaustive. At various stages in our lives one of these approaches may dominate over others. Human development does not cease once one reaches the age of maturity—rather, it is an ongoing process throughout our lives. What is particularly difficult about the changes wrought in chronic illness and pain is that they are distinctly involuntary. Changes, including pain and low energy, are not the kinds of changes we would choose. Not surprisingly, then, most resources dealing with chronic pain and chronic illness address the very real and sometimes overwhelming grief that accompanies the loss of identity when one can no longer carry out the roles and functions around which life meanings have been organized. Over and above the direct losses associated with illness are the deeper losses of a sense of belonging and place, and the risk of slipping into a life stance characterized by meaninglessness and pervasive bitterness or regret. To speak of choosing or discovering meanings may seem incredibly insensitive when just getting through the day is a daunting challenge.

For example, Monette has chronic pain and a job that requires her to sit at a desk for long periods. Carrying out repetitive computer tasks contributes to her symptoms, which she relates to limited opportunities to move. She said:

> I know I should be grateful for the days that are better than the worst ones. But I can't seem to get past being angry—I'm so angry that I can't do the things I used to be able to do. I'm angry that this happened to me and that I have to work in a place that not only probably put me in this condition, but treats me like a slacker when I can't do the things I used to be able to. It's misery to even have to come here and if I didn't have to I would leave in a heartbeat.

☐ Creativity and Creative People

In the next chapter we describe how to recognize the stage/phase of clients in their process of living with chronic illness/pain. People who have become at least occasional searchers/seekers have already begun the process of creating a meaningful life. They have determined to try to make the best of the situation and to carry out the necessary adjustments to make life worth living. Certainly one of the first steps people take is trying to figure out which parts of their old life they *can* continue and which they *want* to continue, given new or evolving circumstances. Those whom we have called "recrafters" (chapter 5) are those who have brought artistry and skill to their new life situation. Realistically, most people have some days when they feel more like visitors and some when they have limited energy to seek new ways to do old things or to find new things that even matter. But we recognize craftspersons because—as *craft* implies—they have used or developed the skills and abilities to create something that previously did not exist.

The many meanings of *craft* are represented in Robin's story. His first concerns were about survival and hope of rescue. Only later did he try to make a "craft"—a vessel that might take him around his new home and perhaps beyond its borders. To be creative is to use the skills you have, develop the ones you need, and bring to a project an originality and inventiveness that makes the eventual creation a unique expression of its creator (Cameron, 1992; Maslow, 1960).

Creativity is often seen as something only a privileged few were issued at birth and unavailable to the average (much less the challenged) person. Creativity is, however, a gift accessible to everyone, whether they apply the gift to building exotic monuments to time, to nurturing relationships, or creating a peaceful corner in the midst of chaos. Research on exceptionally creative people has identified the characteristics they share in common (Csikszentmihalyi, 1996). Creative people are complex—by which we mean they do not seek to be "average" or to present themselves as singular. They may manifest extremes in many characteristics. What seems to make them unique is that they embody traits often considered to be mutually exclusive. They are not bound by either/or choices, and usually operate from both/and positions that may appear paradoxical when they are actually in dialectic tension. Although most people go through life trying to control or hide their "shadow" side, creative people find acceptable ways to express all the dimensions of their personalities. They often have great energy, but they also tend to sleep a lot and many take naps. Their schedules are defined by internal signals rather than by external calendars and clocks. They appear to have a general intelligence or wisdom that is combined with a childlike naive quality. Similarly, they can be both playful (even irresponsible) and highly disciplined. They have the capacity to engage in rich fantasy and imagination and also have a sense of groundedness. These characteristics make it possible to break away from the present at times, without losing touch with the past.

Most research finds that people maintain stable traits of being extraverted (outer oriented) or introverted (inner oriented). Highly creative people are both. They often do their work alone and are comfortable with being alone. At the same time they value the company of those with whom they can share and exchange ideas. Humility and pride are other paradoxical traits of creative people. They are well aware that their accomplishments are noteworthy and partially the result of luck, *and* that their own achievements have built on those who developed the groundwork. They can be both passionate about their work and objective about it—a necessary asset for receptivity and response to criticism. They can be seen as ambitious *and* selfless, competitive, and cooperative in their efforts to contribute to whatever they choose as their field of endeavor.

Because they tend to focus on current challenges and future projects, creative people spend little time dwelling on the past. Although they can be rebellious and independent, they often display a great appreciation for the rules and values of tradition. They are often androgynous, being more sensitive and less aggressive than most men, and more tough and dominant than most women. Their openness and sensitivity may expose them to more pain and suffering than others experience, and they may be more sensitive to slights and anxieties. On the other hand, their sensitivity may predispose them to the capacity for great enjoyment—and they often take great pleasure in a variety of activities.

Csikszentmihalyi (1996) also identified the major obstacles to expressing the creative potential every individual has. Obviously, those who are concerned with safety and survival are preoccupied with these worries. Other obstacles include having too many demands, being easily distracted and/or having a lack of discipline that saps energy on other activities, and not knowing what to do with one's energy.

Not knowing what to do with one's energy would seem to be an unlikely problem for those with chronic pain and chronic illness. One thing that becomes clear, however, when working with people who have limited energy, is that when they are feeling a bit better they often engage in a flurry of "catch-up" activities as they try to make up for all they haven't been doing. Guilt and perfectionism may then drive their efforts to exceed the limits of the newfound energy, resulting in a relapse and need for a lengthy period of recovery. Seldom are these activities even considered "creative"—rather, they usually fall into the category of necessity and may be engaged in with an understandable resentment that makes it difficult to find whatever creative potential may be hidden in the project.

☐ Consciousness: Raising, Focusing, Ordering, and Expanding

Putting together ideas about creativity and change, we have come to believe that creating a meaningful life involves developing the ability to focus, order, and expand consciousness. The literature about consciousness is vast. We use the term here to particularly highlight the aspects of consciousness that have to do with attention and awareness—having the ability to focus attention, and awareness of thoughts, feelings, actions, situations, and our responses to these. Once these abilities are recognized, it is possible to expand the focus of attention and to become aware of new or different information in the service of health and healing.

Prochaska and Norcross (1994) saw consciousness raising as an essential aspect of any process of therapeutic change. By definition, they saw it as related directly to awareness therapies that emphasize bringing into consciousness that which has been unconscious. However, consciousness raising is equally essential to decision making about change in action therapies, creating the path between precontemplation, contemplation, and preparation. Prochaska and Norcross emphasized that feedback and education can be important sources of consciousness raising. The kinds of feedback and education we see as most important are those discovered by clients. The role of the therapist is to facilitate clients awareness of their unique self-care resources and information, as well as to support clients in whatever actions they deem are appropriate to this knowledge. We help clients notice what *is*, and what makes a difference, and then assist them to notice what difference acting on these new awarenesses makes in their lives. This spiral of attending and becoming aware involves coming to recognize how we focus our attention and what we become aware of as a consequence of that attention.

For example, it may seem obvious that people who are feeling ill or in pain have limited energy to put into creating a meaningful life or any-thing else. Sometimes people have limited energy, at least in part, be-cause they have constricted their lives to manage the illness and, as a consequence, they also may feel bored. In the process of giving up what they can no longer do, they may not have taken the next step to finding out what they can do or what they would truly enjoy doing. One of the first steps that can be taken is becoming aware of what you do or do not enjoy, a task far less simple and obvious than might be expected.

Considerable research has studied the phenomenon of attention to symptoms. Clients are often told to attend to their symptoms to unravel the diagnosis. Sometimes clients feel strongly that they are the only one who could know or truly care what their experience is. They hope that attending to the nuances of their sensations will provide the information needed for a cure. This attention to the symptoms may, in time, become a double-edged sword, leading to the hyperarousal of worried vigilance, a diminished circle of attention, and a compromised quality of life. Many pain-control approaches, then, are based on the idea of distraction—coax-ing the attention to different repetitive thoughts, feelings, or behaviors that compete with symptoms for attentional focus. In our experience, however, the competition, if framed as distraction, has the potential to retain the attention on the problem—a paradox noted by some in rela-tion to development of an identity around a problem (e.g., Alcoholics Anonymous, or other problem-centered groups). Having a problem focus can be immensely helpful to some people, whereas to others it becomes part of the problem—a life now organized around *not* having pain or *not* enacting a behavior (Watzlawick, Weakland, & Fisch, 1974). The energy consumed in such antiproblem nonactivities and mental gymnastics can be exhausting and provide limited rewards. Instead, we have found it much more useful to help people notice what they are doing when they don't have the problem (exceptions) or when they are deeply engaged in an activity that is personally satisfying and moderately challenging—activities characterized by *flow*. Although talking about exceptions is one approach to shifting focus from the problem, we find sometimes it's even more effective to engage in discussions about experiences of flow.

☐ Flow: Doing–Being

What is flow, and why is it important for people living with chronic pain and chronic illness? For the past 30 years, Csikszentmihalyi (1990) and researchers around the world have studied a phenomenon they label *flow*. The characteristics of the flow experience include a narrowing of atten-tion, associated with a feeling of involvement and focused concentration.

In fact, positron emission tomography (PET) scans have shown that when in flow the brain is highly focused and efficient. It appears that flow "orders" consciousness in much the same way that meditation does. Goleman (1988) referred to "flow" as the Western meditation—a form of ordered consciousness based in focused activity—that is, "doing."

When experiencing flow, we often have a diminished awareness of time (it may pass more quickly or slowly). While absorbed in the activity, people tend to be unconcerned about other issues and unself-conscious. Any activity can produce optimal flow (e.g., games, artistic performances, religious rituals, sailing, computer programming, sports, meditating, etc.). These experiences have been described in relation to recreational and other leisure activities (e.g., rock climbing, playing chess, creating art or music, being in nature), alone or with other people, and often in relation to vocational situations, such as for surgeons, artists, or mothers with children. The situations most likely to become flow activities typically involve a clearly defined goal, knowledge about what must be done, and immediate feedback about how well we are doing. There must be a balance between the challenges and demands of the activity and our skills in the activity. Flow experiences are often related to activities that are highly valued or consistent with our sense of meaning or purpose.

The conditions most likely to facilitate flow have concrete goals and manageable rules, and the person involved is able to adjust opportunities for action to capacities. Therefore, we must be able to obtain clear information about our progress and be able to attend to the activity (i.e., the situation permits us to screen out distractions, making concentration possible). Some people are more easily able to experience flow in a range of activities. Such people concentrate easily and are not easily distracted. They are not afraid to "lose themselves" in an activity, and are less concerned with their own "ego" than they are with the activity at hand. They tend to be good at reading feedback (small signs) that others may miss. They are able to set manageable goals and to match their skills to the opportunities available. They often are able to set goals where others would not necessarily see that there was anything that could be done. We find flow activities often take place in nature, or doing hobbies or enjoying aesthetic pleasures, such as playing or listening to music, sewing, gardening, sports, or other activities that "please the senses" and engage the mind.

Flow is the light in the tunnel for many people with chronic pain and chronic illness. Studies have shown there is a strong relationship between quality of life and ability to enter flow experiences. Research on chronic pain management emphasizes the role of distraction—an approach that still leaves the problem/pain in the central role, that is, we are distracting ourselves *from* what demands our attention. The focus on flow creates a subtle and important shift in focus to that which is meaningful and creative. Purposefully nurturing healthy flow experiences has benefits therapeutically as well as developmentally. Some therapeutic interventions are being developed that build on awareness of flow to improve quality of life (deVries, 1992). In our experience, those who have more flow experiences truly do have an improved quality of life. We have found it can be tremendously helpful to tell clients about flow phenomena and encourage them to identify how and when they tend to have these experiences in their lives. Based on these self-discovered experiences of flow, clients can consciously choose to do more of these and fewer of whatever is not rewarding. It may even be possible to identify aspects of flow in activities that cannot be relinquished. Clinical examples of the use of flow are described in chapters 6 and 8.

For example, Jeanine has been on disability for several years now with chronic pain. She also has arthritis and high blood pressure. Asked what advice she would have for others who are suffering with chronic illness, she said:

> Find out what you love. I love my husband and my friends. But I also found out, after I became ill, that I love doing some things—they make life worthwhile. For me it's pottery. I go to the studio everyday and work for at least two hours—I usually can't manage to do any more than that. There's so much to learn and try. No matter how bad I'm feeling, while I'm doing that there is no pain—just the pure enjoyment of doing something I love. And if someone actually likes what I've made enough to buy it, that's a real kick.

☐ Ultradian Rhythms (Being–Doing)

In contrast to focused attention in activity, another approach to focused attention and awareness is Ernest Rossi's ultradian healing response—which he has called a form of "Western yoga" (Lloyd & Rossi, 1992; Rossi, 1996; Rossi & Nimmons, 1991). The ultradian healing response is the hypothesized potential for healing in "naturalistic trance" that accompanies some of the body's *ultradian* (within 24 hours) rhythms. In his work with Milton Erickson, Rossi became aware that Erickson's process of "naturalistic trance induction" used for hypnotic healing was based on Erickson's keen observations about subtle facial, breathing, and attentional differences that occur at regular intervals (see chap. 8 on hypnotic phenomena). Noting when clients were moving into these "natural rest cycles," Erickson would encourage the cyclic process of physiologic slowing and drifting attention to facilitate trance and a focused attention on inner phenomena.

In the years since Erickson's death, Rossi has greatly enlarged his knowledge of psychoneuroimmunology and his understandings about cyclicity and healing in hypnosis. In several books he has outlined his theory of the ultradian stress response—the consequences of continually overriding the body's natural rhythms and ignoring the subtle signals the body offers to "take a break" at regular intervals. Rossi points out that the release of chemicals from the endocrine system (hormones, etc.), autonomic system (neurotransmitters, stress response chemicals), and immune system (natural infection fighters) fluctuates within a 24-hour period. Just as our body has circadian rhythms (day/night), and monthly and seasonal rhythms (infradian), we also experience many physical and mental changes that occur at approximately 90- to 120-minute intervals throughout the day and night. Among the mind activities modulated by ultradian rhythms are attention, concentration, learning, memory, sensations, perceptions, emotions, dreaming, fantasy, imagination, creativity, and a transpersonal sense. Body activities modulated by ultradian rhythms include left–right nasal dominance, autonomic nervous system, gene-cell metabolism, endocrine system, immune system, breast-feeding, hunger and sex, digestion, work and sports, stress response, psychosomatic responses, cellular metabolism, and drug sensitivity (Auvil-Novak, 1997; Turek & Zee, 1999).

At night (during sleep) these rhythms are recognized by changes in sleep phases, including rapid eye movements (REM) observed under the eyelids during dream cycles. During the day (when awake), these cycles may be noticed as subtle shifts that signal the need to "take a break," such as wanting to stretch or loosen up your muscles, yawning, or sighing, noticing your body becoming quiet or still, feeling a desire for a snack, and/or a mild urge to urinate. Others may experience happy memories and thoughts of good times, feel thankful or introspective, or experience friendly fantasies and/or feelings of mild sexual arousal. Many realize outer performance is slowing down, and inner awareness increases. If we don't recognize and respond to these signals, we may find ourselves increasingly experiencing the "ultradian stress syndrome," a sense of stress and fatigue. If we continue to ignore these signals, Rossi believed we may become "high" on stress hormones. These hormones may increase performance in the short run but result in hidden wear and tear over time and possibly in seeking external stimulants (caffeine, nicotine, alcohol, etc.). Mistakes, memory lapses, irritability, and depression may result from ongoing stress. Classic psychosomatic symptoms (e.g., insomnia, asthma, depression, anxiety, compulsive eating, high blood pressure, headache) may begin to be experienced (Rossi & Nimmons, 1991).

To utilize the natural healing inclinations of the ultradian cycle we need to become aware of our natural signals calling for rest and allow time to access the deeper levels of rejuvenation and rest that we so often ignore. There are several ways to utilize this time for healing. Rossi suggested that just beginning to pay attention to these natural signals and when they occur can help us to move naturally into the ultradian healing response by attuning to the body's natural rhythms. Chapters 8 and 9 provide several examples of ways to utilize the concept of the ultradian healing response in therapy by observing the signs of naturalistic trance. Ultradian rhythm experiments are also found in chapter 11.

In our experience, simply telling people about these cycles and encouraging them to notice their own signals to "take a break" can set into motion small but powerful changes. For people who have been focused on body sensations only as symptoms that something is wrong, the reframing of these as benevolent "signals" can be significant. Attending to these signals has the practical application of helping people more effectively "pace" their activities so that they don't overdo and end up energy depleted. These kinds of awarenesses are "first-level" responses that can be sufficient in and of themselves to improve quality of life. There is, however, the potential for second-level benefits from this practice. With or without the support of a therapist, those who take these breaks and also accept the invitation to be "curious" about what they might become aware of will begin to access the unconscious knowledge and resources that some call "inner wisdom." After some time on the island, Robin had his own description of inner wisdom, calling it "Secret Hints and Dictates." He wrote in his journal, "I afterwards made it a certain rule with me, that whenever I found these secret hints, or pressings of my mind, to doing, or not doing anything that presented, or to going this way or that way, I never failed to obey such dictate."

Although for many this access is the primary reason for using the ultradian healing response (H. Erickson, personal communication, 1998), the combined benefits of pacing activities, befriending the body, and trusting one's own deepest inner wisdom can be empowering in ways that simply telling people what they "should" be doing cannot be.

☐ Clinical Example

"I've got to do something fast. I blew up at my boss yesterday and I've missed so much work that I'm going to get fired." Gloria, a 49-year-old computer programmer, had suffered debilitating migraine headaches subsequent to an auto accident that occurred 13 months previous to her first visit. She had been referred for clinical hypnosis by her therapist as a "last-resort" attempt to relieve her chronic pain and possibly save her job. "My whole life has changed since the accident," she said. "I'm in pain all the time. Beside these headaches, my neck has never healed right and for some strange reason I'm sensitive to loud noises and light."

In the period since her accident Gloria had missed considerable work time. On numerous occasions she went to the emergency room for injection treatment. On one occasion she had to be hospitalized for a week, due to severe pain. She also spent considerable work time frantically visiting various health professionals and generally being immobilized from her headaches. She went on, "I've been through all the hoops, all the tests and all the treatments, but nothing has helped. My doctor had the nerve to tell me that because of my age, it was probably my hormones."

Although she was a gifted programmer and a valued employee, Gloria's supervisor had recently informed her that she had "run out of second chances" and would be fired if she missed any more work. "The thing is," she said, "I have tried to make up for the time I've missed by putting in extra work when I can. I'm working on an important project that has an inflexible deadline. Some weeks I've worked 70 hours. Of course it wipes me out so much I get another headache and have to miss the next week."

Responding to the "miracle" question (see chap. 6), Gloria, not surprisingly, emphasized that she wanted to learn to set better boundaries in her life so that "I won't feel this constant pressure." She went on to explain that although she loved the intricacies of programming, she no longer liked her job. "There is so much pressure to finish this project, and I know that I have put us far behind schedule. To escape I go back to my cubicle and code the whole day long. I'm able to get away from the pressure of the project, even though I'm working on it. I completely forget what I'm doing. I drink water all day but I never need to urinate more than twice, even when I arrive at the office at 6:00 a.m."

Clearly, Gloria's engagement in this focused activity meets many of the characteristics of the flow state. She "left" her body while in this process and only returned when she absolutely had to urinate. Even then, she would return back to her former state in just a few minutes. This kind of daily detachment certainly raised the possibility that she was suffering from ultradian stress syndrome. Sensing this, the therapist, after informing her of her symptoms' possible relationship to ultradian cycles and teaching her two simple self-hypnotic techniques, suggested the following task assignment:

> Between now and the next time we get together, I would like to try a little experiment. I'd like you to take your alarm clock to work and set it to ring 90 to 130 minutes from the time you begin coding. When you hear the alarm you'll know that it is time to take a break. How long of a break you take is up to you; however, I would suggest that you do the following things: Check in with your body and ascertain what it might want—food, a bathroom break, stretching, a change in body position, etc. I'd also like you to

briefly practice one of the techniques that you learned today. Again, how long you spend doing this is up to you. The best way to determine this, of course, is to listen to your body. When you're ready to begin coding again, set your alarm for another 90- to 120-minute break period.

Gloria, commenting that she wouldn't consent to such a strange request "If I weren't so desperate," agreed that she would try to experiment. A week later she returned to the office delighted with the results. "I haven't had a headache for four days. I felt so good that I was able to walk for two hours. I haven't done so much since the accident." Gloria fully followed the experiment's instructions, setting her alarm and taking breaks for around 10 to 15 minutes. The structure of the two self-hypnosis experiments gave her the sense that even though she was taking a break, she was actively doing something useful.

In reviewing what difference the experiment made to her, Gloria said, "Well, I think that there is a pretty direct relationship between my work state and my pain. But you know bringing my alarm clock in was an indirect way for me to get my boss to leave me alone. It says to him, 'Stay out of my business. I can get it done if you'll just let me be. I'm doing my work, and I'm going to take breaks when I need to.'" As she continued, it became apparent that her "public" assertion of a self-care need created an invisible, yet effective, boundary between her work and her health. This was a first, significant step in achieving her "miracle" (see chap. 6).

Scaling the amount of confidence she had in relation to continuing this solution, Gloria said that she was a "7." Responding to the follow-up question of "What would you be doing differently if you were an 8?" she answered, "I think that I would probably turn down an overtime request [in the next week]." Gloria and the therapist spent the remainder of the session strategizing how this might be done and speculated on what difference such an act might make in regard to her health. At the conclusion of the session, the therapist asked her to continue the experiment, and asked her to pay attention to her ability to assert these helpful "health boundaries" in other parts of her work and home life, reiterating her example of refusing overtime.

Returning two weeks later, Gloria said, "Well, my boss was pretty surprised when I said 'no' to overtime. I explained that I was really starting to feel better and I didn't want to 'blow' it. He was very respectful and thought that refusing extra work 'made a lot of sense.'" She went on to say that she had continued headache free, adding, "Which is surprising because I left my alarm clock at home. When I got to work I got upset because I've become so dependent on it for my breaks. But I wrote myself a note and stuck it on my computer. The funny thing was I never noticed the note. I did notice my neck hurting, however. At first I got real scared thinking that I was about to get a headache after all these weeks. But then I noticed that it had been over two hours since I began working. I stopped, did my hypnosis, went to the bathroom, and it went away. I figure maybe I should listen to the alarm clock in my body from now on."

The therapist and Gloria talked about the importance of listening to the needs of the body and acting accordingly. The therapist informed her that ultradian breaks are most effective in the healing process when they occur as a result of listening to our bodies. He said, "It looks like you're ready to let go of your training wheels," referring to the alarm clock. Continuing, he complimented her on her assertiveness in relation to her own health and wondered aloud how these new boundaries might continue to grow and increase her level of self-care. "That's what I'm looking forward to," Gloria said. "Before, if I wasn't working, I would organize my time around my headaches or in anticipation of having one. Now, I can get back to doing what I used to do—work out, be with friends, and go to the mountains." The remainder of the third session with Gloria focused on the preceding self-care ideas as well as some new ones. At the end of the session, Gloria and the therapist agreed that, because of her successful solution, this third session would be their last, leaving open the possibility that she could return for a "tune-up" any time she chose.

The therapist heard from Gloria 11 months later in regard to a report she needed for her insurance company. He asked how she had been feeling. "I still haven't had a headache," she said and went on to say, "If I did, it would be only temporary, just like everyone else." She reported that she faithfully listened to her body and took her ultradian breaks. At the end of the encounter, the therapist remembered at least six headaches that he had had over the past year.

☐ Putting It Together

The movements between insight and action, solitude and community, internal and external are the rhythms of a meaningful life. The particulars of the insights and the actions will be unique for each person, as is the balance between the time people choose to spend alone and with others. The beneficial rhythms between flow in activity and restoration in rest are apparent in figure 4.1.

☐ Consciousness Raising, Focusing, and Expanding

The Experience Sampling Method (ESM), used by Csikszentmihalyi for his research on flow (Csikszentmihalyi & Csikszentmihalyi, 1988), is sometimes called ecological momentary assessment (EMA) in health psychol-

FLOW   FLOW   FLOW

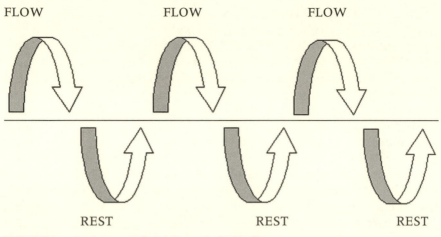

REST   REST   REST

FIGURE 4.1. Basic rest and activity cycle for healing.

ogy research. Originally used to collect data for research (Shiffman & Stone, 1998), it can also be a powerful tool for developing awareness "in-the-moment." Once this ability is developed, attention can more successfully be focused, shifted, and (sometimes) expanded. This flexibility of consciousness is a skill long identified with meditation practices and a valuable tool for anyone, whether or not they live with a chronic health problem. The ESM process involves signaling study participants at intervals (regular or random) for a period of time and having them complete a form about their thoughts, moods, activities, concentration, and motivation, at the moment at which they were signaled. They may be asked to note whom they are with, the level of challenge required, and skills available, as well as other data, depending on the focus of the study.

In our ongoing studies, we have used a combination of several of the above approaches to gather data about interventions that might be useful in several different conditions. The process involves having people first complete the Self-Care Responses (SCR) tool and the Solution Identification Scale for Health (SISH) (chapters 7 and 11). For the first week they are signaled up to eight times a day at random times programmed into watches provided by the researcher. The ESM response form (see part III) takes about two minutes to complete each time and incorporates questions about the phenomena associated with flow and ultradian rhythms (described earlier). Because these are seen as two phases, a basic rest and activity cycle, it is possible to present the phenomena as semantic differential scales that simultaneously measure both experiences. For example, one can simultaneously rate oneself on a scale contrasting feeling cheerful versus irritable or outgoing versus solitary.

During the second week participants complete a daily diary that documents how often, for how long, and under what circumstances they had experiences of flow. During the third week attention is focused on awareness of ultradian cycles and signals to "take a break." They note how often these occurred, what the signals were, and if they were able to take a break. If they took a break, what difference did it make? Did they become aware of any new information if they spent some time engaged in an inner focus? During the fourth and last week, participants complete a daily diary that tracks both flow and ultradian rest signals.

At the start of the project and at the end of each week, the therapist/researcher does a solution-focused interview, seeking information about what clients have noticed, and if they did anything different as a result of that awareness. If so, what difference did it make? We also asked what they thought the likelihood was that they would continue these new behaviors.

During the first interview two additional important questions were, "Why do you think you became ill?" and "What do you think would need to happen for you to begin to heal/feel better?," using their language for an improved experience. This combination of consciousness raising (ESM) following by consciousness focusing (on flow and ultradian rhythms) has been life-changing for many of the participants. Chapter 11 contains copies of the diary and experience-sampling questions that can be used as "experiments" along with other experiments that have the potential to expand consciousness—by trying something new and being curious about what they may learn.

Our preliminary findings are quite promising using this approach. One example that stands out was Judy's experience. Judy, described in chapter 3, has fibromyalgia, chronic fatigue, and grand mal seizures. In an interview about one month after completing the process just described, she reported changes she could already see in her life. While on a trip to visit her family, she was able to be aware of "recognizing whether the thing that I was doing was supporting me or 'cutting me down.'" She said the first (ESM) exercise had been illuminating, because she learned how she was really spending her time and what the costs were. Consequently, in interactions with others that would normally exhaust her, she was able to be with others and also take care of herself a bit more. When her sister wanted her to join her in the kitchen, she was able to ask if they could sit, have tea, and spend time together that way. She found it was her company that her family wanted, more than her participation in activities that were likely to exhaust her.

The ultradian exercises were particularly helpful in alerting her to the subtle signals that she needed to take a break—and the benefits of taking them. "Then, as I got better at it, I could continue the process because I was taking the breaks when they did me good rather than when I had to recover. . . . And so when I'm aware of what I'm doing and I'm aware that I need a break, then I can continue the process. But I'm still not really good at that...to say I need a break and I take a break . . . that's a big step forward from what I did before which was continue the process until I was just a little ragamuffin," she laughed. "And would take three or four days before I could face that task again."

She recalled:

> The thing that I remember about completing the self-care responses tool is that the part of it where it asked whether it was useful. . . . You had to rate its effectiveness . . . that was *really* useful because I would list things (and some of the things required a lot of time). . . . Some of the things I was doing very regularly weren't very effective at all. And some of the things I was doing very rarely . . . were *extremely* effective and . . . it brought up the question, well why am I doing this? And oftentimes the things that weren't all that effective were things that *other* people suggested that I do and were talking to me about and I felt like I needed to do, for whatever reason. And oftentimes the things that were extremely effective were these things that I had labeled as feeling narcissistic.

She added:

> And what I got out of the flow one was a recognition that it was actually a healing time . . . that a number of the activities that I . . . almost felt silly about helped . . . I felt, gee I'm laying in the bathtub for an *hour*? . . . Shouldn't I be doing something for someone else? . . . I felt like I was being bad by doing these things for me, and the flow discussions helped me to realize that a number of those were activities that encouraged the flow experience. And recognizing that that was actually a health-building experience . . . helped me to recognize that it wasn't something to avoid . . . and I started adding those to my life because I felt so much better, I felt so much clearer, not only just physically better but I felt clearer about who I am.

Judy was asked whether she thought others could do the process on their own. Although she felt that was possible, she also felt the relationship was really important. She said, "It feels like you are a trainer . . . a therapist trainer. I guess I felt like I had a personal trainer to help [me] recognize what I was doing and what was helping me and what was not helping me. And uh, 'by the way here are some natural rhythms that exist and how do they work *with* you, how do they work *for* you?'"

Judy wrote the primary investigator (DW) six months later. She had moved to another part of the country, after noticing that she felt a lot better in a different climate.

> This move has been a catalyst for a lot of other thinking. Since one change is happening, other changes are more possible. I have done quite a lot of thinking about the process we went through. I'm hoping to apply more of

it as I settle. I certainly know that it allowed me to move to another level of thinking about what I do and what it does to me (good and bad), and consequently what control I can have over my condition—or at least over the impact it has on my life in general. This is a pretty big deal.

Take care, Judy

The entire process, as described here, is time-consuming and usually needs to be modified for use in clinical practice. Different aspects of the process seem to be helpful alone or in combination. Sometimes we use just the self-care tool and solution-focused questioning. If someone has little interest in activities, we may suggest noticing the times they do have interests and then exploring when times of flow are occurring, even briefly. These activities might then be increased. The awareness of ultradian "take-a-break" signals are particularly helpful for those who tend to overdo when they are feeling better. They can be helped to notice that pacing themselves means they are actually more productive in the end. For those who have great difficulty recognizing their patterns, the Experience Sampling Method (ESM) can be a powerful "wake-up" call. Often people discover that they really don't dislike certain activities as much as they thought—and become aware that some activities and some people really contribute to their overall sense of well-being. Solution-focused questioning is an essential aspect of the process, helping clients focus on what they have noticed, what difference that makes, and what they might do with that information. It is the process of becoming aware and making conscious choices that allows one to recognize what is important and to craft a meaningful and creative life.

In part II, we describe clinical applications of self-care and consciousness approaches to healing, emphasizing the use of solution-focused approaches and approaches to changing states of consciousness. Several approaches to self-hypnosis and the related concepts of flow and ultradian rhythms are described with examples from clinical practice.

☐ References

Allport, G. (1959). Preface. In V. Frankl, *Man's search for meaning: An introduction to logotherapy* (p. 9). New York: Simon & Schuster.

Auvil-Novak, S. (1997). A middle-range theory of chronotherapeutic intervention for post-surgical pain. *Nursing Research, 46*(2), 66–71.

Bresler, D. (1979). *Free yourself from pain*. New York: Simon & Schuster.

Cameron, J. (1992). *The artist's way: A spiritual path to higher creativity*. New York: Jeremy Tarcher/Perigee.

Carlsen, M. (1988). *Meaning making: Therapeutic processes in adult development*. New York: W. W. Norton.

Csikszentmihalyi, M. (1990). *Flow: The psychology of optimal experience*. New York: Harper/Collins.

Csikszentmihalyi, M. (1996). *Creativity: Flow and the psychology of discovery and invention* (p. 57). New York: Harper/Collins.

Csikszentmihalyi, M., & Csikszentmihalyi, I. (1988). *Optimal experience: Psychological studies of flow in consciousness*. New York: Cambridge University Press.

Dethlefsen, R., & Dahlke, R. (1993). *The healing power of illness: the meaning of symptoms and how to interpret them*. Shafesbury, Dorset: Element.

deVries, M. (Ed.). (1992). *The experience of psychopathology: Investigating mental disorders in their natural settings*. New York: Cambridge University Press.

Frankl, V. (1959). *Man's search for meaning: An Introduction to logotherapy*. New York: Simon & Schuster.

Goleman, D. (1988). *The meditative mind: The varieties of meditative experience*. Los Angeles: Jeremy P. Tarcher.

Griffith, J., & Griffith, M. (1994). *The body speaks: Therapeutic dialogues for mind-body problems* (pp. 50–64; 112–133). New York: Basic Books.

Heatherton, T., & Weinberger (Eds.). (1994). *Can personality change?* Washington, DC: American Psychological Association.

Jung, C. (1961). *Memories, dreams and reflections* (p. 340). New York: Random House Books.

Kabat-Zinn, J. (1990). *Full catastrophe living*. New York: Delta.

Lloyd, D., & Rossi, E. (Eds.). (1992). *Ultradian rhythms in life processes: An inquiry into fundamental principles of chronobiology and psychobiology*. London: Springer-Verlag.

Maslow, A. (1960). *Toward a psychology of being*. Princeton, NJ: Van Nostrand.

May, R. (1967). *Psychology and human dilemma* (p. 180). Princeton, NJ: Van Nostrand.

McNamee S., & Gergen, K. (Eds.). (1992). *Therapy as social construction*. London: Sage.

Prochaska, J., & Norcross, J. (1994). *Systems of psychotherapy: A transtheoretical analysis* (3rd ed.). Pacific Grove, CA: Brooks/Cole.

Random House. (1967). *Random House dictionary of the English language* (p. 1460). New York: Author.

Rossi, E. (1996). *The symptom path to enlightenment*. Pacific Palisades, CA: Palisades Gateway.

Rossi, E., & Nimmons, D. (1991). *The 20-minute break*. Los Angeles: Jeremy Tarcher.

Rush, M. (1994). *Decoding the secret language of your body: The many ways our bodies send us messages*. New York: Simon & Schuster.

Seligman, M. (1994). *What you can change and what you can't*. New York: Alfred Knopf.

Shiffman, S., & Stone, A. (Special Eds.). (1998). Special issue: Assessment of health-relevant variables in natural environments. *Health Psychology, 17*(1), 3–52.

Strong, T. (1999). Macro- and micro-conversation in conspiring with chronic pain. *Journal of Systemic Therapies, 18*(3), 37–50.

Turek, F., & Zee, P. (Eds.). (1992). *The regulation of sleep and circadian rhythms*. New York: Marcel Dekker.

University of California, San Francisco School of Nursing Symptom Management Faculty Group. (1994). A model for symptom management. *IMAGE: The Journal of Nursing Scholarship, 26*(4), 272–276.

Watzlawick, P., Weakland, J., & Fisch, R. (1974). *Change: Principles of problem formation and problem resolution*. New York: W. W. Norton.

Webster, D., Dan, A., & McElmurry, B. (1984–1987). *Self-care responses to threats to women's sexuality*. Unpublished findings from Nursing Research Emphasis Grant, Doctoral Programs in Nursing (NU 0 1049).

Wilber, K. (1991). *Grace and grit* (pp. 46–49). Boston: Shambhala.

Yalom, I. (1980). *Existential psychotherapy*. New York: Basic Books.

THERAPY

Stages of Recrafting a Life

Before Robinson Crusoe ultimately recrafted his life on the island, he passed through a variety of identifiable adaptive stages of change ultimately enabling him to transform from someone with few resources into a self-reliant individual equipped to embrace the daily challenges of his environment. Initially experiencing a period of utter disbelief and confusion, Robin progressed though (and occasionally back to) stages of suffering feelings of abandonment and victimization into phases of exploration and retreat, eventually engaging in the process of experimental trial and error to provide for his needs.

Clients stranded due to circumstances of chronic pain and illness navigate similar passages in the journey of recrafting their lives as well. They often experience initial periods of denial and/or feelings of victimization that may lead them to embark on a voyage seeking immediate rescue from their condition. If rescue (in the form of a cure) doesn't eventually materialize, they are faced with the challenge of exploring a bewildering landscape of alternatives in hope that they might discover something that might (even remotely) improve their condition. In turn, this process requires them to engage in a practice of trial and error with the objective of discovering what works and what doesn't. This dynamic process of change often necessitates passages between stages and is seldom linear, requiring the client to endure periods of success and progression along with disappointment and relapse. However, clients who can persevere and meet this challenge are rewarded with the skills and resources necessary to live a recrafted life.

For the therapist, individuals suffering from chronic conditions often present a particularly daunting challenge. Caregivers know that therapeutic progress often means that clients need to take action to do something different. Doing something different, however, frequently requires an increase in the degree of the client's motivation. Readily observable in this client population is the extraordinary amount of energy required to manage chronic pain and illness, even at minimal levels. Accordingly, therapists are presented with the task of motivating members of a client population that feels as if they have consumed much of their available resources.

At the core of our approach is the notion that clients suffering from chronic pain and illness come to therapists at many different levels of readiness for change. Directly fueling their readiness is the amount of energy required to embark on a journey that will involve both risk and reward. Respecting and utilizing clients' (often variable) energy levels and meeting them at their "model of the world" are essential for this journey to be successful.

The remainder of this chapter describes five stages that reflect the available energy, hopefulness, curiosity, and willingness to risk that are necessary for recrafting a life. Paralleling this are interventions to encourage transitions from one stage to another, as well as specific lessons to be learned from clients at each stage.

☐ The Challenge: "Just Getting out of Bed in the Morning"

"I used to measure my life in my daily accomplishments. Even silly little things like cleaning the basement or cooking a really good meal. Now I measure my life in doctors' appointments." Doug, heroically struggling to delay the onset of end-stage heart disease, let out a disgusted sigh as he gingerly eased himself into an office chair. His appearance had radically changed from just a few months ago. Pale and 50 pounds lighter, he was a mere shell of his former 65-year-old energetic self. He continued, "It seems like I have little time for anything else. It never ends, the more specialists I see, the more exhausted I get. The more I get exhausted, the sicker I feel. The sicker I feel, the more I start to think that I should being seeing yet another specialist. Sometimes I feel lucky to just get out of bed in the morning, much less get the simple stuff like paying my bills done."

Doug is the norm rather than the exception. Living with chronic pain and illness devours energy. Varying levels of fatigue may be the result of the physical and emotional demands of the condition as well as a side effect of its treatment (Stewart, Hays, & Ware, 1992). Like crop fields that burn out from overuse, clients' energy becomes quickly exhausted without careful planning. Every day, they are faced with the challenge of marshaling all their resources to try to manage their condition, navigate the complex maze of health care providers, and meet economic and social needs for themselves and their families. This, combined with overcoming the stigmatization of having a medical condition, intrusive questions from everybody from health care providers to insurance companies to family members, and the resulting feelings of diminished self-worth, can significantly sap the energy required just to carry out simple daily tasks of living. At best, clients suffering from chronic pain and illness learn to delicately manage to balance periods of exertion and rest so that they can maximize the quality of their lives (Charmaz, 1991). At worst, they find themselves in a frightening free fall through ever-diminishing levels of available energy accompanied by increasing degrees of hopelessness.

Not surprisingly, health researchers have discovered that clients suffering from chronic pain and illness often experience significant reductions in their energy levels. Ryan and Fredrick (1997) found that clients in enrolled pain clinics consistently observed themselves as having less available energy when compared to matched control subjects. This perceptual gap grew substantially wider when they believed their condition to be disabling or frightening. Energy-reducing health-related stressors, especially those that threaten one's autonomy, may significantly lower clients' sense of self-efficacy as well. Self-efficacy, in turn, can be a critical variable in a client's response to any health challenge (Keefe et al., 1997).

☐ Client Motivation and the Importance of "Fit"

The consideration of the role of client motivation in psychotherapy has burgeoned in the last 15 years. Prochaska and DiClemente (1984), pioneers in this area, developed a stage-of-change model that assessed the degree of readiness people experience in relation to the challenges of engaging in new adaptive behaviors. They identified six distinct stages that occur over the life cycle of an intentional change in behavior. The initial stage, *precontemplation*, is followed by *contemplation*, *preparation*, *action*, *maintenance*, and *relapse* stages. The model assumes that change is a nonlinear process with starts, stops, progression, and relapse until the satisfactory achievement of a behavioral goal occurs. Underlying this assumption is the belief that each stage poses different tasks for individuals to address before they can advance to the next phase of adaptation. Using these concepts to assess clinical progress, researchers have successfully used this stage-of-change model as a predictive indicator of treatment success rates with various clinical populations (Prochaska, DiClemente, & Norcross, 1992).

Some clinicians have found this stage-of-change framework useful for identifying and understanding shifts in attitudes and motivation, whereas others have used it to match treatment interventions to a client's level of readiness within the change cycle. Miller and Rollnick (1991), in their book *Motivational Interviewing*, described interview procedures and intervention methods that enhanced substance abuse clients' motivation to progress from one stage to another. They found that tailoring specific interventions for each stage of readiness substantially increased the success of their treatment outcomes with substance abuse clients.

Recently, Jensen (1996), believing that the lack of effectiveness pain treatment programs for some individuals is due to motivational problems, adapted these techniques to treating chronic pain clients. Noting that most clinical interventions by their nature require active involvement, he suggested that addressing the client's motivational challenges holds great promise for improving treatment effectiveness and reducing relapse rates.

Taking a different tack, Steve de Shazer (1988) and his colleagues at the Brief Family Therapy Center in Milwaukee became interested in the different types of relationships that evolved out of the clinical interview. They identified three relationships—*customer, complainant*, and *visitor*—that are possible between the therapist and client (DeJong & Berg, 1997). Customer-type relationships develop during and after the interview, when client and therapist jointly develop a problem and/or a solution to work toward. In complainant-type relationships the therapist and client are able to jointly develop a problem on which to work but are unable to identify a role for the client in constructing a solution. Visitor-type relationships occur when during and after the interview the therapist and client fail to identify a problem or goal on which to work.

It is important to note that these distinctions in no way constitute a label reflecting the capacity of the client to change. Rather, they begin to identify the ways in which the therapist can respect the client's position in relation to the problem and possible solutions. Most importantly, they provide a useful framework enabling the therapist to make adjustments to insure that the therapeutic discourse will better fit the client's goals.

Tailoring interviews and interventions to the client's model of the world is at the core of all solution-focused therapy. de Shazer referred to the critical importance of finding a proper "fit" for the client within the goal-setting process.

> Fit is a mutual process involving both the therapist and the people that he is conversing with during which they come to trust each other, pay close attention to each other, and accept each other's world view as valid, valuable, and meaningful. By accepting the client's world view the therapist is

able to be useful and help resolve the complaint as simply and easily as possible. (de Shazer, 1988, p. 90)

Because our approach is (client) goal driven, it is critical for the therapist be able to make a clear distinction between what on the surface may appear to be a lack of motivation to improve the client situation and the depletion of energy levels that accompany chronic pain and illness. The remainder of this chapter outlines the different stages that clients pass through, along with intervention strategies that encourage progressive passages into increased levels of energy and consequently motivation.

☐ Stages of Recrafting a Life

Visitors

We have appropriated de Shazer's *visitor* category as our first stage of recrafting. Clients in this stage don't view themselves as having a problem, nor do they have a goal on which they wish to work on with the therapist. Despite their health care providers' best intentions, these individuals appear to be uninterested in participating in any kind of therapy. In fact, visitors frequently express some confusion as to why they are in a therapist's office. This is understandable in view of the fact that they have often been sent by someone else and rarely share the concerns of the referring source, whether it is a family member, someone in their health care system, or a case manager.

There are several good reasons why visitors may have difficulty in identifying a problem, much less a therapeutic goal on which to work. They may have been suffering from a condition for a long time with little relief. When an individual has experienced the continual defeats associated with a chronic condition, energy is depleted and hopelessness becomes a constant companion. Instead of risking defeat one more time, visitors may politely turn away from talking about problems as if they just "don't want to be a bother." Another reason for this status is a client's natural inclination toward avoiding making things worse. The person may have a deteriorating condition and believe that risking an interruption of a current state of maintenance, however low, might jeopardize his or her ability to sustain the little control that the person now has over the condition.

Visitors are often sent to see a therapist because of their reluctance to participate in some kind of medical self-management regime. Traditionally, these clients have been labeled as "noncompliant" or "in denial" due to their refusal or failure to follow a proscribed course of action (Rapley, 1997). In some cases this failure can threaten a client's health or significantly exacerbate a serious medical condition. Often these clients have been deemed "resistant" and "not knowing what is good for them" by referring health care providers. Thus, they are assigned a negative label without ever having a chance to participate in the therapeutic process.

The visitor stage is difficult for both the therapist and the client. Therapists get caught between the demands of the referral source to "fix" the client and at the same time the need to develop a therapeutic relationship with an individual who isn't interested in being "fixed." Clients often feel frightened, ashamed, or disrespected. Complicating matters for visitors is the fact that refusal to follow medical advice may risk a loss of benefits or an interruption in the continuity of their care. Therapists treating individuals in the visitor stage have the unenviable position of helping both sides "rebuild burned bridges."

Interventions for Visitors

The paradoxical relationship between therapist (wanting to help) and client (not looking for help) in this stage requires a great deal of delicacy within the intervention process. The most effective initial intervention with visitors is to simply "just visit." The key at this stage is for the therapist to respectfully talk with the client rather than engage in any kind of direct confrontation. Ultimately, the therapist's goal is to seek a complaint on which to work with the client; a problem that, once resolved, would make a difference in the quality of her life. If the client and the therapist cannot (collaboratively) construct a complaint, further progress will be highly unlikely (Table 5.1).

Ironically, the quickest way to develop movement toward constructing a complaint in the visitor stage is to avoid directly mentioning one. Accordingly, it is necessary to abandon the role of "expert" or assessor while at the same time empathizing with the client about the inconvenience of the situation. Validating the client's experience is critical in this stage. Miller, Duncan, and Hubble (1997), in their examination of successful psychotherapy, emphasized the importance of affirming the client's experience throughout the therapeutic process. Ericksonian practitioners re-

---

TABLE 5.1. Interventions for Visitors

Seek a complaint to address.
Avoid confrontation or challenges to "denial" or noncompliance.
Agree on the inconvenience of the circumstances.
Develop curiosity about the client, his or her story, and coping abilities.
Compliment the client on:
  Staying in the struggle.
  Willingness to put up with a "strange situation."

fer to this type of client affirmation as "pacing" and note its indispensability in the process of successful hypnotherapy (Gilligan, 1986). Acknowledging the client's thoughts and feelings about the situation is the first step toward engaging him or her in a therapeutic conversation. It relieves the pressure arising from anticipation of the unknown and allows the therapist to begin to develop some legitimate curiosity about the client's story.

It is helpful at some point in the initial interview with visitors to invite them to relate (at least a portion of) their story. Along with listening to their story, it is important to express some curiosity about what the concerned third party might have been thinking when suggesting a visit to the therapist. For example, a therapist might ask, "I'm curious, if I were to ask your wife what she had in mind when she made the appointment, what do you think she would say?" Or, "What do you think needs to happen for your case manager to get off your case?" Or, "What would be different in your life that would convince your physician that you don't need to come here any more?"

This kind of interactional questioning, adapted from solution-focused therapy (DeJong & Berg, 1997), allows clients to lower their defenses by focusing on the concerns of a third party rather than on their own. The client may have a complaint about the third party's concerns or, conversely, may be inspired by them. Naturally evolving out of interactional interviewing is information about relationships, perceptions of others about the client's condition, and some details about his or her coping strategies.

In some cases clients may respond negatively to these questions. This may occur because it is too early in the interview to discuss such matters, or the client may be responding to a negative history of compliance problems of which the therapist is not aware. In these cases it is important for the therapist to shift the conversation to a neutral area, assessing the possibility of "weaving" it back to more clinical matters at a later time.

Finally, the first session with visitors is concluded with a series of compliments (chapter 6) in regard to the their willingness to attend the interview, coping skills, and "for tolerating a strange situation." Compliments should always be sincere and directly relate to the material that the client has presented in the interview.

The following case example illustrates interview interventions that are used to discover usable complaints from an initially "noncompliant" visitor.

Case Example: Developing a Complaint from a "Noncompliant" Visitor

Michael was referred by his hospital social worker who was concerned that he had "compliance" issues. He had recently lost a transplanted kidney. This was the result in part, the transplant team believed, of his marginal compliance in an antirejection drug treatment program. As a consequence, he was required to participate in psychotherapy before being reinstated on the transplant eligibility list. Michael arrived for his first session angry that he had drive across town for therapy and bewildered about what he was supposed to accomplish. He began the interview by stating, "There is absolutely nothing wrong with me. I might have 'fudged' a little on the timing of my medication, but that's no reason to for me to spend my time and money with you examining my life. I may have to spend the next month or so with you to get back on the list but I'm not going to tell you anything personal."

After supporting him in his idea that this seemed unfair, the therapist complimented Michael on his willingness to be so forthright about his opinions. Commiserating with him about the fact that he had to drive all the way across town and pay money to "just sit in someone's office," the therapist confessed that he really didn't know much about transplants and antirejection drugs and about their benefits and side effects. In detail, Michael recounted his battle with kidney disease, his struggle to get disability benefits, and seemingly interminable hours on the dialysis machine. "After that transplant I thought—now I'm free. But now, I have to start all over again. And you are what stands between me and a new kidney."

As the session wound down, Michael was complimented for maintaining a hopeful attitude in the midst of a serious medical situation and being willing to tell part of his story in an unfamiliar setting. He was further complimented on the degree to which he coped with a serious medical situation and his willingness to do what needed to be done to get back on the transplant list. Then the therapist, pausing, wondered aloud, "If seeing me somehow could be useful, how do you think that we would spend our time together?" After a period of silence Michael answered, "The only thing that I can think of is that I would like to sleep better." He explained that his medical condition had resulted in a serious sleep disorder, adding, "I don't think spending four hours three times a week on a dialysis machine helps much either."

Discovering a problem and a goal on which to work, the next few therapy sessions focused on a series of self-care and self-hypnosis "experiments" (chapter 8) that were specifically aimed at relieving Michael's sleep disorder. He quickly learned a number of helpful interventions to address his complaint. In addition to improving his sleeping, Michael learned to utilize his newfound abilities to more easily pass the time during his lengthy dialysis sessions.

While he participated in these experiments, without prodding, Michael began to talk about the fact that taking the steroids and other drugs necessary to prevent organ rejection caused him significant and uncomfortable side effects. He went on to say that in the past he had manipulated the timing of taking the drugs in an attempt to feel better. "Now," he admitted, "I feel guilty that I wasted a kidney that could have gone to someone else." When asked whether he could apply his newfound hypnosis skills to managing the side effects next time, he answered, "I know now that I can get through it. I have to. Next time I'll be prepared, I'm not going to lose another kidney. These techniques will help me sleep and, when I start feeling lousy from the drugs, can help me dull the side effects so I can get on with my life."

At the termination of therapy, five sessions after its beginning, Michael felt confident about his new aptitude and expressed some relief in being able to talk about his feelings in regard to losing the kidney. He was able to honestly tell the transplant staff that he "got a lot out of therapy," and they in turn were impressed enough with his new perspective to immediately reinstate him on the transplant eligibility list.

Directly confronting clients in the visitor stage over compliance issues or lack of motivation almost always ends in failure. Instead, expressing sincere empathy for a client's predicament, complimenting the client on his or her struggle, and searching (curiously) for a complaint are effective in circumventing the resistance so commonly associated with the visitor stage. Likewise, developing a workable complaint strengthens the therapeutic alliance and ultimately allows both client and health care provider to coconstruct a goal that "fits."

Although Michael is a representation of a visitor who is (initially) negatively motivated by a third party (the transplant team), other clients may make transitions out of this stage through the positive concern of a loved one. The source of the motivation in this stage is less important than the process that the therapist and client engage in to construct a complaint.

The following case example illustrates the motivational possibilities presented through a concerned loved one.

Case Example: Utilizing the Complaint of a Concerned Third Party

Looking intently at his watch, Max appeared painfully out of place as he sat in the waiting room. A case manager from his insurance company referred him. After reviewing his extensive medical records, she was concerned that his recent auto accident might exacerbate some chronic pain that was a result of a number of previous injuries. When his therapist asked him what might be helpful, he shrugged his shoulders and said, "I don't know, my lawyer told me to come. There's really nothing wrong. He just wants me to take advantage of the insurance company's offer in case there is a question about my benefits later."

Appearing puzzled, the therapist asked, "So what do you think she [the case manager] had in mind when she referred you?" Barely taking time to think, Max replied flippantly, "I can't tell you, she just told me to come. I thought *you* were supposed to know." As the session progressed, Max deftly avoided talking about any physical or psychological problems. Every time the subject was broached he would stare ahead wide-eyed and say, "I'm doing fine." He was more than willing, however, to talk about the fact that he worked as a heating and air-conditioning repair specialist. He talked about the long hours that he spent working two jobs and the fact that his wife would "like me to come home at a decent hour every once in a while." He went on to talk about two children from a previous marriage and how the visitation agreement with his ex-wife made him angry.

The therapist, continuing to try to develop a complaint, asked, "Suppose I were to ask your [current] wife how coming to a therapist might be helpful, what do you think she would tell me?" Pausing, shifting his body position forward and intensely focusing, he said, "Well, that's another kettle of fish, isn't it?" Momentarily staring at the ceiling, he continued, "Yes, she'd want you to cure me of my moods." He went on to describe periods of depression and anxiety subsequent to his accident as well as the persistence of troublesome stomach problems. His refusal to medically attend to his symptoms had come between him and his wife, and the resulting conflict had become so serious that he delayed going home at night by obtaining a part-time job after work.

As this conversational path continued to develop, the therapist casually wondered, "Is that something you would like to change—your relationship with your wife?" He nodded and went on to say, "I'd really like to make this marriage work. It's not fair. Either I'm flying off the handle or I'm so sad that I don't feel like talking. She just doesn't know what to do with me." This statement was the beginning of a complaint description and naturally developed into linkages to the accident, the state of his marriage, and possibilities for relief in the future.

Max was a hardworking man and one of those clients who avoids talking about their problems because it just isn't in their nature. He had survived being a helicopter gunner in Vietnam and a long list of on-the-job injuries. For him, talking about his problems risked making them worse. He never saw the direct connection between his marital problems and his reluctance to address the symptoms arising from his accident. By the time the session was over, Max had shifted from being confused about how therapy might be helpful to gallantly agreeing to invite his wife to the next session and address his mood swings, "for my marriage."

Not every visitor will develop a complaint by the end of the first session. Indeed, from time to time a session will end with the therapist complimenting the client while leaving open the possibility of getting together at a later time. Or, after complimenting the client, a therapist might say, "I enjoyed talking to you. I'm wondering if you would be willing to meet again sometime?" If the client has experienced respect from the therapist within a nonconfrontational atmosphere, he or she will often agree to come back for another visit. If the client flatly refuses, the respectful manner in which he or she was treated by the therapist will significantly increase the possibility that the client will return in the future.

Learning from Visitors

We provided several case examples for the visitor stage because it presents the greatest challenge for both clients and therapists addressing chronic pain and illness. "Visiting" with clients teaches therapists the value of patience and listening. Moreover, visitors help therapists develop interview skills that incorporate timing as an essential component. Further, visitors inform their caregivers that there may be a variety of good reasons for not being interested in psychotherapy. Finally, and most importantly, therapists learn that they will be rewarded by simply respecting the position clients have adopted in relation to their (sometimes long and arduous) journey through the health care system.

☐ Sufferer/Victims

"I'm beginning to think that I'm never going to get over this. I can't remember the last time that I felt good. My kids and husband think that I do nothing but complain. They're really scared. So am I." After years of suffering (on and off) from a variety of mysterious neurological complaints, the impact of Virginia's diagnosis of multiple sclerosis (MS) was just starting to set in. She originally came to therapy as a visitor. Don, her husband, brought her in a year earlier after her neurologist told both of them that he suspected that her recent symptoms indicated that she was suffering from MS. Don had hoped that psychotherapy would help her accept the diagnosis and open up a doorway to psychological treatment. Virginia, however, had no such idea, stating, "I've got no problems, except sometimes my legs fall asleep and it lasts for days."

Unable to find a complaint on which to work, the therapist complimented Virginia on "having chosen a husband that cared about her so deeply" and "politely putting up with such strange questions for an hour." As she left she was encouraged to return if she thought therapy might be useful. In the next year she consulted a number of health care professionals and participated in a variety of treatment schemes (some quite bizarre), including having all her dental fillings removed and replaced with nontoxic substitutes. Now, beginning to accept what she was up against, she returned to therapy facing a lifetime of living with a chronic condition.

It took Virginia a year to make the passage from being a visitor perceiving that she had no problems to that of a sufferer/victim with a well-defined complaint. Sufferer/victims are in a transitional stage in which they realize that their acute problem is converting into a chronic one. Once the shock has worn off from an accident, surgery, or medical diagnosis, they begin to recognize that they might very well have to endure some level of pain and discomfort forever. They often feel victimized by the failure of their body or a specific event such as an accident or unsuccessful surgery. Sufferer/victims have often spent a good deal of time pursuing the promises of allopathic treatment, only to be (frequently) profoundly disappointed in the end. The experience of continually seeking and failing to find relief leaves them feeling "cast away." It is this element that plays a central role in significantly reducing the amount of energy that they have available to successfully address their condition. Fruitlessly traveling from provider to provider, surgery to surgery, or treatment to treatment depletes resources and may destroy hopefulness. This, in turn, constructs a pessimistic barrier between them and openness to trying something new. Ultimately, they feel "seduced and abandoned" by the experience, which in turn can result in a self-fulfilling cycle of failure that significantly impacts future treatment possibilities for both client and therapist.

Health care providers have heard sufferer/victims complain for thousands of years. They are understandably unhappy about their condition, disrespect from family and the health care system, and the fact that "nothing seems to work." In response to this, therapists may try "even harder" to meet these (seemingly impossible) demands or become so jaded that they stop listening or, at worst, caring. In addition to feeling physically and psychologically exhausted, clients in this stage still see the solution to their problems as being outside them. On some level they continue to have the hope that they will "rescued" or find the right provider to "cure" them. At this juncture, practitioners of nonallopathic therapies such as hypnosis can be placed in a particularly difficult position. Responding to (inaccurate) claims of "miracle" cures presented in the mass media, these clients frequently arrive at therapists' offices expecting complete relief from their condition. One need merely scan the tabloid newspapers at most grocery store checkout stands in order to find spectacular testimonials about miracle cures for supposedly incurable conditions.

Another key characteristic of the sufferer/victims stage is the difficulty they have in identifying periods when they may have experienced some (even the slightest) relief from their condition. The experience of their condition thus far is overwhelming and contains very few distinctions that separate the "bad times" from the "good times." They frequently tell their therapists, "I always feel the same—terrible!" Or, "The pain never ceases, it never changes." Nevertheless, solution-focused therapy's focus on recognizing the exceptions (de Shazer, 1985) to the chronic symptoms is the first step in moving out of this stage.

The final characteristic of the sufferer/victim stage is an initial disinterest in attempting solutions outside a professional's office. Their expectation, especially for hypnotherapy, is that any commitment to addressing their condition will be limited to the hour or so that is spent with their therapist. This may be a result of a lack of energy or of magical belief that the therapist's skill or the treatment modality won't require their active participation. Unquestionably, in either case, this view is a recipe for treatment failure.

Interventions for Sufferer/Victims

The experience of sufferer/victims, like that of visitors, needs to be validated (table 5.2). This means listening to their story and sincerely complimenting them on their willingness to seek out yet another health care provider. Respectfully listening to a client's story also gives the therapist the opportunity to attend to aspects, however small, of his or her struggle that indicate some hopefulness. At the very least, the client can be complimented on the fact that, in spite of his or her condition, he or she has enough hope to "try something different." Listening to the client's story also begins the process of demystifying the therapist's expert or "magician" status. This, along with sincerely complimenting the client, implies that his or her story is important and the client's resources are

---

TABLE 5.2. Interventions for Sufferer/Victims

Shift to "solvable" complaint.
Politely decline the expert/"magician" role.
Observe small exceptions and signs of hope.
Respect energy levels.
Go slow.
Compliment sufferer/victims on:
    Survival thus far.
    Willingness to talk to yet another health care provider.
    Small signs of hopefulness.
    Having found a voice to tell their story.

becoming evident. This represents the initial stage of empowering the client to be the ultimate "expert" on his or her unique condition and its successful treatment.

Attempting to completely address a complaint in the sufferer/victim stage typically ends in disaster. Of immediate concern is that any therapeutic intervention, however small, be successful. Brief therapy pioneer John Weakland (Fisch, Weakland, & Segal, 1982) said that of all the interventions he and his colleagues at the Mental Research Institute used, the injunction for clients to "go slow" was the tactic that they utilized most frequently.

Previous treatment failures with clients in this stage have often been the result of trying to accomplish too much in too little time. Utilizing a "small and slow" approach requires the therapist and client to collaborate on the possibility of constructing the most modest of tasks that might make a noticeable difference to her quality of life. Sometimes, however, the therapeutic discourse reveals that even the smallest task may appear too daunting for a client. In these cases it is best to gear the intervention strategy toward having the client observe the times in his or her daily routine when he or she might be most likely to have an adequate amount of energy to "try something different."

The following case example illustrates the engagement of a sufferer/victim in the process of committing to small steps enabling him or her to experience some small successes, ultimately improving the quality of his or her life.

Case Example: Constructing Achievable Goals

"You have got to help me get rid of this damn thing," Shirley said, contorting her face as she adjusted the oxygen tube in her nose trying to gain a little more comfort. Once a model for a cosmetics company, 30 years of smoking had finally caught up with her in the form of life-threatening emphysema. In the last year she had deteriorated from using oxygen a few hours a day to requiring it constantly. Despite this obvious decline and her physician's admonition that she would need to use oxygen for the rest of her life, Shirley expected hypnotherapy to magically transform and free her from this reality.

Beginning to sob, she continued, "Cure me of my dependence on this miserable thing so that I can go out and live my life again. I know that I can beat this. If the doctors would just stop giving me a death sentence I know I could get off it." Embarrassed at having a tube in her nose, she had stopped seeing her friends and had given up a number of physical activities that had previously brought her a great deal of joy.

Feeling trapped in a downward spiral of declining health and increased separation from the world, Shirley experienced her life as growing more out of control every day. Formerly a gregarious woman, she became almost totally isolated from the outside world when her husband Frank wasn't home. This isolation, in turn, increased the frequency and intensity of her panic attacks, a condition that she had sporadically suffered from for most of her adult life. Paralleling this factor was an increased and unwanted dependence on her husband. "The only time I get out," she sighed, "is when Frank takes me to dinner or appointments like these."

After listening intently to her story, the therapist avoided yielding to the natural yet disastrous temptations of insisting that Shirley directly address the seriousness of her medical situation and offering hypnosis as a remedy for her condition. Instead, he responded by complimenting her courage in making it to the appointment and her optimism about the possibilities of "exploring new territory." As the first session proceeded, the therapist and Shirley successfully navigated through her ultimate goal of being free from her dependence on oxygen down to something more immediately possible. "Really, the thing that I miss the most is going to my yoga class. I haven't gone since I've had to wear this damn thing all the time. My teacher calls me every week to see if I'm coming. She really cares about me, but I can't show up with this," she said, angrily pointing to the tube in her nose.

The therapist, wondering aloud, responded, "What would it take for you to get to class?" Shirley replied, "I don't know. I can't take the embarrassment of carting along my oxygen *and* not having the energy to get through a whole class. It's not that I haven't tried. I can't tell you how many times I have planned on going but my panic attacks wouldn't let me get out the door." Recognizing this statement as an opportunity to coconstruct an obtainable goal from a number of small steps, the therapist asked, "What do you think would be the first step in returning to class?" "Well," she said, "I have to get back in shape to do yoga again. I couldn't even keep up with a beginning class now. I haven't done anything in months. I have a great tape at home that I used to use but I just don't have the energy." Continuing the interview process of sifting through the steps necessary to achieve the client's ultimate goal, the therapist asked, "What needs to happen for you to get the energy to do yoga at home?" Shirley went on to describe unpredictable fluctuations in her levels of energy. When she felt like she had enough energy she would plunge headlong into various household chores that she felt guilty about ignoring because of her condition. Ultimately she overextended herself, became exhausted, and in the end became more depressed and isolated.

By the end of the first session, Shirley and the therapist agreed that it might be helpful for her to observe (but not act on) the times during the day that she felt the most energetic. As therapy progressed, this information would be utilized in enacting a resource management scheme that would ultimately allow her to judiciously allocate a reasonable amount of energy to practicing yoga at home without becoming exhausted.

The practice of yoga at home, not surprisingly, enabled her to significantly expand her energy reserve and at the same time improve her breathing. This, in turn, gave her a sense of control over her body and eventually reduced the number and severity of her panic attacks. Finally, six weeks after beginning regime at home, Shirley was able to begin attending class again.

Although she was far from achieving her goal of being permanently released from the constraints of her oxygen canister, Shirley, like many sufferer/victims, found that even a small amount of success had a direct correlation to an improvement in the quality her of life. Clients in this stage require time and perseverance on the part of the therapist to gently accompany them through the process of reconciling the discrepancy of the reality of their medical condition with the unrealistic hopes they may bring to the first therapy session. The journey is eased considerably when it is coupled with gradual improvements in one's quality of life.

Learning from Sufferer/Victims

Sufferer/victims teach therapists that despite their experience of being firmly entrenched in a web of seemingly nonresolvable symptoms, relief is possible if it is achieved one small step at a time. Moreover, these clients inform therapists that when they are aided in taking the first few steps, they gain enough momentum to transport themselves into the seeker/searcher stage on their own power. Clients successfully transcending the challenges of this stage inform themselves and their therapists that they are capable of generating sufficient resources for change.

☐ Seeker/Searchers

"I read where hypnosis was good for arthritis. My friend said that it really worked for her. I've tried acupuncture, a change in my diet, therapeutic touch, chiropractic, magnets and just about everything else under the sun to make my pain go away." Molly, now in her sixties, had suffered from arthritis since she was 40. Cycling between the sufferer/victim and seeker/searcher stages over many years, she had sought out a number of remedies with mixed results. Concerned about the cumulative effects that 20 years of analgesics and other medication might have on her body, she was interested in exploring the potential that hypnosis might offer in re-ducing the amount of medication she required to manage her pain.

Molly is in the seeker/searcher stage of recrafting. Clients in this stage are often experienced health care consumers. Seeker/searchers like Molly frequently experience recurring cycles of success and failure in their search for the "right" treatment. Given the (sometimes numerous) alternatives currently available in the health care marketplace, it is not unreasonable to expect that clients seeking relief will experience varying levels of suc-cess and failure while navigating the vast landscape of traditional and nontraditional remedies.

Seeker/searchers emerge from the sufferer/victim stage after develop-ing enough curiosity about possibilities for change to risk leaving their self-imposed confinement. Clients often move back and forth between these two stages, engaging in a cycle of advancement and retreat. The key characteristic that distinguishes the two stages from each other is the will-ingness of seeker/searchers to try something new. Marshaling enough energy and confidence to take a risk, they expose themselves and their conditions to treatments that range from the conventional to the exotic. If they are rewarded with even partial success they will more than likely continue to seek out additional resources. However, if the particular treat-ment modality is not helpful, they may quickly retreat back to the more familiar confines of the sufferer/victim stage, feeling that, at least tempo-rarily, "nothing works." Months or even years may go by before they are willing to take another risk.

For seeker/searchers the therapist may be just one more stop on a crowded highway of health care providers. Like sufferer/victims, clients in this stage initially don't view themselves as being directly part of the solution. Nor do they expect to actively participate in their care outside the therapy session. Moreover, they present themselves wanting relief "now!" Their focus is on the ultimate outcome of rapid release from the painful symptoms of their condition rather than the process involved in achieving relief. Seeker/searchers will often view treatment modalities such as hypnosis or acupuncture simply as methods to "take my pain away," rather than components of a dynamic process of healing. This mistaken expectation, as in the sufferer/victim stage, can place the thera-pist and the particular treatment modality in the impossible position of being responsible for the client's success or failure.

Interventions for Seeker/Searchers

After listening to the stories of their journeys through the various stages of chronic pain and illness, the therapist can begin to take advantage of the fact that individuals in the seeker/searcher stage have experienced at least some relief from their symptoms in the past. Although they rarely arrive in a therapist's office bragging about a long history of successes, seeker/searchers have discovered, even if on an unconscious level, that there are some things that work in treating their problem. These periods of respite or exceptions represent times when a client can temporarily put his or her condition in the background or recognize specific actions that he or she has taken to improve daily life, despite the condition. Benson refers to the positive expectancies generated by the interchange of client and therapist as one of the essential components of his concept of "remembered wellness" (Benson & McCallie, 1979). This phenomenon may be due to conscious choices that a client makes in relation to his or her own care, or they may occur on an unconscious level while the client engages in an activity that temporarily distracts him or her from her symptoms. Periods of relief often include activities that improve the client's physical and mental well-being as well as the times when he or she is able to manage her energy reserves so as to maximize the ability to make the most out of any given time span.

Frequently, seeker/searchers, especially those who have spent considerable time cycling between stages, have forgotten or abandoned a number of useful activities that have been helpful in relieving their suffering. As incomprehensible as this might seem, clients often have good reasons for stopping these beneficial self-care activities. One of the major rationales for discarding an initially helpful self-care strategy is the amount of energy that it may require. Even seemingly helpful treatments will be rejected if their energy requirements exceed their ultimate therapeutic benefits. Moreover, a particular method, although initially helpful, may gradually loose its efficacy over time. Rather than making adjustments or combining the activity with other helpful interventions, clients in this stage often determine that it has "outlived its usefulness." Furthermore, self-care activities that once appeared beneficial may not fit into a client's current lifestyle, becoming too inconvenient to continue over long periods.

Paradoxically, the very act of searching and seeking itself can lead to the abandonment of other useful health interventions. Feeling pressed to "try something new" can result in a shift from one relatively successful activity to one that initially appears to offer more promise, only to be disappointed in the end. Investing energy and time in a failed endeavor can take the hope out of the most optimistic of journeys.

It is important to initially approach clients in the seeker/searcher stage by actively assisting in reacquainting them with past and present successes, however small, in addressing their symptoms or condition (table 5.3). This is the initial step in transferring power and responsibility back

TABLE 5.3. Interventions for Seeker/Searchers
Interview for exceptions.
Coconstruct self-care inventory of past successes.
Observation/experience sampling: good days/bad days.
Commitment to a path of treatment.

to the client. There are a number of ways to accomplish this. The solution-focused therapy interview creates an effective vehicle in generating detailed and useable exceptions that can be utilized to treat the condition in the present and future. Self-care inventories (chapter 3) can aid the client in pinpointing specific remedies that have been helpful in the past. The Solution Identification Scale for Health (SISH) (chapter 7) is a tool for identifying and discussing the particular personal characteristics, behaviors, and life experiences that clients have found useful in coping with the condition. Observational task assignments (chapter 7) and experience sampling methods (chapter 4) can be enacted to encourage clients to notice the small things that make a real difference in the quality of their lives.

The goal of all of these interventions is the initiation of a process in which client and therapist construct an inventory of success, however initially small, in obtaining relief from the condition. Eventually, the goal in the seeker/searcher stage is for the client to view him- or herself as an active agent in treating the condition, replete with effective strategies, resources, and hope.

The following case example illustrates the facilitation of a seeker/searcher's ability to marshal his or her energy focus and on specific resources and interventions that will best serve his or her needs.

Case Example: The Importance of Choosing a Path

"I can't wait to get out of here." Sam, recuperating from a recent chemotherapy treatment, tentatively sipped ice water from his cup as he adjusted his body in the hospital bed. "They tell me that I have about a 55% chance of surviving this cancer. I think that hypnosis might help," he said. It had taken about a year for Sam's doctors to determine that his stomach problems and sporadic internal bleeding were the result of a rare form of cancer. Subsequent to this diagnosis he had endured two abdominal surgeries, radiation treatment, chemotherapy, and a variety of experimental drug regimes. Feeling that he had exhausted almost all medical avenues, he had recently shifted his focus to the possibilities that some of the complementary therapies might offer. Unable to return to work following his last surgery, he began feverishly researching a wide variety of alternatives over the Internet.

Sam, like many clients who experience the immediacy of a potentially terminal medical condition, frequently cycled between the sufferer/victim and seeker/searcher stages. Having a great deal of success in business made him a results-oriented individual, unfamiliar with failure on any level. He was sure that if he looked hard and long enough, something useful would turn up. Responding to the immediate internal drive to find help, he dedicated most of his waking energy toward seeking out any possibility that might be hopeful. When he found a treatment that looked encouraging, he would throw his whole being into pursuing its purported benefits. After he found little or no help, he would withdraw, depressed and weakened from his efforts, temporarily unmotivated to pursue further treatment possibilities. A few weeks later he would emerge from his bedroom ready to try something else.

"I don't know how much time I've got left," he said. "I'm trying as many things as possible. I want to learn hypnosis for my pain, but I really hope that it can help me get well." In addition to longing for pain relief, Sam hoped that hypnosis would reduce his bouts with anxiety, eliminate his sleep disorder, help him determine which treatment route to follow, and, most of all, help train his body to fight the cancer. He had read numerous articles on psychoimmunology, impressing the therapist with the depth of his knowledge.

After complimenting him on the breadth of his knowledge and his willingness to try something new, the therapist commented, "Those all sound like worthwhile goals, but I'm wondering what do you think would be best to focus on first?" He replied, "If I could get a handle on this [discomfort], I could reduce some of my pain and sleeping medication. That would make a big difference in how clearly I would be able to think, especially in the morning." He recounted his struggle with his surgical wound, the pain that it had caused, and the inconvenience of managing the intricacies of the accompanying drainage tube. Agreeing that this more manageable goal would be the best starting point, Sam learned enough self-hypnosis over the next three sessions to begin to successfully address the physical pain, which in turn contributed to his getting an adequate amount of sleep at night. A beneficial side effect was a gradual reduction in his level of anxiety. Encouraged by his ability to think more clearly, he felt energized enough to redouble his efforts considering even more alternatives. Predictably, rapid energy depletion and the chaos that resulted from his relentless search recreated enough anxiety to return him to his previous state.

Fearing that the cycle would start all over again, Sam told his therapist, "I'm feeling really overwhelmed. I've got this pressure to do something but I don't know which way to turn. I don't have time to get lost in all these blind alleys. I'm starting to loose sleep again and my pain is getting worse." Complimenting him on the energy that he was willing to dedicate to his search, the therapist asked, "It sounds like there are a lot of possibilities out there. How do you make a decision about what to investigate?" Looking perplexed, he hesitated for a long while, finally stating, "I've never really thought about that much. Usually I just depend on my instinct about what might work. It's always worked for me in my business. I'm not sure that it is working for me here though." He continued, describing cycles of frenzied searching and engaging in various nutritional, herbal, and mind/body programs followed by disappointment, exhaustion, and withdrawal. The therapist, reasoning that there might be exceptions to this cycle, suggested that "Between now and the next time we get together, pay attention to the times that you experience yourself as being on the right track in your search."

After observing his own process for two weeks, Sam concluded, "The best times are when I'm looking into something that has a spiritual component." He noticed that when he focused solely on investigating and participating in activities that had a spiritual aspect, he actually felt energized rather than exhausted and disappointed. "Even if it doesn't work out, I feel like I have participated in a worthwhile activity. I'm less anxious because I know that I am going to get something out of it, even if it doesn't directly apply to my situation." Looking much more relaxed, he concluded, "I now know the path that I need to take. Either the practitioner or the program (or both) need to be spiritually based."

Using this template, Sam had narrowed the number and scope of programs that were available, conserving his energy and feeling that his search was purposeful rather than random. He was ultimately able to participate in a spiritually based psychoneuroimmunology program that addressed his goal of making mind–body–spirit interventions to treat his cancer. Discovering a path that represented his needs, beliefs, and resources empowered him to continue his journey within a framework of hopefulness.

Learning from Seeker/Searchers

Seeker/searchers like Sam are expert at teaching therapists the real immediacy of needing relief from a particular condition. They are inspiring individuals who are frequently willing to throw themselves completely into searching out solutions. They have innate abilities to address and solve their problems, and once they are able to manage their energy reserves, they can set clear goals, develop a specific plan, and become capable of moving to the explorer/experimenter stage.

☐ Explorer/Experimenters

"I haven't looked around much lately. I thought that I'd come in and see if there was anything new. Some of the stuff that I have been doing doesn't work as well as it used to. Maybe I need a tune-up." Brenda had success-fully managed her chronic back pain for a number of years. Her willingness to engage in a process of trial and error had rewarded her handsomely. She had developed a dependable yet flexible self-care routine that met most of her needs. She long ago had abandoned actively searching for the ultimate "miracle cure," instead focusing on the actions that she could take, however small, to directly improve her quality of life. Brenda is an explorer/experimenter. Rather than withdrawing and isolating herself after a particular treatment had failed to meet her expectations, she would continue her search. "At least I know I don't have to waste any more time on that," she would say, disappointed but not defeated.

Explorer/experimenters emerge from the seeker/searcher stage after shifting toward viewing themselves as being primarily responsible for the care of their condition. This worldview is often achieved after a long, hard-fought journey in which they have become much more assertive in the management of their care. This leads them to primarily rely on pro-viders for specialized services or consultation. Explorer/experimenters appear to be eager to navigate through new territory, optimistically be-lieving that there might be something useful for them just around the next turn. Likewise, these clients have developed a set of criteria that can be applied to determine whether they should expend their time, resources, and, most importantly, energy on any given treatment alternative.

Explorer/experimenters are actively involved outside the therapy of-fice, viewing the process of treatment as beneficial in itself. This dynamic process constructs a map that will enable them to acquire a new skill that can be integrated into their self-care routine. Accordingly, many times, for explorer/experimenters, the journey itself is often as compelling as its ultimate destination. Prior to arriving at a therapist's office, explorer/ex-perimenters frequently have done a great deal of research on the particu-lar treatment for which they are seeking consultation. As they engage in therapy they may continue to investigate the process on their own, ask-ing for supplementary reading material or taking classes. Explorer/ex-perimenters often (pleasantly) surprise their therapists by arriving at a session with material that is exciting and new to both of them.

Interventions for Explorer/Experimenters

Explorer/experimenters are interested in immediately engaging in a pro-cess that has a definable therapeutic outcome (table 5.4). Consequently,

---

TABLE 5.4. Interventions for Explorer/Experimenters

Set clear goals/future orientation.
Learn criteria for success.
Survey energy and resources.
Encourage experiments.
Construct tool kit.

---

it is important to address these expectations in the first session, learning the client's criteria for a successful intervention, developing a well-defined goal, and investigating the resources and energy available for its completion.

Explorer/experimenters, by definition, seldom have unreasonable expectations for a particular treatment modality. Similarly, these clients rarely need to engage in lengthy descriptions of how they came to have their particular condition. Instead, emerging from the first interview is a therapeutic discourse that focuses on "What needs to be different?" The structured solution-focused interview (chapter 6) is utilized to generate goals and develop signposts of progress that will inform the client that she is on the "right track" as the therapy progresses. Complementing this is therapeutic conversation that identifies the various successful interventions the client has engaged in over the course of her journey. Engaging in this process enables the client and therapist to coconstruct a map that will clearly identify resources (as well as areas to avoid) that will enhance the achievement of her goal. By the end of therapy, clients in the explorer/experimenter stage should have a reliable tool kit (chapter 7) that consists of durable resources, new and familiar, that can be relied on when the need arises.

The following case example illustrates interventions that reacquaint explorer/experimenters with resources that have been helpful in the past, thereby engendering hope.

Case Example: Rediscovering the Tool Kit

"I've had a lot of bruising lately. I'd have to say that I am more than a little worried." George, a 45-year-old college professor, was referring to his hemophilia. Recently, he had experienced an increase in the frequency and severity of the bleeding episodes commonly associated with the disease. Successfully using a combination of meditation and self-hypnosis since his early twenties, he had managed, up to this point, to reduce the number of transfusions that his condition required while substantially increasing his sense of control over the his health. An enthusiastic learner, he had personally researched the role that hypnosis and meditation played in improving the functioning immune system and directly applied their benefits to his medical condition (LeBaw, 1992). "It doesn't seem to be working like it used to," he said, furtively looking at a bruise on his arm. "I thought that I was doing really well when I avoided the AIDS crisis. Now, I'm not so sure. I know worrying about it just makes it more likely to happen, but lately, it's always in the back of my mind."

To the questions "What would be different for you as a result of therapy? How would you know it was useful?" George responded, "I wouldn't let my anxiousness get me. I'd feel like I was back in control again." Halfway through the session George had identified numerous periods (some long forgotten) over the last 20 years in which he felt "in control." Impressed with both George's knowledge of psychoneuroimmunology and the wide variety of successful options he had employed in the past, the therapist asked, "What would it take to get you back to that state of being in control?" He replied, "Well, I'd have to stop projecting myself so far into the future and concentrate on calming myself down in the here and now. I get so concerned about what might happen that I actually think that I make it more likely that it will."

By the end of the first session, George and therapist had constructed a map of past successes and committed to working on upgrading his current resources with a specific skill set that would enable him to situate himself in the present when he found himself anxiously projecting himself into the future. At the conclusion of therapy, four sessions later, George had learned some new skills and reacquainted himself with some old ones. He thoroughly enjoyed the process of learning how to, as he put it, "put my head back on my body" through a variety of hypnotic techniques. Never one to limit his horizons, he experimented in applying these interventions in ways that far exceeded his immediate personal health needs. Moreover, he was readily able to identify the set of self-care tools that he needed to utilize to meet the demands of his condition, commenting, "I think that I just needed to be reminded of 'what works.'"

Learning from Explorer/Experimenters

Explorer/experimenters teach therapists about perseverance, utilization of available resources, and that they frequently already have the solution to their problems. On occasion, they become separated from their resources and need to be reminded of their past successes as well as future possibilities. The task of the therapist is to aid them in rediscovering (and occasionally redrawing) their map.

☐ Recrafters

Rarely requiring psychotherapy, individuals in this final stage have recrafted themselves a unique and valuable life in spite of, or perhaps because of, extremely difficult circumstances. One need to look no further than popular cultural figures such as Stephen Hawking (White & Gribbin, 1993) or Christopher Reeve (1998) to find individuals who have overcome seemingly insurmountable physical and psychological circumstances to lead creative and inspiring lives. Recrafters are individuals who benefit from their successes and view failure as an opportunity to learn something new. Because the process of change itself is so valuable to them, they can easily identify specific steps that enabled them to arrive at this stage. Moreover, a review of their passage (back and forth) through the different stages of recrafting their lives often reveals parts of the experience to be helpful and even vital to their continuing ability to meet the daily challenges of their condition. As inconceivable as it might be for those of us who are able-bodied, many recrafters wouldn't trade their journey for anything.

Interventions for Recrafters

By definition, recrafters need no therapeutic intervention. Unfortunately, however, there is no guarantee that they will remain in this stage indefinitely. Circumstances beyond their control can thrust them back into any of the other four stages. Even George (in the previous case example) drifted into the explorer/experimenter stage when he temporarily got off track in relation to managing his hemophilia.

One intervention that universally benefits recrafters is their seeking out a relationship with the therapeutic community impacted by chronic pain and illness. Training professionals, giving hope to other sufferers, and aiding in research or fund raising can give their struggle significant meaning. The innovation of Internet chat rooms and newsgroups has been particularly helpful in this regard. Daily, one can observe the real concern and caring emanating from clients suffering chronic pain and illness helping other clients.

Case Example: Recrafting a Life

The first time Ellen met her therapist she was reading a magazine while lying in the middle of the waiting room floor. "I bet you're wondering what I'm doing down here," she said, smiling as she looked up. "I need relief from gravity after a few hours. Getting horizontal feels better on my back and if there is one thing that I have learned, it's not to deprive my back of anything," she laughed, self-assuredly. Using one hand to carefully support herself on a nearby chair as she slowly eased herself off the floor, she held out the other one to shake hands with her therapist. "So I'm told that you can help me get off my drugs long enough to have a baby," she said.

Ellen, an explorer/experimenter at the time of her first session, was eager to add hypnosis and other pain management strategies to her already abundant collection of self-care resources. She and her husband wanted to have a child, and she was investigating the possibility of discontinuing her use of pain medication and antidepressants during pregnancy. "The doctors and everyone else tell me that it's impossible and that I shouldn't do it. But I've heard that before," she winked, gesturing as she threw up her hands.

Ellen had beat seemingly insurmountable odds in the past. She had survived two life-threatening automobile accidents and crippling back surgery. Initially losing almost all of her physical mobility as well as her career as a dance instructor, she became firmly entrenched in the sufferer/victim stage. Experiencing continual pain and severe depression, she isolated herself for two years before she took the first few small steps in search of some alternatives. Like Robinson Crusoe, this was the starting point of a long and arduous journey in which she cycled back and forth between stages. A gifted amateur artist, she established herself as painter and eventually as an art teacher while supplementing her income as a day-care provider. "You can take care of little kids while you are lying on the floor," she observed. Overcoming significant physical handicaps in the past convinced her that she could once again defy the odds and have a baby. In the next nine months she learned a variety of self-hypnosis and pain management skills that enabled her to eliminate her regime of pain medication and antidepressants, making it possible to have a child.

Exhibiting one of the defining characteristics of the explorer/experimenter stage, Ellen demonstrated resilience over this period, bouncing back from the occasional failed self-care experiments and inevitable periods of (sometimes extreme) discomfort. She accomplished all this while remaining committed to the process. Even though it was a difficult and often exhausting journey, she prevailed in the end with a healthy baby boy. Ultimately, skeptical health professionals, inspired family members, and friends would eventually agree that Ellen had entered the recrafter stage.

The excerpts that follow are from a video interview (developed for training psychotherapists) that was conducted two years after Ellen had her baby. More illustrative than a case example, Ellen's own words demonstrate the struggles and characteristics of the recrafter stage.

The Cycle of Recrafting a Life

Interviewer: Was there a time in your life when you felt that what you are doing now was out of the question?

Ellen: Sure. If someone would have told me that I would be in the shape I am in now, I would have thought that it was an impossible and silly. Totally out of the question to even dream such a thing. Because I was a dance instructor, I felt like my accident took everything away from me. Day after day, all I focused on was the fact that I could never dance again.

Interviewer: How did that change?

Ellen: The big turning point for me happened when I realized that I needed to start including things in my life rather than excluding them. This didn't come easily. I had been focusing so much on confining my physical activities so that I could live within my limitations that my life just seemed to stop. I got very depressed and suicidal. When I look back at it now I was really angry. And it was a dangerous kind of anger because it was so self-righteous. That kind of anger makes you feel entitled to do just about anything, including taking your own life.

One day I noticed that my dog really needed a bath and there was no one else but me to do it. For some reason I couldn't stand to have him that dirty and I just went ahead and did it without thinking. Afterwards I was sore and exhausted but I realized that I could do something physical and not permanently hurt myself. I continued to do small things that were just a little physically challenging and my depression started to lift a little bit at a time. I became more open to possibilities and began to find more and more things to include in my life. Now every day is an adventure. When I wake up, I think about how far I can push myself. Can I do just a little bit more?

A lot of the treatment I received for my pain centered on adapting to the limitations of my condition. Anyone who has experienced chronic pain for a period knows this. But there is some part of me, the human spirit part of me that says, "You just can't get her down. She won't sit down and shut up in the corner. She just has to be out there and doing it." Even if they (limitations) push me back, at least I learned something.

Interviewer: Were there times along the way that you felt like giving up?

Ellen: Sure. There are times like that now. Being in chronic pain means struggling with that alternative every day. When you're alone with your pain it makes it even worse. Some days I cut myself a break and allow myself to just feel bad for a few hours. I think I'm entitled. When I'm done I go back to whatever I have planned that day.

Interviewer: You seemed to do the impossible by giving up your pain medication and antidepressants to have your baby. How did you do that?

Ellen: Well, first you have to come to he conclusion that you *can* do it. I think that focusing in a spiritual direction was most helpful in convincing me that I could do it. I knew once I got pregnant that there was no turning back and that I was going to have a lot of extra pain. Having a spiritual focus really helped me during the tough times.

Interviewer: On a self-care level what were some of the more helpful things that enabled you to manage the pain?

Ellen: Having a baby without being able to depend on my medication really pushed my inner resources to the limit. Most of the day I focused my attention elsewhere. I knew that I would have to moderate my activity, so about halfway through I farmed out my day-care business. Even though I reduced my activity I found things to focus on that would take my mind off my back. Then I scheduled regular breaks during the day to check in on my body, seeing if there was anything that it needed. This gave me the opportunity to determine whether I was pushing myself too hard. For me this was like checking in—letting my body know that although I can step away for a time, I won't abandon it. During those check-in times, when I noticed my body in pain, I would breathe into the areas that really hurt. I also directed light into these places. After I reduced the pain, I would close my eyes and take myself to a nice place in the back of my mind. If I were really comfortable I would memorize the sensations so that I could use them later. I got really specific with this, memorizing what the water felt like between my toes and the smell of the ocean. Pretty soon I would be ready to go back to what I was doing before the break.

Learning from Recrafters

Recrafters inspire hope in able-bodied and disabled people alike. They demonstrate the possibilities that exist within our fragile existence. They prompt the question in all of us: "I wonder how I would react in that situation?" Clearly not all clients will become recrafters like Ellen. Nevertheless, individuals in the stage have much to teach both therapists and other clients. Their extraordinary courage and motivation lies not in the achievement of a goal, but in the challenging process required to reach and maintain this stage. Recrafters frequently possess a level of spirituality combined with real humility. Often, they express their appreciation for the fragility of life while putting a high value on the lessons learned in the process of managing their condition. Inspiring to both clients and therapists alike, recrafters can engender hope in even the most hopeless of conditions.

☐ Summary

In no way do we mean to present the five stages of recrafting a life as diagnostic categories. In fact, our purpose is just the opposite: to look beyond labeling clients as being "resistant," "noncompliant," "in denial," or "psychosomatic." Instead, this perspective considers the level of energy required to manage the condition, the client's personal struggle with her illness, and the ability of the therapist to engage in a relationship that she might find helpful.

We don't intend to suggest that these stages represent a linear progression originating at the visitor stage and ending at the recrafting stage. Rather, the process is dynamic and may begin in any of the first four stages and shift between stages for the life of the condition. Clinicians may observe clients moving between any and all the stages during the course of therapy.

Finally, the most valuable contribution in using this framework is its ability to begin to inform therapists of types of interventions and therapeutic relationships that will be most helpful in relation to the client's current view the world, level of energy, and access to available resources. These interventions, combining solution-focused therapy and clinical hypnosis, are outlined in the following chapters. No intervention however is likely to be successful if it doesn't "fit" the client.

☐ References

Benson, H., & McCallie, D. P. (1979). Angina pectoris and the placebo effect. *New England Journal of Medicine, 300*(25) 1424–1429.

Charmaz, K. (1991). *Good days, bad days: The self in chronic illness and time.* New Brunswick, NJ: Rutgers University Press.

DeJong, P., & Berg, I. K. (1997). *Interviewing for solutions.* New York: Norton.

de Shazer, S. (1985). *Keys to solution in brief therapy.* New York: Norton.

de Shazer, S. (1988). *Clues: Investigating solutions in brief therapy.* New York: Norton.

Fisch, R., Weakland, J. H., & Segal, L. (1982). *The tactics of change: Doing therapy briefly.* San Francisco: Jossey-Bass.

Gilligan, S. G. (1986). *Therapeutic trances: The cooperation principle in Ericksonian hypnotherapy.* New York: Brunner/Mazel.

Jensen, M. (1996). Enhancing motivation to change in pain treatment. In R. J. Gatchel & D. C. Turk (Eds.), *Psychological approaches to pain management: A practitioner's handbook* (pp. 78–111). New York: Guilford.

Keefe, F. J., et al. (1997). Pain coping strategies that predict clients' self-efficacy. *Pain, 73*(2), 191–199.

LeBaw, W. (1992). The use of hypnosis with hemophilia. *Psychiatric Medicine, 10*(4), 89–98

Miller, S. D., Duncan, B. L., & Hubble, M. A. (1997). *Escape from Babel: Toward a unifying language for psychotherapy practice.* New York: Norton.

Miller, W. R., & Rollnick, S.(1991). *Motivational interviewing: Preparing people to change addictive behavior.* New York: Guilford.

Prochaska, J. O., & DiClemente, C. C. (1984). *The transtheoretical approach: Crossing the traditional bounds of therapy.* Homewood, IL: Dow Jones-Irwin.

Prochaska, J. O., DiClemente, C. C., & Norcross, J. C. (1992). In search of how people change: Applications to addictive behaviors. *American Psychologist, 47,* 1102–1114.

Rapley, P. (1997). Self-care: Rethinking the role of compliance. *Australian Journal of Advanced Nursing, 15,* 20–25.

Reeve, C. (1998). *Still me.* New York: Random House.

Ryan, R. M., & Fredrick, C. (1997). On energy, personality, and health: Subjective vitality as a dynamic reflection of well-being. *Journal of Personality, 65,* 529–565.

Stewart, A. L., Hays, R. D., & Ware, J. E., Jr. (1992). Health perceptions, energy/fatigue, and health distress measures. In A. L. Stewart & J. E. Ware, Jr. (Eds.), *Measuring functioning and well-being: The medical outcomes approach* (pp. 143–172). Durham, NC: Duke University Press.

White, M., & Gribbin, J. R. (1993). *Stephen Hawking: A life in science.* New York: Plume.

The First Meeting:
Exploring the Landscape:
The Solution-Focused Approach

Upon his unplanned arrival on the island, Robinson Crusoe immediately discovered that he had few skills to address the challenges of survival in a harsh environment. Raised within the wealthy merchant class, he knew little of farming, the use of tools, or the engineering involved in constructing a simple shelter. Yet his survival depended on an ability to adapt to the harsh requirements of an unknown environment. This required him to engage in a process of exploiting the resources immediately available to him. Success in this process, in turn, was dependent on an ability to transform his attitude from that of a sufferer and of "victim of God's wrath," to a "seeker" and "searcher" of opportunities that would substantially increase the quality of his life. Once engaged in this process, Robin was able to take advantage of the resources that remained from the shipwreck as well as those that abundantly presented themselves from the island, ultimately enabling him to recraft his life.

Initially, clients suffering from chronic pain and/or debilitating medical conditions are equally unprepared. Like Robin, they must navigate an unfamiliar and often frightening landscape with few (initially) recognizable resources. Unaccustomed to (often radically) changed circumstances, they are understandably anxious and confused as to solutions that might address part of or their entire problem. Fear, unfamiliar circumstances, and a general disorientation may obscure practical solutions and resources that have existed in the past or may exist in the present or future. This challenge demands a therapeutic strategy that overcomes a client's natural tendency to experience powerlessness and hopelessness in the face of seemingly overwhelming odds.

We have adopted the solution-focused model (Berg & Miller, 1992; de Shazer, 1985, 1988; de Shazer et al., 1986) as the core of our therapeutic approach because it most closely serves the needs and utilizes the available resources of those individuals suffering from a chronic condition. Its emphasis on goal-oriented, resource-sensitive, present- and future-focused interventions makes the most effective use of time for those professionals who are concerned about meeting the increasing demands of the health care system (Johnson, 1995). Because its intervention strategy is client constructed, solution-focused therapy is effective at any stage of change. The remainder of this chapter introduces the reader to the principles of the solution-focused approach and the utilization of the initial clinical interview as a direct intervention to enhance client-centered solution construction. Specific interview questions are presented, along with case examples highlighting detailed applications for clients suffering from chronic pain or illness.

☐ The Solution-Focused Approach

The solution-focused approach to psychotherapy was first developed in Milwaukee at the Brief Family Therapy Center (BFTC) in the early 1980s. Evolving out of the early brief therapy contributions of Milton Erickson (1954) and the Mental Research Institute (Watzlawick, Weakland, & Fisch, 1974), Steve de Shazer, Insoo Kim Berg, and their colleagues discovered that shifting from a traditional problem-oriented approach to one that focused on solutions yielded better therapeutic results in a shorter amount of time for their clients (Beyebach, Morejon, Palenzuela, & Rodriguez-Arias, 1996; Cockburn, Thomas, & Cockburn, 1997; DeJong & Hopwood, 1996). This was a radical departure from traditional psychotherapy that sought to change the essential character of clients while viewing their presenting problems as the result of some basic pathology (Budman & Gurman, 1988).

Instead of developing solutions from problem descriptions and speculating on causality, de Shazer, Berg, and their colleagues completely reversed the interview process by beginning the initial clinical interview by asking clients to describe a (detailed) resolution to the problem that brought them into therapy. Characteristically, this novel question was asked before any description of the problem was sought. This served to immediately shift the client's focus away from pathological problems to possible solutions (table 6.1).

Similar to stage-of-change theorists (chapter 5), the BFTC group viewed psychological change as a dynamic process. Instead of assuming that real psychological change, by its very nature, was a slow and belabored process (if possible at all) often dependent on the client's insight, they viewed it as an inevitable and dynamic part of the life process (Fisch, Weakland, & Segal, 1982). Believing that "you can't step in the same river twice" (Omer, 1996), they discovered that utilizing the dynamic nature of change substantially shortened the time that clients required to solve their problems. This resulted from their adoption of Milton Erickson's principle of "inventing a new theory for each client (Lankton & Lankton, 1983), rather than limiting themselves to one particular theoretical model."

Therapists found that this reversal of the traditional starting point of the clinical interview encouraged their clients to consider possibilities in the present and the future instead of becoming entrenched in the past. Continually stressing outcome-oriented, collaborative interaction, the solution-focused model shifted the responsibility and authority for problem resolution from therapists to clients. This factor not only shortened the duration of therapy, it yielded consistently successful results across cultural, gender, and class lines (DeJong & Hopwood, 1996). Their success, the BFTC staff members believed, was due to the emphasis on clients setting their own goals, utilizing existing resources, and measuring their own progress. A parsimonious intervention process that emphasized the simplest and most straightforward path to a successful end, maximizing the use of available resources, further enhanced this client-centered approach. This respectfully attuned therapy to the client's "voice" and made the assumption that he or she has the resources needed to improve his or her situation. Most significantly, it gave clients hope. Instead of being told what to do and where to go, they (many for the first time in therapy) determined their own destination, plotted their own route, and discovered the "points of interest" along the way.

TABLE 6.1. Principles

Focus on solutions rather than problems.
Concentration on the future rather than the past.
A new theory for each client.
Change is inevitable.
Client-determined goals.
Parsimonious, ecological process.

☐ What a Difference a Difference Makes

Gregory Bateson (1972), in his groundbreaking work *Steps to an Ecology of Mind*, stated: "Difference, which occurs across time, is what we call 'change.'" Clients' observations about the differences between problem states and solution states are central to the solution-focused approach. Facilitating these observations is a structured interview in which questions are designed to help the client create solutions from existing resources and successful life experiences, and coconstruct (with the therapist) possibilities in the future. Rather than simply obtaining historical information for assessment purposes, the therapist uses the first session to begin to facilitate the client's generation of achievable goals. Illuminating these goals is "difference" questioning (de Shazer, 1991). These interview questions focus on contrasting the differences between states of conscious that maintain problems and solutions, symptoms and exceptions, and ultimately, hopelessness and hope. It is the client's ability to recognize and, more importantly, act on these differences that represents success in therapy. As de Shazer stated:

> It is the difference itself that is an important tool for therapists and clients. It is not simply that there are "differences which make a difference." Most frequently differences do not work spontaneously. If they are not recognized, they make no difference, but once recognized, they can then be put to work to make a difference. Differences that count, differences that are significant to the client, are the effects or signatures of a difference put to work. (1991, p. 156).

De Shazer, Berg, and their colleagues have embedded this concept into virtually all their interview questions. From the beginning of the first interview through the end of the last therapy session, questions focus on encouraging clients observing the essential differences their actions and thoughts make in breaking down the barrier between problem and solution. This results in creating vital links in a virtual "chain of difference," allowing clients and therapists to coconstruct workable solutions. It is the recognition of this "news of the difference" that enables both clients and therapists to move beyond the limitations of the problem while illuminating a more hopeful future.

Beginnings: Listening to the Story

As we begin the millennium, more individuals find themselves caught in a crowded intersection where the promises of modern medicine collide with the limitations of the postmodern world. As technology and the need to hold down costs shift health care from a human-based system of care to a more information-based system of recording, assessing, and managing, clients frequently find that they do little more than recite details about themselves that specifically relate to physical symptoms. For many clients, the experience of having someone listen to the story of their illness can represent a major therapeutic breakthrough in itself. The emphasis on the present and the future of the solution-focused approach does not negate the need to reflect empathy when listening to a client's story. Simply telling the story can often transform the isolation and abandonment that often accompany a chronic condition into an interactive helping relationship between client and therapist. Listening (the basic element of any interview) and reacting in an empathic manner rather than simply recording information demonstrate a caring framework (table 6.2).

A cornerstone of our approach is an intentional "not-knowing" stance mixed with a healthy dose of curiosity. Combs and Freedman (1996) provided a compelling description of this:

> We are most successful in achieving a not-knowing stance when we concentrate on listening and when our talking is guided by and secondary to listening. As we listen, we notice and question the assumptions we are making. We ask ourselves, "Am I understanding what it feels like to be this person in this situation, or, am I beginning to fill in the gaps in her story with unwarranted assumptions? What more do I need to know to step into this person's shoes?" (p. 45)

The question "What would be helpful for me to know to be able to best understand your situation?," put forward by Griffith and Griffith (1994, p. 95), addresses the client as a whole person rather than just a diagnosis. It takes the first step in informing the client that he or she will be considered separately from his or her symptoms and authority over the problem, and its solution will be respected above all. This is often the first time that a client has been encouraged to utilize his or her own "voice" in regard to the struggle and represents the beginning of an empowerment process that will follow (or lead) the client throughout treatment.

TABLE 6.2. Listening

"What would be helpful for me to understand?"
Validation of the struggle.
Perspective on the problem.
Listening for coping ability.
Exceptions to the problem.

There are as many ways to respond to this question as there are clients. Some will respond with a list of symptoms, whereas others will need not only to inform to us about the illness but also to recount their struggles to get help (or unsuccessful attempts to be heard). Some clients will acknowledge how the condition (often profoundly) impacts their relationships. Still others will want to explain their particular theories about the cause. This initial session represents a significant point in the intervention process because it begins to define the kind of relationship the therapist will have with the client.

When listening to clients tell their story, it is important for the therapist to identify and appreciate their perspective on the problem. Do they describe themselves as hero, victim, or someone having bad luck? Is this condition one of a long string of unfair life experiences, or is this time different? Do they see the solution as being inside or outside their control? Do they see coming to a therapist as a last resort, as an admission that the problem is "all in their mind"? Do they see themselves as not coping well or do they see their struggle as a natural part of the mind–body connection and thus the healing process? One of the most important outcomes of any first meeting is that the client feels validated in his or her struggle with the health care system, illness, and circumstances.

In addition to giving clients a voice, listening to the stories gives the therapist the opportunity to begin the process of identifying the clients' (self-described) coping abilities as well as instances when they might have experienced exceptions (described later) to the condition. Also, at this point it important to note (at least to oneself) the ways the client has persevered in spite of his or her condition.

Case Example: The Importance of Listening

Martha was eventually diagnosed with a terminal illness. However, when she first sought an explanation for her symptoms, she only was able to describe a few of them before her physician interrupted. He then pronounced her as having a "classic" case of hiatal hernia and sent her home with antacids and instructions to raise the head of her bed by six inches (on blocks). After a few days with no results, she realized that this advice was useless and sought another opinion. Following a series of tests, she was told that she had less than six months to live and that the only chance of extending her survival was immediate, experimental surgery. Despite pressure to make the decision without delay, Martha decided that she needed more information before making up her mind.

Martha began her first interview by describing these experiences and then said, "First I'm told that I'm going to die, then I'm told that I have to make the most important decision of my life *right now*, when I can't think straight about anything." After carefully listening to her story, her therapist gently asked, "How can I help you?" She responded, confidently, "You already have. You listened. You gave me the time to hear myself so I can decide what I need to do."

☐ Drawing the Map: Goal Statements

In a population that is often defined by what it can't do rather than what it can, establishing clearly defined, achievable, and sustainable treatment goals is critical to any successful therapeutic intervention. It is important to establish goals (table 6.3) as early as possible in the therapy process without alienating the client (Cade & O'Hanlon, 1993). Typically, this begins by simply asking, "How will you know that your therapy is finished?" This question begins to orient the client to the fact that her idea of a successful end to therapy is important and is possible.

Most critical to goal setting is the relevance of the goal to the client, or the principle of *fit* outlined in the last chapter. Ignoring fit in the goal-setting process almost always results in a failure in therapy and can destroy a client's hope. The solution-focused interviewing process is saturated with opportunities for clients to describe their goals in detail. However, not surprisingly, clients suffering from a chronic illness, especially those in the sufferer/victim and seeker/searcher stages, will often declare, when first describing their goals, that "the pain will be completely gone forever," or "I'll forget that I ever had this condition." Although these are worthy and understandable ambitions, they may not be realistic given the physical capabilities and parameters of the chronic condition from which the client suffers. In order to be most effective, goals should be achievable within the client's physical context and be within his or her control. Overlooking this fact will not only result in failure but may increase the client's feelings of hopelessness, self-blame, and abandonment. When a totally unrealistic goal is proposed, one that is physically impos-

TABLE 6.3. Well-Formed Goals

Saliency to the client—"fit."
Small, specific, and achievable.
Stated in behavioral terms.
Described as the start of something.
Presence rather than absence.
Recognizable by client and others.
Acknowledged as hard work.

sible, it is important to acknowledge the client's wishes while asking about the possibility of scaling down the goal for the purposes of the beginning stages of therapy.

Beginning of the Journey: Small Steps

Solution-focused therapy dictates that goals should be small rather than large (de Shazer, 1991). This not only substantially increases the chances for success, but also encourages the completion of a goal within a reasonable time period, often giving the client some much-needed relief. Furthermore, goals should represent the beginning rather than the ending of a process. Focusing on the first few steps of the journey, rather than its final destination, often circumvents seemingly impossible barriers that the client may have constructed in relation to a goal.

Clients with a chronic condition routinely describe goals in terms of what won't be happening. They are likely to say something like, "I won't have headaches any more," or, "I won't have a problem sleeping." Noting the impossibility of achieving a negative goal, solution-focused therapy dictates that desired therapeutic outcomes are best stated in positive behavioral terms that will be easily recognizable to both client and therapist. When a client told Milton Erickson that he no longer wanted to experience phantom limb pain, Erickson had him describe in detail the characteristics of "phantom limb pleasure" (Erickson & Rossi, 1979). Discovering what the client will be doing *instead* of experiencing the troubling symptom(s) is critical to success. For example, a client, after being gently reminded how difficult it is to achieve a negative goal, might respond by talking about the possibility of employing pain-management techniques for headaches or constructing a self-care routine that encourages a good night's sleep. A client who is suffering increased pain from exhaustion might consider scheduling regular ultradian breaks (chapter 4) during the day to conserve energy and facilitate the healing response.

Enriching Goal Descriptions

Because the clarity and the mutual understanding of a goal between client and therapist are so vitally important, we have adapted a familiar interview process that enriches goal setting by employing *who, what, where, when,* and *how* questions. These simple questions, recognizable from high school and college journalism classes, supplement the client's descriptions and enable both the client and the therapist to begin a process of understanding of where a goal fits within the client's relationships and social context.

Using these enrichment questions, a client might answer a *what* ("would I [the therapist] hear and see you doing instead?") question by stating, "Instead of pushing myself past the 'point of no return' and burning up all my energy during the day, I would stop what I was doing and take a break." When asked *how* he or she would accomplish this, the client might answer, "I would set the alarm on my watch. That's the only way I would remember." In response to a *when* question, the client might reply, "Maybe every two hours." When asked *where* he or she would accomplish this break, the client might answer, "Outside, sitting on the bench in the garden." When asked *who* would notice this accomplishment, the client might answer, "My kids would notice me just stopping what I am doing and going outside and sitting down." As we show later, combining enrichment questions with "difference" descriptions substantially increases the chances that solution-focused interaction between therapist and client will be a good "fit."

Cade and O'Hanlon (1993) developed an effective question to complement this process. They routinely asked clients to imagine what would be viewed and heard on videotape as the goal was being achieved. We have found this to be useful in helping clients describe the specific actions (and reactions) that would represent success. The "videotape question" can also begin to decipher a vague goal statement in the vein of, "I'd be feeling better." In response to such an answer, a therapist might ask, "I can understand how that would be helpful, but I'd like to get a clearer picture so that you know that I really understand what you mean. What if you were to show me a videotape of you feeling better, what would I hear and see you doing differently that would lead me to the conclusion that you were, in fact, feeling better?"

We don't intend to discount the importance of a particular client's feelings, but it will be difficult to help the client if we can't elicit a behavioral description of what he or she means by "feeling better." These questions help construct a map that will help both the client and therapist recognize progress and realize when they have reached their destination. Likewise, detailed descriptions of solutions are critical when employing hypnotic suggestions (chapter 9).

Finally, it is important to acknowledge that achieving these goals will involve hard work. Because our approach provides interventions that go well beyond "just talking," clients, at times, expect to "have something done to them." This involves thinking that the process will somehow occur outside of them, separate from their volition. When these issues arise, it is important to let clients know that the journey will involve hard work and that they will be at the center of it. Above all, clients should be convinced, as a result of the first interview, that their effort will result in a beneficial and meaningful difference in their lives.

Case Example: Listening to the Client's Voice

Her managed care company referred Grace because she was having suicidal thoughts relating to a feeling that her life was out of control. Her
history included many physical problems and a series of psychiatric difficulties. Her current physical complaints included asthma and possible
fibromyalgia as well as intolerance of a variety of foods. Over the phone,
the client's case manager demanded that the therapist quickly resolve the
current crisis. Additionally, the case manager wanted consolidation of the
client's many specialists and an end to her "overutilization" of the HMO's
resources. At the end of the conversation the therapist was cautioned
that the client's MMPI results indicated that Grace had little credibility.

Grace began the first session by stating, "I want to change my name
and move somewhere my children can't find me." Her adult children had
recently accelerated their many demands on her time and resources. She
believed that the resulting stress put her physical and mental health in
jeopardy. Unfortunately, her children were not convinced that she had
these illnesses. She described a long history of instances of her children's
unhealthy dependence on her. As the first interview progressed it became clear that Grace's goal was to maintain her independence from her
children. She viewed this as crucial to maintaining her health. With this
goal in mind she identified several things that she could do for herself
that would simultaneously maintain her health and relieve her of many
of her children's demands.

Accepting Grace's view of her health and what she needed to do to take
care of it proved to be a validating intervention in and of itself. She subsequently enacted a plan that preserved her independence and increased
her sense of competence. This resulted in diminishing some of her dependence on the services of multiple health care specialists.

Case Example: Achieving Compliance through Acceptance of the Client's Goal

"My therapist sent me here so that you could hypnotize me to be able to
swallow these pills," Rose said as she emphatically pointed her finger at a
small clear plastic bag containing an assortment of about 25 multicolored
tablets and capsules. On the previous day Rose, a health care worker, had
been accidentally "stuck" with a needle containing traces of HIV-positive
blood. She was rushed to the hospital's emergency room, where she was
told that she would be required to ingest a "cocktail" of about 25 pills a
day for the next month to reduce the possibility of infection. When she
informed the physician that she had a tremendously difficult time "just

swallowing water," she was told to "get over it" and take the pills. Her ongoing therapist thought that hypnosis might provide a quick solution to her problem.

Rose immediately identified herself as a *visitor* when she stated, "I'm just here to make my therapist happy. I can't even take an aspirin, much less a handful of pills. My tongue is a gatekeeper for my throat and my throat doesn't want to let those pills in. And before you ask me whether I've been sexually abused, I'll tell you that I haven't. I've had this problem all my life and my mother has it as well."

Sensing that there probably had been enough "pill swallowing" talk for the present, the therapist shifted the conversation in a different direction and stated, "Suppose coming to see me could be helpful—how would you know?" Thinking for a full two minutes, Rose said, "Well I'd get over my fear of *not* taking these pills." After spending the rest of the hour addressing the odds of her becoming infected with HIV, Rose decided that her fear of taking the pills was less than her fear of not taking them. By the end of the session she had devised a way of masking the unpleasant experience of ingesting the pills with the idea of submerging them in chocolate ice cream. "After all," she said, "I'll only have to do it for a little while."

Rose followed through with her plan and adhered to a prescribed medication regimen for the next month. To date, she has remained HIV free and views her solution as a jumping-off point for progress in her own therapy. If the consulting therapist had plunged ahead against Rose's wishes and attempted some kind of hypnotic intervention, he would have failed miserably. This not only would have resulted in a complete loss of rapport but also would have jeopardized Rose's relationship with her regular therapist. More importantly, it would have thrust her into a situation in which she would need to engage in struggle with the therapist that paralleled the experience that she was having with the medical establishment.

☐ Orienting Toward the Future: Suppose a Miracle Happened?

Problems often impose such heavy constraints on clients that solutions become almost impossible to imagine. This is especially true for those individuals suffering from a chronic condition. Dealing with the pain, discomfort, and limitations of their condition 24 hours a day often leaves them with the belief that even the smallest change is impossible. This defeating factor can destroy hope for both clients and their caregivers.

Solution-focused therapy's miracle question constructs a framework for well-formed goals (Berg & Miller, 1992; de Shazer, 1988). Like a compelling narrative, the most potent of all solution-focused interview questions, the miracle question, encourages clients to temporarily suspend their disbelief in regard to solving their problem while considering new solutions. This future-focused intervention enables them to indulge in the benefits of the change process without being constrained by attitudes of "impossibility" of achieving it. The question is constructed to allow them to "work backward" from a seemingly impossible solution endowing them with a miraculous kind of hindsight that ultimately facilitates a radically different perspective on a remedy to their difficulties. Moreover, as Miller commented, the miracle question makes "problem definition superfluous once clients have specified the details of their miracles" (Miller, 1997, p. 81).

As de Shazer (1991) stated:

> The framework of the miracle question and other questions of its type allows clients to bypass their structural, causal assumptions. They do not have to imagine the process of getting rid of the problem, only the results. This then allows them to bring more of their previous non-problem experiences into the conversation; thus, the goals developed from the miracle question are not limited to just getting rid of the problem/complaint. (p. 113)

The Miracle Question

The miracle question, as developed at the Brief Family Therapy Center, is asked as follows.

> Suppose that one night there is a miracle and while you're sleeping, the problem that brought you in here today is solved: How would you know? What would be different? What will you notice different the next morning that will tell you that there has been a miracle? (de Shazer, 1988, p.5)

Therapists working with clients suffering from a chronic condition recognize that the word *miracle* might have a particularly sensitive connotation. Clients continually hear about the miracles of modern medicine and may have spent a great deal of time pursuing "miracle cures." For some individuals the word *miracle* might evoke a religious implication that could confuse the treatment process. If these kinds of concerns arise, the therapist should remember that the question makes direct reference to "the problem that brought you in here today," and not a "miracle cure" to the client's medical problem. However, those health care professionals (e.g., physicians, nurses, physician's assistants, etc.) who provide direct medical services such as surgery and drug therapy in addition to psychotherapy may encounter confusion in relation to their dual role. In these cases it is important to remain linguistically flexible to make adjustments to accommodate each client's unique situation.

Staying Flexible: Adapting the Miracle Question

Taking these factors into consideration, we have adapted the miracle question for those situations that require more specificity in the client's responses. After preparing the client for a "question" that will require him or her to use imagination, the question is typically phrased in the following manner:

> Suppose a miracle happened overnight and while you were asleep you were endowed with the skills to make this (problem) better, ultimately resulting in a higher quality of life for you. What do you think you would notice the next day and in the following days that would give you the idea that this miracle had actually happened?

It is important for therapist to communicate to client that this occurs overnight, during sleep, unbeknownst to the client, emphasizing that the next day (and following days) would result in the client becoming convinced that, indeed, a miracle did happen. "Convincing" initial observations are often represented by details that would make a small difference in a client's life, such as waking a little earlier in the morning, taking the dog for a walk, meditating, and so on.

Other adaptations commonly used to better address specific client conditions and attitudes are: "Suppose a miracle happened overnight and you gained the ability to move beyond the problem that brought you here today." Or, " . . . and you had enough energy to do things that matter to you." Or, " . . . and you gained more hope." Or, " . . . and you could give yourself a trait, attribute, or quality that enabled you to move beyond this point." However, in our experience in considering any adaptation of BFTC's original miracle question, it is worthwhile to note that the more general is the reference to the miracle, the more possibilities are generated by the question.

TABLE 6.4. Suppose a Miracle Happened?

And you had the skills to manage this.
And the quality of your life was better.
What is the first thing you would notice?
What else would you notice?
Who else in your life would notice the changes?
What difference would the miracle make?

Flexibility is also particularly important if a client responds negatively, saying something like, "I can't possibly imagine something like that." Or, simply, "I don't know." At such times we have found it helpful to agree with the client, replying with something like "I know it sounds silly, after all, we're talking about a miracle, but the question is helpful for me. Would you be willing to guess at what it would be like to have that miracle happen?" In the (very) rare case where a client refuses to respond to any form of the miracle question, we suggest that the therapist proceed directly to exception questions (described later).

After the Miracle: The First Thing

After identifying the miracle, it is important for the client to begin associating it with steps toward an achievable goal. The therapist accomplishes this by expressing genuine curiosity toward the small details that might be involved in the miracle. Often, it is useful to ask, "What is the *first thing* that you think you would notice after this miracle has happened?" A client might respond, for example, "Well, I'd wake up and not be so depressed." Another might respond, "I'd look in the mirror and not hate myself." A young mother might reply, "I wouldn't ignore my kid." The initial negative goal reference in the answers to these questions is typical.

As previously noted, it is a very natural thing for someone suffering from chronic pain and illness to wish to immediately experience an absence of their condition. Maximizing the potential of the miracle question dictates that its description needs to be worded in terms that represent the *presence* of something different rather than simply the *absence* of a symptom or troubling situation. Thus, it is imperative that the therapist and client shift to a description that represents what will actually be happening *instead* of the problem. For example, using the responses given earlier: "I'd wake up and look forward to the day," or "I'd look in the mirror and notice my good features." Or, "I'd take the time out to listen to my son and find out what is on his mind."

After the client identifies the first sign of change, the therapist immediately follows up by asking the client to describe, "What difference would that change make?" At this point the client is encouraged to elaborate fully on the difference that the small change would make in terms of his or her lifestyle, the alternate series of events that would accompany the initial change, and the changes that would occur in relationships, job status, self-esteem, and so on. For example, in applying difference questioning to the first example just given, the therapist curiously inquired, "What difference would it make for you to look forward to the day?" The client, speculating on this "miraculous" distinction, responded, "Well, I'd probably get out of the house a lot faster in the morning." The therapist then simply repeated the question, "What difference would *that* make?" to which the client replied, "I'd get to work earlier." Responding repeated times to essentially the same question, client and therapist learned that punctuality at work meant that instead of "rushing" around to complete projects on time, the client would have less pressure. This in turn, the client related, would allow enough time to take breaks during the day, possibly eliminating afternoon headaches, enabling the client to get a good night's sleep and ultimately wake the next morning looking forward to the rest of the day.

Reviewing the details of the miracle is helpful for both client and therapist. As the therapist reads back the fine points of the miracle along with punctuating the difference it would make for the client, the client has the opportunity to enhance the therapist's understanding through refining the description. In addition to informing the client of the importance the therapist attaches to client's vision of the future, a detailed review reinforces the client's entitlement to it.

In teaching this approach, we occasionally encounter students and therapists who fear that the miracle question is naively optimistic in its approach to the very serious problem of chronic and sometimes terminal illness. On the contrary, our consistent experience with this population has shown it to be effective in encouraging achievable aspirations (Berg, 1994b). Likewise, the miracle question represents a unique opportunity to build a progressive narrative that will lead to future possibilities. Finally, as the following case example illustrates, miracle questions can generate hope and empowerment in the most serious medical circumstances.

Case Example: A Difference That Matters

Recently, a student therapist found herself in a hospital room full of crying people. It was her job to treat a woman, Christine, who had been told that she only a few weeks to live. Presented with an apparently hopeless situation, Christine and her family were understandably upset. The therapist, feeling a need to make some kind of useful intervention, responded, "We never know exactly how these things will work out. Even though you are very ill, I'm wondering, what if a miracle happened, and you were able to make the most of the remaining time that you have left. What do you think that you would do?" The client's face lit up and she immediately responded, "I'd get married to Mario," the father of her two-year-old child. She went on to explain that she had been previously unwilling to make this commitment, adding, "But I know that it would make a difference to my daughter and that's important to me." As her mood continued to improve, Christine went to describe how different family members would be involved in the event and who would conduct the service. Knowing that Mario would be delighted about the idea, she spent the rest of the session happily planning the details of this momentous event.

Christine's family enthusiastically got involved as well, hurriedly executing the plans that she made for the wedding scheduled for the following week. Upon the chosen day, their priest married Christine and Mario in the client lounge at the hospital. All of the hospital unit's staff and clients and many of the couple's family and friends attended. There were flowers, a cake, music, and some dancing. The celebration lasted way beyond normal visiting hours. Christine died a few weeks later. In response to the miracle question, she and her family were able to shift from the dread of her death to the celebration of her life. Their memories of her last weeks are happy ones. Her miracle was that she was able live the last few weeks of her life to the fullest, on her own terms.

Christine's miracle had nothing whatsoever to do with "curing" her terminal condition. Instead it related directly to the quality of her life as well as her family's. This is the essence of the purpose of the miracle question. For Christine, responding to the miracle question meant taking an active part in her (albeit foreshortened) own future. Because it was *her* miracle, its impact was greatly enhanced. The importance of this level of empowerment for clients suffering from serious conditions cannot be overstated.

Exception Questions: "Has This Ever Happened Before?"

Exception questioning (Berg & Miller, 1992; de Shazer, 1985, 1988) begins the search for a small part of the solution. After identifying examples of the miracle and noting that a particular example represents a difference that would make a significant difference to the client, it is important to follow up by asking, "Has this ever happened before?" A majority of clients will immediately answer, unthinkingly, "No, never!" It is not surprising that individuals suffering from chronic illness and frequent pain cannot immediately shift their attention from their seeming intractable situation to a time when the problem has not been present. After a period of silence, we have found it helpful to follow up the question by gently and curiously asking, "Has it ever happened, even a little bit?" followed, again, by a respectful period of silence. The goal of asking this question is to enable the client to consider the possibility that his or her experience might include at least some small pieces of the miracle or a time when the symptoms were experienced at a lower level of intensity.

As in miracle questions, clients often initially describe exceptions in terms that reflect an absence of pain or symptoms rather than the presence of an experience that enabled them to enjoy (at least temporarily) some relief. In order for exception questioning to be most effective, the therapist facilitates the client describing experiences that occurred instead of the symptoms. As described earlier in this chapter, these behavioral descriptions can be further enriched with questions aimed at finding out what occurred, when, where, how, and who else was involved. Determining the difference that the exception made is vital as well. An exception that does not make a difference in the client's quality of life is not worth pursuing.

Exception questions are an excellent intervention in sessions where the client's partner, other family members, or friends are present. Often, they will note exceptions a client has forgotten. This was demonstrated recently when a wife, responding to her husband's "amnesia" for exceptions, recalled, "Last week, don't you remember when we were looking at our scrapbook, putting in the pictures of the kids' wedding? You got so involved in arranging and pasting the pictures that you didn't complain about your back for the rest of the evening. In fact, you didn't complain about it the next morning either." To which her husband responded, "Now that you mention it, I didn't have any pain! I must have completely forgotten about it."

This exception opened up a whole line of questioning for the therapist, focusing on the times that the client was able (albeit unconsciously) to distract himself from his pain. For the client, answering the question initiated a process of convincing him that he did, indeed, have the ability to manage his pain. After fully developing the first exception and identifying the differences it made to the client's quality of life, the therapist can further proceed by (expectantly) asking, "When *else* has this happened (even a little bit)?"

Focusing on exceptions allows clients to shift their attention and memory. They begin to see that the problem is not always present and/or that the intensity of a symptom is less. As these observations accumulate,

---

TABLE 6.5. Exceptions

When has this happened before?
Even a little bit?
What difference did it make?
Who else noticed?
What did you/they notice?
When else has it happened?

a kind of therapeutic chain reaction builds in which clients discover resources, notice positive differences, and develop possibilities for future self-care interventions. Ultimately, the goal is for the client to generate enough exceptions for them to no longer need to be considered exceptions.

Together, miracle and exception questions provide a powerful vehicle for coconstructing a different set of options that enhance the future for the client. This powerful combination amplifies the client's success while allowing him or her to suspend, at least temporarily, memories of defeat, hopelessness, and fear. As the miracle and exceptions are reviewed during the first interview and the differences are amplified, the client gradually gains confidence that he or she might have more control over the problem than was first apparent (Furman & Ahola, 1992).

☐ "X" Marks the Spot—Scaling the First Step

Scaling (Berg & de Shazer, 1993; Berg & Miller, 1992; de Shazer, 1991) is a close cousin of miracle and exception questions. It allows both therapists and clients to concretize descriptions of past, current, and future states of health. It helps clients move from a statement of the complaint to a description of an incremental step toward solution. Utilizing numbers as a therapeutic tool, scaling invites the client to orient to his or her current state of health and then consider the next small step that would represent progress. In the first meeting, scaling is often used to determine where the client stands in relation to his or her miracle, and what action might potentially represent a small step toward that destination. However, scaling can be used for practically any purpose within a solution focused interview.

After learning about a client's version of the miracle and beginning to coconstruct a realistic goal, a therapist might ask: "On a scale of 1 to 10, where a 10 represents a time after the miracle has happened (or your goal has been achieved), and a 1 represents a time when you have been at your worst, where would you say that you are now?" After identifying a number, the client is asked, "What do you think that you would be doing differently when you are one point higher?" At this point the client is encouraged to describe the specific details of this incremental change. As with miracle and exception questions, it is important to invite the client to describe what he or she might experience that would be *different* from the lower number. In other words, "What do you think that you will be doing *instead* or *in addition to* . . . (the experience of the lower number)?"

As with other solution-focused questions, it is important for the therapist to become curious about the differences that these changes would make at this higher level of functioning. This is accomplished by asking about possible changes in relationships, quality of life, hopefulness, and so forth that might occur as a result of moving up the scale. The therapist can further strengthen the impact of this higher number by using enrichment questions (given earlier) to more fully develop the next step.

Other Scaling Applications

Scaling questions can also be employed in the first session to illuminate the progress that a client has already made toward a solution by asking, "Are you higher on the scale now than you have been in the past?" This begins a sequence that shifts attention away from the problem to the past successful steps the client has taken thus far. Clients can also be asked, "Have you ever been higher than this?," beginning a sequence that further elicits the details of past useful exceptions.

Scaling in the first meeting can be used to inquire about the effort a client is willing to put forth toward a goal as well. For example, the therapist might inquire: "Given your current level of energy, on a scale of 1 to 10, where a 1 represents your not being willing to put any effort into this (goal, 1-point improvement, etc.), and, a 10 represents the fact that your are willing to do absolutely anything to take this step, where are you now?" Typically the client's answer signals a beginning of a commitment toward a goal. Or it can indicate to both client and therapist that this particular step is perhaps too big, will not produce a meaningful difference, or that a new goal needs to be constructed. Employing the process in this manner enables both clients and therapists to construct realistic scales.

Using Realistic Scales

Realistic scaling is as important as realistic goal setting. Understandably, many clients are in a hurry to get better. This can result in their descrip-

---

TABLE 6.6. On a Scale of 1 to 10

Where are you now?
Where were you before?
How did you get here or there?
What would be one point better?
What will you be doing instead?
What difference would that make?
How hard are you willing to work?

tion of a "giant" step that might not be easily reachable from their current position. For example, someone recovering from a recent auto accident might describe a "6" (representing a 1-point improvement) as, "I'll be able to play tennis on the weekends again." At this point it is important for the therapist inquire about the number by saying (sounding mildly confused) something like, "That sounds great, but to me and I could be wrong, that sounds more like an 8 or a 9. What do you think just one point better would be?" If that fails, the therapist always can make the increments of improvement smaller, using half or quarter points.

Realistic scaling is important when the chronic condition has resulted in the client's hope doesn't manifest itself in the miracle question. Clients who have experienced a great deal of defeat or appear to be firmly entrenched in the sufferer/victim stage can profit from having the scale represent a smaller scope. In these cases the therapist can compress the range of the scale, indicating that a 10 represents a time when things are "just somewhat better" and that "a 1 indicates that time that you have been the absolute worst you have ever been."

It would be a mistake for the reader to think that the scaling process yields anything other than the client's own, unique view of the problem and solution. Therapists must accept that scales are content free (de Shazer & Berg, 1993). They are not psychometric measurements of pathology or health. Only the client knows what he or she means by a "3." Scales do, however, give therapist and client a unique opportunity to engage in a conversation about what constitutes movement away from the problem toward solution and the differences that such movement could make in improved functioning and quality of life.

Case Example: Putting It All Together— Miracles, Exceptions, and Scales

Darla was a personal trainer until she severely injured her right biceps while demonstrating weight lifting. This injury resulted in severe pain in her right shoulder. Subsequently, she had three operations in an attempt to eliminate the pain. Each operation made her shoulder progressively worse until, ultimately, her left shoulder became involved. She then suffered through additional procedures on her left shoulder until her physicians ultimately told her, "There is no more we can do for you." Darla went on to explore nonsurgical techniques of acupuncture, biofeedback, antidepressants, and the use of a Tens unit with mixed results.

The Miracle.   When Darla arrived for her first session, her posture and demeanor suggested that she viewed the interview as just one more stop on a train that was going nowhere. Beginning the interview as a sufferer/victim, she described feeling abandoned by the health care system that had promised to heal her. In addition to losing a profession that she really loved, she was now dominated by physical and emotional pain. Darla responded to the miracle question with the typical and general answer, "I'd wake up the next day and all this would be over." After being reminded that the miracle "wouldn't necessarily take away her physical condition," but "would involve you being endowed with skills that would substantially improve your life," she answered, "I would be able to manage my situation much better." When asked "What do you think would be the first thing you would notice?" she answered, "I would be able to attend to little domestic things like washing my daughter's hair, walking my dog, and fixing my family dinner. Now, either I am in too much pain or too tired to do any of those things." She went on to say that she felt guilty for "not really being there for my family any more."

The Exception.   Linking this answer (to the miracle question) to an exception, the therapist followed up by asking, "Have you ever been able to attend to these things, even a little?" Darla paused for a minute and replied, "Well, last week when I was volunteering at my daughter's school, I was able to come home and take my dog for a walk. I got so involved in helping the teacher that I forgot about my pain. This lasted through the ride home and when my basset hound met me at the front door, I just couldn't refuse him a walk. We had a great time even though he pulled hard on the leash and dragged me around the neighborhood. I hardly noticed my pain until I went to bed."

As the conversation continued, it became apparent that Darla's exception, helping the teacher, came in the form of had been in a *flow* state (chapter 4). This focused, productive, and meaningful activity allowed her to step away from her pain and experience a little part of her miracle. As the session progressed, it was learned that in addition to her dog, her children and her husband positively noticed the difference. She also commented on the fact that she felt more a part of the family that night. Even though she had some pain the next morning, Darla remembered waking up, laughingly recalling her overweight basset hound leading her around the neighborhood. Additionally, she felt that she took some of those good feelings with her into the next day. "Although, at the end of the day," she said, "I was completely exhausted and I hurt for a few days after that. Maybe it was my dog pulling so hard on the leash."

Even though this exception eventually resulted in discomfort and exhaustion, it deserved to be expanded because of the differences it appeared to have made in the client's life. Continuing, Darla explained the phenomena she experienced during this flow state along with what she thought it was about that state that allowed her to step away from the pain for a while: "When I am doing something important," she said, "something that means something to me, my pain just goes somewhere—in the background maybe. I was never happier than when I worked as a personal trainer. I loved the physical parts of it and I could see the results in my clients in just a few weeks." She went on to describe a number of other times that she had been able to put her pain in the background. All of Darla's exceptions involved some kind of flow experience that included her helping other people. She became quite animated at this discovery and seemed invested in trying to make these exceptions the rule.

Returning to the miracle, the therapist asked Darla, "What else would you notice, after this miracle happened?" "The major thing," she answered, "would be that I would have more energy inside, extra concentration and boost to make those [exceptions just described] things happen more." When asked to link this aspect of the miracle to an exception, she said, "That's hard to say, I seem to have the most energy after I have taken it easy for a while." When asked to further expand, she said, "After I slow down for a while, I notice that my batteries are recharged. I feel like I can take the risk to do something productive. Maybe play with my kids." Upon additional examination, Darla identified herself as a "perfectionist." In the past, she had been a high achiever in school, on her job, and at home with her family. As other exceptions were explored, Darla discovered a vital fact that most chronic illness and pain sufferers learn—pacing oneself is crucial for energy conservation and healing.

The Scale.   When Darla was asked to scale her current position in relation to the miracle, she declared, "Right now I'm at a 6. That's pretty good considering that after my third operation, I was at a 1." She described the details of her journey from a "1" to a "6," recalling how "crippled" she was after the accident and operations, remembering the many small steps that she took to arrive at her current level of functioning.

Darla thought that a "7" would be characterized by her ability "to really concentrate on deliberately taking the time to recharge my batteries so that I will have more energy to do things with my family." She answered the *how* question by stating, "That's going to be hard. I just can't sit around. I'm just going to have to find productive things to do while I take it easy. If I feel that I am doing something that means something, I think I can slow down enough to build up enough energy." She went on to describe *what* she would do: "I have some unfinished quilting projects. I haven't touched them since the accident. I used to like to quilt when I was 'able-bodied.' I don't see how my condition would keep me from picking it up again."

Darla proceeded to elaborate the details of her "7." She joyfully spoke of the pleasure that she used to get from assembling colorful blocks of fabric into creative geometric shapes. As she continued, it became obvious that quilting was also a flow state for her as well. The difference this time would be that she wouldn't exhaust herself or put herself in physical jeopardy. She could get all the benefits from a productive, focused, and challenging activity while replenishing her energy supply. This in turn would mean that she could do even more at a later time with her family.

When asked *who* would notice this difference, she said, "My husband wouldn't feel like he had to 'walk on eggs.' He worries a lot about me and he's afraid of upsetting me. He would see that I had enough energy to hold my own." Responding to the question "What other differences would people notice?" Darla said, "My family would smile a lot more. My kids would get their mom back again. We all would get closer. Instead of staying home all the time and watching television, we could all go out and do something fun, like we used to." The therapist complimented her on "knowing yourself and your family well."

As the session wound down, it was apparent that Darla had made a major shift. Her body posture had straightened, her voice had grown stronger, and her affect had changed from hopelessness to one of increased enthusiasm and optimism. She stated, "Maybe I should give that 7 a try." The therapist, trying to gauge Darla's perceptions of her current motivation and energy to be a "7," asked, "How much effort do you think that you should put into being a 7?" suggesting that she scale it. She answered, "A 9!" As a rule, when a client answers a motivational scaling question with a high number we ask, "What makes you a 9?" In this case, Darla answered, "I remembered some things that I had forgotten about. I think that I can keep busy and take care of myself at the same time."

At the end of the interview, it was apparent that Darla suffered from a predicament that accompanies clients distressed by a chronic condition— a substantial lack of energy. Using a standard psychoeducational approach, early on in the interview, some therapists might have informed Darla of the necessity of managing her energy levels. However, the use of the solution-focused interview with its emphasis on miracles, exceptions, scaling, and related differences interactively empowered Darla to discover this factor for herself. As a result, she was able to construct her own unique solution, applying existing and forgotten resources.

Discussion

It has been our experience that this kind of collaborative interaction results in significantly better treatment outcomes than just listening and giving advice alone. The reason for this, we believe, is that the solution-focused approach requires that the intervention "fit" the client, rather than making the client fit the intervention. This is especially important in the initial clinical session when the client's first impressions of the therapist can be critical to success of treatment. "Leading from behind," the therapist demonstrates the utmost respect for the client by listening and engaging her in a process that utilizes her own resources and unique experiences.

☐ Concluding the First Session

One of the hallmarks of solution-focused approach is the intrasession consulting break taken to consider what has transpired in the session (Berg & Miller, 1992; de Shazer, 1985). This initially occurred because therapists at BFTC principally worked as a therapy team observing from behind a one-way mirror. About 40 minutes into the interview, the therapist would take a break to discuss possible interventions with the team. He or she would then return and compliment the client, deliver a message (constructed with the help of the team behind the mirror), and assign a task for the next session. This break proved useful for both clients and therapists. The break indicated to clients that their therapist cared enough to take some time to think about their case. For therapists, this brief interruption allowed them to collect their thoughts and consult with the team.

Although few therapists have the luxury of working with a team, we have found taking a "think break" to be helpful (Walter & Peller, 1991). Before we take our break, however, we inquire, "Is there anything that I forgot to ask?" This allows the client to fill in any details of his or her story that the client feels are important. It also signals to the client that he or she is, in fact, the authority on the situation. The break in the process allows us to reflect on what we have noted about the client's story and his or her coping strategies, along with answers to miracle, exception, and scaling questions. The break can either be taken by leaving the room or by asking the client to excuse the therapist (in the room) while reviewing clinical interview notes. This is an excellent time to collect one's thoughts and consider how to proceed. Likewise, it respectfully informs the client that the therapist is taking what he or she has said seriously.

Returning from the break, the therapist begins by thanking the client for sharing his or her story and compliments the client on his or her journey thus far. Offering compliments should not be confused with any intervention attempting to manipulate the client in some way. Rather, solution-focused compliments are sincere responses to the parts of the client's story that have impressed the therapist. These compliments should be in relation to the client's coping ability, goals, exceptions, motivation, and/

or resources. This intervention provides the opportunity for the therapist to review some of the positive things along with the accompanying differences the client has revealed. If nothing else, a client can be complimented on willingness to tell his or her story to a complete stranger. Arguably, a therapist who cannot find something on which to compliment a client shouldn't be working with that client.

After delivery of the compliments, there are several options at the end of the first session. The therapist might give the client the Self Care Inventory or the Solution-Focused Inventory of Health or Solution Identification Scale for Health (SISH, chapter 7), a simple observational homework task, or be assigned the first session formula task—all covered in detail in chapter 7. If time doesn't permit a complete interview, or the interview has not produced any workable answers to miracle, exception, or scaling questions, the client can be complimented and invited to think about what has been said (thus far) until the next meeting. Finally, the client might be given a combination of these options. The implementation of these options and their relationship to recognizing readiness is discussed in more depth in the next chapter.

Summary

The solution-focused approach utilizes the client's unique resources and characteristics to enable the client to address his or her problems in a more effective manner. The first clinical interview in this approach is fundamental to the facilitation of a critical shift in the client's focus away from an ineffectual entrenched view of the problem in the past and toward a proactive and hopeful outlook in regard to solutions in the present and future. This is accomplished by interventions that acknowledge the client's struggle, facilitate the discovery of forgotten resources, and enable the construction of future possibilities. These components form an intervention matrix of "differences that make a difference," resulting in observable improvements in the client's quality of life. Finally, these first-session interventions complement and expand self-care potential (chapter 3) while substantially increasing the possibilities for the success of tools and real-world experiments covered in subsequent chapters.

☐ References

Bateson, G. (1972). *Steps to an ecology of mind*. London: Jason Aronson.

Berg, I. K. (1994). *Dying well*. (Audio tape). Milwaukee: Brief Family Therapy Center.

Berg, I. K., & de Shazer, S. (1993). Making numbers talk: Language in therapy. In S. Friedman (Ed.), *The new language of change: Constructive collaboration in psychotherapy* (pp. 5–24). New York: Guilford Press.

Berg, I. K., & Miller, S. (1992). *Working with the problem drinker*. New York: Norton.

Beyebach, M., Morejon, A., Palenzuela, D. L., & Luis Rodriguiz-Arias (1996). Research on the process of solution-focused therapy. In S. D. Miller, M. A. Hubble, & B. L. Duncan (Eds.), *Handbook of solution-focused therapy* (pp. 299–334). San Francisco: Jossey-Bass.

Cade, B., & O'Hanlon, W. H. (1993). *A brief guide to brief therapy*. New York: Norton.

Cockburn, J. T., Thomas, F. N., & Cockburn, O. J. (1997). Solution-focused therapy and psychosocial adjustment to orthopedic rehabilitation in a work-hardening program. *Journal of Occupational Rehabilitation, 7*(2), 97–106.

DeJong, P., & Hopwood, L. E. (1996). Outcome research on treatment conducted at the Brief Family Therapy Center, 1992–1993. In S. D. Miller, M. A. Hubble, & B. L. Duncan (Eds.), *Handbook of solution-focused therapy* (pp. 272–283). San Francisco: Jossey-Bass.

de Shazer, S. (1985). *Keys to solution in brief therapy*. New York: Norton.

de Shazer, S. (1988). *Clues to investigations in brief family therapy*. New York: Norton.

de Shazer, S. (1991). *Putting difference to work*. New York: Norton.

de Shazer, S., Berg, I. K., Lipchick, E., Nunnally, E., Molnar, A., Gingerich, W., & Weiner-Davis, M. (1986). Brief therapy: Focused solution development. *Family Process, 25*(2), 207–223.

Erickson, M. H. (1954). Special techniques of brief hypnotherapy. *Journal of Experimental and Clinical Hypnosis, 2*, 109–129.

Erickson, M., & Rossi, E. (1979). *Hypnotherapy: An exploratory casebook*. New York: Irvington.

Fisch, R., Weakland, J. H., & Segal, L. (1982). *The tactics of change: Doing therapy briefly*. San Francisco: Jossey-Bass.

Freedman, J., & Combs, G. (1996). *Narrative therapy: The social construction of preferred realities*. New York: Norton.

Furman, B., & Ahola, T. (1992). *Solution talk: Hosting therapeutic conversations*. New York: Norton.

Griffith, J. L., & Griffith, M. E. (1994). *The body speaks: Therapeutic dialogues for mind-body problems*. New York: Basic Books.

Johnson, L. D. (1995). *Psychotherapy in the age of accountabilitiy*. New York: Norton.

Lankton, S., & Lankton, C. (1983). *The answer within: A clinical framework for Ericksonian therapy*. New York: Brunner-Mazel.

Miller, G. (1997). *Becoming miracle workers: Language and meaning in therapy*. New York: Aldine De Gruyter.

Omer, H. (1996). Three styles of constructive therapy. In M. F. Hoyt (Ed.), *Constructive therapies II* (pp. 319–333). New York: Guilford Press.

Walter, J. L., & Peller, J. E. (1991). *Becoming solution focused in therapy*. New York: Brunner-Mazel.

Watzlawick, P., Weakland, J., & Fisch, R. (1974). *Change: Principles of problem formation and problem resolution*. New York: Norton.

Solution Building

Robinson Crusoe had never touched a tool before his castaway experience, much less had the need to invent new ones for his own survival. He did, however, have keen observational skills that enabled him, after some experimentation to utilize the resources from both the shipwreck and the natural environment of the island. He engaged in a process of trial and error ultimately enabling him to grow crops, build shelters and boats, and observe and exploit the differences in weather patterns to maximize the yield of his harvest. Following a methodical process of exploration and experimentation he crafted furniture, pottery, and even a dugout canoe. Impressively, he invented a hands-free grinding wheel—a device of which he had no previous knowledge. Progressing to the explorer/experimenter stage, Robin managed to endure failed experiments and stayed on track in his quest to improve the quality of his life. This dynamic process involving small steps, finding encouragement from (even partial) successes, and learning from mistakes eventually transformed him from suffering from a "poor miserable existence" into someone who celebrated the blessings and the abundance of his circumstances.

Clients suffering from pain and chronic conditions discover that their journey is made up of many challenging (yet small) steps as well. Akin to Robin's transformational passage, their journey will encompass a process of dynamic discovery requiring them to recover and move ahead from setbacks (relapse) as well. Providing a map to navigate this challenging terrain, the second and subsequent sessions of solution-focused therapy construct opportunities to further develop and enhance the progress initiated thus far. Utilizing material generated from miracle, scaling, and exception questions, the therapist and client continue to construct a framework of solutions specifically tailored to the client's motivation and resources, resulting in the invention of new tools as well as the adaptation of old ones.

This chapter presents three (interrelated) methods to effectively facilitate this process. The first utilizes a structured solution-focused interview to elicit, amplify, and reinforce the resources the client is already employing to improve her condition. The second draws upon a familiar ritual (filling out a form) to facilitate solution talk in regard to current and future possibilities not immediately apparent to the client and therapist. Finally we offer a number of "experimental" tasks that can significantly enhance the solution-finding process from the beginning stages experienced by sufferer/victims to the maintenance process employed during the recrafter stage.

☐ Advancing the Journey: The EARS Process

Not surprisingly, shifting focus from a problem state to an exception state can be a very demanding task for someone suffering from painful symptoms or a chronic condition. The phenomenon of living within a chronic condition 24 hours a day can easily interfere with one's awareness of times when things are better. Webster's definition (Guralnik, 1972) of the word *chronic*, as something that is "always present or encountered," aptly describes the degree of sameness that can creep into the lives of some of these clients. Charmaz (1991, p. 4) wrote about the possibility that people suffering from a chronic condition may consequently enter a separate reality that alters and distorts their experience of time. Some clients may experience a day-to-day existence without noticing any particular change. Conversely, if increasing levels of pain or a rapid deterioration is present, clients may spend much of their time focusing on the smallest signal that things might be getting worse.

Frequently, however, clients pay little active attention to the signs that represent an improvement (however small or temporary) in their condition. Yet these signs may often appear spontaneously. As a result of these phenomena, some clients suffering from chronic pain and illness find it exceedingly difficult to recognize those situations where things have been better. Developed at the Milwaukee Brief Family Therapy Center, the EARS process directly and effectively addresses this phenomenon (DeJong & Berg, 1997). The acronym represents a four-step process—eliciting, amplifying, reinforcing, and starting over—designed to engage the client and therapist in a conversation that generates solutions (in the form of exceptions) to the client's problems.

Eliciting

In the acronym from which the name EARS is derived, the E stands for the process of eliciting an exception. Beginning a session by directly attempting to elicit exceptions may not be met with success with a clinical population that frequently views the health care system as "not listening" to their problems. Taking this into account, the first question we ask in the sessions subsequent to the initial one is, "So, what's *different* since the last time I saw you?" This question opens up the possibility for the client to relay any improvements that may have occurred since the last session, without pressuring him or her to improve too quickly. For the population suffering from chronic pain and illness, we have found this preferable to beginning a session by immediately asking, "What's better?" or inquiring about the client's task assignment from the previous session. This indirect approach simultaneously conveys interest in the client's life while relieving any feeling that he or she is expected to "perform" for the therapist.

Some clients begin answering the "what's different?" question by recounting the details of their lives without mentioning any particular problem. They may talk about a trip that they made, helping their children with their homework, or a walk that they took with their dog. Engaging in this kind of conversation provides an opportunity for the therapist to verbally and nonverbally acknowledge and reinforce these (nonproblem) activities. It also opens up the possibility of eliciting further exceptions through questions like "So, I'm curious, what did you notice that was different about your condition (pain, symptoms, etc.) while this (activity) was going on?"

The client, having already described parts of his or her life that are not directly associated with his or her condition then has the opportunity to reflect back on the problem within the context of normal daily activities. The therapist can then elicit direct exceptions by following up with the question "How were you able to step away from your condition when you walked the dog (took a car trip, helped you child with his homework, etc.)?" As outlined in the previous chapter, the process of eliciting exceptions can be enhanced through determining *who* else noticed (the exception), the client doing *what* (instead of having the problem), *when* (did it happen), and *how* did the client experience it?

In attempting to elicit more specific exceptions the therapist may ask these questions: "Were there some days that were better than others?"

"When is the last time that a part (even the smallest part) of the miracle happened?" "If I were to ask your partner to describe one of your good days, what do you suppose he (or she) would say?" "How were you able to distract yourself from your discomfort since we last met." "When (in the recent past) has the problem (or symptoms) been less severe?" If, as often is the case, the client replies, "I had no good days whatsoever in the last week. My pain was terrible," the therapist can follow up with, "It must have been very difficult, perhaps more so than words can express, and yet somehow you managed to get through this terrible time. How did you manage to do this?" Clearly, the specific wording of these questions should be adjusted for the client's particular context.

Amplifying

The A in the EARS acronym represents the process of *amplifying* a particular exception. Amplification allows the client and therapist to further illuminate its details and to discover "what difference" the experience made to the client. Exploring the sensory details of the exception can be especially valuable for someone enduring the discomfort of a chronic condition. For example, clients may describe helpful sensations of being more or less connected with their body. Or, they might relate sensory experiences such as: "Somehow I put my pain somewhere else when I took my walk. I didn't notice my pain at all." "I felt energized, my body just took off and did things on its own." "I didn't forget that I had a headache, but it just went into the background somewhere." "My legs just stopped hurting and went to sleep."

The therapist can help the client amplify the experiential description of the exception with follow-up questions such as: "What else strikes you about that experience?" "What were you aware of (or not aware) in your body?" "What was your body experiencing instead of the pain (or symptom)?" "What happened when you stopped being afraid and just let yourself experience your body?" "How did time pass differently (more quickly or more slowly) when your headache went into the background?" "What did your body do or experience that was unusual when it 'just took over' and forged ahead in an energized way?"

Difference questions (chapter 6) are vital to the amplification process. They give an exception increased dimension and meaning. As previously noted, exceptions that do not make a difference in clients' lives are not worth pursuing. However, exception states that illuminate a clear difference from the problem state can be a powerful clinical tool in building solutions. Some of useful difference questions are: "What difference did this (exception) make for you?" "How did it affect the remainder of your

---

TABLE 7.1. EARS

Elicit—Exceptions.
Amplify—What difference did the exception make?
Reinforce—Positive changes and their resulting
    differences.
Start over—"So what else is better?"

---

day?" "What did you do that you were not normally able to do?" "How did it affect your interaction with those around you?" "How do you think that they would describe that interaction?" "What difference do you think it made to them?" "How did it carry over into other parts of your life and what difference did that make?" As a rule, we follow the *chain of difference* of a particular exception until the client signals that it no longer makes a difference.

As we show in chapter 9, obtaining amplified descriptions of exception states can be extremely helpful when using clinical hypnosis as a therapeutic intervention. The sensory details elicited by the interview process represent real resource states that can be easily incorporated into the hypnotic process. It is much easier to hypnotically elicit a state of "remembered wellness" (Benson, 1975) than an imagined one.

Reinforcing

The R in the EARS acronym represents the therapist verbally and nonverbally reinforcing the client behavior the exception entailed, along with the positive differences that resulted. In this phase, the therapist acknowledges the exception on verbal and nonverbal levels. The therapist verbally and nonverbally reinforces the client by expressing interest in the details of the exception, encouraging the client to further explore the exception, and commenting on the differences that it made to the client.

Generally, the best way to do this is to paraphrase the client's description of the exception and repeat it back to the client, acknowledging and emphasizing the particular meaning it had for him or her. For example, the therapist might say "So, you walked twice as far as you usually do and your back felt great. And, afterward, you talked to your son about that squirrel that came up to you in the park. It seems that just being able to talk to him about something positive for a change really made a difference in your relationship and allowed you to feel good for the rest of the day."

The compliments that the therapist gives to the client in relation to the exception further supplement the reinforcement process. For example, a therapist might say: "Wow! That sounds like a great walk. I'm impressed with the difference it made with your son and it must be nice to reconnect on that kind of positive level." Like the compliments given in the initial clinical interview, those used in the amplification stage should be sincere and realistic. It is critical that all methods of reinforcement be earnest and directly relate to the exceptions that the client is conveying.

The verbal process of reinforcement is paralleled by the therapist's nonverbal punctuation of an exception. This would involve the physical actions that we naturally exhibit when we are actively listening to someone's story—leaning forward, smiling, raising an eyebrow, taking notes, nodding the head, and so on. Again, it should be a realistic signal that further reinforces the risks that the client has taken and the rewards that he or she has reaped for courage.

Start Over

Finally, the S in the EARS acronym represents the process of *starting over* by asking, "When else have there been times when things have been better?" Given that the chronic pain population has often had to struggle to be recognized as merely having a legitimate complaint, it is important for the therapist to employ the process of starting over judiciously. This is especially true for those clients residing in the sufferer/victim stage. They may react negatively to (misperceived) aggressive questioning if they feel that the therapist has not heard their story. An effective way to approach this type of client is through exhibiting subtle curiosity, asking questions like "I'm curious, are there other times when you don't notice (the problem or symptom) so much, even a little?" Above all, it is vital that the client not mistake asking about exceptions for the therapist not taking his or her problems seriously.

Case Example: Utilizing the EARS Process to Uncover Hidden Exceptions

Fred had sought therapy in the hope of getting some relief from his physical symptoms emanating from post-polio syndrome. He was experiencing increased fatigue, muscle soreness, and a substantial reduction in his endurance. He had spent years working diligently to recover his muscular strength. This had eventually allowed him to lead a relatively normal life, in which he had taught school, climbed mountains, and played in a local Dixieland jazz band. Now post-polio syndrome threatened his hard-earned accomplishments. He spoke in a halting, choked voice, stating, "I thought that all that was behind me." "Now I feel like I'm moving backwards in time," he added forlornly. His goal was to: "Get this under control so that I can go back to living my life again."

Beginning his second session by answering the *eliciting* question "What's different since the last time we met?" Fred responded, "Well, I finally perfected this (musical) piece that I've been working on for months. I never thought that I'd get it down, but finally it just came to me one night." The therapist complimented him on his ability to stick with such a long-term and difficult task and wondered aloud, "How were you able to focus your energy to accomplish this?" Fred answered, "I was getting frustrated about never really completely learning it, but I also knew that I would really need to be fresh to practice. I decided that the only way to do this was to take some time to recharge, so I took a couple of days off and just rested. Looking back, the rest gave me time to think about what I needed to do to learn it. When I looked at the music again, I don't know, somehow I had the energy to just focus on the piece, and forget about everything else. It came to me."

The therapist encouraged Fred to *amplify* the exception by asking, "What did you notice differently about your muscles while this was going on?" After pausing for a full minute while he pondered the question, Fred responded, "Well, I guess I didn't notice any pain at all. My fingers worked fine, and in fact, I practiced for about two hours in the same (body) position and just walked away without noticing any pain. Usually when I stay in one position for more than a few minutes I get stiff and sore."

Reinforcing Fred's accomplishments with compliments, review, and non-verbal gestures, the therapist *started over* by utilizing *difference* questions to enhance the *elicitation* and the *amplification* process, asking, "What difference does it make for you when you approach something you want to do in this kind of recharged manner?" After thinking for a while, Fred recounted the fact that when he was teaching, he always felt better on Mondays after he had "taken it easy" over the weekend. He also noted that he felt better in the mornings and worse at night. This led to more examples and further "solution talk" about the benefits of energy management in relieving his symptoms.

At the conclusion of the session, Fred was convinced that carefully conserving and judiciously expending his energy would significantly impact his life and his chronic condition. He devised a plan to schedule breaks during the day and resolved to "listen" to his body when it told him to slow down. After a few weeks of experimenting with conserving and managing his energy, he was convinced that he "had it under control."

Although the EARS process is generally effective in generating solution states, it may not always maximize the possibilities for both the client and therapist. Complementing the interview process is the Solution Identification Scale for Health (SISH) (described next). Taken together, these produce a detailed map for the client in the journey through chronic pain and illness.

☐ Uncovering Hidden Possibilities: Solution Identification Scale for Health (SISH)

Evident to "seasoned" therapists working with individuals suffering from pain and chronic illness is the fact that not all clients are like Fred. Some clients, especially those in the sufferer/victim stage, have a difficult time relating anything different about their experience from week to week. When asked the question "What's different?" they may respond, "Nothing has changed, I always feel the same—lousy!" In light of this we have developed an instrument to address this phenomenon. The Solution Identification Scale for Health (SISH) is a simple, two-page questionnaire that serves as a vehicle to elicit, amplify, and reinforce exceptions. It is made up of 34 positive and declarative general statements about health, coping ability, and effective self-care. As a rule, it is given to the client to take home and complete as early in the therapy process as possible, preferably after the first session. The client has the option of checking the answers of *never, rarely, sometimes,* or *often* for each item. Additionally, a client can choose not to answer a particular item or indicate those that do not apply.

The concept of encouraging clients (Berg & Miller, 1992; Dolan, 1991; Johnson, 1995) to indicate areas of their lives that are less impacted by their condition radically differs from many current instruments that seek to assess psychopathology, physical deterioration, or pain. In fact, the SISH wasn't designed to assess anything at all. There are no norms and there are no protocols for scoring it. No single question carries any more or less weight than another. Although the SISH can be implemented to track progress over the course of therapy (between sessions), it is primarily used as a tool to generate a "solution talk" between therapists and their clients about the details of exceptions. This is accomplished by providing a familiar structure and ritual—of filling out an evaluation form—to facilitate the conversation. Presenting the option to answer in the affirmative substantially eliminates the temptation for both therapists and clients to fall into "problem" talk.

Therapeutic benefits can accrue from implementation of the SISH at every stage of the recrafting process. For example, using the SISH with sufferer/victims allows them to realize that they already have developed some ways of coping that were outside of their immediate awareness. Seeker/searchers can rediscover helpful strategies that they have successfully used in the past (and perhaps forgotten). This enables them to create a very valuable self-care inventory. The SISH can be used to further validate and reinforce explorer/experimenters for their willingness to take risks and actively seek out "new territory." Even recrafters can use the SISH as a vehicle to gain additional perspective on their accomplishments, and can be further encouraged to share them with others.

Case Example: Utilizing the SISH to Enhance the EARS Process

Audrey's first session found her slumping dejectedly into her chair, confiding to the therapist, "I really thought that this was under control. After my first attack subsided I tried to put it out of my mind. My medications managed everything pretty well. For a time living with lupus seemed no more than an inconvenience. Now, I never know from one day to the next whether I'll be able to get out of bed in the morning." She continued to describe her decline after her second major episode. In addition to being extremely fatigued, she had pain in her joints, often ran a fever over 100°F, and had painful skin rashes.

When her therapist began the second session by asking, "What's different since the last time I saw you?" Audrey responded in a discouraged tone, "Nothing, nothing has changed at all." She looked up at the ceiling as she handed him the Solution Identification Scale for Health she had completed between sessions. Carefully examining Audrey's responses to the SISH, the therapist noticed that she marked only one item as occurring *often*: "I manage to maintain a good attitude" (number 34). Expressing surprise, her therapist pointed to the item and gently asked in a tone of respectful incredulity, "I'm curious, how in the world, despite all you have been through, do you manage to maintain a good attitude?" After thinking for a minute, Audrey answered, "Well, it's all I have. Just because you hurt a lot doesn't mean that you can't try to have a good attitude. I know I complain a lot in here. But I figure," she smiled, "that's what you're here for." Continuing, she explained, "I can't have a great attitude all the time, but I know that if I completely lose that ability, I might as well as give up."

The therapist further explored this "attitude" exception by inquiring, "Who else notices that you have a good attitude?" "My husband is a dear," she said. "He is amazed at the things that I can do despite my condition. He's always saying, 'Audrey, why don't you let me help you more?' He thinks that I'm stubborn, and he's right. He notices that I work hard not to be so much of a burden on him and the family."

Seeking to further amplify this exception, the therapist asked, "What, specifically, do you think that your husband notices about your attitude?" Audrey paused and then answered, "Well, I'd guess that he'd say that I work hard to not let things get me down. I can't do some of the things that I used to, but I try to pull my weight as much as possible in the family." Her voice now contained a note of pride.

Continuing to amplify with *difference* questioning, the therapist pondered aloud, "What difference do you think a good attitude makes?" This time Audrey immediately answered, "Oh, everything! Sometimes I just will myself to get out of bed and open the curtains and let the sun shine in. Just doing that can change my day. Other times, even though I'm exhausted, I'll try to make conversation at the dinner table. It makes me feel more 'whole' and connected to my family. I'm really tired by the time that I go to bed, but feel happy."

The therapist respectfully *reinforced* what Audrey had identified by enthusiastically paraphrasing her affirmative statements, repeating her exact words when appropriate. To further validate and punctuate her accomplishments nonverbally, he leaned forward and made eye contact before complimenting her as follows: "I'm impressed with your perseverance in the light of such a serious illness. It's obvious that you're not going to let this thing beat you. I'm especially struck by the positive differences that you notice when you're able to 'push through' and have a good attitude."

Moving on, the therapist mentioned that Audrey marked *sometimes* for item 7, "I can tell when I'm going to have a good day." "I can tell by how my joints feel in the morning," she explained. "They always hurt, but the pain sometimes subsides after about 20 minutes. If it decreases to a point where I think activity won't make it worse, I try to get my body moving." Audrey and the therapist then *amplified* the differences between good days and bad days. This led to discovering that, occasionally, Audrey was able to transform a "bad" day into a "good" day. By the end of the session, in response to the therapist's *eliciting* questions, Audrey could positively identify various times when she was able to maintain a sense of hopefulness (item 13), enjoy being with friends (item 17), and experience increased levels of comfort (item 10). Each item was *amplified* and *reinforced* before *starting over* and moving on to the next one.

Audrey left the session convinced that the ongoing experience of her illness was variable rather than static. In subsequent sessions she was able to use various experimental task assignments (discussed later) observing the differences between her "good" and "bad" days, gauging her energy reserves, and increasing her self-care activities. Later, in another conversation with the therapist facilitated by the SISH, Audrey was able to quickly reestablish a heightened awareness of her resources and hope.

Enhancing the Administration of the SISH

Several factors enhance the successful administration of the SISH. At the outset, it is important to reassure clients that the purpose of the instrument is "to just see where you're at" and that "there is no real 'score' involved." Clients respond most positively when therapists maintain a level of positive expectancy along with genuine respect for their struggle. This is particularly true when amplifying an exception; the therapist should express respectful enthusiasm tempered within a framework of sincere curiosity. This informs the client that his or her condition isn't being taken lightly even though he or she is affirmatively engaging in solution talk. Correspondingly, items marked *never* need not be discussed.

It is important to note that exploration of exceptions need not be limited to the items indicating *often* or *sometimes*. For example, a client who checked *rarely* in relation to item 4, "There times when I don't notice my symptoms as much," discovered that she was able to significantly distract herself from her pain when she went down to her basement and painted. However, since the onset of her condition she just hadn't done it very much. When she was asked the *difference* that painting made, she was able to access numerous positive instances of different types of "creative distraction" that had significantly enhanced her life. In effect, the very act of engaging in this conversation engendered significant visible signs of hope in the client, enabling her to leave the office with the single purpose of utilizing a "rare" exception.

Finally, it bears repeating that the SISH is not a psychometric instrument that produces any kind of objective clinical measurement. Rather, it is simply a tool that enhances the interview process through generating additional possibilities for "solution talk." Accordingly, successful shifts away from "problem talk" generally occur within a subtle conversational context rather than one in which the therapist directly and enthusiastically "leaps" on an exception. This is especially true for sufferer/victims and seeker/searchers, who may view the health care establishment as indifferent to their problems, merely geared toward the quick disposal of their complaints and symptoms.

Preceding the identification of exceptions by silently reviewing, (visibly) pausing a bit, and demonstrating nonverbal agreement can significantly enhance the conversational context when utilizing the SISH. Following this, the therapist can use language that indicates sincere interest. For example: "I'm curious about (item number) . . . could you tell me a little more about it?" Or, "I know that this might only happen rarely but I was wondering what difference it makes when . . . " Or, "As I was reviewing your answers, I tried to imagine what it might look like on videotape when you . . . " (chapter 6).

To some, these indirect conversational methods may appear to "coddle" and encourage denial in the client. However, in considering the experience and views of this clinical population, it is our view that a more subtle approach is required to maximize the possibilities for the discovery and utilization of useful exceptions and resources. Thus, the client has the opportunity to view the process as one of mutual discovery rather than one attempting to "catch" him or her without serious symptoms.

Occasionally, despite a therapist's best efforts, utilizing the structured methods just described yields little success. In these cases we have found it most effective to shift the clinical focus toward the client's current ability, however small, to cope with his or her condition.

☐ Coping Questions: Addressing a Client's Lack of Engagement

Coping questions (Berg & Miller, 1992) are employed in situations in which the solution-focused interventions already described result in nonconstructive outcomes. Generally employed in the first and second interviews with visitors and sufferer/victims, coping questions are useful when the client declines to become engaged in the interview or when usable solution descriptions or exceptions cannot be developed.

Occasionally, despite the therapist's best intentions, clients fail to engage in the interview process outlined thus far. There could be a number of reasons for this. For some clients the length and degree of their illness may have resulted in the construction of rigid associations that block out hope. Others may misperceive the therapist as "just another professional who won't listen." Moreover, the client may view his or her immediate environment—family, institution, or society in general—as restricting the client to a (seemingly) insignificant role. Finally, the client may legitimately feel that nothing has worked thus far.

These views, understandably, result in the belief that "nothing (in the future) will ever work." In addressing this negative position we refrain from initiating further conversation about why the client feels this way. Instead, we assume that there are good reasons for his or her attitude and shift the solution-focused interview toward (curiously) exploring the client's coping ability with the hope of developing some usable exceptions that can be utilized therapeutically. Thus, within casual conversation, we might gently ask, "I'm curious, given all you have been through, how have you managed to keep things from getting worse?" Or, "I was wondering, given all you have been through, how have you managed to keep your attitude as good as it is?"

At first glance these coping questions might appear counterintuitive to the solution-focused model with its emphasis on the future and hopeful-

---

TABLE 7.2. Coping Questions

How have you managed to keep things from getting worse?
How have you kept your attitude as good as it is?
How come you haven't given up?
What do you currently (specifically) do to maintain your current level (of coping)?
What trait do you have that enables you to function on this level?
What trait would other people say you possessed for coping?

---

ness. However, this intervention is consistent with the stance of meeting the client at his or her (self-perceived) level of functioning. Of course, common sense and clinical judgment should be used when asking these questions. For example, it would be disrespectful to ask the first question of a client who feels that his or her condition is out of control and rapidly deteriorating. Similarly, a client who directly states that he or she has a "terrible attitude" shouldn't be insulted with the second question. Rather, the therapist must adjust questions to the client's unique situation, remembering that it is the concept of the client's coping that matters most.

Additional coping questions that have proven useful are "How come you haven't just given up?" and "What do you do to maintain your (current) level of functioning? These questions, aimed at generating conversations centering on any of the client's self-care activities, can produce more consistent (usable) exceptions to her complaints. Questions about specific traits that the client possesses are also useful for respectfully generating coping information. For example, asking "What trait would you say that you have that allows you to cope as well as you do?" can generate talk about specific attributes in which the client takes pride. These may be spiritual beliefs, values passed down from generation to generation in her family, or simply being a "survivor." Others in the client's social system can be helpful in enhancing coping questions. In some cases, asking a spouse, relative, or support group member, for example, "What trait do you think that (the client) has that allows (him or her) to cope as well as (he or she) does?" can provide both the therapist and client with valuable coping information. Asking the client to speculate on other people's observations of his or her coping ability is equally helpful. For example, the therapist might ask, "What traits do you think (your partner, best friend, sister, etc.) would identify that enable you to cope so well?"

Amplifying Coping Abilities

In order to be most useful, as with all other solution-focused interventions, answers to coping questions need to be amplified until the client identifies meaningful exceptions. For example, when a client suggests that her spirituality "gets me through the day," the therapist might gently inquire about how that happens. Are there times when the client is praying that her symptoms will be less intrusive? Does her spirituality help put the minor daily annoyances of life into better perspective? Does she recognize "good days" and feel thankful for them? What difference does it make when she engages in conversations about spirituality with friends and relatives? In addition to generating exceptions, amplifying these answers provides ample opportunities for the therapist to compliment the client on possessing valuable and meaningful traits.

Amplifying coping ability also provides a natural opportunity to scale the client's current level of functioning with the goal of discovering the client's idea of small improvement. When a client was asked what it would take to move from a (coping level) of "2" to a "3," she explained that "In addition to being thankful for those few 'good' days I'd be able to take advantage of them more." When asked how this might occur, she said, "Instead of sitting around, I think that I would get a little exercise." After exploring the differences exercise would make, the therapist and client decided that it would be worthwhile to experiment with a gentle half-hour walk the next time the client experienced one of those "good" days.

Case Example: Transforming Dysfunctional Coping Skills into Useful Exceptions

A friend who was concerned about Pam's marriage referred her to a therapist for pain management. Beginning the interview in the sufferer/victim stage, it became obvious that chronic illness was causing significant problems in her relationship with her husband. She had suffered from debilitating migraine headaches for most of her life. She began the first interview by confiding to the therapist: "I don't like being in this body. It's never been my friend." Then she began to cry. She couldn't remember a period of time when she had not endured severe pain that would incapacitate her for several days at a time, usually once a week. "If I'm not having a headache I'm thinking about the next one. I don't know what's worse, the anticipation or the headache itself. I organize my life around it. It's either pain or fear every day, all day long," she continued.

At one time firmly entrenched in the seeker/searcher stage, Pam had experimented with a number of things, including sinus surgery, having five teeth extracted, EST training, and meditating for several months, with little success. "I do all this stuff but nothing ever gets fixed," she sighed. After failing to produce meaningful answers to miracle, exception, and scaling questions, the therapist stated, "You've had this condition for a long time, how do you cope with this as well as you do?" "My body stays in the bed while my head just goes somewhere else," she said. "Actually,

I learned it in reaction to my mother. She was always sick and demanded that we [Pam and her brother] be quiet at all times."

Pam survived an abusive childhood and early in her life developed ways of effectively "getting away" from her pain. "I've always isolated myself and tried to stay out of the way," she said. She continued, "Now my husband is having problems with me separating from the family when I'm in pain, which seems like most of the time. He doesn't think that I'm 'here' enough. He says that he doesn't know how much longer he can stand it. My kids are worried about me too."

When the therapist complimented her on her ability to get away from her pain, Pam tearfully responded, "But *that's the problem*, I'm stuck between choosing between relieving my pain and my family." The therapist agreed that this was an unacceptable choice for anyone. Continuing, the therapist asked Pam what dissociative mechanism she actually used at times when she "went away for a while." In answering, Pam described what was clearly a self-induced hypnotic state, saying, "I can just stare out in space for a time and go away." The therapist then wondered aloud, "Are there any times that you experience this ability, even unconsciously, and still manage to stay connected to your family?"

After a long thoughtful pause, Pam identified two regularly occurring distinct occasions where she was able to accomplish "going away" while simultaneously remaining connected to her family. The first involved her planning and preparation of Sunday dinners. She enjoyed thinking about elaborate meal plans and successfully executing them: "I can have a headache and become so involved in my recipes and cooking that I don't notice the pain." The other instance involved a weekly television show that all the family watched together.

Continuing to participate in this process of "mutual discovery," the therapist and Pam engaged in a conversation designed to amplify these two exceptions while exploring the differences they made, her family's reaction, and the hope of expanding their range and frequency. At the conclusion of the session the therapist asked Pam to scale her coping ability. She said, "Thirty minutes ago I would have said a zero. But now I'd say that I'm a three." When asked what a "four would look like," Pam identified the goal of eventually extending that experience all the way through Sunday dinner.

In subsequent sessions the therapist utilized Pam's dissociative abilities through the application of self-hypnotic techniques (chap. 9) to address her pain. This classic hypnotic intervention allowed her to both "go away" and stay connected to her family when she had her headaches. At the conclusion of her fourth and final therapy session she enthusiastically commented, "I'm glad I was able to finally learn how to put all that childhood stuff [dissociating from painful experience] to good use."

Ironically, in some instances a client's coping mechanisms can cause more problems than the condition itself. This is most frequently demonstrated in inappropriate uses of medication, alcohol, and/or dissociative abilities. Tragically, nonfunctional coping mechanisms that effectively alleviate a client's pain can inadvertently cause the client to become psychologically distant in relationships with loved ones. With a few adjustments, however, and a little knowledge, in this case Pam was able to transform a troublesome coping behavior into a useful self-care skill.

Although coping questions are most frequently employed as a lifeline back to usable exceptions for both therapists and clients, they can be utilized throughout the course of therapy. Positively punctuating the therapeutic experience, they can be used as a springboard for compliments from the therapist reminding the client of his or her strengths and courage. Combined with scaling they can be used to indicate progress over time. Additionally, coping questions can become useful in illuminating functional exceptions that may not be readily apparent to either client or therapist. Finally, as we show later; coping questions can be utilized in one of the most common situations encountered by therapists treating clients suffering from chronic pain and illness—relapse.

☐ Relapse Management: Recovering from the Fall

Sometimes, despite the best efforts of clients like Pam and their caregivers, relapses can and do occur. Individuals addressing the challenge of adapting to life with pain and chronic illness are periodically confronted with "bumps in the road" that threaten hard-won progress. Relapse, a dynamic element of the stages of recrafting a life (chapter 5), is common with this clinical population. Physical and psychological setbacks can be a critical turning point in the client's life. If he or she can meet the challenge, the client will gain new confidence in his or her ability to successfully respond to the condition. On the other hand, if the client becomes overwhelmed by a setback, he or she may fall into despair and lose much of the progress that achieved through previous hard work and commitment.

Relapse can come in several different forms. A client may let his or her self-care routine gradually slip, ultimately paying the price in decreased functioning and increased discomfort. Paradoxically, this may occur as a result of the client feeling better, perhaps thinking that the original routine needn't be followed so completely. A client may be faced with a temporary, yet seemingly overwhelming, physical and/or psychological challenge that revives old, dysfunctional ways of coping. Often clients find a self-care routine that once enhanced their daily lives eventually falling short, complaining "it just doesn't work like it used to." Finally, if the course of the illness is unpredictable and/or deteriorative, the client may

---
TABLE 7.3. Relapse Management

Possible turning point.
Focus on "getting back up" rather than the "slip and fall."
How did you manage as well as you did?
Review what worked in the past.
Scale past, present, future.
Combine best of the old and promise of new.
Compliments on past hard work and present commitment.
Normalize the dynamics of change.
Reexamine past and current coping strategies.
Review skills gained from the recovery.

---

experience a series of setbacks resulting in feeling as if he or she were in an uncontrollable downward spiral.

In the vast majority of these cases, clients experience some hopelessness in response to a relapse, often slipping back to the sufferer/victim stage. Typically, they have worked hard at overcoming the debilitating effects of their condition, and understandably feel grief, rage, even desperation in the face of their current reduction in functioning. When a relapse occurs, the immediate temptation for both therapist and client is to focus on what, how, and why it happened. Although at first glance it seems to be logical to analyze the "slip and fall," focusing extensively on the details of the relapse can actually worsen the client's despair.

Shifting Focus: Getting Back Up

In addressing relapse we attempt to shift the focus to the process of "getting back up." After respectfully listening to the client's story and validating his or her concerns, we begin by gently asking questions such as "What was working before the relapse?" and "How did you manage as well as you did?" Once again it is particularly useful to use enhancement questions that focus on *what* the client was doing that enabled him or her to maintain her previous state, *how* exactly the client went about sustaining his or her level of functioning, *who* else noticed, and so on. These questions can help her become reacquainted with real resources that recently worked, giving her hope that they can be utilized again.

Scaling is a particularly valuable tool following a relapse because it allows the client to determine where he or she was before the relapse, his or her current state, and what (specifically) needs to happen to improve one point. Like most processes in solution-focused therapy, recovery from relapse proceeds in incremental steps. If the client identifies his or her

current level as several points from where he or she was before the relapse, the therapist should focus on the next small step (one point better)
rather than immediately facilitating a large change. Moreover, it is important for the therapist to normalize the processes of "slipping and falling" in the course of addressing the challenges of a chronic condition,
emphasizing that the process of "getting back up" will be easier this time
because "You've already been down that road before; and, you know
where all the potholes are."

The experience of relapse can be devastating for a client, particularly
after he or she has made a considerable amount of progress toward improving his or her condition. The following case demonstrates the ways
in which relapse management can be used as an opportunity for such
clients.

Case Example: Bouncing Back from Relapse

"I can't believe that I'm back up to 12 again. For a while there I felt so
energized and positive. Now I feel like I'll never get back down again."
Barbara, who suffered chronic pain from a degenerative spinal disorder,
was referring to the number of pain medication pills she had recently
been taking. Previously, as a result of diligent effort, working along with
her therapist, Barbara had succeeded in reducing her medication from 18
to 8 pills a day. Although she knew that her condition probably would
always require some daily medication, her goal had been to reduce it to a
point in which she could sufficiently minimize the cumulative side effects
that interfered with the quality of her daily life. These side effects—drowsi-
ness, poor concentration, and lack of energy—significantly interfered with
her personal relationships as well as raising her children. Over the course
of therapy she learned to effectively utilize self-hypnosis and other pain
management techniques, enabling the gradual reduction of her medication. At the time of her relapse she had achieved a balance between her
daily medication and self-care techniques that enabled her to be alert and
more engaged with her family.

Ironically, her efforts had backfired. A gifted amateur athlete, Barbara
had recently felt so good that she managed to seriously exacerbate her
condition by jumping on her son's trampoline, an action that was completely contrary to medical advice. "It was the stupidest thing. I can't
believe I did it," she groaned. "I knew it was dangerous but I just couldn't
help myself. Everyone else was having so much fun." Barbara's significant increase in pain resulted in her increasing her medication by 50%.

After commiserating with her for a while, the therapist asked, "How
did you manage to keep from taking 14 or even going back to taking 18
pills a day?" Momentarily speechless, Barbara eventually answered,

"Well . . . I just told myself that I wasn't going to take more than 12, no matter how much I hurt." The therapist, visibly impressed, complimented her on her ability to cope with such an unpredictable disaster. Continuing, he asked her to amplify on her coping abilities by asking, "Exactly how did you endure those times when the medication wore off?" She began to describe utilizing what she had learned, some self-hypnosis, biofeedback, and gentle stretching techniques in response to the pain. "I threw everything at it but the kitchen sink," she laughed.

During the remainder of the session Barbara and the therapist reviewed, in detail, all the things that she had done "right" before, during, and immediately after her relapse. Not once did the therapist mention what caused the relapse or chastise Barbara about the consequences of future risky behavior. This was information she had already learned—the hard way. Instead, he complimented her on performing admirably under extremely difficult circumstances.

Knowing that her increased discomfort was temporary, the therapist wondered aloud, "Given that your back will eventually return to where it was before your accident, how do you think your experience of your relapse (only increasing the medication by four tablets in response to excruciating pain) will affect your ultimate goal of reducing your medication further in the future?" Barbara thought for a moment before answering, "Now that I can look at it that way, I know that if I can make it through this, I can do just about anything."

When Barbara and the therapist scaled the next small step toward recovery, she identified the goal of a reduction to 10 tablets a day and devised a plan to reincorporate many of the self-care techniques that had worked for her in the past. She was further able to reduce her medication to six tablets a day, resulting in improved pain management skills and increased daily functioning. Both Barbara and the therapist wondered whether this reduction would have taken place so quickly if Barbara's relapse had not presented such a good opportunity.

Paradoxically, when a relapse is treated as an opportunity (by both therapist and client), it can serve as a springboard for further progress. However, the very nature of chronic pain and illness can condition clients to view their improved functioning as temporary and "too good to be true," anticipating a relapse. This "waiting for the other shoe to drop" view appears to be especially true when the client makes rapid improvement. Thus, clients and therapists may be required to address the fear of relapse as well.

Interventions for the Anticipated Relapse

Johnson (1995), in addressing relapse in the general clinical population, regularly asks clients to imagine having a setback and subsequently invites them to speculate on what might be learned (in advance) from such an experience. Thus the client is given the opportunity to discover and solidify current competencies from rehearsing and recovering from a relapse without actually having to endure one. Although we don't ask this particular clinical population to imagine such a negative event, we do feel that solution-focused interventions are indispensable when clients openly express fear about having a setback.

In addressing the understandable fear of relapse, we employ a three-step process. We begin by shifting focus to the (imagined) details of the recovery. Notably absent from this description are the details of the feared relapse. Unless the client insists in reviewing these (imaginary) details, it is sufficient for the therapist to have a general idea of what it would entail. Examining recovery from a potentially frightening future event from the relative safety of the present significantly facilitates the client's ability to generate useful solutions. Given the client's (past and current) participation in the solution-focused process, this task is relatively straightforward.

In utilizing interventions akin to the miracle, exception, and scaling questions (chapter 6), we begin the process by asking: "Looking at a (possible) future relapse from the safe haven of the 'here and now,' what do you think your first step toward recovery would be? On a scale of 1 to 10 what would represent a one-point improvement? What difference do you think that first small step might make? What would other people notice that would let them know that you were on the road to recovery? If you were to show me a videotape of this, what would I see and hear to let me know that you had taken that first step? "

Second, the therapist can amplify the client's answers through asking difference questions to highlight and compare his or her skills and adaptation before therapy to the client's current level of functioning. This not only underscores what the client has learned and achieved up until now, but infuses him or her with self-confidence as well. Typically we begin this difference questioning by using scaling to compare current and past levels of functioning, emphasizing the journey that the client has made thus far. Then we follow up with: "How do you think you would handle a relapse now compared to when you were a . . . (lower number on the scale)? What do you know about yourself now that would help you recover from a possible relapse? What (specific) steps do you want to remember to take if such a setback might happen? What difference do you think taking those steps will make?"

Relapse—A Final Word

In situations where the relapse is associated with the declining value of the once effective self-care routine, the client and therapist can focus on combining the "best of the old with the promise of the new." This may involve reviewing what has been learned thus far as well as repeating some of the exception, scaling, coping, and even miracle interventions that were previously helpful. Commenting on this, the therapist can note that the changing nature of the client's condition—and most medical conditions, for that matter—requires the dynamic implementation of resources. Moreover, clients should be complimented on the hard work that they have been willing to do in the past and the fact that they are willing to reengage in it in the present.

In some cases, however, a relapse may be the result of the unavoidable progressive deterioration that accompanies the client's condition, possibly resulting in death. Although clients are typically aware of the inevitability of this deterioration, its arrival is never easy (for client or therapist). There are no simple answers or unique interventions for these kinds of relapses other than to continue to respectfully acknowledge the client's ongoing experience and validate whatever positive actions the client is taking in order to go forward with life in the best way possible under the current circumstances.

The final step in addressing an anticipated relapse lies in the next section on experimental tasks. These assignments—Roadside Repair Kit, Rainy Day Letter, and Memory Virus tasks—serve to solidify the client's gains and provide the client with a specific set of practical tools that complement the interventions already outlined.

☐ Experimental Tasks—Broadening Therapy's Impact

In addition to complementing relapse prevention, experimental tasks can significantly enhance the solution-focused approach at virtually any stage of therapy. They can extend the impact of the therapeutic process beyond any individual session. They serve to add an additional dimension to the therapeutic process that transcends the structured interview process. Additionally, experimental tasks generate exceptions that can be utilized by both therapists and clients to further clinical progress.

We consistently emphasize the "experimental" nature of any task assignment request we make of a client. Underscoring the experimental context is the fact that, frequently, clients suffering from pain and chronic illness have experienced what they considered to be failure to address their problems. These "failures" may have occurred in relation to compliance issues, an individual procedure, or a self-care regime that proved to be inadequate. Thus, presenting an assignment as "just an experiment" serves to head off self-criticism that a client may experience in relation to his or her anticipated failure. Instead of viewing the task as representing "something else that didn't work," the experimental context informs the client that the task or action is something that "I know I don't need to try that again."

Observational "Doing," and Metaphorical Tasks

Experimental tasks come in three basic forms, observational, "doing," and metaphorical. Observational tasks invite the client to pay attention to small signs of improvement within the everyday environment. Here the emphasis is on improvement and paying attention to "what works" rather than on what doesn't. These tasks are ideal for sufferer/victims and those seeker/searchers who are not yet interested in taking an active role in their treatment outside the therapist's office.

The value of observational tasks lies in the fact that a client's lack of compliance outside the office doesn't prohibit the possibility of completing the task inside the office. For example, if a client failed to complete a task to observe the difference between good days and bad days over a week's time, the client can take a moment in the office to remember those differences. The therapist might simply state, "Well that's perfectly fine and understandable, but I'm still curious about those differences. What were they anyway?" If the client thinks it is a reasonable task, he or she will comply in the office. If the client doesn't, it tells us much about his or her stage of readiness to change and informs us that adjustments must be made (discussed later).

"Doing" tasks simply invite the client to participate by repeating an activity that has been helpful in the past or experimenting with something new that appears to be (to the client) promising. These proactive tasks generally relate to exceptions that the client has found helpful, assigning the client to "do more of that." Metaphorical tasks are "doing" assignments that encourage clients to participate in a specific symbolic activity that is in some way representative of a solution to the client's problem. "Doing" tasks are ideal for seeker/searchers who have begun to do (or are committed to doing) things for themselves outside the therapist's office. Generally, metaphorical tasks are helpful for clients in explorer/experimenter and recrafter stages.

Rules for Successful Task Assignment

Typically, when a therapeutic experiment fails, it is a reflection of a mismatch between the client's stage of readiness (chapter 5) and the energy and motivation required by the task. This is reflected in the experimental tasks outlined next. As a rule, successful task assignment can be represented on a continuum with one side representing the most general, and therefore most likely to succeed, observational tasks and the other side representing the most specific and therefore possessing more risks, "doing" and metaphorical tasks. Characterized by increasing complexity, this continuum roughly parallels the stages of recrafting characterized by differing levels of readiness, motivation, and available energy.

Thus, visitors get no assignment other than an invitation to return if they think it might be helpful. Sufferer/victims are assigned the most general of observational tasks that have a very low failure probability. Seeker/searchers profit from general observational task assignments as well as those that specifically target their exceptions. As they make progress closer to the explorer/experimenter stage, they can be assigned to "do" something to make the exception occur more often. Finally, explorer/experimenters and recrafters, characterized by an enthusiastic willingness to do something outside the office, may be assigned virtually any kind of observational or doing task.

In considering factors that contribute to successful task assignment, we would caution that any task, no matter what the stage of recrafting, will fail if it doesn't fit the client's model of the world or respect the limits of his or her condition. Thus, a client who has religious objections to hypnosis shouldn't be given the task of applying self-hypnotic techniques to his or her symptoms. Likewise, clients with limited mobility shouldn't be required to do anything that would inappropriately tax them physically.

Before describing specific task assignments it is important to note that if a task, for some reason, should fail, it is critical for the therapist to take responsibility for suggesting the wrong assignment and to thank the client for his or her willingness to participate in the experiment. This position is based on several factors. First, blaming the client for the failure will significantly reduce or entirely eliminate the possibility of assigning tasks in the future. Second, a failed task informs the therapist that adjustments need to be made to better accommodate the client's worldview and stage of recrafting. Finally, exhibiting the behavior of apologizing and thanking the client for her willingness to take a risk can serve to positively surprise him or her, creating new possibilities for the therapeutic relationship in the future.

Experimental Observational Tasks

Experimental observational tasks center on the act of inviting the client to pay attention to the exceptions, small signs that the miracle is occurring, and movement on a (previously constructed) scale. Sufferer/victims and seeker/searchers generally profit from these tasks because there is little risk of failure. Clients cannot help but observe whether they're doing better or worse, even if it after the fact. Observational tasks that target specific helpful phenomena are most successful in cases where the client's exceptions occur randomly (de Shazer, 1988). In these cases clients generally report the existence of helpful exceptions but cannot describe when or how they occur.

By and large, these tasks have a *difference* component built in to the observation. Thus, the therapist might suggest that the client notice what difference it makes when an exception occurs. The therapist can amplify this suggestion through suggesting that in some cases the exception might make a clear difference, that is, directly contributing to symptom relief. In other cases, the therapist might suggest the exception might make more indirect and subtle differences, such as, a good night's sleep providing more energy during the day, which in turn allows for more engagement in family activities.

Ironically, in some situations, the act of observing exceptions and other helpful phenomena can interfere with their effectiveness. This is especially true in cases of successful pain-management strategies (Eastwood, Gaskovski, & Bowers, 1998). Proving the adage that "A watched pot never boils," clients excessively focusing on these types of observations may actually prevent exceptions from occurring or, worse, decrease their actual level of functioning. To address this dynamic, we routinely suggest to the client that he or she need not make a record of the observation at the time of the exception, but sometime later when it is more convenient. This is particularly important to stress when utilizing hypnosis to address chronic pain. In these cases we note to the client that "your unconscious mind can notice the differences it makes and inform you at a later time."

First-Session Formula Task.   Originated by the staff at BFTC, the first-session formula task represents the most general and therefore one of the most useful of all observational tasks (de Shazer, 1985). It is best assigned when goals are not well formed and/or the client's exceptions are unclear or nonusable. In utilizing this intervention, the therapist asks the client whether he or she would be willing to, as an experiment, "between now and the next time we get together, pay attention to the things in your life that you would like to continue." If the client is somewhat confused by this invitation, it is helpful to clarify that the client need not focus on what he or she doesn't want to continue, but rather the things that he or she does. Further, we state, "This can be anything from the smallest thing that you enjoy to the most significant factor in your life. We suggest that you might find it helpful to write these things down as they occur to you, or perhaps you might prefer to simply store them in the back of your mind." Whatever way works best for the client will be the "right way."

In the following session, the therapist carefully notes the activities, friendships, and even (seemingly) inconsequential details of life that the client wishes to continue. For added emphasis, the observations may be carefully recorded in the client's presence as a way of nonverbally communicating the importance of the information. The client's responses to the first-session formula task typically generate some potentially usable exceptions to his or her symptoms and condition, enabling the therapist to engage in the EARS process with each item.

For example, a client with irritable bowel syndrome reported that she wanted to continue reading, walking her dog, and going out to lunch with her best friend. The therapist inquired about how the experience of her illness was different when she engaged in these activities, especially going out to eat with her friend. She reported, not surprisingly, that she couldn't remember experiencing her symptoms during those times. "Now that I think of it," she said, "I really should be having some problems when I go out to eat with Jody (her best friend)." The therapist and client spent the remainder of the session eliciting and amplifying more exceptions as well as exploring the difference they made to the client. By the next session she was able to utilize this information and substantially reduce her discomfort from her condition.

The first-session formula task is particularly helpful in generating exceptions from sufferer/victims who, in the initial session, relate vague answers to miracle and exception questions. This occurs when the therapist is sure that the client has a complaint but is sure of little else at the end of the first session. At the conclusion of the session, although the therapist has listened to the client's story, the caregiver may have the impression that little else has been accomplished.

Such seemingly unsuccessful sessions are quite familiar to experienced health care professionals. In these cases we suggest that the therapist compliment the client on his or her ability to relate the details of his or her story to a stranger and for coping as well as the client has. This can be followed up by the statement, "It's obvious that you know yourself really well. Given that fact, I'm wondering if you would be willing to conduct a small experiment." Subsequent to this, the first-session formula task can be assigned.

In eliciting the details of his or her observations, as previously mentioned, it's best to approach the sufferer/victim with cautious curiosity instead of "jumping" on the first exception generated by the assignment. Rather, after listening and nonverbally responding for a while, the therapist might say, "I'm curious, what difference does it make when you (experience a clear exception) . . . " Subsequently the therapist can use the structured EARS process to amplify the possibilities these exceptions represent. Once these exceptions have been sufficiently explored more standard observational tasks can be assigned.

The Standard Observational Task: Pay attention to the times and difference it makes when you . . . This simple task simply invites the client to experimentally observe the difference it makes when he or she experiences times when the symptoms are better or nonexistent. Useful for seeker/searchers and those sufferer/victims who have responded well to the first-session formula task, these assignments are most successful when they directly reference (previously defined) usable exceptions, miracles, and scales. For example, it is better to suggest that a client "notice the times (and what difference it makes to your pain) when you play the piano," than to "pay attention to times when thing are better." Also, as previously mentioned in regard to amplifying exceptions, it is helpful to know details what the client was experiencing *instead* (chapter 6) of the symptoms.

In the case of entire miracles or exceptions that seem too large to occur, clients can be directed to notice any part of their occurrence. For instance, one client who had severe chronic nerve pain and had as her miracle "the ability to completely leave my body when I need to" was directed to observe any portion of the miracle occurring, even the smallest imaginable part. She remembered letting her mind wander during a routine yet uncomfortable procedure. She had no physical sensation of the procedure until it was brought to her attention that it was completed. This informed her that she did, indeed, have this "miraculous" ability, further encouraging her to employ structured, self-hypnotic techniques (doing tasks).

A client suffering from crippling arthritis observed experiencing a different kind of flexibility in her limbs when she least expected it. This random exception surprised her and resulted in her enrollment in a yoga class. Yoga in turn became a daily self-care activity, significantly improving her quality of life.

For a client suffering cancer pain, the next step on her scale (a 6) was to spend one hour a day pain free (without medication). When she returned for the next session she excitedly observed, "I was a 6 for at least two hours a day, sometimes, three or four." This gave her hope and the motivation to make the exception occur more regularly and for a longer period of time. In each of these cases the observations made by these clients resulted in their ability to expand their range of options in relation to their condition. Virtually any positive client trait can be used in an observational experiment. This might be a positive attitude, a sense of humor, or the ability to "put all this into perspective."

Another standard observational task is to invite the client to "pay attention to the differences between good days and bad days." Requesting that the client simply observe "what makes some days better than others" can broaden this assignment. This works best when the client takes some time out at the end of the day to review whether it was better than previous days, and, if so, what specifically made it better. If the client returns reporting "all the days were exactly the same," the therapist can inquire about which day was the "least bad" (even by a infinitesimal margin), using the information to find out what made it different.

Having clients observe how they "stay on track" is also a reliable observational task assignment. Walter and Peller (1994) suggested that the phrase *on track* serves as a metaphor for the course of therapy, particularly when it may involve a long-term process. Implemented after the client has made some progress (as defined by the client), the therapist suggests that the client "pay attention to the (specific) things you do to stay on track." This not only generates helpful solution-focused dialogue but it permits mutual discovery of what the client did to overcome specific obstacles that he or she overcame to "stay on track."

It is quite possible to exclusively utilize observational tasks throughout the entire course of therapy in all stages of recrafting. Even suggesting to a visitor that he or she is welcome to return when the client thinks that he or she might be helped by therapy is an indirect observational task. However, in cases where a client express a desire to "do" more or consistently demonstrates a motivation to achieve tasks outside the therapist's office, experimental "doing" tasks are called for.

Experimental "Doing" Tasks

In assigning these tasks the therapist simply suggests that the client "do" something, experimentally. These tasks are constructed from (primarily exception-related) information developed from the solution-focused interview, the Solution Identification Scale for Health (SISH), and the Self-Care Response (SCR) tool. Clients who succeed at "doing" tasks view themselves as part of the solution. Primarily these tasks are reserved for seeker/searchers and explorer/experimenters. Recrafters, by their nature, continually generate these types of tasks on their own but can always profit from new ones. "Doing" tasks can be particularly satisfying because the client has an immediate experience of actively impacting her condition.

Two factors are critical in assigning successful "doing" tasks. First, the client should demonstrate that he or she is willing to do something outside the office that is directly related to his or her condition. Clients who can identify past exceptions and are interested in making them occur again are generally good candidates for this kind of assignment. Although explorer/experimenters, by definition, fall into this category, the same cannot be said for all seeker/searchers. In the beginning of this stage these clients may cycle between the sufferer/victim and seeker/searcher positions, not quite ready to make a motivational commitment. In these cases it is best for the therapist to assign only observational tasks. However, as the seeker/searcher begins to view him- or herself to be part of the solution, the client will profit from "doing" tasks.

The second critical factor in assigning doing tasks is the (apparent) available energy reserves of the client. Even explorer/experimenters and recrafters can experience periods of low energy. Energy can be calibrated with scaling before proceeding with any assignment. For example, the therapist can direct the client, "On a scale of 1 to 10, how much how much energy/motivation do you have to try something experimentally?" Once the client expresses his or her current position (on the scale), the therapist can engage the client in solution-focused dialogue in regard to the present number, where the client was before, and where he or she would like to go next on the scale. If, after this process, the client concludes that he or she doesn't have the requisite amount of energy required for the task, a less taxing one can be assigned.

The Standard "Doing" Task: "If it works, do more of it!" In assigning the standard "doing" task the therapist simply invites the client to "do more" of what has worked in the past de Shazer (1988). These tasks primarily utilize (frequently forgotten) exceptions that have consistently worked in the past. If exercise consistently reduces a client's pain, for example, the therapist suggests that the client develop a regime to include more exercise in his or her life. The therapist supplements the suggestion by aiding the client in developing specific objectives that will ensure the success of the task. The same thing holds true for scaling assignments. If the client can deliberately achieve a higher number, and that number will make a difference in his or her functioning, the therapist assigns the client to "be" that number, suggesting that, as an experiment, "Between now and the next time we get together—be a 6." Again, the therapist reviews the characteristics and differences represented by that number, reinforcing the client's the goal.

As with observational tasks, virtually any exception, scaled (higher) number, and/or miracle (or part thereof) can be assigned as a "doing" task. "Doing" tasks should be carefully reconsidered, however, in those rare cases where they might represent a risk to the client's health. Simple common sense comes into play in this consideration. For example, a client who has degenerative joint problems shouldn't be encouraged to exercise in a manner that risks further degeneration, even though such exercise has helped in the past. Finally, if the client manages to accomplish only part of the doing task, perhaps because the client and/or the therapist is shooting too high, the subsequent focus should only on the benefits of what the client has accomplished. Utilizing this dialogue, the therapist can reinforce accomplishments and suggest that the client might "scale back and take it more slowly the next time."

Experimental Metaphorical "Doing" Tasks

Metaphorical tasks invite clients to participate in solution-focused "doing" activities within a nonordinary frame. These assignments use metaphorical activities and rituals to represent, discover, remember, and reinforce exceptions. Because they are tasks that request clients to carry out a specific activity, the same rules for assigning "doing" tasks apply. That is, they should only be assigned to clients who are motivated to "do" something outside of the office. Typically, this means that they will succeed with explorer/experimenters, recrafters, and proactive seeker/searchers.

The Roadside Repair Kit.   This metaphorical task centers on the development of a resource kit that will be available during a relapse and other times of need. Generally, it is utilized toward the middle or end of therapy. It is suggested to the client that, like a well-equipped car on an extended road trip, with its spare tire, jack, safety flares, and other emergency equipment, it might be helpful for the client to construct a repair kit for him- or herself. The therapist suggests that the client include objects and ideas that will provide aid and comfort in a time of need. Although it is the client's task to assemble the specific tools for the kit, the therapist can supplement the assignment by mentioning previously discussed exceptions as examples. Additionally, the therapist can invite the client to take his or her time in assembling these tools, using observational skills to enrich his or her selection.

The task of constructing the Roadside Repair Kit is therapeutic in itself. It requires the client to seriously consider the important things that contribute to his or her quality of life. Moreover, it gives the client and therapist an opportunity to discuss those self-care activities that can prevent relapse or, at worst, soften the landing somewhat. After therapist and client have discussed the contents (and their meaning) of the kit, specific applications can be constructed to enhance the client's journey.

Some Roadside Repair Kit applications directly address the fear of relapse. In these cases the therapist and client discuss how the tools would be used and under what circumstances. Additionally, it is critical in these cases to highlight the differences that these tools might make in relation to managing a relapse. Often, the process of assembling the kit and engaging in a conversation about its meaning and uses will substantially reduce a client's fear of relapse.

Other applications of this metaphorical task might center on a client remembering what's important. Understandably, some clients suffering from chronic pain and illness can become separated from their resources. For example, Erin, who suffered from muscular dystrophy, included a number of objects in her kit to remind her "I am not my disease." She included a favorite picture of her grandmother, who gave her the idea that she should never give up. Also she had a whistle she used to coach the girls soccer team, an old identification tag from a dog that she rescued from the pound, and various aphorisms, poems, and self-affirmations that were important to her. She used her kit daily, often adding tools, as a vehicle to maintain her dignity in the face of a serious illness.

The Rainy Day Letter.   Our adaptation of Dolan's (1998) Rainy Day Letter is beneficial for those clients firmly entrenched in the explorer/ experimenter stage. Generally, it is best assigned close to the termination of therapy. Like the Roadside Repair Kit, it functions as a "remembering" task that is beneficial for clients who may become temporarily separated from their resources. Used in addressing the of fear of relapse or for smoothing the inevitable "bumps in the road clients are bound to encounter," this task is designed to reacquaint clients with the successful steps that they have taken on the journey thus far.

In assigning this task, the therapist requests that the client, before the next therapy session, write him- or herself a letter from the present time to his or her future self. It is further suggested that the letter reflect the significant gains the client has made thus far in the struggle with a chronic condition. The Rainy Day Letter is to serve as a kind of "wish you were here" communication that outlines all the things that the client is currently doing that significantly enhance his or her quality of life. These might be self-care activities, helpful attitudes and traits, and/or relationships with friends and family that make a difference in the client's ability to meet the challenge of chronic pain and illness. Additionally, the client should be encouraged to give him- or herself wise advice in relation to surviving the occasional "dips" that are bound to occur along the way.

When the client arrives for the next session, he or she can review the letter with the therapist. In addition to reinforcing progress, the Rainy Day Letter provides opportunities for the therapist to compliment the client on "staying on track" through the challenging times. Moreover, it provides the option for the therapist to ask the client from his or her current functional state, "What advice would be most helpful if you ever found yourself in a 'tight spot'?" After the client and therapist have reviewed the letter, taking the opportunity to make any additions (or subtractions), the client is directed to seal the envelope. Without using the word *relapse*, the therapist suggests that "a few bumps in the road are inevitable," and that these bumps can temporarily "separate us from our resources." "If that happens," the therapist continues, "you can take this letter out, open it, and remember this time and listen to the advice of the one who knows you best. Remember that you haven't changed as a person and have the same traits and skills that have served you well in the past." Finally, the client is instructed that after he or she uses this particular Rainy Day Letter, the client is to repeat the letter writing process again so that he or she is once again prepared—this time with the experience of recovering from the bumps in the road included in the narrative.

Like the Roadside Repair Kit, the act of writing, reading, and discussing the Rainy Day Letter serves to solidify therapeutic gains and engender confidence. The act of simply carrying the letter around serves as a symbolic reminder of the client's victories on the journey.

Memory Virus.   For seeker/searchers and explorer/experimenters, the Memory Virus task focuses on eliciting and developing the client's knowledge of inherent beneficial traits that serve to enhance both his or her life and the management of the chronic condition. In assigning the task, the therapist suggests that the client "Sometime, before our next session, spend 15 minutes in a quiet place where you will not be disturbed. I'd like you to imagine what it would be like to know that 15 minutes from the time you sit down, your memory would be completely erased. Your task is to use the 15 minutes to write down the things that you would want to remember about yourself. After the primary things such as your family members, the job, and perhaps critical things about managing your condition, what would be most important to recall about yourself?"

Like the first-session formula task, this metaphorical assignment focuses on the important things that the client wants to retain in his or her life. In discussing this task the therapist can point out that it will not be particularly useful to bring nonhelpful memories with the client into the future. For example, failed surgeries, an abusive childhood, or unsuccessful legal battles will be of no use for the client, as he or she builds a new memory in the future. Instead, the client is directed to collect positive traits, personality characteristics, and life skills that will be vital for him or her as he or she builds new memories. These can also include specific things "that work," such as helpful self-care activities, nurturing friendships, and energizing pursuits.

Upon returning with this information, the client and the therapist engage in the EARS process; amplifying usefulness, differences, and meaning that these memories represent. Subsequently, the therapist can suggest "doing" or other metaphorical tasks to make these memories and traits more accessible.

The Fortune Cookie Task. The Fortune Cookie Task is for explorer/ experimenters and recrafters. It requires motivation, commitment, and discipline. In assigning the task the therapist requests that the client, on separate slips of paper, write down every conceivable self-care activity that he or she finds useful. These activities can be identified by the SISH or SCR instruments, previously identified exceptions, scales, and so on. In all cases, however, they should represent activities that the client will find comforting and is willing to do.

The client is then instructed to put the slips in some kind of readily available container. It is suggested that the client choose one, at random, when the situation calls for it. This Fortune Cookie Task need not be restricted only to relapse situations. Indeed, it can be utilized when the client knows that he or she will be helped by doing something different (Walter & Peller, 1994). The resulting framework is a type of self-care fortune cookie jar that contains many of the client's available resources while retaining an element of surprise. Adventurous clients can solicit suggestions from family and friends to enhance the impact of the task.

The serendipity inherent to the Fortune Cookie Task can be quite effective. For example, a client who was experiencing an increased level of pain from overworking randomly selected a slip that stated, "Take tomorrow off." "I was expecting to read something like 'take a hot bath or go for a walk,'" she said. "This was the thing that I was the least willing to do. But I said that I would do anything that came out of the jar, and I'm glad I did. I really needed rest. I went back to work on Monday feeling really great."

This task can be adapted to suit the client's specific needs. For example, the therapist and client may identify time periods or symptomatic symbols that would trigger the task. Additionally, clients can make multiple jars to better suit their lifestyle. These could be jars for weekends, work days, vacations, and so on. The time requirements of the activity may also determine how the jars are utilized. The client may separate activities that take several minutes, several hours, or more than a day.

☐ A Final Word about Experimental Tasks

The clinician is encouraged to construct original experimental tasks that meet the specific needs of her clients. The principles of good task construction are: Tasks should have a high probability of success, always tak-

The Solution Identification Scale for Health (SISH): Pain and Chronic Illness

The following questions may be helpful to consider as you scale your improvement. They may be answered in terms of frequency during the day, week, or globally. Add the items that would indicate, to you, evidence that you are improving.

	Never	Rarely	Sometimes	Often
1. I get enough sleep at night.				
2. I get enough rest.				
3. I am able to enjoy eating.				
4. There are times when I don't notice my symptoms as much.				
5. I am able to maintain my appearance in a manner that is satisfying to me.				
6. I am able to maintain my concentration and attention on activities that are important to me.				
7. I can tell when I am going to have a good day.				
8. I am comfortable with my relationship with my health care providers.				
9. I have enough energy to get through the day.				
10. Even though I am aware of symptoms associated with my illness, I also am aware of areas of relative comfort.				
11. I am able to function adequately at work. (If applicable)				
12. I continue to pursue enjoyable activities, hobbies, and pleasurable pastimes.				
13. I am able to maintain a sense of hopefulness.				
14. My relationship with my partner is satisfying. (If applicable)				
15. I am curious about how my life will unfold.				
16. I feel I am able to contribute to meeting the family's needs. (If applicable)				
17. I am able to enjoy time with friends.				

	Never	Rarely	Sometimes	Often
18. I am able to function adequately at school. (If applicable)				
19. I am able to calm myself when I need to.				
20. I have ways to cheer myself up.				
21. I am aware that it's normal to have periods of sadness.				
22. I have ways of relaxing.				
23. I am satisfied with my life as a whole.				
24. I am able to function adequately at home.				
25. I find life interesting.				
26. My relationship with my children is satisfying. (If applicable)				
27. I am able to carry out self-care to meet my daily physical needs.				
28. I am able to carry out activities necessary to manage my illness.				
29. I am able to ask others for help when I need it.				
30. I get as much exercise as I would like.				
31. Despite the challenges of my situation, I realize I have grown in some ways from this experience.				
32. I am able to distract myself from my condition when necessary.				
33. I have enough energy to do things I'd like to do.				
34. I am able to maintain a good attitude.				

ing into account energy and readiness; they should involve the client's goals, wishes, and desires; and they should be constructed to utilize and further develop the exceptions, positive traits, and resources that are unique to the client. Finally, the clinician is reminded once again why they are called experimental tasks—sometimes they fail. When this happens, we apologize to the client for assigning the wrong task and engage in a dialogue with the client about what might work better next time. Of course, the converse is true when a task is successful. We never take credit for assigning a successful task. Instead, we "blame" the client.

Summary

Solution building in the second and subsequent sessions is the process of "framing in" the foundation constructed by the therapist and client in the first session. The interventions and instruments involved in this process complement the answers to the miracle, exception, and scaling questions from the initial interview. This results in the client generating additional, diverse avenues to meet the challenge of chronic pain and illness. No intervention in the solution-focused tool kit, however, is as important as the resources of the client him- or herself. Enhancing these "natural" resources are solution-focused experiments that enable the client to further develop the solution-building process outside the therapist's office. In the following chapters on clinical hypnosis, further interventions are presented to utilize the client's natural consciousness resources.

☐ References

Benson, H. (1975). *The relaxation response*. New York: Avon.

Berg, I. K., & Miller, S. (1992). *Working with the problem drinker*. New York: Norton.

Charmaz, K. C. (1991). *Good days and bad days: The self in chronic illness*. New Brunswick, NJ: Rutgers University Press.

DeJong, P., & Berg, I. K. (1997). *Interviewing for solutions*. Pacific Grove, CA: Brooks/Cole.

de Shazer, S. (1985). *Keys to solution in brief therapy*. New York: Norton.

de Shazer, S.(1988). *Clues to investigations in brief family therapy*. New York: Norton.

Dolan, Y. M. (1991). *Resolving sexual abuse*. New York: Norton.

Dolan, Y. M. (1998). *One small step*. San Francisco, CA: Papier Maché Press

Eastwood, J. D., Gaskovski, P., & Bowers, K. S. (1998). The folly of effort: Ironic effects in the mental control of pain. *International Journal of Clinical and Experimental Hypnosis, 46*(1), 71–91.

Guralnik, D. B. (Ed). (1972). *Webster's new world dictionary of the American language, second college edition*. New York: World Publishing Company.

Johnson, L. D. (1995). *Psychotherapy in the age of accountability*. New York: Norton.

Walter, J. L., & Peller, J. E. (1994). "On track" in solution-focused brief therapy. In M.F. Hoyt (Ed.), *Constructive therapies* (pp. 111–125). New York: Guilford Press.

Recrafting Consciousness: Clinical Hypnosis for Pain and Chronic Illness

The major turning point in Robinson Crusoe's life on the island occurred in relation to a severe illness accompanied by a high fever. Suffering from what was most likely an infection, Robin experienced a number of vivid dreamlike states. These altered states of consciousness created a powerful experience that ultimately provided him with the insight to abandon his focus on a return to "civilization" and to adopt an attitude of hopefulness in relation to the possibilities that the island offered. Defoe's (1994) description of Robin's altered state directly corresponds with phenomena that individuals experience within a hypnotic trance state: dissociation, hallucination, and time distortion.

Hypnosis, primarily utilizing the resources of the unconscious mind, has had a long and sometimes controversial history within the healing arts. In the last 50 years, however, this treatment modality has made significant strides in its acceptance and utilization in the treatment of individuals suffering from chronic pain and illness. This factor, combined with solution-focused therapy's ability to successfully utilize more consciously oriented resources, creates a balanced therapeutic framework that significantly expands the treatment options for clients suffering from chronic pain and illness.

This chapter briefly reviews the history of hypnosis, its phenomena, and their applications for chronic pain and illness. Expanding on the clinical applications of hypnotic and nonhypnotic altered states of consciousness, we present a three-stage clinical model integrating the work of Milton Erickson and solution-focused therapy. Finally, specific self-hypnosis applications are provided to relieve clients suffering from pain and chronic illness.

☐ Hypnosis: A History of Healing and Sensationalism

Few scientific endeavors or therapeutic interventions have attracted more controversy or sensationalism than hypnosis. Professional and academic realms have yielded spirited theorizing and disagreement about the definition, applications, and efficacy of hypnosis since its modern inception over 200 years ago with the work of Franz Anton Mesmer (Buranelli, 1975). Hypnosis and hypnotic-like interventions have been used since the time of the ancient Greeks to relieve pain and suffering (Lynn & Rhue, 1991). The phenomenon of hypnotically induced analgesia has played a crucial role in increasing the acceptance of hypnosis as an identifiable altered state of consciousness (Chaves & Dworkin, 1996). From its earliest days, mesmerism was employed to reduce or eliminate the most intractable pain. Throughout the first half of the nineteenth century, surgery, childbirth, and even amputations were performed on clients who had been induced into a "mesmeric sleep." During this time, the most celebrated figure of hypnotic analgesia and anesthesia was the Scottish surgeon James Esdaile (Guald, 1992), who practiced in India in the early to mid 1800s. His own writings and numerous reliable eyewitness accounts reveal the details of hundreds of successful surgical procedures using mesmerism as the only form of anesthesia. Observers and the clients alike reported that little or no pain was experienced during or after the procedure. Moreover, surgery performed using mesmeric techniques appeared to result in less bleeding and shorter postoperative recovery.

Hypnosis, as we now recognize it, was significantly advanced in the 1840s through the writings of the James Braid, who began to differentiate between mesmerism and something he called "nervous sleep," which he later termed *hypnosis* (Guald, 1992). Like Esdaile, he was a Scottish surgeon interested in reducing the pain and suffering of his clients. Unlike some of his more flamboyant predecessors, however, he investigated the benefits and phenomena of hypnosis within a formal medical context. After Braid's death in the 1860s and the adoption of ether for anesthesia, hypnosis significantly declined, only to experience subsequent cycles of acceptance and rejection until the middle of the last century. Notably, some of the most important early explorers in consciousness,

Charcot, Janet, Bernheim, Prince, and Freud, to name a few, found hypnosis important in the development of their psychological theories and understanding of the unconscious (Ellenberger, 1970).

The 1950s saw hypnosis begin to reestablish itself as an effective treatment for pain. While clinicians like Milton H. Erickson (1980a) utilized hypnotic analgesia directly with clients, researchers like Ernest and Josephine Hilgard investigated it as a neuropsychological and psychological mechanism within a laboratory setting. Within this setting, researchers have found hypnosis to be effective in reducing or eliminating pain in a wide variety of experimental studies (Hilgard & Hilgard, 1994).

The last decade has yielded significant clinical research in regard to the effectiveness of hypnosis in the relief of pain (Holyroyd, 1996; Montgomery, DuHamel, & Redd, 2000). As a treatment intervention, hypnosis has been shown effective when compared to a variety of other nonmedical treatment interventions for pain relief (Faymonville et al., 1997; Lang et al., 2000). Currently, through modern neuroimaging techniques, significant data are being gathered about neuroanatomy of the hypnotic trance state. Specifically, researchers using single photon emission computed tomography (SPECT) and positron emission tomography (PET) have differentiated patterns activated in a hypnotic state in the cortical areas of the brain (Lamy & Maquet, 2000; Maquet et al., 1999), visually identifying the phenomenon of hypnotic suggestion.

Hypnosis has had its dark side as well. At times throughout its modern history, hypnosis has been mercilessly exploited in a nonprofessional context to a point at which it is credited with everything from sensational miracle cures to profound spiritual enlightenment. Even its originator, Franz Anton Mesmer, was investigated over 200 years ago for sensational claims, by Benjamin Franklin and a French royal commission of scientists (Guald, 1992). Currently, television, films, and books have built the public's expectancy of the mystical power of hypnosis to a point where some clients become disappointed when it does not provide a miracle cure for which they hoped. This expectation factor makes it imperative that the therapist define hypnosis within a clinical context and demystify any unrealistic views a client may have before proceeding with hypnotherapy.

Defining Hypnosis

There is no commonly accepted definition or unifying theory of hypnosis. It has been variously defined as guided imagery, a naturally recurring yet altered state of consciousness, a relaxed hypersuggestable state, a twilight state between sleep and wakefulness, and even role playing (Yapko, 1990). The richness and complexity of the hypnotic experience significantly complicate its definition. Although theories overlap, investigations in the last half of the 20th century are inclined to divide the observation of hypnotic phenomena into two camps. The first, and more traditional, is the view that hypnosis is a special nonordinary state that is noticeably different from normal waking experience. A more recent, alternative perspective contends that the psychological and physical phenomena created through hypnosis are the product of commonly definable psychological, cognitive, and social variables (Chaves, 1997).

Although these views may differ from the etiology of hypnotic phenomena, the vast majority of experimenters and clinicians agree on their existence. These phenomena, characterized by recognizable physiological and psychological shifts in behavior and experience, belong to what Hilgard (1973) referred to as the domain of hypnosis, presented in detail next.

How one defines hypnosis presents serious implications for its utilization by both clinicians and clients. Our view most closely resembles that of Joseph Barber when he defined hypnosis as "an altered condition or state of consciousness characterized by markedly increased receptivity to suggestion, the capacity for modification of perception and memory, and the potential forces systematic control of a variety of usually involuntary physiological functions (such as glandular activity, vasomotor activity, etc.)" (Barber, 1996, p. 5).

By *altered*, we refer to that state of consciousness accessed by the client that is noticeably different from his or her previous, and perhaps less functional, state of consciousness. Often referred to as a trance state (Spanos & Chaves, 1991), this distinct shift in consciousness may be facilitated through the therapist performing a hypnotic induction (heterohypnosis) or through the client's own practices (self-hypnosis). Thus, utilizing this definition, therapists and clients will expect that the process of altering one's state of consciousness will be associated with (partial or complete) relief of chronic pain and illness.

Defining Nonhypnotic Altered States

In addition to formerly induced altered states of consciousness, it is important to acknowledge those informal altered states of consciousness that are available to virtually all clients on an everyday basis. These informal states are particularly relevant to practitioners of solution-focused therapy as they provide naturally recurring exceptions (chapter 6) for many individuals suffering from chronic pain and illness.

Ludwig (1972) commented on the fact that altered states of consciousness (ASCs) have played a significant role in human functioning through out history. In addition to being actively involved in many of the healing arts and practices, ASCs have been critically involved in the expansion of knowledge, experience, and social functioning. Practices such as meditation, prayer, religious conversion, divinational states, transcendental experiences, creative insights, estheticism, and psychedelic-type experiences have been used adaptively (and maladaptively) by virtually every culture.

Weil (1995, p.19) wrote that altering one's state of consciousness is a basic human drive. He observed that children, before the age where social conditioning intervenes in their behavior patterns, commonly spin themselves into "vertiginous stupors." Erika Fromm (1979, pp. 82–83), noting that there are a number of states between wakeful alertness and sleep, placed these identifiable phenomena on a continuum. Between the polarities of simple daydreaming or relaxation states and serious psychotic and hallucinatory activities, she included inspirational creativity, hypnogogic and hypnopomic states, hypnosis, sensory deprivation states, nocturnal dreams, psychedelic states caused by drug use, concentrated and mindful meditation states, states of mystical rapture, shamanistic ecstasy, dissociative states, depersonalization states, and fugue states.

There are similarities between hypnosis and some of the more formally induced states of consciousness as well. Barmark and Gaunitz (1979), when comparing transcendental meditation and relaxation-oriented heterohypnosis, found that both modalities generated similar physiological states. Moreover, both states generated shifts in attentional processes, body image, and the experience of time. Physiological similarities between hypnosis and a relaxation state exist as well. Benson, Arns, and Hoffman (1981) found that neutral hypnosis (that state produced through induction without or before suggestion) and the relaxation response produced similar shifts of autonomic functioning: decreased blood pressure, heart rate, and respiratory rate.

Milton Erickson (Erickson & Rossi, 1979), the originator of the hypnotherapeutic approach (discussed later) outlined in this book, assumed that distinct, naturally recurring altered states of consciousness are experienced by virtually everyone. Believing these beneficial shifts occurred both inside and outside the therapist's office, Erickson assumed that the sensory experience organic to the client was much preferable to one solely elicited by the therapist. Thus, like solution-focused therapists who followed him, Erickson utilized the client's unique recurring sensory and psychological experiences to enhance the impact of his therapeutic interventions.

Integrating Altered States and Solution-Focused Therapy

Key to the clinical approach presented in this book is our view that problem and solution frameworks can be represented as states of consciousness that are distinct from each other. Most important to therapists are the "solution states" that deliberately or spontaneously manifest themselves in the context of the client's daily life. As previously noted in this volume, they present themselves in two major forms: flow and ultradian states. Although they may not directly recognize it, clients suffering discomfort from a chronic condition can experience a number of opportunities to utilize these distinct states on a daily basis. Whether focusing on an enjoyable activity (flow) or letting their mind wander to a past, pleasant experience (ultradian), these states are characterized by a (beneficial) shift in consciousness that can represent significant relief from a painful condition. Consequently, it is the task of the therapist to facilitate the integration of the client's ability to consciously (through solution-focused interventions) and unconsciously (through generating hypnotic phenomena) access these solution states on a consistent basis.

Although perfectly adequate when used separately, integrating the conscious approach of solution-focused therapy with the unconscious tools of clinical hypnosis substantially improves treatment outcomes for clients suffering from chronic pain and illness. The ability to shift into a solution state, most often represented in the form of exceptions, can be facilitated through solution-focused observations of the helpful, naturally recurring hypnotic phenomena. These observations generated by miracle, exception, and scaling interventions can be subsequently supplemented by hypnotic suggestions that recreate the physical and psychological aspects of the phenomena. Working in the different direction, formally induced hypnotic states that separate (employing trance phenomena; Edgette & Edgette, 1995) the client (or client's awareness) from troubling symptoms can be supplemented by solution-focused injunctions that center on observation and utilization of exception states.

This integration is best characterized by the mechanisms involved in answering the miracle question. This simple question beckons the client to consciously suspend his or her current (and often entrenched) experience of the problem state and proactively engage in an imaginary, future-oriented solution state. Paralleling this solution-focused intervention are formal hypnotic techniques that project clients into the future where the phenomena of dissociation, positive hallucination, and time distortion facilitate problem resolution. These interventions, referred to as pseudo-orientation in time (Erickson, 1954), are capable of defeating the despondency and despair so often experienced by clients feeling "at the end of their rope." Milton Erickson, the progenitor of these interventions, was the first psychotherapist to combine conscious and unconscious interventions (Zeig & Munion, 1999) enabling the integration of the clinical interview with formal hypnotic interventions.

☐ The Influence of Milton Erickson

The hypnotherapeutic approach that we utilize in our treatment was initially developed by Milton H. Erickson, M.D. Erickson was one of the most creative and influential investigators and practitioners of clinical hypnosis of the 20th century. He was profoundly influenced by his own personal story of adapting to chronic pain and illness (Erickson, 1983). During his long and varied career, Milton Erickson was generally acknowledged to be the world's leading practitioner of hypnosis. He authored 150 professional journal articles and worked with over 30,000 clients, as well as authoring and coauthoring numerous books. Additionally, he was widely considered a major innovator in the practice of strategic and brief psychotherapy (Haley, 1967). He was the founding president of the American Society for Clinical Hypnosis as well as the founder of the society's professional journal. In 1980, shortly after Erickson's death, the first International Congress on Ericksonian Approaches to Hypnosis in Psychotherapy was held. Attended by 2,000 clinical psychotherapists, this was the largest gathering of clinicians to honor and study the work of an individual therapist. Today, the Milton H. Erickson Institute, located in Phoenix, Arizona, continues to carry on his work, teachings, and research.

☐ Principles of the Ericksonian Approach

Given the numerous current available models of hypnosis, we utilize the Ericksonian approach because of its therapeutic sensibility and respectful approach to clients. In addition to being inspired by Erickson's story, we believe that his approach most closely matches the needs and resources of clients suffering from a chronic condition and chronic pain. Moreover, his focus on the future and facilitation of the unique resources of the client makes the approach a perfect complement to its offspring, solution-focused therapy.

Utilization of the Hypnotherapeutic Relationship

The importance of the therapist–client relationship is well established within the literature of psychotherapy. This relationship is even more critical in the practice of hypnotherapy. How one approaches the hypnotic relationship has a profound effect on the applications and efficacy of the therapy form. Gilligan (1986) wrote that the hypnotic relationship can be characterized by one of three approaches: authoritarian, standardized, and cooperative. The authoritarian approach, popularized in the 19th century and the first part of 20th century, is wholly dependent on the "power" of the hypnotist. A good representation of this approach can be observed in stage hypnosis where audience members often volunteer to do degrading things they wouldn't normally be willing to do, such as "bark like a dog or cluck like a chicken." Unfortunately, although rare in professional practice today, the image of the authoritarian hypnotist seems to linger in the mind of the public.

In the standardized approach, the hypnotic subject is presumed to possess a continuous level of measurable susceptibility to hypnosis. Susceptibility is evaluated through behavioral testing, and subjects are divided into categories ranging from those who cannot be hypnotized at all to those who are "highly hypnotizable" (Evans, 1991). In this approach, primarily developed in experimental laboratories, the subject's ability to achieve a trance state is essentially determined by his or her innate level of "hypnotizability" rather than by the hypnotist's ability. This is illustrated by the fact that hypnotic inductions are often standardized and derived from scripts. Although the phenomenon of hypnotic susceptibility and its laboratory investigation have their merits, we find that this has little practical application in a day-to-day clinical context. It has been our experience that the naturalistic nature of the Ericksonian approach bypasses many of the problems associated with low hypnotizability.

The Ericksonian approach is based on the ability of both therapist and client to utilize their unique resources within a clinical context (Zeig & Munion, 1999). Gilligan referred to this as a "cooperative effort in which responsibility is mutually assumed" (1999, p. 3). Paralleling the solution-focused model, this approach centers on both the therapist and the client engaging in a process in which the client's unique gifts, resources, and abilities are emphasized and utilized. Dolan (1985, pp. 6–7) defined Erickson's utilization approach particularly well: "Utilization is the process of incorporating aspects of the client's current behavior and perceptions, current and past relationships, life experiences, innate and learned skills, and abilities into the therapeutic change process."

Like solution-focused therapy, the Ericksonian approach is goal oriented, emphasizing the identification of resources and taking "the first few steps" toward success (Zeig, 1985). This relationship of shared responsibility, utilization of the client's strengths and view of the world, and engagement of naturalistic phenomenon (discussed next) creates an effective set of intervention strategies that empower clients rather than categorize them. As Erickson and Rossi put it: "The utilization approaches achieve their results precisely because they activate and further develop what is already within the client rather than attempting to impose something from the outside that might be unsuitable for the client's individuality" (Erickson, Rossi, & Rossi, 1976, pp. 20–21).

Naturalistic Approach

Key to Erickson's ability to utilize the resources of his clients was his naturalistic approach to psychotherapy and hypnosis. He believed that a trance state developed out of intrapsychic phenomena that were dependent on the client's unique internal processes (Yapko, 1990). Instead of using a standardized procedure, he tried to tailor each hypnotic induction to specific aspects of the client's life experience and view of the world. This ability to focus the client's attention on a familiar aspect of his or her own personality or real remembered sensory experience served to depotentiate the common conscious process that inhibits successful trance inductions.

Paralleling his naturalistic induction and utilization techniques was Erickson's belief that trance and altered states of consciousness are naturally recurring events in everyday life. He frequently reminded clients of the everyday experience of trance: "Anyone absentmindedly looking out the window during a lecture is experiencing trance with eyes wide open. You are oblivious to the external lecture and your surroundings as you tune into inner realities. Everyone has had that experience" (Erickson et al., 1976, p. 47). Although Erickson differentiated between the experience of trance and the induction of trance (Erickson, 1980c), he fervently believed in the absolute normalcy of the experience (Erickson, 1980d). The ability to adapt to clients on a naturalistic level along with engaging them in conversations about previous experiences in which they were able to inwardly focus their attention substantially reduces problems that the therapist might encounter in terms of their level of hypnotizability.

The Resource of the Unconscious

Erickson felt that the unconscious mind was the most important resource that any therapist could utilize. To Erickson, the unconscious mind was not a metaphorical construct but a very real component of personality. He postulated that this separate level of awareness represented an enormous resource that clients could tap into directly or indirectly through the process of hypnosis (Havens, 1984). He believed that the unconscious existed separately from the conscious mind, possessing mutually exclusive processes of awareness, learning, and response.

The view that unconscious resources can be tapped and operate generatively and autonomously can provide a tremendous resource to a clinical population that is often characterized by feelings of defeat and despair (Lamy & Maquet, 2000). Erickson frequently utilized this division by assigning the resistive parts of a client's personality and history to the conscious mind, and the resources or solving the problem to the unconscious mind. As he explained in many of his hypnotic inductions, "it doesn't really matter what your conscious mind does because your unconscious mind automatically will do just what it needs to" (Erickson et al., 1976, p. 67).

As we've mentioned in other parts of this book, experiencing the struggle of having a chronic condition can generate therapeutic resistance. Utilizing the resourceful unconscious mind not only bypasses resistance, it gives clients hope that they have the power to make a mind–body connection that will be truly useful. As shown in the remainder of this chapter and throughout the next, utilization of this natural conscious/unconscious division can be helpful in the facilitation of clients' ability to break through the barriers to solutions for chronic pain and illness.

Similarities and Differences between Ericksonian and Solution-Focused Approaches

It is no surprise that the solution-focused approach closely resembles that of Erickson, in that its earliest applications evolved out of his work. Both approaches are atheoretical, resource oriented, and brief in nature. Moreover, both focus on viewing the client as a unique individual and expanding rather than reducing the client's life possibilities. Evolving out of this worldview, neither approach relies on diagnostic categories as part of the psychotherapeutic process.

The two approaches diverge somewhat in how they view the nature of change and therapeutic resistance. Erickson often communicated his belief that change was an integral part of human development. Although neither acknowledging nor disagreeing with the relationship between change and human development, solution-focused therapy adopted the Mental Research Institute view that "change is inevitable" (Watzlawick, Weakland, & Fisch, 1974). Similarly, although Erickson believed that resistance was an asset to the therapeutic process and sought to strategically utilize it, solution-focused therapy employs the interview process to bypass it while discovering the client's "unique way of cooperating" with therapy (de Shazer, 1982, p. 14).

One of the primary differences between solution-focused and Ericksonian approaches is Erickson's emphasis on utilizing the client's symptoms to solve the problem (Zeig & Geary, 1990). In contrast, solution-focused therapy uses the client's idea of the solution to address the problem. Furthermore, although Erickson's therapeutic stance was often one of "expert" (although a permissive one), the solution-focused approach strives to assume a "one down" position, looking to the client for expertise in regard to solution (DeJong & Berg, 1997).

Both approaches make extensive use of client strengths. However, Erickson would use his unique observational skills and powerful communication capabilities to (directly and indirectly) identify and inform the client of his or her resources. Solution-focused therapy relies on the client's own observational skills, making extensive use of miracle, exception, and scaling questions to identify and utilize resources. Erickson facilitated the change process by utilizing hypnosis to aid clients in the process of shifting their state of consciousness and potentiating resources. In solution-focused therapy, the interview process primarily facilitates the shift in the state of consciousness from a problem state to solution state.

Significantly, both approaches are infused with optimism and hope. While maintaining a present and future orientation, both approaches utilize an interpersonal therapeutic interaction that clearly communicates to the client that change is possible.

Indications and Contraindications for Using Hypnosis

Before detailing the therapeutic protocols for the initial hypnosis sessions, it is important to identify specific factors and client characteristics that are useful in determining whether the modality might be an appropriate and effective treatment. Fortunately, hypnotherapy is appropriate and effective for the vast majority of the clinical population suffering from chronic pain and illness. In considering its usefulness for a given client, we ask the question, "Would an altered state of consciousness be helpful for this client in this clinical context?" For the vast majority of clients suffering from chronic illness and pain, the answer is obviously "yes." When the answer is "yes," the therapist and client must work to determine what specific hypnotic phenomena will characterize the preferred state. Goal-oriented, solution-focused interviewing techniques (described later) are extremely helpful in determining the characteristic "state" that the client wishes to achieve.

Hypnosis is both a process and an identifiable shift in consciousness to a different state for the client to experience, instead of the painful symptoms. Chronic illness symptoms other than pain can be treated with hypnosis on a complementary basis as well. If these symptoms can be characterized as an (often involuntary) state of consciousness, such as anxiety, depression, hopelessness, and even boredom, hypnosis can serve as a vehicle to transport clients to a preferred state in which they can experience more functionality.

Like most clinical interventions, hypnosis has the ability to both heal and hurt clients (Lynn, Martin, & Frauman, 1996). Although in the vast majority of clinical situations hypnosis is highly effective for treating individuals suffering from chronic pain and illness, it may not serve the client's best interests in a few instances. In addressing these concerns, we begin by stating the obvious: Clients who clearly don't want hypnosis should never be forced into accepting it. Not only does this kind of coercion violate our therapeutic model (and most others) of working with clients, it won't work. Moreover, hypnosis should never be practiced without the client's knowledge. The hypnotic relationship is a cooperative one. We never attempt it without first informing the client of what we are doing. Additionally, hypnosis is not a substitute for appropriate medical care. Although it can be extremely useful for pain management, hypnosis should not be used in lieu of needed prescription medicine.

Past trauma is also of concern in determining the appropriateness of using hypnosis as a treatment modality. We invariably ask clients whether they have suffered any kind of physical, psychological, or sexual trauma. Traumatic experiences often have dissociative, hypnoticlike qualities. In some cases, untreated victims of trauma may access unpleasant past experiences when initially engaging in the hypnosis. If clients have a history of trauma yet are not receiving (or have not received) treatment for this condition, it is generally wise to limit hypnotherapy to highly structured self-hypnosis interventions that firmly establish a secure orientation in the present.

We never work with clients who cannot securely maintain and orient themselves in real time or to their current surroundings. Serious dissociative disorders such as multiple personality disorder, depersonalization disorder, psychogenic fugue, and psychogenic amnesia are conditions that should be addressed and resolved elsewhere before beginning a course of hypnotic treatments for pain and chronic illness. An inability to maintain appropriate boundaries by either the client or the therapist is also potentially problematic. Barber (1998) commented that the qualities of the hypnotic experience can heighten the effect of transference and countertransference for some clients and therapists. Although rare in our experience, the possibility of this kind of occurrence points to the necessity of forming a strong therapeutic alliance with clear boundaries and goals.

The Importance of the Client's View of Hypnosis

In addition to psychological factors, the client's approach to the concept of hypnosis is an important criterion to consider before proceeding. Prior to working with any client in a hypnotic context, it is essential to determine his or her view of hypnosis. Often the client's ideas about hypnosis are derived from inaccurate depictions in the media. Clients may have been exposed to a form of stage hypnosis and view it with some suspicion or imbue it inappropriately with enormous power (Echterling & Whalen, 1995). Moreover, clients may have had the experience of being "hypnotized" by relative or friend. Alternatively, they may have previously been to a therapist who employed hypnosis. In any case, the client's view of the therapeutic modality can be important in successful outcomes. As mentioned in chapter 5, sufferer/victims and seeker/searchers may have unrealistic expectations for hypnosis resulting in their anticipation that change will occur with a minimum of their participation. Because our model is client centered and self-hypnosis is a core component of our treatment approach (discussed later), it is doubtful whether clients who cannot shift to a more realistic view will experience much success.

It is important to find out whether the client has had a previous negative experience of hypnosis. In our practices we have discovered that, paradoxically, some clients who have been abused within professional or nonprofessional hypnotic contexts strangely seek to utilize the form again. We've come across a surprisingly high number of cases in which clients have been sexually abused by relatives and nonrelatives purporting to practice some form of hypnosis. In such cases it is critical for the therapist and the client to discuss whether hypnosis is the most appropriate intervention. If there is a mutual decision to pursue hypnotherapy, it will be important for both client and therapist to discuss the ways in which the current hypnotic intervention will be different from the previous experiences. Key to the success of this pursuit is the therapist's ability to incorporate safety and security into every hypnotic intervention.

Finally, this discussion would not be complete without addressing the controversy arising out of the relationship of hypnosis to the phenomenon of false memory (Loftus & Polage, 1999). Although we acknowledge that such a relationship, on occasion, can exist, the false memory phenomenon has virtually no relevance to our model of working with clients suffering from chronic illness and pain.

There are several reasons for this: First, at no point in the hypnotherapeutic process is it our goal to uncover repressed memories of abuse. Quite to the contrary, our utilization of the hypnotic phenomenon of age regression (described later) is directed at enabling the client to remember times of comfort and security, not trauma and abuse. Second, our primary approach to induction is through the mechanism of self-hypnosis. As a result, the suggestions we employ specifically relate to the client's present and future.

Clinicians who would like more in-depth discussion about hypnosis and memory should consult the excellent American Society of Clinical

Hypnosis monograph *Clinical Hypnosis and Memory: Guidelines for Clinicians and for Forensic Hypnosis* (1995).

Hypnotic Phenomena

Historically, perhaps because the experience of trance is highly subjective, investigators and clinicians have attempted to categorize the various physiological and psychological characteristics experienced through the process of hypnosis. Edgette and Edgette (1995, p.12) refer to the this group of characteristics, commonly labeled as hypnotic phenomena, as "natural behavioral and experiential manifestations of a trance state." These shifts and distortions of time and place, the experience of remembering and forgetting, alterations of perception, and unconscious automaticity primarily involve a dissociative experience that separates one reality from another. Rituals focusing on inducing these phenomena in the hope of relieving pain and ailments have existed for thousands of years (Edmonston, 1986). Using the modern method of hypnotic induction, therapists seek to suggest and utilize these phenomena with the goal of changing sensations and perceptions of clients suffering from chronic pain and ailments.

Nonadaptive Phenomena

Hypnotic phenomena are not always in the service of the client. Gilligan (1999) noted that the experience of dissociation, as well as most of the other hypnotic phenomena, can be involved in nonadaptive perceptions as well. He presented the thesis that the phenomena characterized in psychological symptoms "are naturalistic versions of classical hypnotic phenomena" (p. 21) and can be utilized to aid the client in solving the problem. Echoing Gilligan's sentiments, Edgette and Edgette (1995, p. 27) remarked that "if it's part of the problem, it can be part of the solution." As a reparative strategy, they suggested that troublesome and symptomatic phenomena can be "balanced" by opposing healing, hypnotic phenomena. For example, a therapist treating a client experiencing "amnesia" for her resources might suggest to her in a trance state that she the experience "hypermnesia" for periods of time when she felt particularly competent.

Although it is difficult to directly "reverse" phenomenological experiences of those clients suffering from chronic pain and illness, we have found it helpful to observe ways in which different psychological and physiological phenomena are experienced with the goal of identifying potential opportunities for solutions. For example, clients who appear overly focused on pain in one area of their bodies tend to dissociate from the other areas of their bodies that remain in relative physical comfort. Moreover, people suffering the sameness of chronic illness often experience time to be infinitely elongated (time distortion). Clients experiencing the onset of a particular symptom may panic and negatively experience themselves in the future (pseudo-orientation in time), anticipating and actually creating a state of needless fear. Clients describing the painful symptomatic phenomena often describe their opposite (related) complements as solution states. Examples include the ability to shift focus and attention away from painful symptoms to more pleasurable activities and thoughts; the ability to experience time more productively; and the ability to orient oneself in a more manageable present rather than feeling overwhelmed by constrictions imposed by the illness.

Defining and Utilizing Hypnotic Phenomena

The capacity to recognize, understand, and utilize these phenomena significantly enhances the therapeutic impact of any hypnotic intervention. Whether seeking naturalistic examples of solution states through exception-finding questions, utilizing their presence within the actual hypnotic experience, or employing them in the construction of posthypnotic suggestions, hypnotic phenomena significantly contribute to a successful hypnotherapeutic experience.

Next is a brief overview of the phenomena relevant to the treatment of chronic pain and illness as well as adaptive and nonadaptive examples of their use. Specific strategies for the hypnotic suggestion of these phenomena are covered in the next chapter.

Dissociation.   Dissociation is a meta-phenomenon that serves as a powerful supportive framework for all the other hypnotic phenomena. The client in a dissociated state experiences the separation of mental mechanisms that are generally associated as being bound together. Yapko (1990, p. 285) defined dissociation as the ability to "break a global experience into its component parts, amplifying awareness for one part while diminishing awareness for the others."

Frequently, clients are able to experience a feeling of separateness from a physical experience or a particular injured body part. The hypnotic ability to separate sensations allows for a cognitive awareness of the physical condition while simultaneously providing for a detachment from it. For example, a client needing to have a broken arm set can have knowledge of the injury and the forthcoming procedure while maintaining the ability to separate the sensation of the pain from the body.

On a less adaptive level, clients suffering from chronic illness and pain can focus so closely and intensely on their symptoms that they literally "become" their condition. Clients experiencing this form of dissociation from the whole self can exclude virtually everything else in their lives except the engulfing experience of their illness. Interventions in these types of cases center around exception and scaling questions contained in the solution-focused interview and self-hypnotic techniques (described later) that focus on the whole of the "here and now" experience.

Analgesia and Anesthesia.   Representing different points on the same continuum, analgesia and anesthesia are the hypnotic phenomenon most commonly utilized for pain management. Hypnotically induced analgesia occurs when clients are able to reduce the perception of their pain through the suggestion of the hypnotist or themselves (through self-hypnosis). These diminished sensations are similar to those experienced through the ingestion of chemical analgesics such as ibuprofen and aspirin. Clients generally accomplish this by shifting the focus of their attention elsewhere, away from the pain. For example, they may become inwardly absorbed with a memory or a physical process such as their own breathing pattern. Clients can also shift their focus to external stimuli such as activities visible outside their window or sounds and sensations within their immediate external environment. In any case, the shifting of focus of attention and perception enables the reduction in the sensation of pain.

Anesthesia is distinguished from analgesia in that it is characterized by the ability to have a complete lack of sensation in a particular part, parts, or the whole of the body. Often people pass through analgesia to achieve anesthesia. This remarkable phenomenon was aptly demonstrated by James Esdaile (mentioned already) in the middle of the eighteenth century, when he successfully used hypnosis to create anesthesia in a wide variety of surgical cases, including amputation.

The potentially dysfunctional aspects of anesthesia and analgesia can be found in those clients who use their abilities to reduce or eliminate their level of sensation to the point of ignoring important physical symptoms. This lack of awareness may result in further deterioration of a physical condition. The clinical intervention we apply in these situations is to facilitate the client' s development of an "early warning system" that will enable him or her to intervene earlier in the process.

Hyperesthesia.   Hyperesthesia is a rarely used hypnotic phenomenon that is the opposite of anesthesia. It is characterized by a substantially increased sensitivity to physical sensations. This sensory experience can be quite vivid. Individuals experiencing this phenomenon notice the smallest variation in internal and external sensations. They often can identify specific sensations they are experiencing in areas not usually associated with profound sensation, such as their hair, nails, the tip of the nose, and so on. For the client being treated for chronic pain and illness, this phenomenon represents an opportunity to develop significantly increased (and comfortable) awareness in parts of the body that are not affected by pain, creating an opportunity to shift focus and sensations away from the affected area to a more comfortable region of the body.

Clients who have journeyed through some of the darker parts of chronic pain and illness sometimes experience this nonadaptive phenomenon. This occurs when clients obsessively focus on the minute real or imagined body sensation. They may have experienced such intractable pain that they literally flinch at the proximity of someone's hand. This can interfere with valued experiences of intimacy, in effect constructing an emotional and physical boundary between the client and loved ones. Hypnotic interventions that address this phenomenon employ the induction and posthypnotic suggestion of both analgesia and anesthesia.

Time Distortion.   Time distortion occurs when the client's subjective experience of time is either contracted or expanded in relation to linear chronological or "clock" time. This "psychological" time can be experienced as being compressed or expanded as a consequence of hypnosis and trance. Cooper and Erickson (1982), early investigators of time distortion, discovered that while in a trance state research subjects were able to hallucinate substantially expanded and compressed periods of time.

Frequently, clients report experiencing time distortion for both events occurring within a trance and the duration of the trance itself (Blakely, 1991). They may report a 10-minute induction and trance as lasting 30 minutes or as little as 5 minutes. Given its common occurrence, the phenomenon of time distortion serves as an effective indicator to clients that trance states exist and can easily be accessed as a resource.

Time distortion is invaluable for the therapist working with clients suffering from chronic pain or illness. The phenomenon provides the clinician the opportunity to construct posthypnotic injunctions that suggest that the client can contract his or her experience of time during painful periods and expand it during comfortable ones. This is a common clinical intervention for women in childbirth.

Nearly everyone who has ever been ill has experienced the nonadaptive side of time distortion. Illness and chronic pain may seem to expand time interminably (Charmaz, 1991). Because time distortion happens so naturally in the trance experience, clinicians have many opportunities to successfully address its more adaptive counterpart, suggesting within a trance and posthypnotically that the client can take the opportunity to compress time.

Age Regression.   Hypnotically induced age regression represents a client's ability to experientially return to a real sensory experience from an earlier time in his or her life. Age regression can be a useful intervention—for example, suggesting that clients remember a comfortable time before their illness. This hypnotic suggestion and phenomenon is similar to Benson's "remembered wellness," requesting that the person revisit the comfort of that experience (Benson & Friedman, 1996). Although a useful intervention, clinicians should use the phenomenon of age regression judiciously. As previously discussed, age regression may be contraindicated in relation to clients suffer from posttraumatic stress disorder.

Age regression typically exists on a nonadaptive level in clients who are unable to "leave the past." These clients may have a difficult time in getting past the fact that their bodies no longer work as well as they once did. Interventions for these types of situations range from solution-focused exception questions to self-hypnotic techniques that orient the client in the present.

Pseudo-Orientation in Time (Age Progression).   Pseudo-orientation in time, or, more simply put, age progression, is a phenomenon in which the client experiences him- or herself in the future through suggestions by the hypnotist. Havens (1984) remarked that the utilization of these particular hypnotic phenomena was one of Milton Erickson's greatest contributions. The goal when utilizing this phenomenon is similar to that of asking the solution-focused miracle question. There is one major difference, however. In a miracle question the future is imagined and constructed (in a nonhypnotic state), whereas in age progression the hypnotic subject projects him- or herself into the future and experiences it as a "real" sensory experience. Although not typically useful for those individuals who are suffering a progressive, debilitating condition, pseudo-orientation in time can be quite effectively employed with clients within a rehabilitation context. Utilizing a trance state such that they can experience themselves in the future as healed can be a powerful intervention to engender hope, maintain goals, and "stay on track."

Unfortunately, there are many opportunities for clients suffering from chronic pain and illness to use this phenomenon counterproductively. Accompanying the experience of having a chronic condition are natural doubts and fears about the future. Sometimes clients needlessly panic in the anticipation of a deteriorating condition and have the experience of projecting themselves into a hopeless future. Interventions helpful in countering this phenomenon center around hypnotic and nonhypnotic activities that ground the client in the present, suggesting that he or she "take one step at a time."

Amnesia.   Weitzenhoffer (1989, p. 268) succinctly defined amnesia as "a reversible inability to remember certain facts or events that can be clearly attributed to a person having been hypnotized." He went on to state that the phenomenon of amnesia can be spontaneous or suggested in relation to intrahypnotic or posthypnotic states. This selective lack of remembering is useful in encouraging clients to forget, at least temporarily, painful sensations. Clients remembering past painful experiences often suffer anxiety in the anticipation of their recurrence. This anticipation frequently makes the experience of their pain more severe. Suggesting amnesia for previous painful experiences can be helpful in controlling pain experienced in the present and future. Hypnotic suggestions engage the client's natural ability to "forget the painful part" of an uncomfortable experience. Finally, suggesting amnesia for painful or unpleasant memories within a trance state is helpful in protecting the client from unneeded, painful remembering.

The phenomenon of amnesia becomes counterproductive in situations where clients have a difficult time remembering their resources. This often occurs when the intensity of pain or the anticipation of its severity serves to separate the client from his or her self-care resources and the perspective that the pain might only be temporary. In these cases, the therapist and client develop posthypnotic cues, symbols for safety and security, and therapeutic rituals to reorient the client's perspective.

Hypermnesia.   The complement of amnesia, hypermnesia is a state of consciousness in which an individual remembers an experience in vivid detail. Hypermnesia is actually a subset of age regression and refers to the vivid sensory detail of the actual memory. Edgette and Edgette (1995) distinguished between hypermnesia and age regression in that the latter phenomenon is characterized by reexperiencing oneself in the past. They suggested that this phenomenon is gradually developed with the client, first age-regressing to a previous time and then more fully developing the experience and the associations that naturally rekindle memory.

For example, an individual might remember spending summers at the beach and upon further exploration develop this into a specific memory of a specific day, enabling him or her to hear the sounds that were present, fully experience the kinesthetic sensations, vividly remember the visual details, and even reexperience the tastes and smells.

The phenomenon of hypermnesia can be extremely helpful in enabling clients to more fully develop memories of comfortable and pleasurable dissociation and distraction from chronic pain and illness. Clients developing this ability can be given a posthypnotic suggestion that they can use the phenomenon to recall and utilize these memories for comfort and relief.

Hypermnesia becomes counterproductive in cases of posttraumatic stress disorder when clients revivify traumatic memories in the form of a flashback or hypnotic abreaction. These memories may be of the details of a painful procedure, a car accident, or a traumatic experience unrelated to a physical condition. These types of flashbacks should be treated in a manner that securely and comfortably orients the client to the present.

Ideomotor Movement.   This physically based phenomenon occurs when one body part, usually a finger, hand, or arm, effortlessly moves autonomously and independently from other parts of the body as a result of suggestion. The client experiences the movement as being automatically directed by the unconscious mind. Classic hypnotic arm levitation is a good example of this. The procedure enables the subject to experience his or her arm moving without conscious volition, as if it were disconnected from his or her body. Although these movements are experienced as effortless, they present themselves in a kind of jerky motion, making the experience appear to be all the more unconscious to the client.

Ideomotor movement represents a powerful encounter with the unconscious mind, enabling the subject to experience the classic dissociative split, simultaneously feeling a part of and apart from something. This convincing demonstration of the power of dissociation encourages clients to respond to suggestions that they have the ability to "separate" from their pain and illness, compartmentalizing body parts, movement, and physical sensation as needed. Moreover, it builds confidence that their unconscious mind can operate autonomously and independently for their benefit.

Demonstrating the client's hypnotic ability to separate unconscious movement from the conscious mind, Rossi and Cheek (1986) expanded on Erickson's early work using ideomotoric signaling to access psychobiological sources of problems, reframe their meaning, and ratify therapeutic gain.

Unfortunately, ideomotoric movement can be counterproductive when it exists as a "muscle memory" of a traumatic experience. For example, an individual (unknowingly) driving by the scene of a previous accident may experience small, uncomfortable involuntary twitches and jerks completely outside his or her consciousness. This may also occur in relation to an unconscious association to a previous medical procedure, hospital stay, or painful therapeutic process. Hypnotic interventions for these negative associations center around utilization of a positive associational suggestions of selective amnesia, and orientation to the "here and now."

Positive and Negative Hallucination.   Positive hallucination is the phenomenon of perceiving something that is nonexistent. Its complement, negative hallucination, is the inability to perceive the existence of something in the environment. Both are extremely useful hypnotic phenomena in treating individuals suffering from chronic pain and illness. Representing opposite points on the same continuum, both these phenomena involve altering or abandoning one association or perception to embrace another. Experiencing these phenomena can involve any of the five senses—visual, auditory, kinesthetic, olfactory, or gustatory. The simplest way to suggest positive hallucination is to add a different dimension to a perception or experience. For clients experiencing arthritic hand pain, for example, injunctions suggesting a change in temperature, comfortable catalepsy, on lightness or heaviness can significantly interrupt and change the experience of pain.

Negative hallucination can help clients achieve distance or separation from painful sensory experiences. Using the preceding example, the therapist might suggest that the hand could go into a deep sleep so that it will feel nothing. Alternatively, the hand may be left behind to heal while the client is projected into the past or future in order to have amnesia for the injury. Negative hallucination is useful as well for those clients who must endure painful procedures. Hypnotic suggestions can be made to diminish awareness, sending the affected part to another dimension while the work is being done in order to create selective anesthesia.

Counterproductive examples of negative and positive hallucination should be obvious to most clinicians. In any instance in which these phenomena are experienced in a way that is not beneficial to the client, such as a failure to be grounded in reality, interventions should center on establishing concrete boundaries in the present.

Posthypnotic Suggestion.   Posthypnotic suggestion occurs when a client subsequently carries out an injunction in a nontrance state suggested by the hypnotist during a trance state. Generally, the posthypnotic suggestions are linked to amnesia suggested during a trance state. Clients typically experience posthypnotic suggestions as occurring automatically and without their conscious volition. Using the client's everyday reality, posthypnotic suggestions are constructed to occur within specific time frames, in conjunction with a predictable future or undeniable event, or in relation to a specific symptom. Given that a client's pain and discomfort are invariably experienced outside the therapists office, posthypnotic suggestion is a valuable and often essential tool in treating chronic pain and illness.

For example, within a trance state the therapist might suggest to the client that when he or she begins to experience the first signals of discomfort, "Take a deep breath, sit down, close your eyes, take a moment to engage that comfort that comes from your self-hypnosis exercise." Using solution-focused interview techniques to discover helpful trance phenom-

ena (described later) makes constructing effective posthypnotic suggestions very simple. Moreover, it insures that the suggestion will be appro-
priately ecological and respectful of the client' s view of the solution.

Posthypnotic suggestions can be counterproductive in two ways. First,
on a naturalistic level, when trying to break out of old patterns, many
clients experience (involuntarily) past injunctions from parents, authority figures, and failed relationships. Responding to repeated past statements such as "You'll never be able to do this" or "This will never change,"
they find themselves stuck in a rut of hopelessness.

On a more purely hypnotic level, it is important to insure that clients
do not engage in posthypnotic behavior that would endanger them in
some way. Because the hypnotic experience can be quite literal, language
must be carefully constructed in delivering posthypnotic suggestions. In
the preceding example, it would be prudent to insure that the client not
execute the injunction while driving a car. This is easily accomplished by
building safety factors into all posthypnotic suggestions, delivering the
injunction that they are only to be executed within a safe context.

Three Stages of Engaging Clients in the Hypnotic Process

We employ three distinct stages in successfully engaging clients suffering
from chronic pain and illness in the hypnotic process. These stages can be
represented on a continuum beginning with indirect reference to hypnotic phenomena and ending with its direct suggestion. The first stage
involves utilizing solution-focused interview techniques to elicit, amplify,
and reinforce the naturalistic trance phenomena that clients have experienced in the past. Emphasizing the naturalistic nature and the difference
that these exceptions create sets the stage for more formal hypnotic interventions in the future. Once the client is convinced that helpful, naturalistic altered states of consciousness exist, we employ the second stage—
self-hypnosis (described later). Utilizing the hypnotic phenomena elicited
in the first stage, the modality of self-hypnosis creates a natural bridge to
the third stage of engaging the client in the hypnotic process—
hetrohypnosis. This treatment modality, stressing hypnotic suggestion, is
presented in detail in the next chapter.

**Interviewing for Phenomena: Setting the Naturalistic
Stage.**   Similar to the solution-focused interview, the goal of this stage
is to establish that the client does have the ability to experience different
states of consciousness and the ways in which those phenomena have
been helpful in the past. Moreover, this stage presents a perfect opportu-

nity for the client and therapist to explore the ways in which natural shifts in consciousness are helpful in enhancing the client's ability to meet the challenges of chronic pain and illness.

After explaining our approach to hypnosis and assessing the appropriateness of its application to the client's current problem, we inquire about naturally recurring and helpful states of consciousness that the client may have experienced in the past. This process begins to build a framework in which the client associates naturally recurring states of consciousness with more formal ones that he or she will experience in the therapist's office later. We begin by asking questions about the client's life that reflect his or her general experience of altered states of consciousness. As a rule, we avoid making immediate direct inquiries into the (naturalistic) exceptions the client may have experienced in relation to his or her condition. When this is conducted in a conversational style, clients are relieved of pressure to remember something specific. There are questions about losing track of time, pleasant absorption in an activity, periods of distraction that may stand out in the client's mind.

Answers to general questions of this type begin to orient the therapist to the client's sensory world. Further, they provide basic information about how the client uses imagination, the client's abilities to move from one state into another, and the specific qualities of these states that he or she most enjoys. Information gathered in this context can also be helpful to utilize in regard to suggestions when the client and therapist engage in the second and third stages of the hypnotic context. The act of remembering and describing real sensory experiences also makes it easier for the therapist to elicit specific naturalistic phenomena in the past (in the form of exceptions) that have proven helpful to the client's condition. Once the existence of the client's naturalistic experience has been established, the therapist can elicit examples that are more specific.

Amplifying and Reinforcing the Client's Naturalistic Exceptions. As in the structured solution-focused interview, it is important to reinforce and expand on the helpful phenomena that the client has experienced in the past. This is accomplished by inquiring about the specific sensory experiences from common everyday activities that indirectly represent hypnotic phenomena. For example, we might pose the riddle: "Have you been ever been in a darkened room with hundreds of people for several hours without noticing time passing, the proximity and the sounds of the other people, or the fact that you have been sitting in an uncomfortable seat?" Less important than the client's guessing the answer to the riddle (a movie theater) is the act of illuminating the client's experience of being "taken away" by a movie. Following up on this, the therapist can discuss times when the client lost track of time, was un-aware of physical discomfort, and had the ability to separate from his or her environment and join a different reality.

The converse of this question is equally valuable: "On the other hand, have you ever been a theater watching a movie that you absolutely hated and noticed that time seemed to stand still, there were a number of people talking and coughing, and you felt that the seats were so uncomfortable that you couldn't stay one more moment?" These questions demonstrate to the client that substantially different states of consciousness are pos-sible within the same space.

Naturalistic states of consciousness abound. Other examples include: "Have you ever had the experience of driving from one part of town to the other without really noticing stopping at stoplights or signaling to make turns or operating the gas and brake pedals with just the right amount of pressure? Yet your unconscious mind can get you from one part of town to the other quite safely. Or have you ever been sitting some-where and let your mind wander into a completely different place and really enjoyed yourself?" Alternatively, "Have you ever been so immersed in a book or listening to music that you didn't hear the phone ring or remember to keep an appointment?"

The types of experience, as long they are pleasant, are less important than the meaning the client attaches to them and the differences that they make. For example, does being taken away by a movie make a posi-tive difference in his or her life? Does immersing him- or herself in read-ing or listening to music allow the client to experience an "island" of peace and comfort, allowing him or her to step away from problems for a while?

Incorporating some of the components of the solution-focused inter-view into the hypnotic context is an excellent way to identify states of consciousness that have been helpful to the client in the past. The major difference between interview interventions in nonhypnotic and hypnotic contexts is that the latter focuses on facilitating the client's utilization of his or her unconscious resources, enabling the client to overcome the obstacles and difficulties that may be preventing him or her from attain-ing a goal.

Within the hypnotic context, the goal of the interview is to translate answers from exception and scaling questions into state-specific descrip-tions that more closely parallel the physiological and psychological phe-nomena available to the client within the trance state. In interviewing for these phenomena, exception questions are presented in a two-part ma-trix. The first part repeats the classic solution-focused question, "What happens instead (of the experience of pain and discomfort)?" As in the traditional solution-focused interview, the therapist will want to amplify these descriptions with enhancement questions. Thus it will be important to know *what* the client was doing at the time of the exception along with the specific type of phenomena she experienced; *how* the exception actually occurred; *where* the client was located at the time; *who* else noticed the occurrence; and what *difference* the occurrence of the exception made to the client's condition.

The second part of the matrix involves following up the client's answers to the exception questions with inquiries that focus on the microdynamic psychological and physiological characteristics of the experience. This part of the process provides important information that can be can utilized later in the hypnotic induction, hypnotherapeutic interventions, and posthypnotic suggestions. The goal is to generate information about naturally recurring hypnotic-like phenomena that have relieved the client's symptoms in the past.

Specific attention should be paid to the language the client uses to describe this experience. For example, a client describing feeling comfortably numb, cognitively aware but physically removed from his or her condition, as leaving one's body behind but taking one's mind with her, or having the ability to reduce the pain to a much smaller concentrated area, provides the therapist with enormous resources for suggestions. The following case examples illustrate this.

Three Short Case Examples of Utilization of Phenomena Elicited in the Interview.

Mary, a sufferer from debilitating arthritis, realized in her clinical interview that she completely "forgot" about her symptoms when she was in the park with her granddaughter. When she mentioned that she forgot her pain, the therapist complimented her on her ability to have therapeutic amnesia and wondered aloud what that experience was actually like for her. Mary responded, "It was like I forgot anything else existed in that moment but my granddaughter. I had no pain, no doctors to think about, and my body could do what I wanted it to."

When the therapist asked Mary about other times when she might have experienced this phenomenon, she remembered a time when she was traveling to a doctor's appointment and was listening to some Big Band music on the radio. "When I started out I was really dreading the monthly experience of being poked and examined," she said. "I heard a particular song, 'In the Mood,' and I started to remember the first time I heard it. That was a great time. After a while, I looked up and I realized I was four exits past my doctor's office, even though I know that I looked directly at that exit sign. For just a moment I thought about turning back, but then I thought 'What the hell!' and kept going to spend a great day in the mountains."

After listening to Mary's description, the therapist remarked on the fact that she was able to develop amnesia (for her pain) by remembering something else. "Hearing that song put me right back to that time. It was amazing, " she replied. She continued, describing how she spent the rest of the day in a small Colorado mountain town free from pain, window-shopping, eating in a small restaurant, and conversing with the local townspeople. In subsequent sessions, her therapist utilized the details of these descriptions to enable her to consistently achieve a trance state.

Barbara, on the verge of losing her job because her incapacitating headaches contributed to frequent absenteeism, described "floating away" when she took a bubble bath. When the therapist asked Barbara, "What is it like to have your pain just slip away when you take a bubble bath?" Barbara responded, "The pain just floats away because it has nowhere else to go. It's like I have a head, but I don't. For me it stops time completely. It's as if I can string a hammock between two moments. I figure that because there is no time there can be no pain."

When the therapist commented on Barbara's ability to "stop time," and wondered when else it might happen, she responded, "There is no sense of time after my bath. I even forget to take my pills. If I can get right into bed, I can read or get to sleep easily. Unfortunately, the next day, I know exactly what time it is."

Bob, who had suffered seemingly intractable referred pain in his neck following a major back surgery, described being aware of "nothing but my hands" when he played flamenco guitar at a local Mexican restaurant. His referred pain was quite a mystery to him. "I can't believe it doesn't hurt where I had my operation," he said. Curious about his experience playing the guitar, the therapist asked Bob, "Where do you think the pain goes when you play?" "I don't know," he said. "The only thing I'm aware of are my hands and the sound coming out of the guitar."

"You're not aware of anything else in your body?" the therapist asked. "Absolutely nothing," Bob replied. "My hands just play automatically, on their own. I really don't think of anything in particular. It's like the rest of my body doesn't exist." The therapist asked Bob whether he was able to drive home after playing at the restaurant, with "only a pair of hands." "I've never thought of that," he said. "I always get home safely. My wife says I get right into bed and sleep like a baby but I don't remember driving or getting into bed."

All three of these examples are rich with psychological and physiological characteristics that closely resemble phenomena formally induced in a trance state. These distortions of time, remembering and forgetting, alterations of perception, and unconscious automaticity involve a primary dissociative experience that separates one reality from another. Yet they all occurred without a formal hypnotic induction. Mary experienced the phenomena of age regression (returning to a pleasant time by listening to a song), amnesia (forgetting about the pain), and negative hallucination (missing her exit). Barbara experienced time distortion (time slowing down to a stop so that she could enjoy herself), dissociation (separating from her pain and having it slip away), and amnesia (forgetting to take her pills). Bob was able to experience automaticity of movement (his fingers playing on their own), dissociation (hands separated from his body), and amnesia (no memory of how his separated hands drove him home).

Amplifying and reinforcing the naturalistic exceptions of these clients served to convince them, beyond any doubt, that they were capable of experiencing a variety of altered states of consciousness in relation to their condition. They were further convinced that their ability to shift their consciousness made a difference to their condition.

Thus, interviewing for phenomena acts as an initial, powerful intervention, implicitly acquainting clients with past and present resources that can be utilized in the future. This indirect approach sets the naturalistic stage for the second portion of the process of engaging the client within the hypnotic context: self-hypnosis.

Self-Hypnosis

Self-hypnosis acts as a natural bridge between the first step—setting the naturalistic stage—and the third stage—heterohypnosis—of engaging clients in the hypnotic process. Continuing to inform and assure the client of our naturalistic approach to hypnosis, we present the modality of self-hypnosis as our primary introduction to more formally induced altered states of consciousness. Although some writers such as Weitzenhoffer (1957) and Sanders (1991) stated that clients should be trained in heterohypnosis before attempting self-hypnosis, Johnson (1979) found essentially no differences when measuring the behavioral outcomes in heterohypnotic and self-hypnotic subjects. He was also able to confirm the research of Ruch (1975) indicating that inexperienced individuals are equally capable of achieving a trance state through self- or heterohypnosis. Moreover, he found, not surprisingly, that self-hypnosis research subjects experienced a sense of having more control than their heterohypnotic counterparts.

Defining Self-Hypnosis.   Defining self-hypnosis is almost as difficult and confusing as defining heterohypnosis. Some theorists deem all hypnosis as self-hypnosis (Aroz, 1981; Hilgard, 1977; Spiegel & Spiegel, 1978). Alternatively, Fromm and Kahn (1990) prefer a more research-oriented definition of self-hypnosis in which the experimenter is not present and all suggestions are initiated by the subject after previous training by experimenters. Sanders differentiated self-hypnosis from clinical self-hypnosis when she stated that, in clinical self hypnosis, "The client is given the opportunity to participate actively because the therapist, by providing a safe environment and support to facilitate psychological help by suggesting helpful words and images to which the client ascribes meaning" (Sanders, 1991, p.4).

Our approach requires that the self-hypnotic experience include the following components:

- The client is an active participant in a structured process initially presented by the therapist.
- The structure of the process insures that all suggestions, whether initiated by the client or the therapist, originate from the client's own experience and model of the world.
- All hypnotic experiences are viewed as experiments.
- All frameworks used to teach self-hypnosis are easily replicable outside the therapist's office and actually enhance the client's quality of life.

Key to our choice of this treatment modality is the fact that clients suffering from chronic pain and/or long-term illness invariably experience a loss of control emanating from both their condition and their perceptions of the system that treats it. In addition to returning control, self-hypnosis training begins to inform them that they have the unconscious resources to address their problems. This kind of empowerment, similar to that achieved within the solution-focused interview, demystifies both the process and the role of the therapist while informing the client that he or she will be in charge (and responsible) from the beginning. Utilizing self-hypnosis as a naturalistic bridge substantially reduces resistance to the idea and process of heterohypnosis. Thus, because clients don't have the experience of having "something being done to them," they are more open to embracing a formalized process that may be unfamiliar to them later.

Finally, and most importantly, clients learning self-hypnosis skills have an immediately accessible tool to take home to relieve their condition. Practicing of these skills between sessions significantly shortens the length of treatment.

Self Hypnosis Protocols.   After engaging in a conversation about the clients' naturalistic experiences, we inform them of our wish to introduce them to some self-hypnosis "experiments" before proceeding with a more formal, therapist-directed trance induction. These experiments are typically conducted over two clinical sessions. The following three self-hypnosis procedures are initially demonstrated by the therapist with the client engaging in them after each demonstration.

Therapist-Demonstrated Self-Hypnosis

We realize that some readers may have some difficulty with the idea of therapist-demonstrated self-hypnosis. However, in 25 years of practice no client has ever encountered problems with boundary or transference issues in relation to our demonstration of these protocols. Because the techniques are primarily devoid of any revealing personal information and because they are presented in a completely professional manner, clients naturally accept the normalcy of their therapist "hypnotizing" him- or herself in the office.

Moreover, continuing the naturalistic approach of our work, demonstrating self-hypnotic techniques indirectly informs the client, "If it's safe for my therapist to do, it probably is safe for me to do." Frequently, clients "follow along" during the demonstration, exhibiting an increasingly relaxed state often accompanied by eye closure. It is important to note that therapists need to only briefly demonstrate these techniques while maintaining a sufficient conscious focus. Finally, all of the self-hypnosis procedures illustrated in this chapter can be adapted to and supplement heterohypnotic utilization, discussed in the next chapter.

☐ 54321 Technique

Purpose

The 54321 Technique is excellent for those clients who need to establish themselves in the present. It is particularly helpful in quelling anxiety arising from (realistically or unrealistically) anticipated pain. Moreover, it is beneficial for those individuals who anxiously project themselves into a foreshortened future because of a progressively deteriorating condition. In addition to serving as a good general technique to achieve a "neutral" state of hypnosis, this procedure has the ability to aid clients in shifting their attention from disturbing internal thoughts and sensations to a neutral external awareness, eventually allowing them to return to a more adaptive internal state of consciousness. This is especially true with nonorganic forms of insomnia. Finally, because it involves the client "distributing" awareness over a wide range of sensory observations, the 54321 Technique has proven effective in altering and diluting painful perceptions.

Procedure

The therapist begins by explaining the details of the technique before demonstrating it. It is not necessary or advisable (for the purpose of time) for the therapist to work completely through the technique in the demonstration. The therapist need only demonstrate one or two "rounds" (as follow) for the client to understand the procedure.

1. After asking the client to make any adjustments necessary to be more comfortable, the therapist suggests that he or she need only to breathe normally. The therapist should further suggest that she comfortably fix her eyes on an area in front of her. This technique seems to work best when the eyes and *especially the head* are kept relatively stable and comfortably focused toward the front.
2. Out loud, the client acknowledges five things that he or she sees in her field of vision, followed by five sounds that he or she hears (inside or outside the room), followed by a sequence of five sensations that he or she physically feels. It is important that sense modalities are acknowledged together within their given group, avoiding mixing, for example, three sights and two feelings with four feelings.
3. After the client has finished the first round, acknowledging five examples of the three sense modalities, the client immediately begins the second round, again acknowledging out loud four things he or she see, hears, and feels.
4. The client continues working through "three," "two," and "one," or until he or she seems to achieve a more desirable shift in his or her state of consciousness.
5. When, in the office, the therapist observes the client slowing, or momentarily stopping, it can be suggested that he or she "take a moment to enjoy that feeling for a while." This may be supplemented with suggestions that are relevant to the client (chapter 9).

Case Example: 54321 Technique

To illustrate, we include a short portion of a recorded transcript of Sheila, who suffered from migraine headaches. After a brief demonstration by her therapist, she fixed her gaze outside the office window and began: "I see the steeple in the distance. I see the trees along the creek. I just saw a bird fly by the window. I see the large black building far off in the distance. And I see someone bicycling along the creek."

After pausing a moment to listen to the sounds in the room, she continued: "I hear the clock ticking. I hear the air-conditioning system circulating air through the room. I hear the computer humming." Briefly hesitating while trying to hear a new sound, she resumed, "I just heard the building creak. And I hear a horn honking outside."

In acknowledging the kinesthetic sensations she continued, "I feel the weight of my body in the chair. I feel my arms on the armrests of the chair. I feel one foot crossed over the other on the ground." Again hesitating while accessing another physical sensation, she said, "I feel an ache in my head. And I just felt my shoulders relax a little."

Sheila worked her way through the next round, eventually stopping in the middle of the third round after experiencing a little confusion as to whether she should be noticing two or three feelings. Noticing her slightly bewildered (yet comfortable) shift in consciousness, the therapist suggested that she "take all the time in the world to just hang out with that comfortable feeling until you feel like returning here refreshed and relaxed."

After giving Sheila a moment to fully reorient herself, the therapist asked her whether she would be willing to share her experience. "Well," she said, "I started out wondering how this would help my headaches but then I got involved in noticing different things. At one point, I couldn't keep track of where I was supposed to be and I heard your voice and just gave up and enjoyed it. After a while I didn't notice my head as much. I'm more aware of it now but I know it went away for a while."

The therapist congratulated her on her ability to alter her own state of consciousness and suggested that she practice the technique at home. She agreed and over the next three sessions, supplementing this technique with some heterohypnosis and some other self-hypnosis techniques, made so much progress in managing her own pain that she no longer required therapy.

Important Considerations in Using the 54321 Technique

There are four major considerations that enable the 54321 Technique to be successful. First, it is imperative that clients keep their eyes and especially their heads stationary and oriented to the front when engaging in the procedure. Looking right to notice one thing and turning left to notice another will not work. The general injunction that we have found helpful is to suggest to the client that he or she find a comfortable field of vision to focus on so that the client will not need to shift his or her eyes or head. It is natural and acceptable for clients to shift this focus slightly from one round to the next, but the head should remain fixed.

A second critical factor to make this technique successful is to ensure that the client not rush through the sensory observations too quickly. This becomes evident when a client, perhaps trying to excel at the procedure, rattles off several observations within just a few seconds. When this becomes apparent, it is important for the therapist to interrupt and request that the client start over, taking the time "to really notice the detail of the observation."

For example, the client could notice the coloring on the bird that flew

by the window, or take the time to listen to the pitch of the sound emanating from the computer, or appreciate the degree to which his or her
shoulders drop when they experience that relaxation. If, after this injunction, clients still can't slow down, the therapist can suggest that the
client take a normal breath between each observation. It is important to
emphasize that breathing be normal to avoid hyperventilation. Punctuating the process with deliberate breathing will naturally slow the procedure down to a therapeutic pace.

Another important consideration in applying this intervention is to inform the client that the experience of confusion while engaging in the
process can be quite desirable. This seemingly paradoxical information is
conveyed before initiating the procedure. We inform clients that one of
the goals of the procedure is for the conscious mind to "let go just a little"
while the unconscious becomes operative. In fact, we inform them the
phenomenon of confusion is a sign that the procedure is working.

The conscious mind is exquisite for focusing one's internal awareness
on the phenomena of pain, anxiety, or even insomnia. It does this at the
expense of other sensory experiences that may be available to the client.
Depotentiating the conscious mind through confusion has long been considered an effective technique in shifting internal focus (Gilligan, 1986).
A client (comfortably) experiencing confusion through trance can effectively break that linear focus and shift to a more neutral awareness. Thus,
clients must be reassured that they are "being successful" when this occurs. This information encourages their acceptance not only of self-
hypnosis experiences, but of more complex heterohypnotic interventions
as well.

Finally, clients suffering from chronic pain invariably inquire whether
they should include it (the uncomfortable sensations) in their observation. The therapist should suggest that instead of ignoring bothersome
sensations they should "stop by for a moment, notice what needs to be
noticed, and (with emphasis) move on to other sensations." Suggesting,
at this point, that the client ignore pain is like asking someone not to
think about pink elephants. However, the emphasis of the intervention is
to "dilute" the pain by adding other neutral or pleasant sensations. This
results in the sequential shifting of awareness allowing the uncomfortable sensation to become less figural.

Encouraging Flexibility

In addition to the preceding considerations, there are several other factors that enhance the effectiveness of the 54321 Technique. Generally,
we try to encourage flexibility in our clients and in ourselves in relation

to hypnotic activities. Although clients are encouraged to replicate the activity in the office in a structured way, we suggest that they make any adjustments at home that they might find helpful. For example, they may find it helpful to repeat an observation in the same round. They may want to expand the sense modalities to include gustatory and olfactory phenomena. This would be especially true if they come from a culture that highly values these senses. Some clients find it helpful to increase the number of repetitions or group them together in a different way. Additionally, some clients appear to benefit from multiple repetitions of the structured procedure. Thus, clients reaching "1," but failing to achieve the desired state, should be encouraged to start over again. This, of course, assumes that they deem that this experiment might be useful in relieving their condition.

There is one caveat, however, in relation to adjusting the structure demonstrated in the therapist's office. Clients who experience intense symptoms seem to benefit from adhering to a more strict structure to distract them from their discomfort. This would include individuals suffering from acute pain, extreme anxiety, or severe insomnia. In fact, we have found that the more severe the experience of the symptom, the more the client is aided by adhering to the strict structure.

Given that this particular technique is helpful in treating a sleep disturbance, clients ask what they should do in relation to keeping their eyes open or closed. We suggest that either they can keep their eyes open until they feel like closing them using the available light in the room, or they can close their eyes and notice the patterns that they see on the backs of their eyelids. Alternately, they can keep their eyes closed and imagine what they would see if their eyes were open. Finally, as in all hypnotic procedures, they can combine some of these ideas into their own unique procedure.

☐ The Here–There Technique

Purpose

The Here–There Technique is a structured intervention that encourages separation from current, uncomfortable experiences. It is an excellent method to formally introduce the client to the phenomenon of dissociation. The goal is for the client to begin to shift between states of consciousness while having a successful experience of dissociating from pain, anxiety, and discomfort. Utilization of this technique results in the rapid induction of a state that Dolan (1991, p. 100) referred to as an "associational cue for comfort and security."

Procedure

As in the 54321 Technique, the therapist briefly demonstrates the procedure for the client. In instructing the client, the therapist informs him or her that this technique is similar to the 54321 technique with an "extra twist."

1. The procedure begins with the client observing out loud three to five things that he or she can see in her field of vision, or *here* (as in the 54321 Technique).
2. When the client is finished, he or she is instructed to close his or her eyes and take a deep breath and notice three to five things that the client sees *there*. The *there* in this case is a previous sensory experience that the client has had that represents comfort and security. It should be a real sensory experience that has been enjoyable and pain and anxiety free.
3. After the client has finished making the visual observations *there*, the client opens his or her eyes and returns back *here*, to make three to five auditory observations. Again, after finishing with the auditory portion, the client is instructed to take another deep breath, close his or her eyes, and observe three to five sounds that the client notices *there*.
4. When the client has finished, he or she returns *here* to repeat the procedure with the kinesthetic sensations *here* and *there*. When he or she has completed this round, similar to the protocol for the 54321 Technique, the therapist can suggest that the client might want to spend some more time *there*, "taking all the time in the world and returning back *here* refreshed and relaxed when you are ready."

Further Considerations

Most of the considerations that make the 54321 Technique work apply to the Here–There Technique. These would include encouraging clients to keep their heads and eyes focused forward, to take their time with observations, and to include appropriate, uncomfortable sensations and then move on. In describing their experience of *there*, it is helpful to encourage clients to be as specific about their sensory experience as possible. For example, feeling the sand between one's feet is a much more powerful sensory experience than the description of merely walking on a beach. Clients can be informed of this fact directly and/or observe it in the therapist's demonstration.

This technique differs from the previous one in the actual process of shifting between *here* and *there*. Actively engaging in this shifting process can be quite dissociative, which, of course, is the goal in most pain-management contexts. Also, instead of confusion, clients often experience a desire to remain in the *there* portion of the procedure rather than shifting back to the *here* portion. This is perfectly acceptable; however, if the therapist believes that additional dissociation might be helpful, the client can be encouraged to shift back and forth "just a little while longer." Once the therapist observes signs that the client is sufficiently dissociated, it can be suggested that he or she stay there for as long as he or she needs to.

This procedure relies less on strict compliance with a specific number sensory observations than the 54321 Technique. This is especially true in the *there* portion of the intervention. We have found that three sensory observations appears to be a minimum for adequate development of meaningful details. However, we encourage clients to notice as many things that are necessary to fully immerse themselves in the *there* experience.

Clients sometimes ask whether they can shift to a different *there* location between sense modalities. We have found this to be ineffective and encourage them to stay in one place, or if their *there* isn't particularly useful, to stop and find a better one. The Here–There Technique offers flexibility in its application for both therapists and clients. The therapist can limit it to one "round, " for reasons of time, a desire to combine it with heterohypnosis, or because the client appears to be satisfied with the results.

The procedure also presents an option to continue to subsequent rounds with the client experiencing additional sensory images in the *there* state. Finally, the client can shift to a different *there* after each round. Regardless of which option the client chooses, he or she should be convinced of the ability to "go somewhere else," dissociating from his or her discomfort and associating with a context of calmness at the conclusion of the exercise.

☐ Eye Breathing

Purpose

Eye Breathing is a technique with the goal of enabling clients to rapidly gain an orientation in the present while effectively separating from disturbing thoughts, emotions, and physical feelings of discomfort and pain. Its simplicity and "no fail" protocols are generally successful, even when other self-hypnosis techniques have failed for clients in the past.

Uses

Because of its brevity, therapists and other health care personnel find that Eye Breathing serves as an excellent intervention in circumstances that require an emergent response. Clients find it useful in times of acute pain or anxiety when they feel unable to employ some of the more complex self-hypnosis interventions. As will become apparent in the next chapter, in addition to serving as an excellent general self-hypnosis vehicle, Eye Breathing serves as a reliable bridge between self-hypnosis and hetero-hypnosis. Finally, because it is brief and easily executable, this technique is can be effectively suggested posthypnotically.

Procedure

The therapist suggests that the client get into a comfortable position and breathe normally.

1. The procedure begins with the therapist inviting the client to follow along during the demonstration.
2. Then, with the therapist demonstrating, the client is directed to link his or her eye closure to his or her breathing rhythm. Specifically, it is suggested that the client leave his or her eyes open when inhaling and allow them to close when exhaling. It is further suggested that the client continue this, establishing a distinct rhythm as he or she listens to the therapist.
3. The therapist, visibly demonstrating the action, then falls silent, giving the client a few moments to get breathing and eye closure in synchro-nization.
4. Observing this synchronization and minimal shifts in the client's ex-ternal state (slowing of breathing, muscle tension, reduction in body movement, etc.), the therapist suggests that the client, while continu-ing to synchronize breathing and eye closure, inhale a color. The thera-pist suggests that the color be one that the client finds soothing and even healing, adding, "It can be any color at all, just as long as it rep-resents the kind of peacefulness and comfort you are looking for."
5. Again, after observing minimal shifts in the client's external behavior and giving the client a few moments to comfortably add the color to the process, the therapist suggests that the client consider coloring the breath that he or she is exhaling as well. "But," the therapist suggests, "it might be helpful for you to choose a color that represents some-thing that you would like to eliminate. Many people like to assign a toxic color to their exhalation."

6. After giving the client a few more moments to establish a rhythm, the therapist summarizes the procedure by saying something like "At this point you can comfortably allow your eyes to remain open when you inhale that healing color and close your eyes when you are ready to exhale that toxic color. Why don't you take a few moments to enjoy your ability to bring in the good and eliminate the bad? You can return here comfortable, refreshed, and relaxed when you're ready."

Further Considerations

There are several factors to keep in mind to insure that this technique will be successful. First, clients are instructed to breathe normally. Excessively deep breathing can cause hyperventilation. Second, if clients wish to reverse the order of the rhythm, closing their eyes on the inhale and opening them on the exhale, they should be encouraged to do so. The most critical factor is that they engage in a rhythmic pattern capable of distracting them from an uncomfortable experience.

Eye Breathing has proven effective in emergency medical contexts and when a client's pain and anxiety are so overwhelming that other hypnotic interventions may prove too lengthy and complex. When using this technique in acute situations, however, care providers need not worry about suggesting that the client "color" the breath. Simply maintaining eye contact, speaking in a calm voice, and gently engaging the client in the process should be sufficient.

Finally, because this particular technique is useful in emergency situations, it is important that the therapist "pace" the client's physical experience. Discussed in more detail in the next chapter, pacing is simply a process of feeding part of clients' sensory experience back to them. In clients suffering from immediate and acute anxiety or physical pain, it is important for the therapist to verbally acknowledge the client's situation and environment while simultaneously attempting to interrupt the pattern of the discomfort. Specific examples are presented in the next chapter.

Fractionation

The process of suggesting that clients open and close their eyes in the last two self-hypnotic interventions serves two purposes. First, it provides a reliable procedure for the client to "check back in" with both the therapist and the client's present reality. This can prove especially reassuring to those clients experiencing hypnosis and trance for the first time, allowing them to safely dissociate.

Second, the procedure serves to introduce fractionation to the client's hypnotic experience. Fractionation is a method used in heterohypnosis to increase trance depth through a series of consecutive inductions, each subsequently followed by reorientation, and followed by further reinduction of a trance state (Weitzenhoffer, 1989). Thus, the technique of "checking in and checking out" can effectively provide the client with a valuable way of deepening his or her trance.

It is important for both clients and therapists to understand that trance is a dynamic, not static, experience. Clients frequently report this nonlinear state as one of feeling themselves, at times, deeply in trance and, at other times, not in a trance all. Edgette and Edgette (1995, p. 282) rightly pointed out that when clients initially produce hypnotic phenomena, the experience may tend to "lighten" the trance and have an orienting response. Therefore, the experience of fractionation "paces" the client's natural experience of the varying depth of the trance experience.

Reorientation

Reorientation, variously referred to as dehypnotizing or disengaging the client from trance, is a relatively simple process in all forms of hypnosis. It is simply the process of (gently) inviting the client to return from his or her altered state of consciousness. Maintaining a context of self-determination, the therapist suggests to the client that he or she can "return back here when you're ready, at your own pace, refreshed, relaxed, and energized." It is further suggested that "once you're back here, there is no reason to say anything until you're ready."

The speed of reorientation will vary considerably between clients. The therapist can facilitate a client's reorientation in those rare cases where the process appears to be exceedingly slow. After giving the client a period to reorient, the therapist can direct him or her to notice the immediate environment, suggesting, "You can become more aware of the sound of my voice, the fact that you have been sitting in the same position for a while, and the sounds in the room." Continuing, "Perhaps you would like to stretch, move around a little, or become curious about what's on the other side of your eyelids."

After giving the client a little more time, the therapist can continue to feed back cues from the client's immediate environment, raising his or her voice slightly. This can be complemented by slowly counting to 10, suggesting that the client can increase his or her awareness with each numeric progression. Touching a client should be a last resort and should only be done after informing the client ahead of time. We repeat that reorientation problems occur extremely infrequently, and in our combined 60 years of practice, we have never been required to touch a client in the course of reorientation.

Post-Reorientation Discussion

When the client appears to be fully reoriented—engaging in eye contact, conscious body movement, and logical conversation—the therapist can ask some general questions about the client's experience. However, asking too many specific questions may depotentiate the value of the experience. Generally, asking whether there "is anything that you want to share about your experience" is sufficient. The critical factor in any post-reorientation discussion is reinforcing the client's experience of the hypnotic process. Even small phenomena such as temporarily losing track of the therapist's voice or "just slipping away for a while" can be framed within a hypnotic context. If the client found the process helpful, it is important to discuss the different possible contexts in which he or she might apply it in the future. In recounting the client's experience, it is valuable for the therapist to listen to the way the client describes his or her shift in consciousness. For example, the client may describe him- or herself "leaving my body for a while," or enjoying it so much "I didn't want to come back," or "not really sure where I went to while I forgot about my pain." Noting the language of these descriptions, the therapist can later use them in facilitating further hypnotic utilization or in a self-hypnosis task assignment that the client can accomplish outside the office.

☐ Sending Self-Hypnosis Home

Once the client has learned any of these techniques, he or she can be assigned to experiment with it between sessions. As a rule, we suggest that the client practice self-hypnosis techniques in a variety of contexts. Thus, it is important to stress that the client not wait for a particularly painful or stressful situation to employ it. In fact, it will be preferable for the client to practice it in relatively stable circumstances, enabling him or her to become familiar with its benefits under stress-free conditions.

If the therapist and client wish to immediately employ a technique in relation to acute or chronic pain, time and care should be taken in the office to insure its efficacy first. That is, the therapist should directly observe and inquire about its effectiveness. This can be supplemented by employing scaling procedures measuring its effectiveness in regard to relieving specific symptoms. This can be followed by a discussion about the technique, which can amplify and reinforce its use.

No single self-hypnotic intervention works for every client. As discussed in the previous chapter, framing these assignments as simply an experiment allows the client who doesn't profit from a particular intervention to quickly move on and attempt something that might prove more useful. Even though the interventions presented in this chapter and the next have generally proven to be quite successful, they will not be effective in every case. When this occurs, it is important for the therapist to take responsibility for the lack of efficacy of the experiments, thereby releasing clients from feeling that they have "failed once again."

A Final Word on Self-Hypnosis: The Role of Suggestion

The self-hypnotic interventions presented in this chapter may or may not be accompanied by suggestion. This may be an important distinction when treating some individuals suffering from chronic pain and illness. Although the vast majority of clients desire the suggestive benefits of clinical hypnosis, some religions and cultural traditions strictly prohibit its practice. Likewise, hypnosis as a clinical intervention may be controversial within some agencies or clinics. In these cases, we suggest that the practitioner engage these interventions without utilizing any process of suggestion. Given that, by definition, hypnosis is a suggestive therapy, the absence of formal suggestion eliminates the implication of (perceived) therapeutic manipulation that a particular group might find objectionable.

In cases where hypnosis may be considered controversial, clients and other concerned parties are notified of this distinction from the beginning. We inform them that clinical activities that do not contain suggestion, by their nature, can't be considered hypnosis. Instead, the authors, working and teaching in various contexts and countries over the years, have variously labeled these interventions as relaxation exercises, self-soothing procedures, and developing an ability to "walk away from it all."

Specific suggestion strategies within a self-hypnotic and heterohypnotic context are outlined in detail in the next chapter. For those clinicians seeking written material to recommend to their clients in regard to self-hypnosis, we suggest Alman and Lambrou's (1992) excellent *Self-Hypnosis: The Complete Manual for Health and Self-Change* and *Self-Hypnosis Plain and Simple* (Simkins, & Simpkins, 2001).

☐ Summary

This chapter has presented the first two stages of successfully engaging clients suffering from pain and chronic illness in the hypnotic process.

The first stage utilizes many of the interview techniques developed in solution-focused therapy to discover and utilize the hypnotic phenomena for change. Using the clinical interview integrates the naturalistic principles and practices of Milton H. Erickson with more formal hypnotic interventions.

This integration sets the stage for the second stage of engaging clients in the hypnotic process—self-hypnosis. Employing the naturalistic experience of the hypnotic phenomena, self-hypnosis utilizes the client's unconscious resources to directly address symptoms arising from a chronic illness or condition. Upon mastering the ability to alter his or her own state of consciousness, the client is ready to engage in the third stage and final stage of clinical intervention: hypnotic and posthypnotic suggestion, presented in the following chapter.

☐ References

Alman, B. M.,& Lambrou, P. (1992). *Self-hypnosis: The complete manual for health and self-change* (2nd ed.). New York: Brunner/Mazel.

American Society of Clinical Hypnosis Committee on Hypnosis & Memory. (1995). *Clinical hypnosis and memory: Guidelines for clinicians and for forensic hypnosis.* Des Plaines, IL: American Society of Clinical Hypnosis Press.

Aroz, D. L. (1981). Negative self-hypnosis. *Journal of Contemporary Psychotherapy, 12*(1), 45–52.

Barber, J. (1996). A brief introduction to hypnotic analgesia. In J. Barber (Ed.), *Hypnosis and suggestion in the treatment of pain: A clinical guide* (pp. 3–32). New York: W. W. Norton.

Barber, J. (1998). When hypnosis causes trouble. *International Journal of Clinical and Experimental Hypnosis, 46*(2), 157–169.

Barmark, S. M., & Gaunitz, S. C. (1979) Transcendental meditation and heterohypnosis as altered states of consciousness. *International Journal of Clinical and Experimental Hypnosis, 37*(3), 227–239.

Benson, H., & Friedman, R. (1996). Harnessing the power of the placebo effect and renaming it "remembered wellness." *Annual Review of Medicine, 47,* 193–199.

Benson, A. H., Arns, P. A., & Hoffman, J. W. (1981). The relaxation response and hypnosis. *International Journal of Clinical and Experimental Hypnosis, 35*(3), 259–270.

Blakely, T. A. (1991). Orientation in time: Implications for psychopathology and psychotherapy. *American Journal of Clinical Hypnosis, 34*(2), 100–110.

Buranelli, V. (1975). *The wizard of Vienna: Franz Anton Mesmer.* New York: Coward, McCann, & Geoghegan.

Charmaz, K. (1991). *Good days, bad days: The self in chronic illness and time.* New Brunswick, NJ: Rutgers University Press.

Chaves, J. F (1997). The state of the "state" debate in hypnosis: A view from the cognitive—behavioral perspective. *International Journal of Clinical and Experimental Hypnosis, 45*(3), 280–290.

Chaves, J. F., & Dworkin, S. F.(1996). Hypnotic control of pain: Historical perspectives and future prospects. *International Journal of Clinical and Experimental Hypnosis, 45*(4), 356–376.

Cooper, L., & Erickson, M. H. (1982). *Time distortion in hypnosis: An experimental and clinical investigation* (2nd ed.). New York: Irvington.

Defoe, D. (1994). *Robinson Crusoe*. London: Everyman. (Original work published 1719.)

DeJong, P., & Berg, I. K. (1997). *Interviewing for solution*. Pacific Grove, CA: Brooks/Cole.

de Shazer, S. (1982). *Patterns of brief family therapy: An ecosystemic approach*. New York: Guilford.

Dolan, Y. (1985). *A path with a heart: Ericksonian utilization with resistant and chronic clients*. New York: Brunner/Mazel.

Dolan, Y. (1991). *Resolving sexual abuse: Solution-focused therapy and Ericksonian hypnosis for adult survivors*. New York: W. W. Norton.

Echterling, L. G., & Whalen, J. (1995). Stage hypnosis and public lecture effects on attitudes and beliefs regarding hypnosis. *American Journal of Clinical Hypnosis, 38*(1), 13–21.

Edgette, J. H., & Edgette, J. S. (1995) *The handbook of hypnotic phenomena in psychotherapy*. New York: Brunner/Mazel.

Edmonston, W. E. (1986). *The induction of hypnosis*. New York: John Wiley & Sons.

Ellenberger, H. F. (1970). *The discovery of the unconscious: The history and evolution of dynamic psychiatry*. New York: Basic Books.

Erickson, M. H. (1954). Pseudo-orientation in time as a hypnotherapeutic procedure. *Journal of Clinical and Experimental Hypnosis, 2*, 261–283.

Erickson, M. H. (1980a). An introduction to the study and application of hypnosis for pain control. In E. L. Rossi (Ed.), *The collected papers of Milton H. Erickson: Innovative hypnotherapy* (Vol. 4, pp. 237–245). New York: Irvington.

Erickson, M. H. (1980b). Basic psychological problems in hypnotic research. In E. L Rossi (Ed.), *The collected papers of Milton H. Erickson: Innovative hypnotherapy* (Vol. 2, pp. 340–353). New York: Irvington.

Erickson, M. H. (1980c). Hypnotic psychotherapy. In E. L Rossi (Ed.), *The collected papers of Milton H. Erickson: Innovative hypnotherapy* (Vol. 4, pp. 35–48). New York: Irvington.

Erickson, M. H. (1980d). Naturalistic techniques of hypnosis. In E. L Rossi (Ed.), *The collected papers of Milton H. Erickson: Innovative hypnotherapy* (Vol. 2, pp. 168–176). New York: Irvington.

Erickson, M. H. (1983). Healing in hypnosis. In R. L. Rossi, M. O. Ryan, & F. A. Sharp (Eds.), *The seminars, workshops, and lectures of Milton H. Erickson* (Vol. 1). New York: Irvington.

Erickson, M. H., Rossi, E. L., & Rossi, S. I. (1976). *Hypnotic realities : The induction of clinical hypnosis and forms of indirect suggestion*. New York: Irvington.

Evans, F. J. (1991). Hypnotizability: Individual differences in dissociation and the flexible control of psychological processes. In S. J. Lynn & J. W. Rhue (Eds.), *Theories of hypnosis: Current models and perspectives* (pp. 144–168). New York: Guilford Press.

Faymonville, M. E., Manbourg, P. H., Joris, J., Vrijens, B., Fissette, J., Albert, A., & Lamy, M. (1997). Psychological approaches during conscious sedation. Hypnosis versus stress reducing strategies: A prospective randomized study. *Pain, 73*, 361–367.

Fromm, E. (1979). The nature of hypnosis and other altered states of consciousness: An ego psychological theory. In E. Fromm & R. E. Shor (Eds.), *Hypnosis: Developments in research and new perspectives* (2nd ed., pp. 81–104). New York: Aldine.

Fromm, E., & Kahn, S. (1990). *Self-hypnosis: The Chicago paradigm*. New York: Guilford Press.

Gilligan, S. (1986). *Therapeutic trances: The cooperation principle in Ericksonian hypnotherapy*. New York: Brunner/Mazel.

Gilligan, S. G. (1999). *The legacy of Milton Erickson, M.D.: Selected papers of Stephen Gilligan*. New York: W. W. Norton.

Guald, A. (1992). *A history of hypnotism*. Cambridge: Cambridge University Press.

Haley, J. (Ed.). (1967). *Advanced techniques of hypnosis and therapy: Selected papers of Milton H. Erickson, M.D.* New York: Grune & Stratton.

Havens, R. A. (1984). *The wisdom of Milton H. Erickson*. New York: Irvington.

Hilgard, E. R. (1973). The domain of hypnosis with some comments on alternative paradigms. *American Psychologist, 28*, 972–982.

Hilgard, E. R. (1977). *Divided consciousness: Multiple controls in thought and action.* New York: Wiley.

Hilgard, E. R., & Hilgard, J. R. (1994). *Hypnosis and the relief of pain* (rev. ed.). New York: Brunner/Mazel.

Holyroyd, J.(1996). Hypnotic treatment for clinical pain: Understanding why hypnosis is useful. *International Journal of Clinical and Experimental Hypnosis, 44*(1), 33–51.

Johnson, L. S. (1979). Self-hypnosis: Behavioral and phenomenological comparisons with hetrohypnosis. *International Journal of Clinical and Experimental Hypnosis, 37*(3), 242–263.

Lamy, M., & Maquet, P. (2000). Neural mechanisms of antinociceptive effects of hypnosis. *Anesthesiology, 92*(5), 1257–1267.

Lang, E. V., Bentotsch, E. G., Flick, L. J., Lutgendorph, S., Berbaum, M. L., Berbaum, K. S., Logan, H., & Spiegal, D. (2000). Adjunctive non-pharmacological analgesia for invasive medical procedures: A randomized trial. *Lancet, 29*, 355(9214), 1486–1490.

Loftus, E. F., & Polage, D. C. (1999). Repressed memories. When are they real? How are they false? *Psychiatric Clinics of North America, 22*(1), 61–70.

Ludwig, A. M. (1972). Altered states of consciousness. In C. T. Tart (Ed.), *Altered states of consciousness* (pp. 11–24). New York: Anchor Press.

Lynn, S. J., Martin, D. J., & Frauman, D. C. (1996). Does hypnosis pose special risks for negative effects? A master class commentary. *International Journal of Clinical and Experimental Hypnosis, 44*(1), 7–19.

Lynn, S. J., & Rhue, J. W. (1991). Theories of hypnosis: An introduction. In S. J. Lynn & J. W. Rhue (Eds.), *Theories of hypnosis: Current models and perspectives* (pp. 1–15). New York: Guilford Press.

Maquet, P., Faymonville, M., Degueldre, C., Delfiore, G., Franck, G., Luxen, A., & Lamy, M. (1999). Functional neuroanatomy of hypnotic state. *Biological Psychiatry, 45*, 327–333.

Montgomery, G. H., DuHamel, K. N., & Redd, W. H. (2000). A meta-analysis of hypnotically induced analgesia: How effective is hypnosis? *International Journal of Clinical and Experimental Hypnosis, 48*(2), 138–153.

Rossi, E. L., & Cheek, D. B. (1986). *Mind–body therapy: Methods of ideodynamic healing in hypnosis.* New York: Norton.

Ruch, J. C. (1975). Self-hypnosis: The result of hetrohypnosis or vice versa? *International Journal of Clinical and Experimental Hypnosis, 23*, 282–304.

Sanders, S. (1991). *Clinical self-hypnosis: The power of words and images.* New York: Guilford Press.

Simpkins, C. A., & Simpkins, A. (2001). *Self-hypnosis plain and simple.* Boston: Journey Additions.

Spanos, N. P., & Chaves, J. F. (1991). History and historiography of hypnosis. In S. J. Lynn & J. W. Rhue (Eds.), *Theories of hypnosis: Current models and perspectives* (pp. 43–78). New York: Guilford Press.

Spiegel, H., & Spiegel, D. (1978). *Trance and treatment: The clinical uses of hypnosis.* New York: Basic Books.

Watzlawick, P., Weakland, J., & Fisch, R. (1974). *Change: Principles of problem formation and problem resolution.* New York: Norton.

Weil, A. (1995). *The natural mind: An investigation of drugs and the higher consciousness* (2nd ed.). Boston: Houghton Mifflin.

Weitzenhoffer, A. M. (1957). *General techniques of hypnosis.* New York: Grune & Stratton.

Weitzenhoffer, A. M. (1989). *The practice of hypnotism* (Vol. 1). New York: Wiley.

Yapko, M. (1990). *Trancework*. New York: Brunner/Mazel.

Zeig, J. (1985). *Experiencing Erickson: An introduction to the man and his work*. New York: Brunner/Mazel.

Zeig, J. K., & Geary, B. B. (1990). Seeds of strategic and interactional psychotherapies: The seminal contributions of Milton Erickson. *American Journal of Clinical Hypnosis, 33*(2), 105–113.

Zeig, J. K., & Munion, W. M. (1999). *Milton H. Erickson*. London: Sage.

Suggestive Therapeutics: Hypnotic and Posthypnotic Suggestions to Treat Chronic Pain and Illness

The experience of Robinson Crusoe's altered state of consciousness (arising from his severe illness) affected him throughout the remainder of his stay on the island. His experiences within this trancelike state continued to influence him long after he recovered from his illness. He would recall the messages that he received in this unconscious experience in a variety of ways as he recrafted his life on the island. These messages, in the form of unexpected insights, reminded him of the importance of maintaining hope and exploring the possibilities that the island presented to him on a daily basis.

Robin's experience of the process of the spontaneous insertion of useful insights into his consciousness closely resembles the ways in which clients experience hypnotic and posthypnotic suggestion. From its earliest origins, hypnosis has proven to be an effective framework for delivering therapeutic suggestions to clients suffering from illness, distress, and discomfort (Edmonston, 1986). Because their (frequently noxious) symptoms are often in the forefront of their sensory and emotional focus, however, clients suffering from chronic pain and illness can present a particularly formidable task to the clinician utilizing hypnosis as an intervention. The clinician can meet this challenge through the effective utilization of hypnotic and posthypnotic suggestion.

This chapter presents principles, components, and techniques of hypnotic suggestion, along with ways to integrate them into the self-hypnosis protocols presented in the preceding chapter. Specifically, a clinical intervention framework for hypnotic and posthypnotic suggestions is presented. This framework is represented by a continuum of suggested strategies ranging from Erickson's microdynamics of pacing and leading to direct behavioral injunctions that provide relief to clients suffering from chronic pain and illness. Additionally, strategies for posthypnotic suggestion are presented with specific applications that address time-, symptom-, and event-related contingencies common to this clinical population. These principles and techniques are illustrated by lengthy case examples.

☐ Defining Hypnotic Suggestion

Hypnotic suggestion is a specific form of therapeutic communication that occurs within the context of a hypnotic trance or induction. In effect, the presence of suggestion is the major factor that differentiates hypnosis from other therapeutic interventions, such as relaxation and meditation, which also involve an altered state of consciousness. Hypnotic suggestions are invitations from the hypnotist to the client to (beneficially) alter his or her current experience. This alteration may be suggested in the form of a change in sensory experience or perception (e.g., your arm is getting numb), a modification of a behavior or an emotional state (e.g., "As your breathing becomes more regular your anxiety will decrease"), or a shift in perspective or conceptualization (e.g., "You can experience the pain as being outside your body"). Posthypnotic suggestions differ from hypnotic suggestions only in their proposition that these therapeutic alterations occur at a future time, *after* the hypnotic session (e.g., "When that pain begins to sneak back into your arm, you can remember to allow the numbness you are experiencing now to reoccur").

☐ A Framework for Maximizing Hypnotic Suggestions

A number of factors maximize the success of hypnotic and posthypnotic suggestions. The rapport building and cooperative utilization strategies outlined in the three preceding chapters are equally critical to maximizing the possibilities for hypnotic suggestions. Additionally, it is important for the therapist to (verbally and nonverbally) create a context of positive expectancy in regard to the beneficial possibilities that exist for the client within the hypnotic process. This is accomplished by the therapist exhibiting confidence in the process as well as by communicating a belief in the client's ability to productively use his or her resources for change. Equally important are the ways in which the therapist wordlessly communicates a belief that the client can change through compassionate facial expressions, gentle yet hopeful sounding voice tone, and a demeanor of respect and positive regard for the client.

Key to the success of therapeutic suggestions is their direct relationship to the goals of the client. As previously stated, the description of the phenomena involved in these goals is best developed through solution-focused miracle, exception, and scaling questions outlined in previous chapters. Moreover, following the solution-focused model of intervention, success is considerably enhanced when hypnotic suggestions represent the presence of positive phenomena rather than the absence of negative ones. Largely, this is accomplished by suggesting specific positive phenomena that alter or replace the noxious symptoms that the client is experiencing. Consequently, instead of directing the client to experience the disappearance of a throbbing ache in an arm, the therapist might suggest that the client remember the comfortable sensation of the arm floating in the water from past summer vacations at the shore. Or it might be suggested that the client experience the movement of the pain to another (less sensitive) part of the body. Alternatively, the client might experience a pleasurable sensation in another part of the body, enabling him or her to have amnesia for pain in the more affected part of the body.

☐ The Microdynamics of Effective Hypnotic Suggestions: An Ericksonian Approach

One of Milton Erickson's major contributions to hypnosis was the way in which he applied the microdynamics of hypnotic induction and trance to enhance suggestive therapeutic communication. The vast majority of his hypnotic communications was suggestive. As Weitzenhoffer (1989b, p. 6) stated, "For post-traditional hypnotism, best exemplified by Ericksonian hypnotism, suggestive effects and hypnosis are inseparable." For Erickson, hypnotic and posthypnotic suggestions ranged from the minutest alteration in the client's experience to grand interventions requiring the client's complete and focused attention. In particular, perhaps due to his own daily bout with pain, he developed a variety of approaches to pain and illness integrating the hypnotic phenomena along with the client's resources (Erickson & Rossi, 1979).

Nonetheless, even the most basic of techniques would have been less successful if it were not for his unique ability to establish rapport with even the most "resistant clients." Key to Erickson's suggestive strategies was his method of selecting a portion of the client's ongoing experience and communicating it back to the client, or pacing (Bandler & Grinder, 1975). This process of matching a portion of the client's (current) experience instilled comfort and confidence in his clients, enabling him to successfully propose a wide variety of hypnotic suggestions otherwise known as leading. Thus, Erickson continually interwove these processes, ultimately constructing a hypnotic framework that the vast majority of his clients accepted.

☐ Pacing

Building sufficient rapport to initially engage the client in an induction is critical to all the hypnotic communication that follows. Pacing in hypnosis parallels the respectful and client-centered interview techniques originating from solution-focused therapy. Both center on the acknowledgment of the validity of client's own real-world experience with the aim of creating a cooperative framework of associations between client and therapist that Erickson and Rossi referred to as the "yes set" (Erickson, Rossi, & Rossi, 1976).

Weitzenhoffer (1989a, p. 52) succinctly defined pacing as the process of "feeding back to the subject, directly or indirectly, verbally or nonverbally, factual data regarding what is currently going on with regard to his overt and covert behavior." These familiar and undeniable associations enable clients to quickly gain a comfort level with the hypnotic process while becoming more open to the suggestions of the hypnotist. Thus, internally processing familiar sensory and psychological experiences enables clients to unconsciously answer "yes" to the therapist's injunctions.

Pacing is accomplished by the therapist simply acknowledging the client's (undeniable) current sensory and psychological experience. Generally, it is most successful when it involves the three major senses. This occurs through verbal acknowledgment of what is in the client's visual field, auditory awareness, and current physical experience (e.g., seeing, hearing, and feeling). The most effective way for therapists and their clients to learn pacing is the engagement in the 54321 Technique discussed in the preceding chapter. Ideally, this "pure" pacing exercise affords the therapist the ability to directly observe the unique ways their clients experience their immediate environment.

Pacing can occur on a conceptual level as well. If the client's psychological state is objectively observable (i.e., the client has verbalized it to the therapist), it can be included as well. This would also be true in regard to the client's immediate outlook on his or her condition. For instance, a therapist, in response to a client's clear expression of hopelessness, might state, "It seems like this will never go away." If the client exhibits excessive anxiety, the therapist might comment that "you are experiencing apprehension about what might happen next." In pacing a client's emotional state, however, the optimism and possibilities derived from the solution-focused interview should never be sacrificed for conceptual pacing. The process of pacing necessitates that the therapist include no new information in the interchange, eliminating the opportunity for the client to say "no" (Gilligan, 1986). Thus, pacing a client's particular experience should be strictly avoided in cases where the therapist has the slightest doubt about its details.

Neutral pacing involves the therapist making statements that are undeniable but unrelated to the client's current physical or emotional state. Similar to Erickson's use of truisms (described later) (Erickson et al., 1976), these neutral observations supplement the pacing process by communicating generalized facts that are indisputable yet unrelated to the client's immediate condition. Statements such as it's five o'clock, it's raining outside, or today is Tuesday serve to invite the client to (unconsciously) say "yes, " with little risk of rejection. Interspersing neutral statements with more condition-specific pacing constructs a framework that avoids the client interpreting therapeutic communication as being mimicry or judgmental observation.

Pacing is most effective when it is kept simple. This is especially true in the beginning of a hypnotic induction. Observations that are brief, straightforward, and true are most effective. Consequently, the therapist begins the induction by observing facts that present themselves in the current environment by stating, for example, "While you're sitting there you might notice your feet on the floor . . . and you can be conscious of the sound of the air-conditioning system above . . . and aware of my presence in your visual field." Continuing: "And your eyes are blinking, and you can become aware of the sound of your own breathing, and you can shift your attention to your body position in the chair"—continuing—"and you can hear the sound of my voice, and I'm sitting in a black chair, and you just adjusted your body position in your chair."

It has been our observation over the years, both in our students and in our own practices, that the vast majority of failed hypnotic inductions are due to inadequate pacing. This is usually due to the specific environmental factors, such as emergent situations, excessive chaos (noise, movement, etc.), or contexts that challenge client rapport. Accordingly, in these situations, it is possible for both therapist and client to fail to utilize the most important mechanism of pacing—"being in the moment." Ironically, the most effective response to difficult environments is to pace their more prominent noxious sensory characteristics.

The following case example demonstrates pacing within the context of chaos and acute pain.

Case Example (Part 1): Acute Pain—Pacing

Bob was recovering from a recent spinal fusion operation. Due to a postoperative heart attack, his physicians were required to (temporarily) withdraw his pain medication. This resulted in his experiencing excruciating, acute pain. Accompanying his pain, not surprisingly, was an intense state of anxiety bordering on a panic attack. He could be heard in the hospital hallway crying out in pain to the nurses. Complicating matters for Bob and the therapist was an inordinate amount of noise in his room emanating from a variety of lifesaving machines and excessive (although necessary) interruptions from the hospital staff.

The therapist began to pace Bob's anxiety and extreme discomfort.

Client	Therapist (ellipses indicate pauses)
(The client, rapidly breathing, indicated his discomfort through a great deal of physical movement.)	(The therapist matched his movement by continually adjusting himself in the chair.)
It hurts, it hurts so bad, I don't know how much longer I can stand it, I'm going to die—I know I'm going to die.	This is really painful . . . and you don't know how much longer you can stand it, . . . and you feel like you won't live through this.
(The client, his face contorted from pain, struggled to catch his breath.) Is this ever going to stop? I don't know how much more I can take.	Your breathing rate has increased, . . . and this temporary period without your medication seems like it's lasting forever, . . . and you have had about enough of this...
(The client continued the movement while falling silent.)	And you can be aware of the noise of the machines in the room . . . while that nurse leaves the room . . . and you can make any physical adjustments you like, to make yourself just a little more comfortable.
(The client reduced his body movement and the rate of his breathing diminished slightly, appearing to focus more on the therapist's voice.)	(The therapist reduced his own body movement and interspersed truisms [discussed later] with more pacing statements.)

Today is Friday, and you're certainly still painfully aware of that discomfort . . . and you can also be aware of the fluorescent light above . . . while your breathing becomes just a little more regular . . . I'm wearing a red tie . . . and you can be aware of the clanging of dinner plates out in the hallway . . . all while you are listening to the sound of my voice.

(The client shifted more focus toward the therapist, engaged in eye contact, while releasing some tension from his body.)

And you can see my eyes blinking over here while I see yours blinking over there . . . while that discomfort hasn't completely left yet . . . your body is making slight adjustments while your breathing becomes a little more regular . . . and you can be aware of the people talking out in the hallway if you like . . . or maybe it doesn't matter.

Continuing to notice Bob's ability to split his focus between his pain and his external environment, the therapist began to increase the number of neutral pacing statements while reducing the frequency of pain-related pacing statements. After a short time, the therapist was able to intersperse some leading statements (see case example part 2, later) interweaving suggestion for relaxation and comfort within the series of pacing statements.

Discussion.   In this example, Bob was able to shift his focus away from his pain in just a few minutes. The therapist accomplished this by acknowledging his painful predicament through the direct pacing of his physical symptoms and emotional distress. This, in turn, enabled the therapist to shift to neutral pacing statements, ultimately setting the stage for therapeutic suggestions (discussed later). There is no precise way to predict how much pacing a client will require. It varies with each individual. Extensive pacing is particularly critical in the circumstances where the client is experiencing immediate and significant discomfort in the therapist's office or in a hospital room. These factors are often exacerbated by the client's (understandable) panic and fear of the future (Barber, 1982). Occasionally there is the temptation for caregivers to react to acute anxiety and pain by stating "relax," or "the pain will go away soon." In these cases, it is far better to say nothing than to make premature leading statements to which the client is completely incapable of responding.

The most critical factor in assessing pacing is the behavior the client manifests in relation to the induction. Inadequate pacing is generally indicated by the client continuing or increasing physical agitation, exhibiting an inability or unwillingness to respond to hypnotic suggestions, and/or direct communication toward the therapist. The therapist has several options in this situation. The first is to simply increase the amount and variety of pacing statements. They should be delivered in a sincere and sympathetic manner that communicates a desire for rapport. A mere rapid increase in pacing with no purpose simply will not be sufficient and may serve to agitate the client further.

A second option is to simply ask the client, "What are you aware of right now?" The client's verbal description can then be utilized within a pacing context. He or she may comment on anxiety, specific location of pain, and/or confusion about the process. This material can then be judiciously interspersed with neutral pacing statements to make the reintroduction of hypnotic communication as natural as possible. Again, the client must be engaged in a sincere manner to maintain rapport.

The third option is to discontinue the intervention altogether. Clearly, this option should be chosen in cases in which the client indicates that he or she doesn't wish this type of intervention. Moreover, in the (infrequent) case where these interventions clearly fall short or serve to agitate the client further, they should cease immediately.

Intrahypnotic Pacing Applications

In addition to being invaluable for introducing clients to hypnotic communication, pacing is useful within the hypnotic induction itself. Clients beginning a course of hypnotherapy frequently experience the nonlinear, dynamic characteristics of trance through varying levels of hypnotic depth. This is especially true when someone is suffering from painful physical symptoms. A client might experience a relatively functional level of dissociation one moment, only to reexperience discomfort a few moments later, ultimately reorienting him or her from trance. This experience acts as a form of fractionation, spontaneously cycling between trance and wakefulness. In these cases, therapists need only to pace the client's experience of increased sensitivity to current physical feelings, visual images, and auditory awareness, with the goal of setting up suggestions to lead the client back to a more dissociated state.

For example, the therapist noticing a client beginning to reorient can preempt the action by suggesting that the client "might want to come back here just for moment and briefly open up your eyes, become more aware of the sounds in the room, and make any physical adjustments necessary to allow yourself to be more comfortable." Continuing, the therapist could suggest, "You may well be aware of more physical sensation than you were a moment ago. And just as it came back it can leave again." Pacing the client's experience in the middle of induction (and later reintroducing trance) produces the deepening phenomenon of fractionation mentioned in the preceding chapter (Weitzenhoffer, 1989a). Thus the client has the experience of briefly "checking back in," being paced by the therapist, and being reintroduced to trance.

Final Thoughts on Pacing

Although, on the surface, pacing appears to be a one-dimensional and simplistic hypnotic intervention, it is considerably more demanding of the therapist than leading. Pacing is a subtle clinical skill that requires the therapist's focus to be totally "in the moment" with the client. This requires continual observation and the flexibility to make adjustments in relation to shifts in the client's physiological and psychological state. Once this focus is in place, however, the therapist and client achieve a rapport that makes the process of leading comparatively effortless. The reader seeking a more comprehensive discussion of pacing is referred to Gilligan's (1986) excellent, *Therapeutic Trances: The Cooperation Principle in Ericksonian Hypnotherapy*.

☐ Leading

Leading is simply the process of offering suggestions within a hypnotic induction. Pacing recounts the client's current reality, whereas leading implies the client's impending reality. Leading represents a microdynamic process within a larger framework of hypnotic suggestion. Thus, leading "minisuggestions" refer to slight shifts, suggested by the therapist, in the client's experience that will occur within the very near future. Leading involves the suggestion of small, progressive steps in the client's experience that invite the client to ultimately embrace a variety of more profound dissociative, hypnotic directives. Consequently, the therapist begins the process of leading by suggesting small psychological and physical alterations in the client's experience, such as eye fixation, a reduction of blink response, a change in body temperature, sensations of lightness or heaviness in the limbs, shifts in auditory proximity, and alterations in breathing patterns.

As a rule, introductory leading suggestions should be general, nonauthoritarian, and always imply that the client has a choice (discussed later). Tightly interwoven with pacing statements, these suggested shifts in consciousness become more specific, ultimately accumulating to the point where the client becomes convinced that he or she is, indeed, capable of achieving an altered state of consciousness. This conviction, in turn, builds a bridge to the client's acceptance of suggestions of major hypnotic phenomena that will ultimately provide relief for his or her condition.

As stated earlier, critical to the success of any (leading) suggestion is the presence of adequate pacing. This is accomplished by ensuring that a leading statement is preceded and followed by a series of pacing statements. Thus, wrapped within the familiarity and safety of pacing, leads suggested by the therapist will be more readily implemented.

Case Example (Part 2): Acute Pain—Leading

As he listened to the induction, Bob became increasingly focused on what the therapist was saying. Pacing and leading, the therapist continued:

Induction	Commentary
Bob, as you look at the clock on the wall, listen to the commotion out in the hallway, and continue to have that awareness of your body . . .	Three statements directly pacing the experience of the client, utilizing the three major senses.
You can notice your breathing become more just a little more rhythmic and regular . . .	Leading reference to a suggested small shift in physical experience.
And while you continue to listen to the sound of my voice . . . notice your body position shifting in the chair . . . and see that another minute has passed on that clock behind me . . .	Two pacing statements that refer to current physical reality followed by a neutral pacing statement.
You might begin to notice those slight changes in your body awareness . . . now . . . or a few moments from now . . .	A permissive lead (implying choice) employing a presupposition (described later) in reference to a physical shift in the future.
While being aware that the commotion has died down in the hall . . . and that your eyelids are fluttering, ever so slightly . . . and,	Auditory and visual pacing surrounding a reference an involuntary ideomotoric action (eyelid flutter) that commonly accompanies trance.

now that the sun is setting, the light in the room has diminished a bit . . .

And . . . I don't know which you'll notice first, . . . the release of some of the tension in your body ... or the increase in the comfortable heaviness your body will experience . . .	A lead that gives the choice between two presupposed physical outcomes.
And your eyes are focused on my eyes over here . . . you can hear the sound of the heater up above . . . and your breathing is more rhythmic and deep . . .	Visual and auditory references followed by pacing the (now accomplished) lead that suggested increased rhythmic breathing.
. . . It can comfortably penetrate those muscles . . . and that comfort can spread to other parts of the body	Direct lead suggesting that the client's rhythmic breathing can contribute to comfort spreading to other parts of the body.
And . . . as this temporary situation moves closer to resolution . . . your body and your unconscious mind can make the adjustments necessary to continue to generate the comfort necessary to get you through this.	Pacing statement referring to the temporary nature of medication withdrawal combined with a general leading suggestion implying the body's ability to produce comfort.

Continuing with the case of acute pain outlined earlier, the continuing clinical example here illustrates the interplay of pacing and leading with a transcript of the induction along with commentary.

Discussion. In this example, sufficient pacing enabled Bob to accept and utilize a variety of leads, ultimately setting the stage for the suggestion of more profound hypnotic phenomena. Frequently, the process of pacing and leading becomes so interwoven that it becomes difficult to differentiate the two. This occurs when a synchronized process is created resulting in sufficient pacing setting up the client's rapid response to a lead, which immediately becomes paced by the therapist. This short sequence sets up yet another lead, continuing the process. This set of responses, in turn, builds a sense of positive expectancy convincing the client of his or her ability to be "led" into more symptom-relieving phenomena.

☐ Integrating Pacing and Leading within the Self-Hypnotic Context

There is great value in combining the process of pacing and leading with the self-hypnosis techniques outlined in the previous chapter. This integration is particularly helpful in clinical situations that demand the economical expenditure of time. It is the pacing nature of these self-hypnotic procedures that bridge the gap between self-directed and heterohypnotic techniques. The 54321 Technique creates a "pure" pacing experience revolving around material generated from the client's actual, current experience. The Here–There Technique shifts between pacing the client's current context and leading (him- or herself) into a real, past pleasant experience. Finally, Eye Breathing serves primarily as a pacing vehicle as well. Even though the therapist constructs the process, the client establishes his or her own rhythms, along with ascribing healing and toxic colors to individual breathing practices.

To facilitate this integration, the therapist first invites the client to engage in one of the self-hypnotic techniques. Then the client is informed that at some point the therapist will accompany him or her with some positive suggestions. If the client and therapist have had the luxury of experimenting with a number of the already mentioned self-hypnotic techniques, the client should be encouraged to choose the one that works best for him or her.

Integrating the 54321 and Here–There techniques into a heterohypnotic context may result in the therapist and client talking simultaneously (shown later). Clearly, the client should be notified of this possibility, along with the suggestion that "There is no need to pay attention to anything in particular, except what suits you at the time." The therapist goes on to state that if for any reason the client doesn't find this intervention helpful, he or she can request immediate termination of the induction and that they will both move on to something else that might more fruitful. Following this, the therapist simply falls silent while the client begins his or her self-hypnotic procedures.

☐ Timing Heterohypnotic Integration

The timing of the integration of suggestions into the client's self-hypnotic process depends on both the client and the situation at hand. If the situation is emergent in nature and/or involves acute pain requiring immediate attention, the therapist should not delay long before integrating therapeutic suggestions into the procedure. In the cases where anxiety is high, pain is intense, and the ability of the client to focus is limited by the context, we have found that Eye Breathing accompanied by adequate pacing and therapeutic suggestion is most effective. It requires less of the client than other, slightly more complex, interventions. Similarly, if the therapist is familiar with the client and the client has demonstrated a general comfort level with hypnosis, integration of pacing and leading statements can begin quickly. In fact, the client may expect this.

If the client is unfamiliar with hypnosis and/or unsure about the concept, it is best to wait until the client establishes his or her own hypnotic rhythms and/or exhibits some initial indications of trance behavior. Carefully observing the client's external behavior, the therapist looks for specific signs that the client's level of dissociation is increasing. Primarily, the signs include reduction or cessation of extraneous body movement, a lessening or cessation of the swallow reflex, more measured and rhythmic breathing patterns, eye fixation and/or what appears to be natural eye closure, a flattening of the facial muscles or a change in skin coloration, an alteration of voice tone, and small ideomotoric movement in the limbs or hands. Rarely do all or even most of these signs manifest themselves in a single session. The therapist need only look for an alteration in the client's consciousness signaled by a shift in the client's external appearance or behavior.

Once having made this observation, the therapist can initiate the heterohypnotic induction by beginning to pace the client's observable experience. This, in addition to serving as a rapport-building intervention, gives the therapist an opportunity to effectively join the rhythm of the client. Shortly after establishing a pacing rhythm, the therapist offers a sequence to the client through a series of general, open-ended suggestions (see Indirect Suggestion, later). Ideally, the therapist should attempt to insert pacing and leading statements within the natural pauses that occur within the client's self-induction. In effect, filling in these natural punctuation points complements the client's pacing process while simultaneously providing for some mild confusion, a beneficial phenomenon that increases dissociation. Alternatively, simultaneous speaking by both the therapist and client is equally capable of producing a comfortable feeling of dissociation, in effect creating a powerful double induction (Gilligan, 1986).

The following interaction is a brief example of what might occur between client and therapist utilizing the 54321 Technique as a self-hypnosis protocol. Ellipses (. . .) indicate pauses.

Client	**Therapist (with commentary)**
I'm aware of seeing the church steeple outside the window . . . and I can see car driving by on the street outside . . . I just saw a bird fly by the window . . . and someone just	And you can also be aware of your feet on the floor . . . And the breeze from the fan in the room . . . Perhaps you can feel your body and chair . . . With your arms on the

walked by in a red coat . . . and the clouds in the sky look like rain.

armrests . . . And your head leaning back against the headrest. (Pacing alternate sensory experiences of the client)

When the client begins to exhibit trancelike phenomena, leading statements can be added:

Client	Therapist (interspersing leads)
I can hear the sound of a fan . . . I can hear the sound of my own breathing . . . I hear a faint sound of some conversation next door . . .	As you continue to experience the rhythm of your own breathing . . . and listen to the sound of my voice . . . and have your eyes fixed directly in front of you . . . you can begin to wonder what your unconscious mind has in store. (Pacing alternate experience, setting up a general lead)
I feel the breeze of the fan . . . I feel the leather on the armrests . . . and my hands feel warm . . .	. . . And that warmth can spread . . . all the way to where will do the most good . . . enveloping that area that needs attention . . . (Leading from the client's experience to suggest pain relief)

Discussion. This truncated example demonstrates the ability of integrating the process of pacing and leading with the client's own immediate sensory experience within 54321 Technique to enhance the impact of hypnosis. As the induction continues, and the increasing signs of trancelike behavior exhibit themselves, the therapist can suggest to the client, "You can fall silent whenever you think it most productive and just listen to me for a while, letting your eyes close on their own." This signals a shift toward a heterohypnotic induction utilizing the suggestive strategies outlined next. Essentially the same procedure can be used with the Here–There Technique, affording the therapist the opportunity to pace and lead both the client's past and current sensory experience. Eye Breathing presents excellent opportunities for integration as well. This is presented in detail in a case example later in this chapter.

☐ Strategies for Hypnotic Suggestion—A Continuum

Hypnotic suggestion exists on a continuum anchored in generalized, open-ended, permissive, indirect suggestions on one end and specific, (moderately) authoritarian, direct suggestions on the other. In the middle of the continuum are specific injunctions that are indirectly suggested through implication and presupposition. Generally, we have found it most effective to begin an induction with indirect open-ended suggestions that (at all times) communicate choice. Such suggestions can be interpreted in a variety of (positive) ways by a client. These "indirect" injunctions serve as a gentle introduction to trance within a pacing context, gradually building up the client's comfort level and a "yes set" that will serve both client and therapist well. These types of suggestions are a particularly good complement to the integration of heterohypnotic and self-hypnotic processes. When the client begins to exhibit external indications of trance-like behavior, the therapist can begin to offer suggestions in the form of implication and presupposition. After the client has achieved (at least) a moderate level of dissociation, the therapist can offer suggestions that directly convey the goals that the client has for the session.

Hypnosis has an abundant and diverse set of strategies for therapeutic suggestion. Milton Erickson's repertoire alone included (but was not limited to) direct and indirect suggestive strategies through interspersal techniques; presupposition, metaphor, ideodynamic processes; double binds; implication and implied directives; and a wide variety of complex multi-level communication (Erickson & Rossi, 1979). The remainder of this chapter outlines specific suggestive strategies that are helpful in the treatment of individuals suffering from chronic pain and illness.

Indirect Suggestions

One of Milton Erickson's most notable clinical gifts resided in the variety of unique ways in which he could indirectly suggest change to his clients. Rather than conveying his therapeutic intent in a direct fashion, Erickson would intersperse hypnotic suggestions within questions, metaphors, and a variety of linguistic devices while pacing the client's model of the world (Erickson & Rossi, 1979; Erickson et al., 1976). This indirect approach invariably bypassed "compliance" and "resistance" issues while increasing the client's ability to utilize his or her resources to beneficially alter his or her state of consciousness.

Characterized by their permissive quality, indirect suggestions are an excellent medium to introduce sufferer/victims and seeker/searchers to hypnosis. Avoiding an authoritarian stance, these open-ended directives communicate choice to a clinical population that views itself as having little. Additionally, an indirect framework of suggestion complements the integration of self and heterohypnosis.

Strategies for Constructing Indirect Suggestions

Fundamentally, at the heart of every indirect suggestion should be an invitation rather than a command. Key to the effectiveness of indirect suggestions is their ability to on the one hand communicate support for self-efficacy through client choice and on the other hand generate more opportunities for the client to say "yes" to any given hypnotic directive. For example, using an indirect strategy to simply suggest that a client close his or her eyes gives the therapist many more options than directly suggesting "close your eyes" or "you can close your eyes now." Instead, the client might be given a variety of choices.

Thus, the therapist might frame the directive in the form of a question, stating, "I don't know whether you are ready to close your eyes yet." Or, the client can be presented with a number of options in relation to the timing of eye closure: "You might want to close your eyes now or a few moments from now, or perhaps you would like to leave them open the entire time, it's really up to your unconscious mind." On the other hand, the therapist might evoke a pleasant sensation from the past to encourage eye closure: "Maybe you remember some time in the past when you stayed up really late and all of a sudden you couldn't keep your eyes open any longer." Alternatively, the therapist might evoke a neutral association in regard to eye closure through telling a story about a student listening to a boring lecture and struggling to keep his or her eyes open.

Using indirect communication as a suggestive strategy allows for the repetition of an injunction in a variety of forms. This results in the client interpreting the suggestion within a positive framework that encourages him or her to say "yes." In the early stages of an induction this affirmative act sets the stage for more complex and direct suggestions that are to follow.

It should be noted that the clinical usefulness of the implied "permissiveness" and creation of choice contained in indirect suggestions is a matter for some debate. In particular, Hammond stated that the use of indirect suggestion conveys a lack of conviction and confidence on the part of the therapist. He went on to challenge "the myth of indirect suggestions," citing research indicating little difference in their efficacy when compared to direct suggestions (Hammond, 1990, p. 23). Our experience, to the contrary, clearly indicates that an indirect approach substantially increases the therapeutic repertoire for both clients and clinicians addressing the challenges of chronic illness and pain. This is especially true in the initial stages of the therapeutic relationship.

Truisms and Open-Ended Suggestions

Truisms and open-ended suggestions are the most generalized indirect hypnotic suggestions (Erickson et al., 1976). Largely, they are used in the initial portion of an induction to build rapport and begin the construction of a "yes set." They serve the dual purpose of orienting clients to trance while at the same time pacing their model of the world.

Truisms are statements that essentially appear to be undeniable to the client. These universal declarations encourage agreement and begin to set a general stage for more specific suggestions that will be offered later in the induction. They differ from neutral pacing statements only in their reference to the client's internal imagery that need not be in his or her immediate experience. In addition to their undeniable nature, truisms indirectly refer to common hypnotic phenomena that occur in everyday life. For example, the statement "Everyone has had the experience of shaking hands with someone without even thinking" indirectly refers to unconscious automaticity. Or in suggesting the existence of amnesia, the therapist might state, "Everyone has had the experience of forgetting a number at one time or another." Or in suggesting the general experience of the unconscious and dissociation, "Everyone at sometime has just let their mind wander . . . pleasantly while doing a chore."

Open-ended suggestions, like truisms, make vague references to general hypnotic phenomena while reducing the probability of direct rejection. This is accomplished by presenting statements the client can interpret, positively, in his or her own unique way. For example, in making reference to the general autonomy of the unconscious, one might state, "Your unconscious mind can go anywhere it wants to." Or suggesting memories of a pleasant time in a previous age, the therapist can declare, "You can remember the experience of feeling the warm sun on a summer day." Or beginning to suggest the mental mechanisms involved in dissociation, the therapist can say, "You can listen to my words with your conscious mind while your unconscious mind can do something else altogether."

Covering All Possible Alternatives

This indirect set of suggestions has the goal of addressing all possible choices a client might have at his or her disposal in relation to a directive (Erickson et al., 1976). Like truisms and open-ended suggestions, they are particularly helpful in the initial stages of an induction in that they can diffuse the natural resistance a client might have to altering his or her current state of consciousness. This is accomplished by implying that the client has a variety of choices in response to the therapist's injunctions. Thus, the framework of the "yes set" continues to be constructed to rarify any choice a client chooses to make, even not going into a trance.

This process is accomplished by the therapist directing open-ended statements toward the client that contain all the possible alternatives (including not responding) that the client has in regard to the hypnotic process at hand. In effect, the client is given a number of suggestive choices within a pacing context. For example, the therapist might say, "I don't know if you want to go into a trance now . . . or in a few minutes from now . . . perhaps it's not time yet . . . or maybe your unconscious can choose a time that works best for you . . . it doesn't really matter." Alternately, the therapist might want to evoke an association to a previous state of consciousness that represented an exception to the client's current symptoms. This would be done by suggesting that the client "remember a time when you felt more comfortable (not suffering from the current symptoms) . . . perhaps a time from that recent vacation, or from a time a while back, maybe a summer long ago. Or maybe it was a time in between then in now . . . or possibly, for now, your unconscious mind would like to keep to that memory to itself."

Suggestions Using Implication and Presupposition

The middle of the hypnotic suggestion continuum is occupied by suggestions embedded within the linguistics of implication and presupposition. This set of hypnotic injunctions represents a bridge between direct and indirect suggestions by communicating that an action will take place without directly suggesting its execution. These injunctions differ from the more open-ended suggestions in their implication of the absence of choice for the client. It should be noted, however, that although unstated, the client can always refuse the presupposition.

These presumptive suggestions are embedded in a framework of words and phrases (*while, after, which, how, during, because, before, when, as*) that imply that something (related to the client's goals) specific will occur in the future. For example, the phrase "*After* you have achieved that level of comfort you can . . . " assumes comfort will be achieved. Alternatively, the phrase, "*Since* your unconscious mind can signal when its time to go into trance . . . " assumes that the client will actually achieve a trance state and that his or her unconscious has the capacity to signal it to do so. Directly stating "I don't know *which* arm will rise first . . . " assumes that one arm, in fact, will rise. "I don't know *how* you first will experience that sensation . . . " assumes that there is a sensation to be experienced. Proclaiming "*During* the period that you are in trance..." presupposes that there will be some period spent in an altered state. "*Because* your unconscious mind already knows how to give you relief . . . " communicates to the client that her unconscious mind has special knowledge that will be useful in providing comfort. "*While* your unconscious mind works on that solution . . . " implies that the unconscious has a solution and that it is not far away. "*Before* you begin to experience that comfort . . . "informs the client that comfort will be experienced. "Your conscious mind may not know *when* it is time to go into trance but your unconscious does . . . " communicates a temporal certainty about the unconscious. Finally, the statement "*As* you continue to relax . . . " assumes that the relaxation process has already begun.

Implied directives are presented by the therapist in a "matter-of-fact" and confident way. Because these suggestions are more specific, they are best presented after the client has demonstrated some visible shift in consciousness. If they are presented before this occurs, without adequate pacing, the client will most likely reject them. Keeping this in mind, two (or more) suggestions containing presupposition and implication should be separated by several pacing statements.

At first glance, especially for the solution-focused and other types of postmodern therapists, the use of implied directives and presuppositions might appear to be antithetical to the process of client-constructed solutions. It is our view, however, that when these implied suggestions directly relate to the client's (previously stated) goals, they are another step in the solution process.

☐ Conscious/Unconscious Splits

Students and therapists can often feel (understandably) overwhelmed at the prospect of learning the variety of language and clinical protocols of Ericksonian hypnosis. However, we have found that simply utilizing the process of conscious/unconscious splits is by far the most effective technique to introduce the hypnotic induction to both therapists and clients. This form of suggestion involves directing pacing statements to the client's conscious mind and hypnotic suggestions to his or her unconscious mind (Lankton & Lankton, 1983). Essentially, it is the heterohypnotic version of the Here–There Technique. The process results in a kind of conscious/unconscious dissociation, enabling the client to acknowledge current uncomfortable sensations and other external stimuli while simultaneously (unconsciously) considering hypnotic solutions. Ideally, this suggestive process allows the concerns of the conscious mind to retreat into the background and the healing and symptom-relieving hypnotic phenomena of the unconscious mind to come to the foreground.

In utilizing conscious/unconscious splits, conscious pacing statements are linked with unconscious leading statements. For example, the therapist might state, "Your conscious mind can be aware of sitting in that chair, listening to me, and watching the clock on the wall . . . while your unconscious mind is doing something else altogether . . . And, while your conscious mind can monitor the level of discomfort in your body, and hear the traffic on the street, and see the shaft of sunlight come through the window . . . your unconscious mind can recall a more comfortable time . . . While your conscious mind can have an awareness of the temperature in the room, and that the traffic sounds outside had died down, and that I am wearing a checkered shirt . . . your unconscious mind has known all along a variety of ways to provide you some relief . . . As your conscious mind has the ability to focus on more than one spot, perhaps noticing that your breathing has become slightly more rhythmic, and you can still hear the sound of my voice . . . your unconscious mind can provide you with valuable experiences."

As the induction continues, and the client exhibits a shift in his or her external behavior (catalepsy, eye fixation, flattening of the facial muscles, a reduction in external movement, a change in breathing pattern, etc.), the therapist can offer statements that are more directly suggestive to the client's unconscious mind. As previously stated, direct suggestions should specifically relate to the client's goals or previous nonsymptomatic experiences (exceptions). For example, if the client has related a past pleasant experience of swimming, it can be suggested that his or her unconscious mind can remember a time when "you were swimming and felt the warm water support your whole body as if it were weightless . . . And now, as then, that floating sensation can spread throughout your entire body."

Utilizing conscious/unconscious splits facilitates the incorporation of all the other indirect techniques within an interwoven structure of pacing and leading. Associating pacing and leading statements within this framework enables the therapist to naturally progress to injunctions that directly suggest shifts in the client's behavior, experience, and/or state of consciousness.

☐ Direct Suggestions

Occupying the far end of the continuum of hypnotic suggestion are direct suggestions. Although one of the myths about Milton Erickson is that he primarily used indirect suggestion, historical examination reveals that he used direct suggestion as well (Hammond, 1984). The oldest form of hypnotic suggestion, these are direct and straightforward injunctions from the therapist to the client to perform a specific behavioral task, experience a hypnotic phenomenon, or alter a sensation or symptom. Accordingly, direct suggestions may be as simple as suggesting that the client close his or her eyes or as complex as suggesting that the client experience anesthesia in a specific area of the body. Direct suggestions have an explicit, linear quality. Because they are, by definition, closed-ended instructions, they inherently are more authoritarian in their tone than indirect suggestions. Moreover, their closed-ended nature results in two general outcomes—success or failure.

☐ Using Caution with Direct Suggestions

In our experience, clients suffering from chronic illness and pain have received and attempted to accept numerous (conscious) direct suggestions over the course of their illness. These suggestions may have involved medication, a rehabilitative procedure, or "just thinking differently." These types of suggestions have met varying levels of success. Because of the volume of directives this clinical population generally experiences, we use direct suggestions very judiciously. Direct suggestions to experience a specific hypnotic phenomenon or alter a painful sensation will generally fail in the beginning stages of a hypnotic induction and/or if the therapist and client have inadequate rapport. We believe that they are most successful when they are employed with clients who have had (at least) a moderate amount hypnotic training and/or those who can achieve a relatively deep level of dissociation (Barber, 1996a).

Strategies for Constructing Direct Suggestions

Barber (1996b, pp. 88–91) outlined five direct suggestive strategies to directly address pain and suffering: anesthesia, direct diminution of sensations, sensory substitution, displacement, and dissociation. The first, anesthesia, is perhaps the most difficult to suggest in that it involves the necessity of constructing a positive hallucination. In using this strategy, the therapist suggests that the painful area become insensitive to pain, generally beginning by invoking the sensation of numbness. Accordingly, the therapist simply suggests that "you can begin to experience a growing sense of numbness in that area . . . until there's no sensation in all." Generally, directly suggesting anesthesia will fail with clients who do not have an exceedingly high ability to dissociate.

Direct diminution of sensations involves the suggestion of the continual reduction of the intensity and degree of pain. Similar to the experience of analgesia, this strategy requires the suggestion of the gradual lessening of a painful sensation. Barber suggested the use of scaling to facilitate the client's observation of the reduction in pain. To suggest the diminution in the intensity of pain the therapist might suggest: "That painful sensation can begin to gradually diminish . . . as that 6 will become a 5 . . . on its way to being a 4 . . . there's no telling how long it will have to stay a 5 before it moves on to a 4 . . . but a 5 is certainly better than a 6 . . . and of course you have to go through 5 to get to 4."

Sensory substitution involves substituting a less onerous symptom for a more painful one. Barber argued that some clients are more likely to accept substituted symptoms that retain some adverse sensory quality rather than the experience of comfort. Therefore a burning sensation may become an itch or a sharp pain can become a dull pressure. For example, therapist might suggest that "continual throbbing can become a constant tapping on the outside of your skin."

Displacement of pain involves the movement of the locus of sensation from the sensitive area to a less sensitive one that can be tolerated and managed more easily. For example, to clients suffering severe headache pain, the therapist might suggest that the throbbing involves movement and vibration and that "ever so slightly . . . you can begin to move it down your neck where the throbbing will continue to be noticed on its way to transporting itself into the shoulders . . . staying there for a while, letting you know it is still around . . . then throbbing and moving into the upper arm, where, of course, it will be experienced differently than in the shoulder . . . on its way to the forearm . . . noticing the movement of that throbbing sensation into the hand . . . ultimately residing in the tip of your index finger."

Clients who can effectively move the locus of their pain can often relocate it outside their body as well. Using the preceding example, the therapist might suggest that, "that throbbing can leave your body like an arrow leaving its bow . . . ultimately landing where it belongs, far away from you."

Barber's final strategy, dissociation, is the phenomenological framework that governs all hypnotic pain management. As outlined in the preceding chapter, dissociation is a set of mental mechanisms that allow clients to divide the experience of their painful symptoms and the rest of their everyday living into separate parts. Thus, the client has a cognitive knowledge of his or her actual injury or illness while simultaneously maintaining the ability to separate him- or herself from its painful symptoms. In constructing direct suggestive strategies for dissociation, the therapist should focus on the client's ability to detach from the pain, taking advantage of the separation of the conscious and unconscious mind. For example, the therapist might suggest that "While your conscious mind stays with your body (during the procedure) your unconscious mind can help you step out of your body for a while . . . where you can watch from a distance . . . from outside the room . . . during that time when you felt safe, secure, and comfortable."

Finally, the critical factor in any suggestion involving direct injunctions is the specific goals of the client. At no time should the therapist attempt to directly facilitate a hypnotic phenomenon, alter a sensory experience, or change a behavior that has not been discussed with the client beforehand. In addition to being unethical, this type of practice reduces rapport and generally insures failure of any hypnotic endeavor. Moreover, in the beginning of any suggestive process, the client should be informed by the therapist that he or she is free to accept, reject, or alter any material that might be presented in the hypnotherapy session. To express this, the therapist might state, "As we proceed you can make any adjustments that are necessary to make what you hear applicable to you. If you hear something that doesn't apply to you, please feel free to pay no attention to it. Or if some of my words and suggestions don't quite fit your needs, your unconscious mind can alter them to better serve you." Statements such as these allow the client the flexibility to discard some of the inevitable statements from the hypnotist that do not "fit."

The following case example illustrates the movement on the continuum of hypnotic suggestion, initially incorporating solution-focused interviewing and the Eye Breathing technique, moving through indirect suggestions and implication through presupposition, finally ending with direct hypnotic injunctions.

Case Example (Part 1)—Employing the Continuum of Suggestion

Mike, suffering from amyotrophic lateral sclerosis (ALS), was a World War II veteran and temporary resident of a Veterans Administration nursing home. The course of his illness had recently taken a turn for the worse. He was experiencing severe spinal pain from the disease and had recently become confined to a wheelchair. "I thought that I wasn't supposed to feel any pain with this damn illness," he said, wincing as he offered the therapist a firm handshake. "I sure hope that you can help me. I haven't had any sleep for a couple of nights. The pain is unbearable. I don't know how much longer I can stand this."

The therapist learned that Mike's miracle would involve his pain "being completely gone" and that his scaled progress from his current low "1" to a "2" would be represented by the fact that he could "get just get a few hours of sleep at night" and that "I could distract myself long enough to finish a crossword puzzle."

Using the solution-focused interview to uncover hypnotic phenomena, the therapist asked Mike about the times in his life when he might have naturally experienced some form of an altered state of consciousness, such as daydreaming, pleasant distraction, or "just spacing out." Visibly puzzled at the question, Mike answered, "Never." The therapist replied, "Even when you are doing your crossword puzzles?" Mike again, more emphatically this time, answered "No!" The therapist, not yet willing to abandon this direction of exception questioning, asked, "When is your discomfort less intense—even for a moment?" "Never," Mike responded with complete certainty. "It's always the same," he continued. The therapist looking for the smallest exception asked, "When are the times that you have been able to distract yourself, perhaps even in the smallest way?" "Never," Mike repeated, almost before the therapist could finish the question.

In an attempt to briefly steer the conversation away from the apparent lack of exceptions, the therapist asked Mike about his World War II experiences. He proudly spoke of (illegally) enlisting in the marines of the age 15, being shipped to the Philippines, and being captured and interned in a Japanese prison camp subsequent to the Bataan Death March. He went on to explain that "the commandant used to send me to the 'hole' [a small boxlike cage where prisoners were kept in solitary confinement] a lot. Hell, you couldn't even stand up in that damn cage. The commandant and I didn't see 'eye to eye' very often," he laughed.

The therapist, curious about how Mike coped with such a traumatic experience, wondered aloud, "In that horribly uncomfortable experience, were there any times when you just let your mind wander to get away from it all?" Mike paused for a full minute blankly staring into the air before responding, "Well, yes, back then I couldn't have survived if I would have let myself think about my situation all the time. The guys that thought too much didn't make it."

The therapist, continuing to probe, discovered that there were a number of times during the war that Mike was able to access unconscious resources to relieve pain and discomfort. Daily, during his internment, he was able to "go away" for hours at a time, often remembering what it was like growing up in a small Ohio town. Intrigued, the therapist was able to discover other experiences during the war in which Mike experienced naturally recurring altered states of consciousness. "I remember being on a crowded troop ship and somehow sneaking my way on to an empty deck, near the top, taking off my shirt and just laying in the sun. The waves were gently rolling and I just closed my eyes and stayed up there for hours. I completely forgot that there was a war on. I know that remembering the war should bother me, but it doesn't at all. Even talking about prison camp."

Mike continued to describe, in detail, other valuable past experiences: growing up in a large, loving family, playing sports, caring for animals. With every illustration he visibly demonstrated a shift in consciousness, finally admitting, "I guess now I am able to distract myself when I do my crosswords. But I haven't been able to come close to finishing one since I've been in this damn place." Glancing furtively at the pile of puzzle books on his nightstand, he continued, "I start every morning and just can't get through even one."

It is not surprising that individuals suffering from acute pain can't immediately shift their attention from a seemingly intractable situation to a time when the problem has not been present or less in the forefront. Pain has a way of obliterating both the past and future. For the person in pain the only time is "now," and "now" really hurts. However, if the situation permits, determining the quality of a client's previous altered-state experience can be quite useful in delivering an induction. Additionally, the act of remembering these experiences has the effect of making trance more acceptable to the client.

Equipped with some information about Mike's previously successful altered (exception) states, and having instructed him in the simplest form of the Eye Breathing technique, the therapist proceeded with the hypnotic induction. Here is an abridged transcript with commentary on the suggestive strategies utilized.

Induction	**Commentary**
Mike, as your breathing and your eye movement continue to get in synchronization . . . you can continue to listen to the sound of my voice . . . and it is very possible that some of the things I say won't seem like they particularly apply to you . . . when that happens, and I'm sure it will . . . at least a little, your unconscious mind has the ability to transform those statements into something more useful for you . . . or perhaps, it will choose to discard them altogether . . . it doesn't really matter.	Introduction to the hypnotic process. Beginning pacing statements using the process of Eye Breathing. Reinforcing the client's physical pacing process and suggesting that he make any adjustments necessary to make the process work for him.
As we continue . . . you can be aware of that man walking across the parking lot outside . . . And as your breathing continues to smooth out . . . and that discomfort hasn't really left you yet . . . as your eyes continue to open . . . and close . . . they are in almost perfect synchronization with your breathing . . . your hands are resting on the cold rails of the chair . . . that man has made it	Simple pacing statements including acknowledgment of physical discomfort along with observations of minimal shifts in the client's external physical process. Timing pacing statements (using pauses) to reflect eyes opening and closing.

all the way across the parking lot and has gotten into his car . . .

And you can be aware of that noise from that machine monitoring your room-mate . . . there's no real reason to tune it out unless you want to . . . you may even want to pay attention to the rhythm of that beeping . . . you can also begin to wonder where your unconscious mind will take you today . . .	Pacing noxious external elements (noise). Open-ended suggestion implying the unconscious mind's ability to act autonomously and benevolently.
And Mike, . . . your discomfort is going to hang around a while longer . . . and that car is now driving out of the parking lot . . . and that beeping has stopped for a moment . . .	Continued pacing statements.
Everyone at sometime has had the experience of just letting go . . . maybe after an exhaustive effort . . . maybe at the end of the day . . . maybe because they could use a little sleep . . . maybe they have made a valiant effort under challenging circumstances . . . everyone who has made that kind of effort deserves a break.	Truism implying the common experience of letting go. Pacing sleep disturbance. Pacing the effort he has put forth and linking it to a deserved rest.
. . . And as the hospital parking lot continues to empty . . . perhaps you can hear the sound of your breathing . . . growing a little more measured and rhythmic.	Pacing of undeniable reality—movement in the parking lot. Observing and pacing progress of a physical process.
Your unconscious mind has the ability to take you to a comfortable place . . . a place that you have been before . . . perhaps a place that you would like to go . . . a place not here . . . but there.	Open-ended suggestion about his unconscious mind's ability to create comfort.
While you listen to the sound of my voice . . . and continue to be aware of your hands on that chrome rail . . . and notice that it has gotten a little darker outside as your eyes open and close . . . I don't know whether you want them to stay closed a little longer.	Pacing immediate sensory experience along with an initial suggestion of the eye closure.
I don't know whether you would like to go to a place that has given you comfort before . . . or, maybe you'd like to stay here	Covering all possible alternatives including no change in all.

just a while longer . . . or, perhaps you're unconscious mind will take you somewhere you haven't yet been . . . or possibly your unconscious mind will take someplace without your conscious mind noticing it all . . . or maybe it will send the pain someplace and bring the comfort here . . . it doesn't really matter . . .

Client exhibits initial signs of natural eye closure, flattening of the facial muscles and a lessening of the swallow reflex.

Your may not care whether your eyes need to be synchronized much longer . . . in fact they might fall behind your breathing a little . . . When they are ready to take a break, for a while, your unconscious mind will just let them comfortably close . . . not too soon . . . not too late.	Pacing an observable physical change. Indirect suggestion for eye closure.

Client closes eyes.

That's right . . . And you have a conscious mind and an unconscious mind . . . your conscious mind can remember that man walking across the parking lot, getting in his car, and driving away, something he does every day . . . while your unconscious mind has known all along how to provide you with comfort . . .	Ratification of eye closure along with pacing statements that introduce conscious/unconscious splitting. Recalling a recent visual experience paired with a general presupposition about the unconscious mind.
Your conscious mind knows that this is Tuesday . . . that my voice is coming from over here and remembers what that noise in the hallway sounded like a minute ago . . . while your unconscious mind doesn't need a calendar . . . can remember experiences from long ago . . . the different ways in which you have been able to make yourself more comfortable in the past . . . without really thinking . . . feeling the sun beat down on your body . . . lying on top of the deck . . . feeling the rhythm of the ship as it rides the waves . . .	Truism, recalling and pacing a recent undeniable auditory experience. Pacing and leading through conscious/unconscious splits. Recalling a past undeniable, comfortable physical experience—age regression.
Some moments can be so enjoyable and captivating that they let us forget everything else . . . at least for a while . . . and a moment can seem to last a long time when	Truism, indirectly introducing suggestions of amnesia and time distortion that will be utilized later.

you're enjoying it . . . it's hard to remember how long a pleasurable experience really lasts because time is so unimportant then.

As your conscious mind continues to listen to the sound of my voice . . . your unconscious mind can hear whatever it would like . . . perhaps my voice has become farther away while other sounds, sights, and feelings can become more vivid.	Pacing. Conscious/unconscious split followed up with suggestion for dissociation and more age regression. Beginning suggestions for hypermnesia.
Your unconscious mind has the ability to offer you comfort from long ago, remembering the exact details of a peaceful experience . . . whether it comes from the feeling of the rhythm of the ship on top of the waves . . . or, the warm sun beating down on your back . . . or the soothing sound of the water . . . or all three ...	Presupposition, implying dissociation, functional age regression, and hypermnesia.

Client exhibits further signs of being in a trance state—rhythmic breathing, cessation of swallow reflex, and cessation of all other external movement.

You can take the opportunity to just enjoy for a moment . . . the ability of your unconscious mind to take you away from here . . . to just float in that sea of comfort while falling silent for just a moment.	Direct suggestion for dissociation—positive hallucination. The therapist takes a moment to give the client the opportunity to solidify the shift in consciousness.
And Mike . . . just as that ship can be in rhythm with a large powerful ocean riding on top of the waves, your unconscious mind can float your discomfort away . . .	Linking past experience of comfort with current, challenging physical situation.
And the rhythm of your breathing can match the rhythm of the ocean . . . just as you did with your eyes . . . and that rhythm can infuse your spine with the warmth from that top deck . . . with each wave of warmth increasing your comfort . . . while washing away those sensations that aren't really helpful . . . the ones you came here to get rid of . . . a little at a time.	Direct reference to past pacing experience. Use of a past association to frame the direct suggestion of diminution of painful sensations.

And as that rhythm continues . . . that in and out motion . . . it can take the flotsam and jetsam all the way out to sea where you really don't need to be bothered by it at all . . . while you can continue to experience the increasing comfort that top deck warmth can provide to your spine.

Furthering the metaphor to indirectly suggest increased dissociation for pain and discomfort, which, in turn, frames the direct suggestion of the diminution of sensations.

Discussion.   This (abridged) case example outlines a variety of hypnotic interventions available within the first session. Of particular note is the persistence used to discover the client's exceptions when engaging in interviewing for past hypnotic phenomena. This was complimented by integrating a simple self-hypnotic technique (Eye Breathing), which in turn set the stage for the utilization of the continuum of hypnotic suggestion.

The remainder of this case example, which focuses on addressing Mike's future comfort, will follow the next section on posthypnotic suggestion.

☐ Posthypnotic Suggestion

Posthypnotic suggestion is the phenomenon in which a client unconsciously executes a hypnotic directive suggested by the therapist preceding its scheduled implementation. Posthypnotic suggestion enables the benefits acquired in the hypnotherapy session to be extended well beyond the confines of any single treatment episode or the locus of the therapist. Posthypnotic suggestions may directly relate to a client's physical/psychological symptoms (symptom contingent), a predictable time in his or her daily life (time contingent), and/or a specific event such as surgery or a painful clinical procedure (event contingent).

The phenomenon of posthypnotic suggestion is especially relevant to clients suffering from chronic pain and illness. Often they will require relief for extended periods of time without the availability of their therapist. Generally, suggestions for these clients are directed toward interrupting symptom patterns, accessing specific hypnotic phenomena to provide relief, and/or executing various self-hypnosis protocols. Additionally, posthypnotic suggestions benefit clients through increasing their confidence in the hypnotherapeutic process as well as a reinforced belief in the efficacy of the unconscious.

Strategies for Posthypnotic Suggestion

Effective posthypnotic suggestions make reference to specific hypnotic phenomena rather than a general state of being. For example, it is much more effective to suggest that a client have the dissociative experience of "being aware of your discomfort gradually being drawn out of your body like a wave going out to sea" than simply suggesting "relaxation throughout your body." Moreover, suggesting a phenomenon that occurred both in the treatment room (through a recent hypnotic induction) and in the client's real-life sensory experience (elicited through the solution-focused interview) significantly increases the probability of success for the suggestion. Thus, a client recalling a helpful dissociative experience from the past within a current therapy session can be directed to experience it unconsciously in the future.

Erickson and Erickson (1941/1980) stated that, ideally, posthypnotic suggestion occurs spontaneously and automatically outside the client's immediate conscious awareness and represents a (brief) reinstatement of the hypnotic state. It was their belief that when a suggestion remained unconscious it was more difficult to resist. However, we have made an observation coinciding with Edgette and Edgette (1995, p. 70), who stated:

> The degree that any such a (hypnotic) reinstatement occurs can be expected to manifest differently outside the office than in. It has not been our experience that clients move into an externally recognizable state of trance upon any posthypnotic cue; rather they experience some facet of previous trance states. Thus, clients might re-experience the numbness to the affected area, a dissociated type of separation of discomfort and functioning, or the local analgesia without needing to fully experience a dissociated trance state.

Posthypnotic suggestions are most successful when they are repeated in a variety of ways throughout a hypnotic induction. Utilizing an indirect hypnotic approach (outlined earlier) the therapist can present the same posthypnotic directive multiple times, using the linguistic formats of open-ended suggestions, covering all alternatives, presupposition, and conscious/unconscious splits. Likewise, suggestions may be offered at different depths of trance applying the same rules (outlined earlier) for hypnotic suggestions; the less dissociation a client experiences, the more indirect and open-ended the suggestion should be. If the therapist is not sure about the client's level of dissociation, it is best to use a variety of open-ended suggestions.

Similar to pacing a client's immediate sensory and psychological experience during a hypnotic induction, posthypnotic suggestions are significantly enhanced by the therapist's familiarity with the client's real world surroundings. Erickson and Rossi referred to this environment as a group of "associational networks," where "the client's own associations, life experience, personality dynamics, and future prospects are all utilized to build the posthypnotic suggestion into the client's natural life structure"

(Erickson & Rossi, 1979, pp. 85–86). Accordingly, because the client will execute these directives in the future, the therapist should have a basic knowledge of the patterns of the client's everyday life that lead up to the time period, event, or symptom requiring the suggestion.

Thus, if the action is to occur during a daily routine it will be helpful for the therapist to know some of the client's (often mundane) consistent behavioral patterns that occur on a daily basis, such as mealtimes, leaving for and returning from work, walking a pet, talking on the phone, and so on. If a suggestion is to occur in relation to a scheduled clinical event or surgery, the therapist should be aware of the salient details of the procedure and the events that will lead up to it. Likewise, if the suggestion is to interrupt a symptom pattern, it is critical to know the sensory and psychological cues that signal its initial manifestation.

Time-Contingent Suggestions

Posthypnotic suggestions that are constructed to occur within a given time period are particularly helpful to clients who experience uncomfortable symptoms in relation to a specific portion of their day. Their discomfort may be regularly experienced on waking, a sleep disorder in relation to a medical condition, or the experience of being regularly exhausted at a certain time each day.

When working posthypnotically, it is most effective to suggest that a future phenomenon will occur within a general time span rather than at a specified time. Employing a variety of indirect suggestions that make reference to the time period will generally work best. For example, the therapist might suggest that a specific hypnotic phenomenon occur "around breakfast time . . . I'm not sure whether it will be before or after . . . maybe while you are eating . . . perhaps before breakfast . . . or just after you wake up . . . or in that time period between breakfast and lunch . . . perhaps closer to lunch . . . I don't know exactly when . . . " This suggestion offers a specific period of time while giving the client flexibility within the time span to implement the directive.

Before repeating the posthypnotic suggestion (in another form), the therapist should insert additional pacing statements as well as suggestions that the client can benefit from amnesia. This will enhance automatic responses in the future, insuring that it initially occurs on an unconscious level. For example, the therapist might make the statement, "Your conscious mind doesn't really need to remember when that will happen, or even what will happen, because your unconscious can provide comfort autonomously and independently of your conscious mind when you need it . . . and you know that you don't always have your phone number on conscious mind . . . but your unconscious has it when you need it."

Time-contingent suggestions can be used in reference to the period immediately following a hypnotic induction. They are most useful when the therapist and client determine that it would be helpful to continue the relief produced by the induction after its conclusion. For example, the therapist might suggest that "Your unconscious mind can memorize those (previously suggested specific phenomena) feelings of comfort and relief . . . and you can take them out my office door, down the hallway, and all the way home. Your conscious mind, on the other hand, need not be bothered with any such memorization. You know that your conscious mind doesn't really need to remember how to operate the brake and accelerator in your car . . . you do that automatically . . . just in time . . . even though it can be critical and life-saving knowledge. Your unconscious mind stored that information a long time ago and provides it just when you need it . . . just in time."

A minimum of posttrance discussion facilitates amnesia for all forms of posthypnotic suggestion. Often, clients will make reference to their pain being gone or a specific hypnotic phenomenon that they experienced while in trance. Although such discussion is helpful in ratifying the trance experience and measuring the reduction in levels of discomfort, it is not suggestive of the amnesia that enhances posthypnotic suggestion. Moreover, frequently talking about the specifics of pain control may negate the phenomena (Eastwood, Gaskovski, & Bowers, 1998).

If the client wants to engage in such a conversation, however, it is best for the therapist to make broad statements referring to the unconscious and power of hypnosis in general. For example, the therapist might state, "Well, now you know that your unconscious is a very powerful thing and can operate autonomously and independently of your conscious mind, providing relief in the most surprising ways. I'm sure that both our conscious minds are curious about what your unconscious will come up with between now and the next time I see you." Finally, in reference to amnesia, if the therapist suspects that the posttrance discussion might in some way be detrimental to the success of posthypnotic suggestions, the therapist can briefly reintroduce the trance state, suggesting amnesia again, subsequently reorienting and concluding the session.

Event-Contingent Suggestions

Event-contingent suggestions are helpful in providing relief in relation to a scheduled uncomfortable clinical procedure or therapeutic process.

Event-contingent suggestions can be utilized in relation to preoperative anxiety and postoperative pain (Lynch, 1999). Likewise, they can be constructed to coincide with a painful, regularly scheduled therapeutic procedure. Additionally, event-contingent suggestions can be utilized in conjunction with the occurrence of the client engaging in a self-hypnosis protocol.

In all cases, event-contingent suggestions are significantly enhanced when the therapist has knowledge of the process of the event and the environment in which it will occur. For example, if the therapist is using hypnosis as an intervention for a painful procedure, it is helpful to know the details of the process from start to finish. This would include the time of day of the procedure, the way in which the client is transported to the procedure, the details of the treatment room along with the type of equipment involved, specific details of the procedure itself, different treatment staff members will be encountered, and so on.

Recently, a therapist facilitating a pain-management program for a client undergoing an extremely painful debriding procedure on a deep, open wound on his arm offered these event-contingent suggestions within the following (abridged) hypnotic induction:

Now you and I know that this is no easy thing . . . and you certainly have memories of how painful this was yesterday . . . but your unconscious mind can serve you well . . . and who knows when your unconscious mind will come to your aid . . . perhaps it will begin when the orderly rolls in that silly wheelchair to take you down there even though you can walk on your own . . . or after he pushes the button on the elevator . . . it could "kick in" while you're waiting for him to come to your room . . . the only thing that's important is that you're aware that your unconscious mind can provide you with a variety of types of relief . . . whether you experience it, just as you did a moment ago, as your arm comfortably separated from the rest of your body floating in a sea of comfortable numbness . . . or, on the other hand, you may notice it slowly building and spreading throughout your arm from the top of your shoulder through the tips of your fingers . . . maybe your arm will go somewhere else completely, unknown to you, getting the treatment it needs to eradicate an infection, while the rest of you stays here . . . and it's difficult to know exactly when a thing begins . . . maybe in the elevator as you look up and watch the floor numbers diminish, from the tenth floor . . . all the way down to the basement . . . I don't know, whether, by the time you arrive in the treatment room . . . that arm will be floating away from your body or your body floating away from the arm. I do know that after you enter the hydrotherapy room you will be aware of the whirlpool tank filling up with water . . . and whether the sound reminds you of a gentle stream, a magnificent waterfall . . . or the time and you were comfortably floating in the Caribbean with the waves softly rocking you "to and fro," . . . or something even more comfortable . . . I don't know . . . and as the technician rolls your chair up next to the tank . . . your unconscious mind is capable of reminding you of all the different ways that you can go into a trance . . . maybe it will begin with simple Eye Breathing . . . or one of the other techniques you just learned . . . it doesn't really matter because you're unconscious can choose the best course for you.

Utilizing these (undeniable) events within this type of intervention positively links the logistics of a (predictable) process to the desired hypnotherapeutic outcome. This phenomenon of "pacing the future" naturally results in the construction of a posthypnotic "yes set" enabling the client to more effortlessly respond to the therapist's posthypnotic suggestion.

Symptom-Contingent Suggestions

Symptom-contingent suggestions address anticipated future physical or psychological discomfort. Similar to event-contingent suggestions, it will be helpful for the therapist to have some knowledge of the ways in which painful symptoms initially manifest themselves. Primarily, this is accomplished through a conversation with the client about his or her obs tions of the ways in which specific symptoms initially become noticeable. Generally, these signs are experienced at the threshold of discomfort for the client.

For example, in the case of a client who experiences (predictable) joint pain, the therapist might suggest that he or she can interpret those first signs of throbbing and aching as a signal to "just for a moment . . . sit down . . . take a breath, and let your unconscious mind infuse your joints with the warmth of the sun that you experienced in Mexico last year. With every normal, measured breath you take, the energy from the sun can increase its penetration in your joints in such a way that transports them to the comfort of lying on a warm beach listening to the waves rhythmically ebb and flow back and forth."

Symptom-contingent suggestions can provide a preventative function with the client suffering from chronic pain and illness as well. Occasionally, these clients ignore the initial warning signs their symptoms provide. This often results in a needless exacerbation of their chronic condition. On the other hand, some clients may experience so much anxiety from the mere anticipation of a symptom that they unnecessarily experience discomfort where none should exist. In both cases, symptom-contingent posthypnotic suggestions can be offered to divert these reactions into a form that enables the client to experience some therapeutic distraction. Construction of posthypnotic suggestions in these cases centers on directing the client to become aware of the earliest warning signals and to engage in an ultradian rest cycle and/or self-hypnosis protocol.

The following example was constructed for a client suffering from migraine headaches. Recently, they had become so frequent that she would become quite anxious just in the anticipation of them, ultimately making things worse. The therapist, aware that the psychological impact of the anticipatory anxiety and the discomfort from the physical symptoms were inexorably entwined, offered the following symptom-contingent suggestions within the hypnotic (abridged) induction:

> Your unconscious can act like radar, offering you an early warning system to repel these attacks before they do serious damage. Of course, you can never be sure where or when these things are going to turn up . . . but you can be sure about what you can do about them. The first sign may be a small "blip" on the screen . . . maybe you will notice your breathing rate becoming slightly elevated . . . perhaps your heart picking up a beat or two . . . or even feeling slightly disoriented . . . these signals, like a yellow traffic light or a stop sign, can indicate the fact that you can slow down or even stop for moment . . . take a second to plant your feet firmly on the ground . . . maybe you will even hear the sound of my voice, just as it is speaking to you now, reminding you to engage in that [self-hypnotic] exercise you did just a moment ago . . . the one that made a difference for you. The one that allowed you to separate your head from your body while keeping all your senses intact. Recognizing a signal can be an automatic thing, like observing an outstretched hand and raising your hand up to shake it without thinking, or, recognizing your luggage at the airport and just going over to the carousel and picking it up. . . . Maybe you'll get the signal through an aura . . . perhaps a little dizziness . . . it's not important . . . those signals are your friends—keeping you out of dangerous traffic until it passes . . . enabling you to pass safely and productively.

Implementing symptom-contingent posthypnotic suggestions increases the options for the client in relation to the ways in which he or she manages the condition. Interrupting symptom patterns not only increases the client's sense of mastery over a painful condition but also serves as a kind of preventative maintenance sequence enabling a client to improve the quality of his or her life.

Continuing with the earlier case example of Mike, the therapist, after fractionating the hypnotic experience by briefly reorienting Mike from his trance, reinduced a trance state with the purpose of constructing posthypnotic suggestions aimed at addressing his specific goals.

Case Example (Part 2)—Posthypnotic Suggestion

Induction	Commentary
And Mike, as you can see me over here directly in front of you . . . listening to the sound of my voice . . . having an awareness of what's important and what isn't . . . you can take all the time in the world to let your eyes close . . . naturally . . . on their own.	Reintroduction of trance, open-ended neutral statements along with pacing current experience leading to presupposing eye closure.

Client closes eyes.

Induction	Commentary
Now your conscious mind can recall the image of me sitting in front of you, just a moment ago, on the other side of your eyelids . . . while your unconscious mind can get back in that rhythm again . . .	Using conscious/unconscious splits to further the reintroduction of trance. Reintroduction of soothing image—age regression.
The waves . . . the sun . . . the soothing sound . . . all completely available to you . . . floating on top of everything . . . not really having to worry about anything in particular.	

The therapist continued to reintroduce induction until the client reexhibited external signs of trance.

Induction	Commentary
And everyone knows the difference between the past, the present, and the future . . . and your unconscious mind can bring the past into the present so you can use it in the future.	Truism setting up the introduction of posthypnotic suggestion, suggesting that the unconscious can effectively utilize all time periods.
And while your conscious mind is excellent at addressing the "here and now," your unconscious mind can record important things for the future that can be recalled later . . . when you need them most . . .	Conscious/unconscious splits further setting up posthypnotic suggestion.
And I'm not exactly sure when, it might be shortly after you leave here . . . perhaps tomorrow morning, after you have had a good night's sleep, before lunch . . . maybe a little bit after . . .	Introduction of a variety of time-contingent possibilities. Presupposing a good night's sleep.

. . . Your unconscious mind . . . without particularly bothering your conscious mind . . . can glance over to that night table to your right and observe that pile of crossword puzzle books sitting there . . . stacked quite neatly waiting to be opened . . .	Suggestion of dissociation and amnesia. Utilization of the client's familiar environment.
. . . And you can wonder which one would bring you the most pleasure. Will it be the May issue, perhaps the June, just in time for summer vacation . . . maybe that one from last winter, Christmas . . . it really doesn't matter . . .	Presupposition about the ability to receive pleasure and relief and the action of picking up a book.
And you can just sit there and wonder what it would be like to lose yourself so completely in a puzzle that nothing else mattered . . . reach over and choose one.	Suggestion of dissociation along with direct suggestion to pick up book.
And whichever month you choose you can open to a clean page . . . a fresh grid . . . columns and rows of boxes waiting for you to fill them up . . .	Pacing a future (undeniable) event
And of course your conscious mind might have that doubt, remembering that discomfort, while your unconscious mind can travel to that top deck, continuing in that rhythm that has been so freeing . . . and what is a four-letter word for "comfort?" . . .	Conscious/unconscious split—pacing inevitable doubt while suggesting positive hallucination. Reference to current trance and past comfortable event. Indirect suggestion of comfort.
As your pen moves across the page . . . automatically . . . filling in each square without really thinking . . . as if it had a mind of its own . . . just like signing your name . . . without thinking, unconsciously . . . that feeling of the top deck can, then, as now, saturate your spine . . . and the feeling of the sun, the sound of the waves, the rhythm of the movement can follow.	Suggestion of ideodynamic (automatism) hypnotic phenomenon. Posthypnotic suggestion for age regression. More suggestions of dissociation specifically directed at the locus of pain.
. . . While you experience that feeling . . . I don't know whether it would be better for you to take the puzzles up to the top deck or bring the top deck down to finish	Presuppositions suggesting dissociation. Indirect suggestion of calm, comfort, and ease, linked to client's envi-

them . . . you may want to leave your back up there while finishing them down here . . . it doesn't really matter . . . and of course tomorrow you will know that four-letter word for comfort is . . . "calm" . . . of course it could be "ease." You'll know tomorrow which . . . maybe both . . .

ronment and inevitable actions.

As you continue to fill in the boxes... tomorrow . . . you might wonder where the time is going . . . whether on a top deck or moving around those columns and rows . . . time really doesn't matter. A minute can seem like an hour, an hour like a day . . . or you can stop time altogether and step in between two moments . . . perhaps swing on a hammock between them . . . anything can be finished when you can stop time . . . never needing to concern yourself with how long you are spending floating on the rhythm of the waves.

Event-contingent suggestion for the phenomenon of time distortion linked to further dissociation. Reference to client's goal of finishing the puzzle.

You have all the time in the world to determine whether "ease" or "calm" means "comfort" . . . or maybe its another four-letter word . . . I don't know.

Suggesting time distortion to enable pleasant experiences.

. . . When you are done filling in that last box you can put your pen down and take just a moment . . . all the time in the world . . . to appreciate your ability to be in two places at once . . . and you know that your unconscious mind can't be confined to stay just in one place . . . the body can stay behind . . . taken care of by the natural healing rhythms . . . but your unconscious can go wherever it wants . . .

Presupposition of completion of a goal. Suggestions for full dissociation following completion of the puzzle. Suggestions making reference to mind–body split with indirect reference to the ability to dissociate during previous confinement.

As the induction drew to a close, the therapist made several time-contingent suggestions referencing a good night's sleep and amnesia. These were framed within the posthypnotic suggestion that immediately after reorienting, Mike could "continue to experience that 'top deck' sensation with all its sensations of floating, warmth, and rhythm, without your unconscious mind needing to worry," continuing with the suggestion that he "take that sensation to bed with you and sleep on it." Upon the therapist visiting several days later, Mike proudly presented a stack of (completed) crossword puzzle books, remarking, "I sleep on that top deck every night."

Discussion.   Posthypnotic suggestion is particularly useful for continuing the client's dissociative experience after the hypnotic session. In addition to the client's immediate posthypnotic relief, the phenomenon serves as a vehicle to persuade the client that he or she, in fact, possesses significant resources that are capable of addressing the condition in the future. Clients who need to drive home after a therapy session should receive suggestions about their ability to remain focused, alert, and awake during the trip, followed by time- and/or event-contingent posthypnotic suggestions referencing the continuation of relief.

In subsequent sessions therapist should look for opportunities to determine the effectiveness of posthypnotic suggestions without making a direct reference to them. Often, clients such as Mike will recount their experience before the therapist makes an inquiry. Once the quality and frequency of the client's posthypnotic experience have been determined, the therapist can incorporate the experience into the next hypnotic induction, further reinforcing the experience.

☐ Supplementing Solution-Focused Tasks with Posthypnotic Suggestions

One of the most effective ways to integrate solution-focused therapy with clinical hypnosis is to incorporate conscious task assignments outlined in chapter 7 with posthypnotic suggestion. This can be accomplished in a variety of ways. Posthypnotic suggestions can be designed to coincide with observational tasks. For example, the task to "observe the times when your symptoms are better" can be supplemented with the event-contingent posthypnotic suggestion to "take advantage of that feeling and expand it by sitting down and just for a moment engage in that technique that worked so well in the office." Alternately, helpful (experiential) observations can be expanded with the posthypnotic suggestion to the client that "your unconscious mind can memorize that experience (observation) and reacquaint you with it at a later time."

Metaphorical and "doing" tasks can be supplemented posthypnotically as well. Both contexts lend themselves to symptom- and event-contingent suggestions. Frequently clients fail to engage in a helpful self-care activity because of the overwhelming apprehension produced by anticipated symptom flare-ups. Thus, on the observation of the recurrence of a symptom, the client's anxiety can be interrupted and quelled with a posthypnotic suggestion about his or her ability to "slow time down . . . remember to breathe so that you can take care of yourself . . . and take back control of your body by doing . . . (the self-care technique)."

Employing the phenomena of age regression (to remember past resources) and amnesia (to forget past failure and disappointment) within the context of posthypnotic suggestion can significantly enhance metaphorical task assignments. They can be very helpful in evoking the central process of the metaphorical task—to represent, discover, remember, and reinforce meaningful resources and exceptions the client has at his or her disposal to address the condition. Thus, whether engaging in the Emergency Roadside Repair Kit, Memory Virus, or Rainy Day Letter tasks, it can be suggested to the client that by engaging in the task he or she can simultaneously "remember those times you were able to fully utilize your resources . . . and forget the things that really don't matter."

☐ Summary

Hypnotic and posthypnotic suggestions are extremely effective in providing relief for clients suffering from pain and chronic illness. Success in employing these suggestions with this client population is dependent on the degree of rapport established by the therapist through interweaving pacing and leading statements. This is accomplished by initiating the induction process through generalized, open-ended, permissive, and indirect suggestions, progressing though presupposition and implication, and ultimately setting the stage for the delivery of specific direct hypnotic injunctions for symptom relief.

Employing this continuum facilitates a hypnotic framework that contributes to the construction of (time-, event-, and symptom-contingent) posthypnotic suggestions enabling the client to utilize helpful hypnotic phenomena outside the therapist's office. Moreover, this framework facilitates the smooth integration of self- and heterohypnotic approaches, thereby expanding the range of options available to the client. Furthermore, hypnotic and posthypnotic suggestion strategies can significantly supplement the solution-focused task assignments outlined in chapter 7. Finally, the limited scope of any general introduction to hypnosis inherently limits a fully comprehensive discussion of suggestive strategies. The reader wishing more information is referred to Hammond's (1990) excellent edited volume *Handbook of Hypnotic Suggestions and Metaphors* for a more exhaustive survey of the subject.

☐ References

Bandler, R., & Grinder, J. (1975). *Patterns of the hypnotic techniques of Milton H. Erickson, M.D.* (Vol. I). Cupertino, CA: Meta Publications.

Barber, J. (1982). Managing acute pain. In J. Barber & C. Adrian (Eds.), *Psychological approaches to the management of pain* (pp. 168–179). New York: Brunner/Mazel.

Barber, J. (1996a). A brief introduction to hypnotic analgesia. In J. Barber (Ed.), *Hypnosis and suggestion in the treatment of pain: A clinical guide* (pp. 3–32). New York: W. W. Norton.

Barber, J. (1996b). Hypnotic analgesia: Clinical considerations. In J. Barber (Ed.), *Hypnosis and suggestion in the treatment of pain: A clinical guide* (pp. 85–118) New York: W. W. Norton.

Eastwood, J. D., Gaskovski, P., & Bowers, K. S. (1998). The folly of effort: Ironic effects in the mental control of pain. *International Journal of Clinical and Experimental Hypnosis, 46*(1), 71–91.

Edgette, J. H., & Edgette, J. S. (1995). *The handbook of hypnotic phenomena in psychotherapy.* New York: Brunner/Mazel.

Edmonston, W. E. (1986). *The induction of hypnosis.* New York: Wiley.

Erickson, M. H., & Erickson, E. M. (1980). Concerning the nature and character of post-hypnotic behavior. In E. L. Rossi (Ed.), *The collected papers of Milton H. Erickson on hypnosis: Vol. I. The nature of hypnosis and suggestion* (pp. 381–411). New York: Irvington. (Original work published 1941.)

Erickson, M., & Rossi, E. (1979). *Hypnotherapy: An exploratory casebook.* New York: Irvington.

Erickson, M. H., Rossi, E. L., & Rossi, S. I. (1976). *Hypnotic realities: The induction of clinical hypnosis and forms of indirect suggestion.* New York: Irvington.

Gilligan, S. (1986). *Therapeutic trances: The cooperation principle in Ericksonian hypnotherapy.* New York: Brunner/Mazel.

Hammond, D. C. (1984). Myths about Erickson and Ericksonian hypnosis. *American Journal of Clinical Hypnosis, 26*(4), 236–245.

Hammond, D. C. (1990). *Handbook of hypnotic suggestions and metaphors.* New York: W. W. Norton.

Lankton, S., & Lankton C. (1983). *The answer within: A clinical framework for Ericksonian hypnotherapy.* New York: Brunner/Mazel.

Lynch, D. F. (1999). Empowering the client: Hypnosis and the management of cancer, surgical disease, and chronic pain. *American Journal of Clinical Hypnosis, 42*(2), 123–130.

Weitzenhoffer, A. M. (1989a). *The Practice of hypnotism* (Vol. I). New York: Wiley.

Weitzenhoffer, A. M. (1989b). *The Practice of hypnotism* (Vol. II). New York: Wiley.

Caring for the Caregiver

This chapter is relatively brief, despite the importance of the topic and the prevalence of caregiver stress and burnout, because the approaches described in the foregoing chapters are those most likely to be helpful for caregivers as well as patients. There are many different caregiver roles: professional and nonprofessional, formal and informal, intermittent and constant. Although each of these roles has its own special stresses, they have more in common than might be immediately apparent. For example, more professionals, patients, and families find themselves providing care in the community and the home. More patients with Alzheimer's disease are cared for at home, and more terminally ill people are choosing to die at home.

In addition to home care as a choice, the institution of cost containment efforts has forced institutions, families, and individuals to find ways to do more with less. The greater prevalence of an aging population with multiple chronic illnesses requires continuous care over long periods, in contrast to earlier periods when acute illnesses were the major health care focus. Despite the worldwide increase of women in the paid work force and the dispersion of extended families through geographic mobility, there is an apparent assumption that even complex medical procedures can and should be delivered in the home by the patient or family members. Although self-care can be empowering for clients who choose to take more control over their situation, it can be an additional source of stress to those who have neither the energy nor the inclination to engage in many self-care activities. This distortion of the concept of self-care has serious consequences for the persons with chronic illness or pain and for those who care for them, professionally and personally.

☐ What Is "Burnout"?

Burnout is defined as a "prolonged response to chronic emotional and interpersonal stressors on the job" (Maslach, 1997). Burnout was first described in studies of nurses, often based on concerns about high absenteeism and turnover rates. Subsequent studies have described the phenomenon in a wide range of care providers. Burnout is usually described as an individual stress experience that exists in a social context, particularly within social relationships. Three components of burnout have been identified: emotional exhaustion, depersonalization, and a reduced sense of personal accomplishment. Emotional exhaustion often includes complaints of depleted energy, fatigue, or feeling worn down as a consequence of feeling emotionally overextended. Depersonalization describes a pervasive loss of idealism, which may be evidenced by a sense of detachment, a negative or callous attitude toward clients, and increased irritability. The tendency to treat others as objects and care as an application of technology reflects depersonalization (Peters, 1997). The concept of reduced sense of personal accomplishment refers to low morale, withdrawal, reduced productivity, and diminished feelings of competence. Peters described the five stages of burnout as idealism and enthusiasm, followed by disappointment, frustration, and eventual apathy.

Even without burnout and with the ability to maintain deep caring and concern, many in the caring professions suffer emotional and/or physical exhaustion related to continuous exposure to overwhelming experiences. *Compassion fatigue* (Figley, 1995) is a related concept that refers to the sense of numbed feelings, withdrawal, and general anxiety responses that may insidiously invade the lives of those who deal with trauma victims or work with continuous suffering and death. Most of us who entered the helping professionals did so because we wanted to help others. When we find ourselves working with people who don't get better or continue to suffer despite our best efforts, it is not unusual to find a sense of hopelessness and personal inadequacy creeping into our daily lives.

Who Experiences Burnout?

The major focus of this chapter is on professional health care providers; however, most of the points made here apply equally to the informal caregiver, partner, or family member who provides care for another. Dealing not only with the ill person but also with the need to interact with professionals can be an overwhelming responsibility for the partner or family member of one who is ill. Too often this role is undertaken without sufficient respite or assistance from others and in addition to other personal and work responsibilities (Jutras & Veilleux, 1991). Similarly, the burden of the illness itself and the need to expend precious energy on just getting through each day mean that patients themselves often become exhausted and apathetic, depersonalized, and incompetent.

Signs and Symptoms of Caregiver Burnout/Compassion Fatigue

The signs and symptoms of burnout share those associated with general stress responses indicating compromised physical and mental health (Lerner, Levine, Malspeis, & D'Agostino, 1994), that is, complaints that are physical (including sleep disturbances), emotional (depression, anxiety, tension), behavioral (withdrawal, denial, aggression, overuse of alcohol or other substances) (Freudenberger, 1990), and cognitive (diminished abilities for decision making, concentration, memory, and perceptual accuracy). Leading up to these signs and symptoms is usually a pattern that reveals an imbalance between work demands and personal resources. "Longer working hours, little time with family, hurried meals, frequent minor illnesses and sleep disturbances" set the stage for acute and chronic stress responses and eventual burnout (Peters, 1997). In contrast to a growing sense of apathy, another risk of overinvolvement with one's work can be problems with appropriate boundaries within the therapeutic relationship. When our work isolates us from others, we may find we are meeting our own needs for companionship in the therapeutic relationship—overidentifying with clients' problems or talking more about our own lives than is helpful to the client (Porter, 1995).

We suspect impending burnout in ourselves and others when we:

- Begin to think of clients as resistant.
- Think of clients' weaknesses rather than their strengths.
- Can't see possibilities or futures for our clients.
- Use the language of pathology to describe clients.

Those we live with may complain that we:

- Can't stop talking about the job, the clients, and managed care, outside the office.
- Are too tired to do anything else at the end of the day.

- Use too much TV, alcohol, and so on, eradicating the time we do have and not getting replenished.
- Have no energy to do anything creative or fun.

Risk Factors and Mediators: Personal and Contextual

Research on the risk factors and mediators of burnout focuses on the separate or interdependent personal and organizational factors. By extension, many contexts of care, organizational or otherwise, can intensify or mediate the experience of stressors related to caring. Burnout is complex, and interrelated variables are multiple and tenacious. A meta-analysis of the correlates of nursing burnout identified as major factors role ambiguity, work load, age, hardiness, active coping, and social support (Duquette, Kerouac, Sandhu, & Beaudet, 1994). Risk factors found in a study of clinical psychologists included low job satisfaction, low range of active coping strategies, high use of avoidance coping strategies involving denial, stressors not externalized and objectified, stressors that threatened other roles/relationships, low experience in job, no quality relationship with confidante or poor quality relationship with partner, and being female (Cushway & Tyler, 1996). In a study of workers in long-term care settings, burnout was related to the fit between the demands and risks of the job, specific professional education, personality traits, and habitual behavior patterns (Sandman & Wallbrom, 1997).

The concept of "misfit with work demands" raises the obvious question of just what strengths and resources would prepare someone to work in close proximity with pain, grief, suffering, and despair without fear of "contagion." A study of "stayers" and "leavers" in a cancer center found both groups were above the norms in despair, social isolation, and somatization, described as "chronic compounded grief" as a consequence of repeated confrontations with death (Feldstein & Gemma, 1995). In addition, the health risks associated with changing shifts are considerable (Taylor, 1997), as are the risks of repeated sleep interruptions experienced by caretakers in the home. Over and above these risks there are growing concerns about malpractice suits, documentation requirements, and standards of care (especially with higher patient acuity and higher patient-to-provider ratios) (Jones, Barge, Steffy, & Fay, 1998). High demands, low control, and perceived lack of social support have been consistently associated with a risk of burnout. Institutional settings appear to provide a greater opportunity for social support than would be likely for the therapist in private practice. Practicing in isolation with the weight of protecting client confidentiality, the therapist has much in common with the family member who may become literally and figuratively isolated from others who "don't want to hear" about the problems. On the other hand, institutions may also be perceived as a major source of work stress, when workers feel unsupported and overwhelmed by work demands. Perception of a threat of unemployment provides yet another potential source of work stress (Toivanen et al., 1996).

Several personal characteristics have been associated with increased risk or as protective factors against burnout. Individual reactivity to stress has been linked to differential burnout rates (De las Cuevas, Gonzelez de Rivera, De la Fuiente, Alviani, & Ruiz-Benitez, 1997), whereas a "negative cognitive style" has been implicated in vulnerability to burnout (Evans, 1991). In one study, trait anxiety combined with a measure of stress accurately predicted over 80% of the workers in high and low burnout categories (Griffin, 1990). An interactive effect was found in one study of social support and burnout in which extraverted nurses required more work-related peer support in order to avoid emotional exhaustion (Eastburg, 1991).

Among personal characteristics most consistently associated with protection against burnout is the concept of "hardiness" or personal resiliency (Duquette, Kerouac, Sandhu, Ducharme, & Saulnier, 1995). "Hardiness" is described by Suzanne Ouellette as comprised of commitment, control, and challenge (Dreher, 1995; Kobasa, 1990). "Hardy individuals are characterized by their personal belief of having personal control and influence over events or stressors in their lives. They have the ability to recognize their goals, values, and priorities and can alter their perception of stressors to minimize personal threat. Hardy individuals view change as an exciting challenge" (Wright, Blache, & Luterman, 1993). Closely related, a "sense of coherence" has also been associated with preventing burnout (Lewis, Bonner, Campbell, Cooper, & Willard, 1994). Antonovsky described a "sense of coherence" as "a global orientation that expresses the confidence that (a) the stimuli deriving from one's internal and external environments in the course of living are structured, predictable, and explicable; (b) the resources are available to one to meet the demands posed by these stimuli; and (c) these demands are challenges, worthy of investment and engagement. These three components are called, respectively, comprehensibility, manageability and meaningfulness" (Antonovsky, 1990, p. 231). Because it is precisely this sense of coherence that is most damaged by the experience of poorly understood chronic illnesses and chronic pain, it is not surprising that both patients and their caregivers often have a diminished sense of competence.

☐ Caregivers and Self-Care

A report of the WHO Guidelines for Primary Prevention of Mental, Neurological and Psychosocial Disorders (Anonymous, 1995) emphasized that recovery and prevention of staff burnout require the same things: new work situations that provide autonomy, organizational support, and interesting work. These guidelines speak succinctly to the institutional level of the problem, but leave open the issue of what caregivers might also do to retain or regain their passion for what they do. Some clinicians have recognized the hazards for the professional caregiver (Reynolds, 1997) and recommend different forms of "therapy for the therapist." Multiple approaches to treating and/or preventing burnout appear in the literature and include, among others, support groups, regular relaxation training, massage, information sessions, music therapy, art therapy, cognitive behavioral programs and skills groups, exercise and meditation, and humor.

One professional group has within its ethical guidelines the expectation that self-care for the therapist is essential to ethical practice: "A feminist therapist engages in self-care activities in an ongoing manner. She [sic] acknowledges her own vulnerabilities and seeks to care for herself outside the therapy setting. She models the ability and willingness to self-nurture in appropriate and self-empowering ways." In contrast to views of self-care that are limited to improving physical function, Porter told a parable about a therapist who had "given everything" to her professional life, only to find one day that her clients were unmotivated, her students no longer intelligent, and her workshop participants ungrateful. When she sought guidance from an older, wiser therapist she was advised to "Walk to a remote hill each evening and watch the sun set. Talk to a friend each day. And sing or dance at least once a week" (1995, pp. 247–248).

The foregoing chapters and the following chapter on "experiments" reflect a similar message: Dare to believe that your situation can be better and then begin to take the small steps that can make it so. Here are some suggestions:

- Ask the miracle question: Suppose your life got a lot better? And scale it and work with that. One step at a time.
- What if it were possible to have a life that included both passion for your work and balance in your life? What would that look like?
- Who would notice what?
- What difference would that make?
- Take *smaller steps*—not just "do what you love"—it's the little things that add up.

- Play the "anthropologist" and study an exotic culture in which people live balanced lives: Ask what others do.

Here's a list of some of the things we found our own colleagues do to stay whole:

- Cultivate creativity and humor in my life.
- Surf the internet for possibilities—stay curious about new ideas "out there."
- Try out being creative in another area, such as, improv, quilting, pottery, painting.
- Take some classes in a topic that interests you.
- Stay in contact with friends who are not therapists.
- Do some experience sampling—find out how you really spend your time and how it feels.
- Running.
- Meditation.
- Golf.
- Enjoy my kids.
- Develop ways to ritualize separating work from the rest of your life, such as, changing your clothes, feeding the dog, taking a shower—moving into a different "place," leaving work behind.
- Take regular mini-retreats (no phone, newspaper, projects, or unfinished work).

If you do many of the things listed in the "experiments" and self-care chapters you should be able to identify the unique solutions to your problem that will best meet your own needs. If you're open to trying some self-care "experiments," we've included a list of those used by health care professionals in a graduate class on health and healing. Some of these are probably familiar, whereas others are highly original, based on the students' "favorite" ways to take care of themselves. At the end of this chapter, we include some of the "experiments"/questions that may help you identify not only how to be a worthy companion, but also how to take care of yourself in the process.

You'll know when it's time for you to begin to take care of yourself. Remember that you need to be a customer and not a complainant. With time you may even become an artist at living your own life.

☐ Experiments for Becoming a Worthy Companion

In addition to the experiments in chapter 11, we list here a few consciousness-raising questions specific to therapists for becoming a worthy companion and creating a meaningful life.

What characteristics make anyone (friend, family, etc.) a good companion—who already is one? What can you ask for from a companion?

What can you ask for from a companion?

What do you have to offer as a companion?

- Fears.

  What are your concerns about working with people who are ill, in pain, or dying?

- Trust.

  What makes someone trustworthy?

  Who and what do I already trust?

  What can clients trust me for?

- Posttraumatic stress disorder.

  If you think of clients as probably having multiple traumas associated with their illness and treatment, does that influence the ways you think about how you can be helpful?

  Do you have ways to calm yourself?

  How can you help clients build on the ways they already are able to calm themselves?

- Helping and coping (self-evaluation).

  Review the points in chapter 2 about models of helping and coping. Do you tend to think about clients from the perspective of the medical model, moral model, compensatory model, or enlightenment model?

  Does it depend on what the illness or condition is?

- Cultural beliefs.

  It can be illuminating to ask older family members some of the questions posed by Spector (1996) in *Cultural Diversity in Health and Illness*. Among the questions are:

  What is health/illness?

  What are signs of being healthy/ill?

  What do they do to maintain health and prevent illness?

  What causes illness?

- Wholeness.

  What does wholeness, as a definition of health, mean to you and for you?

  Does this definition translate into the things to do to maintain your own health?

- Mobilizing hope.

  What are your beliefs about hope?

  Can you give someone else hope?

  How do you mobilize your hope for clients?

- Envisioning the client without limitations (or with limitations that must be worked with, but doing so successfully).

Holding positive intentions for clients can take many forms. How do you hold clients in your consciousness?

Are you able to envision your clients as able to manage their condition? Does the client have to be able to first envision this before you can?

Can you do so when the client's own hope is at low ebb?

- Curiosity about the future.

How do you communicate and model for clients a healthy and hopeful sense of curiosity about the future?

How is curiosity about the future different from fear?

How is open-ended curiosity different from predetermined outcomes such as those reflected in affirmations or five-year plans?

☐ References

Anonymous. (1995). How to prevent burnout. Extracted from Guidelines for the Primary Prevention of Mental, Neurological and Psychosocial Disorders: 5. Staff Burnout, Division of Mental Health, WHO/MNH/MND/94.21. *International Nursing Review, 42*(5), 159.

Antonovsky, A. (1990). The salutogenic model of health. In. R. Ornstein & C. Swencionis (Eds.), *The healing brain* (pp. 231–243). New York: Guilford.

Cushway, D., & Tyler, P. (1996). Stress in clinical psychologists. *International Journal of Social Psychiatry, 42*(2), 141–149.

De las Cuevas, C., Gonzelez de Rivera, J., De la Fuiente, J., Alviani, M., & Ruiz-Benitez, A. (1997). Burnout and reaction to stress. *Revista de Medicina de la Universidad de Navarra, 41*(2), 10–18.

Dreher, H. (1995). *The immune power personality.* New York: Penguin.

Duquette, A., Kerouac, S., Sandhu, B., & Beaudet, L. (1994). Factors related to nursing burnout: A review of empirical knowledge. *Issues in Mental Health Nursing, 15*(4), 337–358.

Duquette, A., Kerouac, S., Sandhu, B., Ducharme, F., & Saulnier, P. (1995). Psychosocial determinant of burnout in geriatric nursing. *International Journal of Nursing Studies, 32*(5), 443–456.

Eastburg, M. (1991). *Social support, personality and burnout in nurses.* Unpublished doctoral dissertation, Fuller Theological Seminary, School of Psychology, Pasadena, CA.

Evans, C. (1991). *The hopelessness theory and the burnout of nurses.* Unpublished doctoral dissertation, Fielding Institute, Santa Barbara, CA.

Feldstein, M., & Gemma, P. (1995). Oncology nurses and chronic compounded grief. *Cancer Nursing, 18*(3), 228–236.

Figley, C. (1995). Compassion fatigue as secondary traumatic stress disorder: An overview. In C. R. Figley (Ed.), *Compassion fatigue: Coping with secondary traumatic stress disorder in those who treat the traumatized* (pp. 1–20). New York: Brunner/Mazel.

Freudenberger, H. (1990). Hazards of psychotherapeutic practice. *Psychotherapy in Private Practice, 8*(1), 31–34. (Original work presented 1988.)

Griffin, A. (1990). *Stress, trait anxiety, and coping strategies indicative of burnout in nursing staff in long-term health care facilities.* Unpublished doctoral dissertation, Texas A & M University, College Station.

Jones, J., Barge, B., Steffy, B., & Fay, L. (1988). Stress and medical malpractice: Organizational risk assessment and intervention. *Journal of Applied Psychology, 73*(4), 727–735.

Jutras, S., & Veilleux, F. (1991). Informal caregiving: Correlates of perceived burden. *Canadian Journal on Aging, 10*(1), 40–55.

Kobasa, S. (1990). Stress-resistant personality. In R. Ornstein & C. Swencionis (Eds.), *The healing brain* (pp. 219–230). New York: Guilford Press.

Lerner, D., Levine, S., Malspeis, S., & D'Agostino, R. (1994). Job strain and health-related quality of life in a national sample. *American Journal of Public Health, 84*(10), 1580–1585.

Lewis, S., Bonner, P., Campbell, M., Cooper, C. & Willard, A. (1994). Personality, stress, coping and sense of coherence among nephrology nurses in dialysis settings. *Anna Journal, 21*(6), 325–336

Maslach, C. (1997). Burnout in health professionals. In A. Baum, S. Newman, J. Weinman, R. West, & C. McManus (Eds.), *Cambridge handbook of psychology, health and medicine* (pp. 275–278). Cambridge: Cambridge University Press.

Paradis, L, Miller, B., & Runnion, V. (1987). Volunteer stress and burnout: Issues for administrators: Special Issues: stress and burnout among providers caring for the terminally ill and their families. *Hospice Journal, 3*(2–3), 165–183.

Peters, D. (1997) Self-care: Stress and the practitioner. In A. Watkins (Ed.), *Mind–body medicine: A clinician's guide to psychoneuroimmunology* (pp. 269–286). New York: Churchill Livingstone.

Porter, N. (1995). Therapist self-care: A proactive ethical approach. In E. Rave & C. Larsen (Eds.), *Ethical decision making in therapy: Feminist perspectives* (pp. 247–266). New York: Guilford Press.

Reynolds, S. (1997). Psychological well-being at work: Is prevention better than cure? *Journal of Psychosomatic Research, 43*(1), 93–102.

Sandman, P., & Wallbrom, A. (1997). Characteristics of the demented living in different settings in Sweden. *Acta Neurologica Scandinavica Supplementum, 94*(Suppl. 168), 96–100.

Spector, R. (1996). *Cultural diversity in health and illness* (4th ed.). Norwalk, CT: Appleton & Lange.

Taylor, E. (1997). Shiftwork and health. In A. Baum, S. Newman, J. Weinman, R. West, & C. McManus (Eds.), *Cambridge handbook of psychology, health and medicine* (pp. 318–319). Cambridge: Cambridge University Press.

Toivanen, H., Lansimies, E., Jokela, V., Helin, P., Penttilae, I., & Haenninen, O. (1996). Plasma levels of adrenal hormones in working women during an economic recession and the threat of unemployment: Impact of regular relaxation training. *Journal of Psychophysiology, 10*(1), 36–48.

Wright, T., Blache, C., & Luterman, R. (1993). Hardiness, stress, and burnout among intensive care nurses. *Journal of Burn Care Rehabilitation, 14*(3), 376–381.

Experiments in Self-Care

☐ Why Do We Call Them "Experiments"?

Many books about self-help are called *workbooks*. The implication is that one must put a considerable amount of effort into certain predefined activities to reap rewards. Although this view has its proponents, we find it inconsistent with our assumptions that people can know what's in their own best interests and, given the opportunity, will develop the unique strategies that are likely to be most successful for them. Others find the prospect of more "work" onerous. On the other hand, sometimes people feel "stuck" or would prefer some kind of structure to help them identify and develop their resources. We have called the following suggestions *experiments* because that's what they are intended to be—things to try and observe what happens. There is no such thing as a "failed" experiment, because any outcome provides information/learning. The story of Robinson Crusoe provides many rich examples of the processes of trial and error that go into recrafting a life. The experiments presented in this chapter parallel the steps highlighted from the story of Robinson Crusoe (chapter 1).

☐ How to Use This Section

This chapter consists of a series of exercises that can be used in several different ways:

1. The therapist can use these questions as part of the therapy session.
2. The therapist can choose some of the exercises to be used as "experiments" or "homework."
3. Clients may choose to use these as self-help guides to questions they
   may want to answer for themselves. They may choose to journal or
   discuss questions with someone close to them. The questions also may
   provide guidance for self-help groups.

Some self-care experiments appear in the chapter on self-care, and other
experiments are specifically for caregivers—primarily therapists—but also
may be helpful to consider for other kinds of caregivers, including the
family. These appear in chapter 10, "Caring for the Caregiver."

The following feedback sheet can be copied for tracking the results of
experiments. It usually can be completed once a week to provide an overview of progress across time. You may wish to simplify or modify some of
these for your clients.

EXPERIMENT FEEDBACK

Name_____Date_____

Name of Experiment:_____ (page)

Were you were aware of having any symptoms prior to this experiment? Yes No

What were they?

If so, how often did you experience the symptom? NA Daily Weekly Monthly Rarely

How many times did you do this experiment in the past week? 0   1   2   3   4

On average, how much time did each occasion take? (minutes)   10   20   30   40

Were you able to follow the instructions?   Yes   No

How would you describe the experience? What was it like?

How easy was this experiment for you?   (circle one below)

1	2	3	4	5
Very hard	Somewhat hard	Neutral	Somewhat easy	Very easy

Have you used this strategy/experiment before this week?   Yes   No

When?   Never   Within past year   More than a year ago

How often do you use it now?   Never   Daily   Weekly   Monthly

Would you be likely to use this again?   No   Maybe   Yes

Would you be likely to suggest this to someone else? No   Maybe   Yes

Comments

Occasion #1 What was your comfort level before doing the exercise? (mark line)

1	2	3	4	5	6	7

Very uncomfortable   Neutral   Very comfortable

What was your comfort level after doing the exercise? (mark line)

1	2	3	4	5	6	7

Very uncomfortable   Neutral   Very comfortable

Occasion #2 What was your comfort level before doing the exercise? (mark line)

1	2	3	4	5	6	7

Very uncomfortable   Neutral   Very comfortable

What was your comfort level after doing the exercise? (mark line)

1	2	3	4	5	6	7

Very uncomfortable   Neutral   Very comfortable

Occasion #3 What was your comfort level before doing the exercise? (mark line)

1	2	3	4	5	6	7

Very uncomfortable   Neutral   Very comfortable

What was your comfort level after doing the exercise? (mark line)

1	2	3	4	5	6	7

Very uncomfortable   Neutral   Very comfortable

☐ Different Types of Questions, Different "Experiments"

Several different and overlapping categories of questions and activities are included under "experiments." Some are questions intended to foster curiosity and openness, and other questions may lead to new insights or understandings. Because many clients coming to therapy will be in the seeker/searcher stage, many of the experiments encourage observation—noticing what is happening and what makes a difference. Fewer of the experiments will suggest doing something different. In our experience, clients often find their own suggestions most helpful. However, some "doing" experiments may expose clients to ways to "do something different" that might not have been part of the past experience or imagination.

Overall, there are more questions about noticing or developing new understandings than about doing, reflecting the preponderance of those who enter therapy as visitors or as seeker/searchers. Some of the questions and suggestions may have similar purposes or outcomes—the decision to ask one question over the other is usually a matter of matching the client's goals, language, and resources to the issue at hand, rather than using a "set" approach that one might use with every client. In the following sections we note situations in which certain questions might be most useful or when to avoid going down a path that may be a dead end.

☐ Self-Care and Care of the Self

As noted in chapter 3, self-care undertaken to manage a health condition can overlap with care of the Self—the process of growing, changing, and/or becoming "whole," with or without the presence of chronic illness or chronic pain. Many of the "experiments," however, are specifically intended to expand frames of reference or to help people "reauthor" their stories. As such, some of the following experiments are likely to be most helpful when they are used outside the therapy session, allowing whatever time it takes to carefully consider, review, document thoughts and ideas, or try something relatively new. We often find that clients are already trying out new things and may have considerable experience with a wide range of alternative or complementary therapies. These experiments may encourage clients to pursue additional information or develop new resources. Although some of these may be best incorporated into the therapeutic relationship, others may be explored totally outside the therapy. At the end of this chapter we list some of the books, tapes, organizations, and websites that clients may want to explore as they increase their repertoire of self-care strategies and enlarge their perspectives on health and living a meaningful life.

☐ Past, Present, or Future?

In addition to classifying experiments as wondering, noticing, understanding, and doing, many can be thought of as linking past resources with the present and/or linking the future with the present. In each case, the circumstances, perspectives, or resources from the past will be linked to the present to build on clients' previous successes and skills. Sometimes revisiting past experiences can provide an opportunity for wondering how the present situation is similar or different, inviting new definitions and possibilities. Many other questions are specifically intended to link present observations or actions with "miracles," future goals, or preferred scenarios. Obviously, most of the observing and doing experiments are present focused; however, there can still be important questions about the "differences" these engender. Questions may be phrased to encourage clients to see the interactions between new views or behaviors and the effects of these changes on relationships at home, at work, or in social situations. Sometimes the expected or actual differences will be deeply personal or difficult to express. However, the opportunity to reflect on possible consequences of these changes can instill a sense of hopefulness and maintain momentum during times when change may be less apparent.

☐ Matching Relevance, Readiness, and Energy

The most important factors to consider when choosing experiments for another person (or oneself) are whether:

1. They make sense to the person trying the experiment, and seem relevant.
2. The activity matches the readiness stage.
3. The experiment will take more energy than the client has at any particular point in time.

Relevance can often be ascertained indirectly by listening carefully to the kinds of stories people tell, the self-care strategies they use (and find helpful), the values they espouse, and the words they use to describe all of these. When the links between the experiment and personal goals are clear, there are fewer questions about relevance. Remembering, however, the wide range of health beliefs and models of self-care, it's very likely that you will be surprised to discover what others may see as "relevant." When family and others may caution the client about the need to rest, it's not uncommon to find the client taking on a new activity. If it's an activity that feeds the soul, or otherwise enriches one's life, it may be uniquely "relevant," personally stimulating, and ultimately healing. When clients express a great need to "understand" what is happening to them, we ask how it is that they usually come to understand things. Those who seek factual information will appreciate being connected with appropriate resources; those who are trying to make connections between the past and present or how their condition can be understood in relation to larger life questions of meaning and purpose may want to consider other questions and different experiments. In either case, it's important to follow up and find out if the match was fruitful and what difference the "new understanding" will make in their lives. Disconnected insights rarely improve one's quality of life.

In chapter 5 we outlined the characteristics of visitors, sufferer/victims, seeker/searchers, explorer/experimenters, and recrafters. In general we have suggested that visitors be complimented on their willingness to consider how therapy might be helpful to them. The experiments described here parallel the story of Robinson Crusoe and reflect the movement and growth that occurred for him during his adventure. Experiments are thus presented in an order that, similarly, reflects movement from visitors to seeker/searchers, to explorer/experimenters, to artists/craftspersons.

☐ Beginning at the Beginning

The following experiments can be helpful both in session and/or to supplement what occurs in the session. The purposes of these are to help both the client and the clinician, helping one get to know the *person* with the condition (rather than vice versa), getting a feel for the client's worldview, and developing trust in the relationship. Clients watch carefully the responses they get when they try to describe their experiences. Inevitably, the first session will carry with it an undercurrent of mutual testing and evaluation of the participants and the process of the therapy. When someone seems overwhelmed with his or her story or gets caught in the details, it may be helpful for them to write it out and/or create a timeline that helps them and others follow the story. When someone appears to feel burdened by having to tell yet another person a long and depressing tale, not pressing for unnecessary information may be what is called for. In any case, the story will give some sense of what has been tried and what has and hasn't worked, and sometimes of the energy the narrator has to bring to this new relationship.

Telling the Story

- If you've never told your whole story before and you think it might be helpful, start at the beginning and tell everything that someone else would need to know to understand what it's been like for you.
- If you have told your story many times before—has it been helpful? When was it most helpful and why? If it is not helpful, what do you think would be more helpful?
- If you've told the story multiple times, it may be worth asking: Has the story changed over time, that is, do you see things differently at this point than you did at other times? In what ways has it changed? What might account for these changes?
- If you were going to tell your story again, how would you like it to be different? How would you like the outcome to be different?

Connecting to Previous Stories

- Listen to (or read) your own story as if for the first time, and as if it were someone else's story—maybe a documentary. What themes seem to stand out for you?
- What form does the story take? Is it more like a mystery, an inspirational reading, satire, a drama?
- As you "stand back" and look at the story, does it seem similar to earlier stories you might tell about your life? If so, how is it similar? If not, how is it different?

Fears

- As you review the story, what fears do you hear/read? List these and number them. Which is most important to you to address first?
- You may choose to consider these fears from several viewpoints—for example, are they primarily about the past, present, or future? Are they about ability to manage? About relationships? About security? Others?
- How realistic are these fears? Which of these could be modified by information? Which are unlikely to be answerable at this time? Which appear to be changeable? What would have to happen for these to be changed?

Gratitudes

- Sometimes people find gratitude in comparing their problems to those who are less fortunate—do you find that helpful? What do you think explains your answer?
- Despite your situation, are there some things for which you can be grateful?
- List the small gratitudes that often get forgotten in the day-to-day efforts. As you look at your list, what do you think it means that you were able to list any of these?

Why Me?—Seeking Meaning

- When misfortune of any kind besets people, they often have questions about why they have been "singled out." List possible "reasons," whether they are logical or not.
- What ideas have others offered (often unsolicited) for your situation? What do you think about these ideas?
- Is it important to you to have some answer to the question "why me?" Why is it important? If this question could be answered, what difference do you think it would make?

☐ Creating a Home

When visitors become seeker/searchers they don't stop looking for rescue, and safety is often a major concern. The following experiments may be most appropriate when clients express multiple fears, appear anxious, or describe other safety-related issues. Obviously, if a client is not expressing fears and seems more concerned with finding out what will work, it might be best to make certain the client has one or more ways to reliably access a sense of safety and security and then move directly to the changes he or she desires. In any case, it can be helpful to take inventory of the available resources (internal and external) for the search. Similarly, if a client seems to become more upset while focusing on when the problem/symptoms occur and what triggers them, it may be more useful for them to track good days rather than symptom patterns.

Sometimes when clients obsess about the problem, the same attention to details can be used to observe slight improvements. Noticing improvement requires some clarity about what would be considered evidence of improvement. Several of the following experiments are intended to help clients define desirable "outcomes" of self-care and to identify their approaches to self-care. Both the Self-Care Responses tool and the Solution-Focused Outcomes inventory can be used to track improvements and the strategies that seem to foster them. These instruments can be used as "homework" assignments with follow-up in subsequent sessions focused on selected indicators that clients find most meaningful. Most of the experiments for seeker/searchers will revolve around being open and "noticing."

Seeking Safety (Related to Immediate Fears)

- Refer to your list of fears and choose one that is an immediate concern. In relation to this fear, how safe do you feel on a scale of 1 to 10?
- What would it take for you to feel slightly more safe in relation to this concern? How would you and others know that you were feeling even slightly more safe?
- Where and how do you feel safety in your body? If you can identify that space, can you associate an image with it? When you concentrate on that image, what does that feel like?
- While in a deeply relaxed state (or using some of the self-hypnosis techniques in chap. 8), recall a time in the past or present when you felt safe and secure. (This may come easily or require more searching over some time.)
- Notice how you feel in your body and mood when you think of this safe and secure experience. Bring back a "souvenir" image or symbol that reminds you of this sense of safety and security. An actual object or a word may be a potent reminder of this experience of feeling safe and secure.
- Practice accessing this symbol several times a day. Notice what difference it makes in the way you feel.

Shelter (Safe Place, Peaceful Time/Place)

- Again, in a deeply relaxed state, recall or imagine a place that felt special to you, alone or with others. Develop a full memory of the place, involving sights and sounds and smells and physical sensations. Once you've created this special place you can go to in your mind, what will you do there? Notice how you make the transitions to and from this special place so you can access the experience whenever you need to.
- You may wish to practice going to this safe place at intervals and notice what difference it makes. How often do you think it would be helpful to do this, or in what circumstances?

Gathering Resources

Recalling Robin's trips back to the ship:

- What are the resources, material and otherwise, that you can salvage and find some use for?
- What are some of the resources you won't need to bring with you? Are you sure?
- If you could "borrow" resources from others, what would these be?

Creating Containers

One of the first skills Robin had to develop was creating a variety of containers for different purposes. "Containers" allow us to separate some things from others—often a valuable capacity.

- How are you able to separate your illness or pain from other areas of your life when you need to?

Storing Resources

- Do you have a way to store your resources (energy, optimism, curiosity)?
- Where do you store them? How can you access them when you need to?

Starting Small

- Choose a small goal—one just for today.
- If you were to take one small step toward your goal—what would that be?
- What difference would it make if you made small steps toward a small goal on a regular basis? Who would notice? Would it affect your relationships? Your outlook? Your energy?

Getting Bearings/Keeping Track (of Symptoms?)

- Some people feel more in control when they keep lists and calendars. Do you? What kinds of lists are helpful for you now?
- If you find lists helpful, start keeping some and notice *how* these are

helpful. Could you use these organizational skills in other parts of your life?

- Some people find it helpful to track their symptoms so they can find patterns about what makes it better or worse. Do you find that helpful?
- If you do, you might begin to chart these; what seems to make them better or worse?
- If you find focusing on symptoms makes them even worse (and many people do), you might see if you can focus on areas of comfort or times when symptoms seem less prominent and notice what difference that makes. Is distraction from the symptoms a better approach for you? If so, what activities are best at distracting you?
- Journaling is a time-honored approach to staying in touch with one-self. If you've never tried it, maybe this is the time. Some people prefer stream-of-consciousness writing, whereas others like to have a word or theme that they find enlightening or uplifting. Try several approaches to learn what works for you.

Counting the Days (Good Days and Bad)

- For nearly every condition, some days are better than others and some times of days or days of the week may be better than others. Choose a term (or terms) to describe what's going on when things are better (i.e., what *is* happening, rather than what is *not* happening).
- First, notice what is happening on a good day.
- Second, what do you "call" a good day? What's your name for it?
- Third, scale your days from 1 to 10 for a reasonable period.
- Fourth, did you notice what makes a "good day"?
- Fifth, is it worthwhile considering a day that would be 1 point better?
- Sixth, if so, describe what it would take to make a day ½ or 1 full point better. If you can't find a pattern, are you able to predict or guess which days will be better?

Notice Small Blessings and Small Changes

- Take an inventory of the small blessings and small changes that signal that life still holds some pleasure.
- Make a game of thinking of the simplest pleasures you can—a cup of tea, the first signs of spring, the smallest of happy memories of the past or hopes for the future.
- What difference does it make when you recognize these small miracles?

Rescue Images

These can be linked to resources actually available. See web resources.

- Nearly everyone has "rescue" fantasies when they feel their lives are out of control. What is your rescue fantasy?
- Is there a particular image you have for the "rescuer"? Is the image distressing or comforting?
- In what ways have you rescued yourself in the past?
- What particular qualities does the rescuer have? Can you recognize these qualities in yourself? Even a little?
- Notice the times you become your own rescuer.
- Make a point of rescuing yourself at least once in the next week.

Self-Care Resources

- Self-care resources can be either internal or external. Internal resources may include skills, abilities, or past experiences that can be built on. Think about a past experience that seemed daunting and that you feel some pride for having handled. What skills and abilities allowed you to succeed? Could they be called on now?
- Identify at least one internal resource to use consciously during the coming week.
- External resources include, for example, social support, concrete forms of assistance, and material resources. List some of these already important ways you manage your situation. Are there others that you may need to develop?
- Choose one possible external resource that you'd like more information about and get that information during the coming week.
- How will you go about developing necessary internal and external resources, given your circumstance?
- After making a list of the resources you need, choose one you will begin to develop in the coming week.

Self-Care Outcomes

What kinds of "outcomes" would let you know your self-care was effective? Would you be able to function better, adjust to your situation, have a reduction in symptoms, or experience an improved quality of life, despite your illness? Would you have better relationships with others? A deepened spiritual connection?

- What unique outcomes are important to you?
- What would be the smallest sign to you that you are experiencing, even to a small degree, the "outcomes" that are most important to you?

Use of the Self-Care Responses Tool (SCR) is described in chapters 3 and 4. It is often completed before the first session or used as homework after the first session.

Self-Care Tool (Short Form)

Fill out the following instrument and then:

- Notice what things you tend to do most often.
- Notice what things are most effective.
- Are they the same?
- Are there some strategies you might choose to do more of?

☐ Self-Care Responses

Instructions: People respond in many ways to the experience of (_____). They deal with this experience through different ways of thinking or doing things to take care of themselves. Please estimate how consistently you have used the following ways of dealing with your own experience DURING THE PAST YEAR. Please place an "X" to indicate how often you use each strategy and how effective it is. **If you don't use an item, check "don't use" and move on to the next item.** Where indicated, please fill in the blanks.

USE KEY: 1 = RARELY 2 = SOMETIMES 3 = OFTEN	EFFECT KEY: 0 = NOT EFFECTIVE + = SOMEWHAT EFFECTIVE ++ = VERY EFFECTIVE

	Don't Use	USE 1 2 3	EFFECT 0 + ++
1. Worry about it.	*		
2. Accept what I am experiencing as legitimate.	*		
3. Pay more attention to dress, grooming, hair.	*		
4. Take vitamins.	*		
5. Drink alcoholic beverages.	*		
6. Smoke.	*		

	Don't Use	USE 1 2 3			EFFECT 0 + ++		
7. Eat.	*						
8. Think through different ways to handle the experience.	*						
9. Do anything, something, even unsure it will work.	*						
10. Seek counseling, therapy.	*						
11. Keep a calendar or journal.	*						
12. Allow myself to cry.	*						
13. Set specific goals to handle the situation.	*						
14. Have faith. (In_____)	*						
15. Throw myself into my work.	*						
16. Look for meaning in the experience.	*						
17. Put it out of my mind, ignore it.	*						
18. Prepare for the worst.	*						
19. Express anger.	*						
20. Accept changes in my body.	*						
21. Isolate myself, spend time alone.	*						
22. Believe in myself, forgive myself, value myself more.	*						
23. Take better care of myself, pamper myself.	*						
24. Keep busy, productive: for example: volunteer, develop new interests, get a job, go to school? (HOW?_____)	*						
25. Improve my diet. (HOW?_____)	*						
26. Seek prescription medication to help me feel better.	*						
27. Take over-the-counter medication to make me feel better. (WHAT KINDS?_____)	* *						
28. Increase physical activity, such as run, exercise, aerobics, swim, cycle, walk. (WHAT?_____)							
29. Increase recreational activities, plays, eat out. (WHAT?_____)	*						
30. Practice body comfort activities such as: special clothing, relaxation, baths. (WHAT?_____)	*						
31. Avoid difficult situations, for example: plan ahead, cancel appointments. (WHAT?_____)	*						
32. Find ways to gain control, for example: explore options, get second opinions. (WHAT?_____)	*						

	Don't Use	USE 1 2 3	EFFECT 0 + ++

	Don't Use	1	2	3	0	+	++
33. Do housework? (WHAT KINDS?_____)	*						
34. Reduce workload. (HOW?_____)	*						
35 Educate myself. Learn about what to expect: for example, read. (HOW?_____)	*						
36. Find ways to feel good about myself. (HOW?_____)	*						
37. Participate in a "support group." (WHICH?_____)	*						
38. Go shopping, for example: window shop, just spend money, buy things for myself. (WHICH?_____)	*						
39. Seek *information* from someone:	*						
a. Significant other/partner	*						
b. Family members	*						
c. Physician	*						
d. Nurse	*						
e. Friend	*						
f. Someone else with a similar situation	*						
g. Self-help books, tapes	*						
h. Other_____	*						
40. Seek *support* from someone:	*						
a. Significant other/partner	*						
b. Family members	*						
c. Physician	*						
d. Nurse	*						
e. Friend	*						
f. Someone else with a similar situation	*						
g. Self-help books, tapes	*						
h. Other_____							
41. Seek *advice* from someone:	*						
a. Significant other/partner	*						
b. Family members	*						
c. Physician	*						
d. Nurse	*						
e. Friend	*						
f. Someone in a similar situation	*						
g. Self-help books, tapes	*						
h. Other_____)	*						

	Don't Use	USE 1 2 3	EFFECT 0 + ++
42. Seek *assistance* from someone:			
a. Significant other/partner			
b. Family members			
c. Physician			
d. Nurse			
e. Friend			
f. Someone in a similar situation			
g. Self-help books, tapes			
h. Other_____)			
1. Specific thoughts that are helpful.	*		
2. Specific things I do that are helpful.	*		
3. Specific people who are helpful.	*		
4. Specific things others do that are helpful.	*		
5. Specific places that make me feel better.	*		
6. My best times are:	*		
7. Other things I've noticed that make a difference.	*		

Now that I've responded to these questions, I would like more information about:

_____

_____

Other methods of self-care which I use are:

_____

_____

_____

COMMENTS:

☐ Solution Identification Scale for Health

The following questions may be helpful to consider as you scale your improvement. They may be answered in terms of frequency during the day, week, or globally. Add the items that would indicate, to you, evidence that you are improving.

	Never	Rarely	Sometimes	Often
1. I get enough sleep at night				
2. I get enough rest				
3. I am able to enjoy eating				
4. There times when I don't notice my symptoms as much				
5. I am able to maintain my appearance in a manner satisfying to me				
6. I am able to maintain my concentration and attention on activities that are important to me				
7. I can tell when I am going to have a good day				
8. I am comfortable with my relationship with my health care providers				
9. I have enough energy to get through the day				
10. Even though I am aware of symptoms associated with my illness, I also am aware of areas of relative comfort				
11. I am able to function adequately at work (if applicable)				
12. I continue to pursue enjoyable activities, hobbies, and pleasurable pastimes.				
13. I am able to maintain a sense of hopefulness				
14. My relationship with my partner is satisfying (if applicable)				
15. I am curious about how my life will unfold				
16. I feel I am able to contribute to meeting the family's needs (if applicable)				
17. I am able to enjoy time with friends				
18. I am able to function adequately at school (if applicable)				
19. I am able to calm myself when I need to				
20. I have ways to cheer myself up				

	Never	Rarely	Sometimes	Often
21. I am aware that it's normal to have periods of sadness				
22. I have ways of relaxing				
23. I am satisfied with my life as a whole				
24. I am able to function adequately at home				
25. I find life interesting				
26. My relationship with my children is satisfying (if applicable)				
27. I am able to carry out self-care to meet my daily physical needs				
28. I am able to carry out activities necessary to manage my illness				
29. I am able to ask others for help when I need it.				
30. I get as much exercise as I would like				
31. Despite the challenges of my situation, I realize I have grown in some ways from this experience				
32. I am able to distract myself from my condition when necessary				
33. I have enough energy to do things I'd like to do				

☐ Other Self-Care Experiments

Treatments for Illness (Medications, Vitamins, Hot Baths, Etc.)

- Write down (if you already haven't) the kinds of things you do to take care of your illness. Include medications, treatments, vitamins, and so on.
- Write down some things you have tried that didn't seem to help.
- Now create a list of things you haven't tried, but that you think might be helpful.

Body Comfort

There are many ways humans and animals have for increasing their sense of comfort. Some of these have to do with the positions we take (standing, sitting, or lying), or using heat or cold, wearing loose clothing, favorite soft pillows, and so on.

- What are the things you used to do to increase body comfort? Are you still doing some of these?
- What things do you do since you've had your condition to increase your body comfort? What are your favorites?

Physical Exercise

Engage in something that you would consider "exercise." This can be anything from a brisk walk to the more athletic endeavors that might be considered "real" exercise. The important thing is that you do something you wouldn't usually do. You might even try something different each day.

- How do you choose an exercise activity? What kinds of thoughts go through your mind while you are engaging in this "exercise"?
- What are the usual reasons you use to not exercise (if you don't)? What are your favorite reasons? Do you enjoy engaging in sports? Why or why not? Do you like to exercise as part of doing real work (e.g., cleaning the house, hauling groceries, doing repairs, building things)? Do you prefer to exercise alone, with a video, or with others (e.g., in classes or as part of a group)?
- Does running around all day on your feet count as exercise? Does exercise only count if you are wearing a special outfit and have a "goal"? What kinds of messages did you get when you were growing up about the place of physical exercise, physical work, and physical exertion?
- At the end of the week, answer: If you were to incorporate some form of regular exercise into your life, what would that be? How would you go about beginning such a practice?

Attending to Dreams

One time-honored way of trying to understand illness and how to handle it is to attend to dreams. From the healing Aesclepian temples in ancient Greece, and shamanic practices of many indigenous peoples, to Freudian and Jungian analysis, there has been a belief that one way the unconscious communicates is through dreams.

- Keep a small blank book and pencil or a tape recorder within reach of the bed and record whatever you can recall as soon as you awake. There are many techniques for remembering and analyzing dreams (Born, 1991).
- After recording these for some time you will notice certain patterns relating to the characters, settings, activities, events, emotions, sensations, and so on. You may find it helpful to share dreams with someone close to you, because others may be able to see patterns that aren't obvious to the dreamer.

Reading (Information, Inspiration, Escape)

Reading is one of the most consistent self-care activities people engage in—but for apparently different reasons. Some read for information, some for uplifting examples, and some for escape. Others find it helpful to learn others' experiences, either to validate their own or to develop perspective by comparing their own situation with that of others. Some read to get new ideas about their own self-care.

- Take note of what kinds of things you are reading now and what effect they have on you.
- Experiment with reading different kinds of materials and notice what effect these have on you.

Aesthetics

This experiment describes a range of experiences and activities that might be considered aesthetic, that is, anything that enlivens the senses or encourages you to immerse yourself in the beauty within and without. In addition to art, gardening, working with clay, doing needlework, sculpting, sewing, cooking, and decorating are some of the traditional and invisible ways to experience the aesthetic. Being at one with nature, the changing seasons, the rhythms of the moon cycles and sunrises and sunsets, the sound of the wind or the shifting of the tides, can also be healing.

- What aesthetic experiences particularly attract you?
- Are there ways you have in your life to be creative? What are these?
- What difference does it make in your life when you are able to spend time in these pleasures?

During the next week, try one of the following (or do something that better fits your own expression). If you do the latter, what is it?

- Music and sounds: Play or listen to music that you particularly enjoy for at least ½ hour at least 3 days during the week. (No fair just having it in the background while you work.) Really allow yourself to experience it.
- Nature: Whatever turns you on. Go to the zoo, or the Museum of Nature and Science, or for a walk outside, or visit a botanical garden, or a florist, or make of point of enjoying the sunrise and sunset for several days.
- Visual arts: Go to art museums or art galleries, or make your own! How long has it been since you finger-painted, or played with clay?
- Your choice (what is it?).

Self-Regulation

There are countless ways to self-sooth or calm ourselves when our bodies are in a high state of tension or to energize ourselves when we're at low ebb. First you must observe the experience of being tense and how you become aware of it—neck and shoulder tension, jiggling, feeling heavy, and so on.

- Notice that you have already developed some ways to deal with these experiences—what are they and how effective are they?
- Experiment with new ways to calm or energize yourself—most require a certain amount of practice before you can tell if they will be helpful (e.g., breathing techniques, meditation, exercise, writing, talking with a friend, warm baths, etc.).

Biofeedback/Autogenics.   Both of these approaches increase relaxation by attending to physiologic changes, and both will become more effective with practice.

- In autogenic relaxation, imagine the arms and legs individually becoming warmer and heavier. You may wish to repeat suggestions, such as, "My right arm is getting very heavy." In a relaxed state, concentrate on whatever personal image you would associate with warming your hands.
- There are many biofeedback approaches. One of the easiest is to use a small finger-held thermometer to help monitor temperature changes in the hands. In a relaxed position, breathing slowly and deeply from your abdomen, repeat slowly, "My hands are getting warmer," many times. Then add a thought or memory of warm hands (lying in the sun, warming by a fire, warm liquids in or around the hands, etc.).

Self-Management

Similar to self-care and self-regulation, many self-management approaches focus on the thoughts and beliefs that affect stress levels and self-efficacy or confidence in being able to manage. First, notice how your thoughts affect how you are feeling.

- Listen to your own thoughts and beliefs as if they were someone else's and write them down.
- Which thoughts and beliefs increase your sense of confidence, peacefulness, or sense of zest ? How can you incorporate these thoughts more consciously to help you take better care of yourself?

Self-Care Knowledge

We all have ideas, logical or otherwise, about why things are the way they are. Answer without great deliberation: Why do you think you became ill? What do you think needs to happen for you to heal? If recovery is not likely, what needs to happen for you to feel you are adapting? Still able to grow as a human being?

Alternative/Complementary Approaches Used, Considered, Effectiveness

People with chronic pain or illness are often led to try a wider range of alternative or complementary healing modalities. These range from vitamins, to prayer, to acupuncture, massage, and other approaches. What have you tried?

- List what you have tried, what has been helpful, and how it was helpful.
- Think of all the other approaches that you have not tried and consider making a list of those that seem worth trying. How would you know one or more of these was helpful? What is it about certain approaches that appeals to you?

Cultural Beliefs

- What culturally congruent things do you do to maintain, protect, and restore health?

- Look at Spector's list of culturally described ways to maintain, protect, and restore health, table 3.1. Which of these do you currently do? How do your own practices differ from those of your parents or grandparents?
- If possible, interview older family members to learn how they would define health. Do they see it as physical only, or related to social, spiritual, and emotional health too? What are signs of being healthy or ill? How do they maintain their health? What do they think causes illness? Who was responsible for the health of family members in their family of origin? Where do they get their information about health and illness?
- How do older family members believe one should handle pain? What does it mean to be in pain? Do they prefer to be with others or alone when in pain? How are your experiences similar to or different from others in your family and others with shared ethnic identities?

☐ Exploring the Terrain and Trying New Things

The explorer/experimenter is open to new experiences and ways of thinking about things and also has the desire and energy to take an active role in finding out what makes a difference. Many of the experiments listed here can build on the previous sections. For example, clients might decide to try out some self-care activities that are new to them. People at this point usually have learned that experiments don't always result in success and that many of them take practice over time. In this category, clients may be trying any number of new things, and many of the questions are directed toward insight as well as doing.

Turning Points

- Sometimes it's a new awareness or something someone says that makes us realize we no longer see ourselves as simply victims of our illness/pain. Can you recognize any turning points in your own story?
- If someone were to ask you when you first came to realize that you could still have a good quality of life, despite being ill, what would you say?
- Identify at least one thing you would be doing that would reflect that you believe you can and should have a good quality of life. Do it (if it's within reason). What difference does it make in your quality of life and how you feel about yourself to have done it?

Exploring the Territory/Landscape (as If Seeing It for the First Time)

- What have you come to know about since you've been ill that you didn't know existed? Is it possible to describe it in neutral or positive terms?
- Consider the possibility that there may be a life out there (or in there) that you never noticed or imagined. What would it look like? What would you be doing?
- If you were able to think of this unknown territory as an adventure, what would you title it? What would you look for?

Venturing Out (Advance and Retreat)

- Sometimes adventures, even planned ones, can be disturbing. What kinds of activities tend to make you feel unsafe? What do you do to regain a sense of safety?
- When you've engaged in an activity that leaves you feeling depleted of energy, what do you do to replenish your energy? Make a list of these things and try them enough to find out what works best in different circumstances. Make a list of things you've never tried—and try at least one this week.
- What positive benefits come from taking risks? What have you learned about finding the right balance between venturing out and staying close to home?

Living with the Seasons (Working with Cycles)

- Often people notice that they have more energy or are more comfortable in different climates or during different seasons. What patterns have you noticed?
- What are the small signs that let you know that you need to "hibernate" or get more rest? To get outside and explore?
- Are you a morning person (a lark) or an evening person (an owl)? What difference does it make when you are able to honor your body's own rhythms?

Food (Comfort Foods, Food Diary)

- Once you begin to pay attention, you may notice that some foods give you more energy, some make you irritable, or some make you feel relaxed. Try keeping track of what foods make you feel better. Note what you ate, and the time of day, and how long it took to eat. How did you choose what to eat? What thoughts and feelings accompanied your choosing these foods?

- What kinds of feelings (physical, psychological, emotional) were involved with the act of eating, and between this meal and the next?

At the end of the week answer these questions for yourself:

- What patterns do you note about your choice of food, time of eating, and how you feel?
- Are there any foods that "don't agree" with you? How do you know something "doesn't agree with you"? What is the difference between your experience with foods that do agree with you and foods that don't? What did you notice that surprised you?
- Do you think you might change any eating patterns as a result of this exercise? What might these changes look like?
- For a week, plan what you eat based on what you've learned and notice what difference it makes in your energy and overall sense of well-being.

Managing Unpredictability

Sometimes "out of nowhere" we have a flare-up or otherwise bad day. Here are several ways to prepare for these:

- The Rainy Day Letter reminder (letter to self) (See chapter 7; also Dolan, 1991). This is a letter written to oneself on a good day. When you are feeling able to manage things, write a letter that can remind you of your strengths and of your ability to handle the bad days, and can provide hopefulness for the future. It's often difficult to remember these things on the "bad" days. Keep the letter with you or have several copies that are accessible in places you are likely to be when you might need these important reminders.
- The Roadside Repair Kit is a collection of resources that can be easily found when you need a lift. The kit might include inspirational literature, favorite music, projects that help distract you, scented oils or candles (if these are tolerated and enjoyed), pictures of loved ones, memories of happy occasions, and so on. Just choosing these things can be healing. Notice how you feel as you try each of articles you're considering.
- First Aid Kit: A client described this approach as a way to handle the tyranny of pain. "When it swoops down on me," she said, "I can't think of anything—I just panic. So I typed out a list of all the things I need to do to handle an 'attack' that have worked for me in the past. For ex-

ample, I should take certain medications, get out my heating pad, try a warm bath, call whoever might be helpful, or take the phone off the hook if I want to be left alone. Reminders to drink lots of water, and a list of distractions to try. It's helped me more than once when my brain seemed to go empty." She taped the list to the inside of a cupboard door in her kitchen, along with phone numbers of people she might need to contact. Sometimes it's hard to remember in the moment!

- A Day with Roger Ebert: Home videos are much more accessible and reasonable these days. More than one client has noticed that watching TV or movies can provide distractions from pain. It's usually not fun to go out to the movies or to rent a film if you're already feeling rotten. So some people purchase films they know they would like to see, either for the first time, or films that they know they enjoy over and over. Some people like old musicals, some adventures, and others dramas, biographies, travelogues, romances, or comedies. Whatever turns you on can be kept in a special place for a time when distraction from pain or discomfort is needed. Other uses of film, for insight or information about conditions, are listed in several movie resource books. Popcorn and candy are optional.

- Live Someone Else's Life for a Day: This experiment will take some advance research. The "someone" can be a person you actually know, or someone you admire from a distance. If it's a person you know, you can interview the person about how he or she spends his or her days (and maybe how the individual personally handles adversity). With a script for this, you can spend a day in another's shoes, trying out how that person spends time, the schedules he or she does or doesn't keep, the things the person enjoys doing. All the time, you can be noticing what you do and don't enjoy yourself. Alternatively, you might read about a person and invent what you think the person's typical day might involve. Maybe you will choose a Thoreau day and notice the tiniest things about the natural world around you (see if you, too, can get your mother to do your laundry and meals). Maybe a novelist, struggling to create characters in your newest mystery. Maybe a gourmet cook, or an eccentric artist—something very different from your own life. If nothing else, it will make a great story to tell others!

☐ Becoming Creative—The Art of Recrafting a Life: Experiments for Survival and Growth

Creativity is not limited to those whom we have called recrafters. In fact, creativity is usually involved in successful seeking/searching and exploring/experimenting. In this section, however, we describe experiments that are oriented primarily toward creating a meaningful life. Many activities overlap with those of the explorer/experimenter, and there is no clear demarcation between them based on what they do. The major difference is that the recrafter has usually come to some degree of peacefulness about his or her situation and has created the life he or she needs to be living—a meaningful life. Recrafters have done enough experimenting to feel more predictability in their lives—if not specifically in relation to their health, then in being confident that they can manage whatever the day brings.

Some of the most creative people developed their newfound skills by being willing to try new things, whether they believed they had the necessary talents or not. They often have a well-developed sense of humor, and although they can be serious, they don't take themselves too seriously. This lack of self-consciousness is one of the hallmarks of the person who is able to experience "flow" in many of his or her everyday activities. The following experiments again focus primarily on doing as well as insight.

Becoming Inventive

- List some "way-out" ways to manage pain and illness that you have heard of but never tried. Identify some of these ways that would be different, not dangerous. If you were to try one of these, how would you go about it?
- Try one.
- Some of the most interesting and powerful changes are the result of thinking "out of the box." What box is your thinking trapped in? What if you thought "out of the box"? Try out some "strange ideas" on someone you trust.
- Inventions can be big or small. What small one could improve your quality of life? Create some of these, try them, and see if others find them helpful.

Life Goes On (Signs of This?)

- Against apparent odds, life goes on. What are the signs you have that you will survive?
- What are the differences between surviving and thriving?
- The one condition all of us will eventually face is death. What are your beliefs about life after death? How do your beliefs affect the way you live your life day-to-day?

Transformation Questions

- Most people believe they have changed as a result of illness or pain. Have you? In what ways?
- Some people believe their illness has fostered growth or has some positive aspects to it. If you were to describe your experience as "mixed," what would go into that mixture?
- How do you explain that some people describe their experience of illness or pain as ultimately or mostly positive? If you were to describe your own experience that way, what would stand out for you?

Self-Care and Care of the Self (Wholeness)

- The concept of health as wholeness (or holiness) is quite different from the idea of health as a state of nondisease.
- If you were to describe yourself as moving toward "wholeness," what would go into that whole?
- You might find it helpful to draw an image of wholeness and indicate/write what would need to be in that "whole." What does not need to be within the image for you to feel whole? Write those outside the image.

Connecting with Others

- How much does your own sense of health depend on your relationship to others?
- How have your relationships changed since your health has changed?
- If you were to define your health in terms of interconnectedness (with others, the environment, etc.), how would that affect your sense of personal health?

Transcendent Experience

- When in your life have you had a sense of transcendence—connection to something greater than yourself?
- Is/was that experience in relation to a sense of connection with nature, a religious or spiritual connection, or a sense of place in time? Something else?
- How important do you think a sense of transcendence is to your personal sense of self?

Fostering Creativity

Based on the characteristics of highly creative people, Csikszentmihalyi (1993, 1996) suggested cultivating curiosity and interest by consciously finding something that is "surprising" every day and trying to surprise others.

- Keep track of what interests and surprises you.
- Flow in everyday life can be cultivated by having specific daily goals that are possible to meet and to increase in complexity over time (vs. simple repetition).
- Develop habits of strength by taking charge of your schedule so that it can include time for relaxation and reflection.
- Create an environment that encourages you to focus your attention effectively. Choose a portable symbol for this psychic "space."
- Know yourself by noticing your likes and dislikes, doing more of what you like and less of what you don't.
- Find a way to express what you find moving.
- Use as many viewpoints as possible in problem solving.
- Above all, aim to live as full and creative a life as possible.

Experiments in Flow

The characteristics of the flow experience include a narrowing of attention, associated with a feeling of involvement and focused concentration (Csikszentmihalyi, 1993). When experiencing flow, people often have a diminished awareness of time (it may pass more quickly or slowly). While absorbed in the activity, people tend to be unconcerned about other issues and unself-conscious. Any activity can produce optimal flow (e.g., games, artistic performances, religious rituals, sailing, computer programming, sports, meditation, even crime). These experiences have been described in relation to recreational and other leisure activities (e.g., rock climbing, playing chess, creating art or music, being in nature), alone or with other people, and often in relation to vocational situations (e.g., surgeons, artists, mothers with children). The situations most likely to become flow activities typically involve a clearly defined goal, knowledge about what must be done, and immediate feedback about how well you are doing. There must be a balance between the challenges and demands of the activity and the skills of the person. Flow experiences are often related to activities that are highly valued or consistent with one's sense of meaning or purpose. The conditions most likely to facilitate flow have concrete goals and manageable rules, and the person involved is able to adjust opportunities for action to capacities. Therefore, one must be able to obtain clear information about one's progress, and be able to attend to the activity (i.e., the situation permits one to screen out distractions, making concentration possible). Before doing the following experiments, answer for yourself:

- When am I likely to find myself intensely concentrating?
- Are there times when I am so focused I don't notice my discomfort or time passes differently? Describe these activities.
- What skills that I have are so well developed that I am unself-conscious in doing them and feel confident I can develop them further? How do I get feedback about my skills in this area?
- What activities do I engage in for the pure enjoyment, with no other expected reward?
- Use the Experience Sampling Method (given later) for several days.
- Keep a daily calendar of flow experiences.

Ultradian Rhythms and the Ultradian Healing Response

This experiment is intended to help you become aware of your individual biologically based cycles of rest and activity (Rossi & Nimmons, 1991).

- First, notice the subtle "take a break" signs that you may usually ignore, such as wanting to stretch or loosen up your muscles, yawning or sighing, noticing your body becoming quiet or still, or feeling a desire for a snack and/or a mild urge to urinate. Others may experience happy memories and thoughts of good times, feeling thankful or introspective, friendly fantasies, and/or feelings of mild sexual arousal. Many realize outer performance is slowing down, and inner awareness increases.
- Once you become aware of these signals, begin to try to honor them. For example, if you are a bit hungry, a light snack may be helpful, as well as gazing out a window at a restful scene, stretching your arms and legs, or taking a few deep breaths. You may wish to lightly massage your neck or back. If possible, find a place with reduced lighting, and either relax in your chair or lie down.
- Then notice what part of your body feels most comfortable. Relax into that comfort and notice how it spreads to other parts of your body. Become aware of your natural mind–body rhythms of breathing, heartbeat, and pulse.
- Allow your mind to wander to a favorite fantasy, image, or remembered restful idea, time, or place.

- When you are ready to return to more alertness, you will notice the greater sense of peace and/or energy.

Typically these breaks take from a few minutes to about 20 minutes. Notice your own pattern. Sometimes you will become aware of information you had forgotten or never knew. This experiment also will become easier with practice.

Experience Sampling Method

The following experiment (Csikszentmihalyi & Csikszentmihalyi, 1988) is often helpful to determine what you really feel and how you spend you time. Denny uses this in research by programming watches to signal the wearer eight times a day for seven days (Webster, 1999). Each time they are signaled, participants complete the following form. Information about sleep is collected at the beginning of each day. Make enough copies of the following instrument to sample your experience for several days (usually about 20 copies). You may wish to set an alarm clock at intervals or have someone else interrupt you at times. Many newer watches have the option of signaling you at regular intervals. Each time you are signaled, complete the following form. You should begin to see some patterns in the ways you think and feel in relation to activities and situations.

At the beginning of each day complete the following:

DAY _____

What time did you go to bed last night?_____

Approximately how long did it take you to fall asleep? (in minutes)

_____

Time you woke this morning _____

How would you describe the quality of your sleep last night? (Circle response)

0	1	2	3	4	5	6	7	8	9
Very poor									Very good

Experience Sampling

Date:_____

Time Beeped:_____am/pm   Time Filled Out:_____am/pm

As you were beeped . . .

What were you doing? (The main thing)

What other things were you doing?

What were you thinking about?

Was time passing: Slowly   Normally   Quickly

Who are you with?_____

Why were you doing this particular activity ( ) I had to ( ) I wanted to do it ( ) I had nothing else to do

Did you wish to be somewhere else?   Yes   No

	Not at all	Very little	Poorly	Some-what	Moder-ately	Quite	Total
How well were you concentrating?	O	o	.	-	.	o	O
Were you in control of the situation?	O	o	.	-	.	o	O
How physically comfortable did you feel as you were beeped?	O	o	.	-	.	o	O
How important was this activity in relation to your overall goals?	O	o	.	-	.	o	O

What were the:	Low			Moderate			High
Challenges of the activity	1	2	3	4	5	6	7
Your skills in the activity	1	2	3	4	5	6	7

Are you aware of feeling (Circle all that apply)

hungry   full bladder   yawn/stretch   sexual arousal   "take a break"

	Very	Quite	Some	Neutral	Some	Quite	Very	
Alert	O	o	.	-	.	o	O	Drowsy
Happy	O	o	.	-	.	o	O	Sad
Cheerful	O	o	.	-	.	o	O	Irritable
Strong	O	o	.	-	.	o	O	Weak
Friendly	O	o	.	-	.	o	O	Angry
Outgoing	O	o	.	-	.	o	O	Solitary
Active	O	o	.	-	.	o	O	Passive
Involved	O	o	.	-	.	o	O	Detached
Careful	O	o	.	-	.	o	O	Forgetful
Creative	O	o	.	-	.	o	O	Apathetic
Free	O	o	.	-	.	o	O	Constrained
Competitive	O	o	.	-	.	o	O	Cooperative
Excited	O	o	.	-	.	o	O	Bored
Open	O	o	.	-	.	o	O	Closed
Clear	O	o	.	-	.	o	O	Confused
Warm	O	o	.	-	.	o	O	Cool
Focused	O	o	.	-	.	o	O	Fantasizing
Present- oriented	O	o	.	-	.	o	O	Having memories
Satisfied	O	o	.	-	.	o	O	Worried
Striving	O	o	.	-	.	o	O	Peaceful
Sociable	O	o	.	-	.	o	O	Lonely
Goal-directed	O	o	.	-	.	o	O	Receptive
Comfortable	O	o	.	-	.	o	O	Uncomfortable
Secure	O	o	.	-	.	o	O	Anxious
Outer focus	O	o	.	-	.	o	O	Inner focus
Energized	O	o	.	-	.	o	O	Slow

Since you were last beeped, has anything happened or have you done anything which could have affected the way you feel?

Miscellaneous:

The experiments listed here are only suggestive. We believe that the best experiments are those clients develop for themselves. Even when guidelines for experiments are provided, we always encourage clients to change the experiment to make it what they need it to be or to reflect something that makes more sense to them. It is unlikely that all of the experiments just described would be utilized by any one client. Some therapists and clients may wish to have even more ideas for managing pain and living with chronic illness. Here is a listing of some resources for additional information and experiments.

☐ Web Sites

From its beginnings, the Internet has been a tremendous source of information and misinformation for individuals suffering from chronic pain and illness. This is a small representation of the health information on the Web. We present it only as a starting point and note the fact that some of the addresses may change since the publication of this book. Each is given with both an URL and an explanation.

Resources for Chronic Illness and Chronic Pain

http http://www.chronicpaincanada.org/	North American Chronic Pain Association of Canada
http://www2.rpa.net/~lrandall/	Chronic Pain, CFS, FMS and other medical resources
http://members.tripod.com/~Catnip100/intro.html	Chronic Pain and Illness Life-Line
http://www.fortunecity.com/millenium/hibiscus/152/index2.html	Chronic Pain Relief Coalition
http://neurosurgery.mgh.harvard.edu/ncpainoa.htm	National Chronic Pain Outreach Association
http://www.ninds.nih.gov/health_and_medical/disorders/chronic_pain.htm	NINDS Chronic Pain Information Page
http://www.chronicpainfoundation.com/	Chronic Pain Foundation
http://ecn.ab.ca/cpac/	Chronic Pain Association of Canada
http://www.medsupport.org/pforum/pain2.html	MedSupport FSF International—Chronic Pain/Pain Management Forum
http://www.painworld.zip.com.au/pwindex.html	Australian pain support clearinghouse
http://www.widomaker.com/~skipb/skiphome.htm.html	American Society for Action on Pain
http://www.ashelter.org/	A Shelter in the Storm (from pain)

http://www.chronicpainsupport.org/	The Chronic Pain Support Group
http://members.tripod.com/cpf-l/	The Chronic Pain Forum
http://www.geocities.com/Eureka/Gold/8967/windex.htm	The Chronic Pain Information Network
http://www.medsupport.com/headache/forumdis.htm	Headache Central Forum
http://www.improvingchroniccare.org/	Improving Chronic Illness Care
http://www.invisibledisabilities.com/	The Invisible Disabilities Advocate—Chronic Illness
http://www.geocities.com/HotSprings/Spa/5081/	Chronic Illness—Thief of Dreams . . . Vandal of Life Invisible to All . . .
http://www.chronicillnet.org/	Chronic Illness Net
http://members.aol.com/SynergyHN/	Chronic Illness Support and Research Association
http://www.aarda.org/coping_art.html	American Autoimmune Related Diseases Association
http://www.aapainmanage.org/index.html	Pain Management
http://www.web-shack.com/dee/	Pain Management

Resources for Mental Health Care Providers

http://www.mentalhealth.com/ or http://www.mentalhealth.org	Internet Mental Health
http://www.mentalhealth.org/	Knowledge Exchange Network
http://www.cmhc.com/prof.htm	Mental Health Net— Professional Resources
http://www.wpanet.org/icd10cas.htm	World Psychiatric Association, ICD-10 Case Studies
http://www.apa.org/	American Psychological Association
http://www.naswdc.org/	National Association of Social Workers
http://www.counseling.org/resources	American Counseling Association
http://www.psych.org/	American Psychiatric Association
http://www.apna.org/	American Psychiatric Nurses Association
http://www.cpa.ca/	Canadian Psychological Association
http://www.socialworkers.org/	National Association of Social Workers

Condition-Specific Resources

http://www.dartmouth.edu/dms/ptsd/	Posttraumatic Stress Disorder
http://www.arthritis.org	Arthritis and related conditions
http://planetq.com/aidsvl/index.html	HIV/AIDS

http://www.nnlm.nlm.nih.gov/pnr/samplers/ aidspath.html	HIV/AIDS
http://nysernet.org/bcic/	Breast Cancer
http://www.diabetes.org/	Diabetes
http://www.diabetesnet.com/	Diabetes

General Health Care Resources-Agency and Government

http://www.nimh.nih.gov/	National Institute of Mental Health
http://www.guidelines.gov	National Clearinghouse Guidelines
http://www.ifla.org/	National Libraries
http://www.cdc.gov	Centers for Disease Control
http://www.nih.gov	National Institutes of Health

Health Information Resources for Consumers and Professionals

http://www.medscape.com	Medscape
http://www.merck.com/	Merck Manual (medication information)
http://www.medscape.com/	Medline–Medscape
http://www.muscat.gdb.org/repos.medL/	Medline–Community of Science
http://www.psych.org/	American Psychiatric Association
http://www.goaskalice.columbia.edu/	Healthwise, Columbia University
http://www.healthatoz.com/	Alternative and complementary health
http://www.hir.com	Alternative and complementary health
http://www.healthfinder.gov/	Healthfinder
http://www.infonet.welch.jhu.edu/advocacy.html	Patient education
http://www.womens-health.com/health.center	Women's health

Community and Self-Help/Support Group Resources

http://mentalhelp.net/selfhelp.htm	Mental Health Net-Self Help Resources
http://psychcentral.com/	Psych Central: newsgroups, listservs
http://www.healthguide.com/	HealthGuide OnLine
http://www.disability.com/cool. html	Disability resources
http//www.thebody.com/mb/relax.html	Relaxation techniques

Miscellaneous

http://www.omhrc.gov/wwwroot/class/index2.htm	Cultural competence standards
http://www.DiversityRx.org/HTML/DIVRX.htm	Diversity
http://www.health.qld.gov.au/hssb/hou/ resources.htm	Multicultural health resources
http://www.nihr.org.education/fica.html	Spiritual history

☐ **References**

Born, M. (1991). *Seven ways to look at a dream*. Washington, DC: Starhill Press.

Csikszentmihalyi, M. (1993). *Living with flow*. Nile, IL: Nightingale Conant.

Csikszentmihalyi, M. (1996). *Creativity: Flow and the psychology of discovery and invention*. New York: Harper/Collins.

Csikszentmihalyi, M., & Csikszentmihalyi, I. (1988). *Optimal experience: Psychological studies of flow in consciousness*. New York: Cambridge University Press.

Dolan, Y. (1991). *Resolving sexual abuse*. New York: W. W. Norton.

Rossi, E., & Nimmons, D. (1991). *The 20-minute break*. Los Angeles: Jeremy Tarcher.

Webster, D. (1999, February). Psychological type and self-care in chronic illness: Experience sampling for activity and rest. *Proceedings of the Second Biannual Conference on Mind, Body and Personality: The role of type in mental and physical health*. Center for Application of Psychological Type, Gainesville, FL.

INDEX